# Old Dublin Photo's

## Martin Coffey

**Copyright © Martin Coffey, 2015**

First Published in Ireland in 2015
in co-operation with Choice Publishing,
Drogheda, County Louth, Republic of Ireland
www.choicepublishing.ie

**ISBN**: 978-1-909154-83-4

All rights reserved. No part of this publication may be reproduced, stored in a retrieval system, transmitted in any form, or by any means, electronic, mechanical, photocopying, recording or otherwise, without the prior permission of the copyright holder.

To Jerry xx

**‘Through his lens he saved our past’**

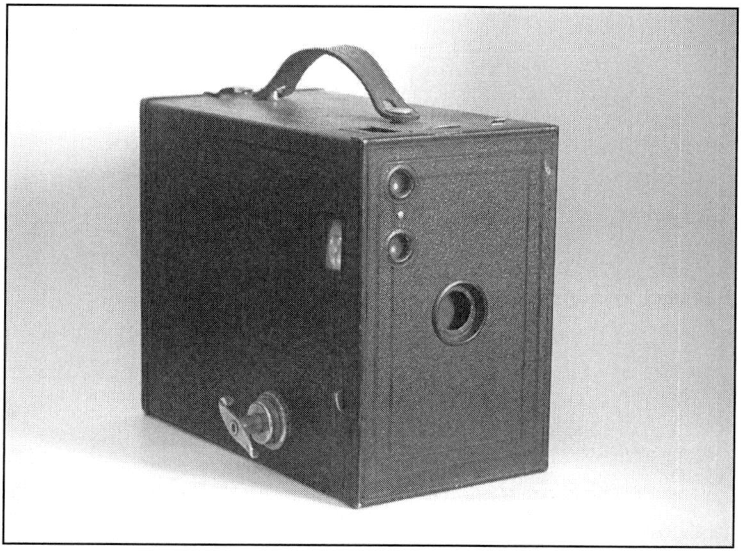

Best Wishes
Martin Coffey

# Dedication

I dedicate this book to the memory of my uncle,

**Paddy Coffey**

**(1905-1989)**

# Thank You

Sometime after the death of Paddy Coffey one of his original photographs appeared in a daily newspaper alongside an article on old Dublin. The article never mentioned Paddy or credited him with being the person who had taken the photograph. It is because of this article that I suggested to some of my extended family that we should safeguard all of Paddy's photographs and make sure that in future he is given full credit for his work. As a result of this, my cousin ***Angela O'Neill*** and her brother ***Paddy Kane*** gave me boxes and bags of photographs, original negatives and paperwork belonging to Paddy Coffey. Also my father's cousin, ***Gracie Doyle Neary*** and ***Maggie Doyle*** gave me many original photographs that they had belonging to Paddy and asked me to keep them safe.

I am very grateful to these people and many more of my relations who have entrusted me to be the keeper of such a magnificent collection of family memorabilia and photographs that have now become such a vital link in the visual and oral history of not only our family but also that of many other families from the north inner City of Dublin and of course Dublin itself. With the exception of a few studio photographs most of the photographs in this publication were taken with Paddy Coffey's old Brownie Box Camera.

# Introduction

The pivotal point in any good story or play is usually the main character or event around which the action revolves. In this instance, for me that character must surely be my father's eldest brother Paddy Coffey, whom I always considered the guardian of our Family History. He was born a subject of the British Crown in the Dublin of 1905. His family roots were firmly planted in the infamous and notorious area known as *'The Monto'*. In 1905 this area of Dublin City was riddled with prostitution, pimps, madams, brothels and shebeens. Paddy Coffey's grandmother, Margaret Doyle owned several houses in this area where she ran shebeens and where she rented out rooms to prostitutes who needed a place to entertain their clients. As a young boy Paddy became involved in this style of family business by running errands for some of the prostitutes and helping out around the shebeens.

In the early 1900's Dublin City had at least one photographic studio on almost every street. This latest invention of recording places, people and events on photographic paper had a great appeal to Paddy Coffey. On the day of his twelfth birthday he asked his uncle to buy him a camera. Instead he was brought to a photo studio where his uncle had Paddy's photograph taken and asked the photographer if he would sell him one of his cameras for Paddy to use. The photographer told him how to make a simple homemade *'Pin-Hole'* camera, which he did. This then was the beginning of a love affair between Paddy Coffey and the world of photography that would never end.

From a very early age Paddy Coffey always had this built-in desire to record his family history and because of his lack of a good education and unable to write too clearly he used his camera as a way of not only recording his family but also that of their neighbours and the area in which they all lived. These were changing times in the lives of Dubliners and in particular the life of this young boy who stood behind the barricades watching British Soldiers firing at the General Post Office and witnessed the tragic scenes of the 1916 Uprising, the shelling by British gunboats of Dublin's main thoroughfare and all its beautiful buildings. Paddy Coffey was very much aware of his uncle William Barter being shot dead by a

British soldier, of the hundreds of men from his neighbourhood, including his own father joining the British Army and heading off to war. It was also to become a time when Ireland was soon to stand on the brink of civil war.

Over a relatively short period of time Paddy Coffey would see even more changes taking place in his own neighbourhood with old and tired tenement houses, small streets, old lanes and alleyways being demolished to make way for the New Ireland and a more modern way of living. The community in which Paddy had grown up in as a young boy was being eradicated, wiped off the face of the earth with families and neighbours forced to change a life style that some of their families had known for almost a hundred years. To most of these people the Monto was like a small village, it was less than a quarter square mile in size where they felt safe but now modernity was creeping in and change was here to stay, nothing would ever remain the same. At an early stage of his life Paddy Coffey became very aware of these changes and how they could possibly alter the whole landscape of Dublin and its people and especially those from his own neighbourhood. So with his camera in hand he set out to record what he could of those changing times. This is his legacy to future generations of Dubliners.

# Contents

Page

# Chapter 1

The early years

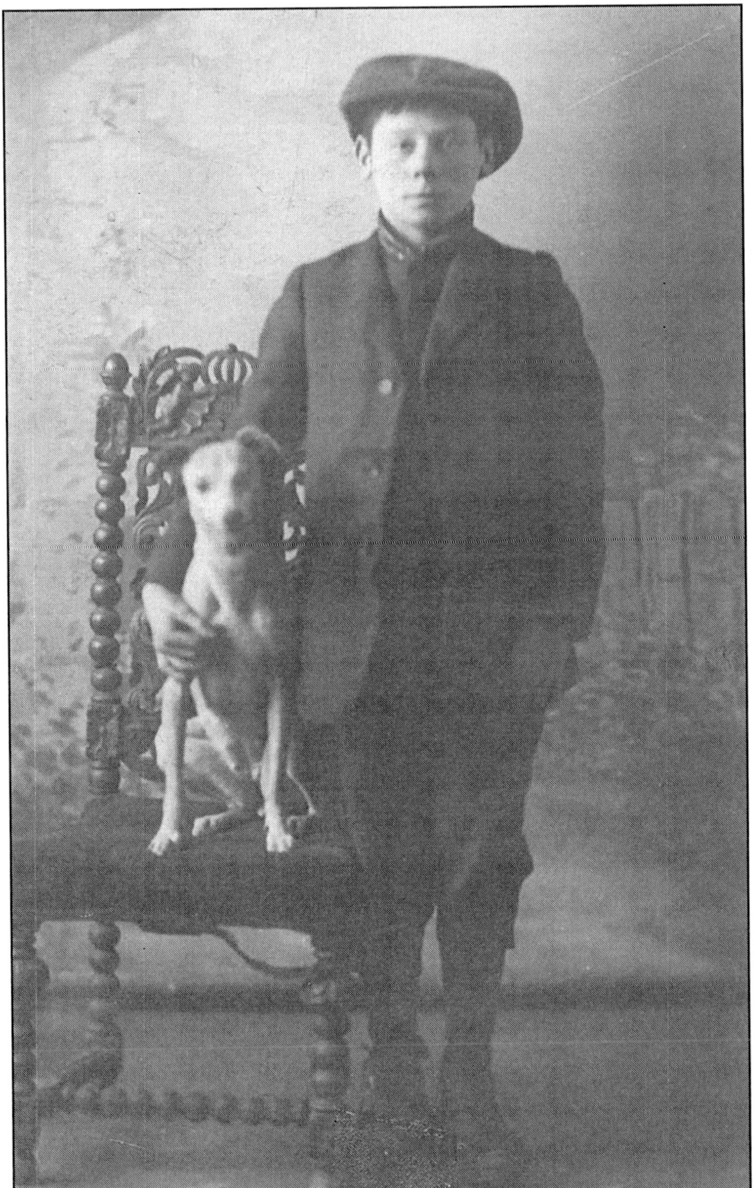

***Earliest known photograph of Paddy Coffey circa 1917.***

The earliest known photograph of Paddy Coffey was taken on the day of his twelfth birthday when his mother's brother, Sonny Doyle brought him to have it taken and to try and buy him a camera. When Paddy was asked what he would like for his birthday he immediately replied that he wanted a camera and it didn't matter what kind of a camera it was as long as it allowed him to take photographs. Now Sonny Doyle was all too aware of the price of a new camera at that time and so decided to try for a second-hand one instead. They went to a photographic studio in nearby Talbot Street where Sonny decided to let Paddy have his photograph taken as part of his birthday present in the hope that if they could not get a camera Paddy might be happy enough with the whole experience of being in a studio.

The photographer told Sonny that all of his cameras were far too expensive to give to a child but he came up with a plan that might solve the problem and save them money. On the advice and instructions of the studio photographer Sonny eventually made a *'Pin-Hole'* camera that allowed Paddy to begin his lifelong passion with photography. This very basic type of camera is a box that is completely dark inside with all light being kept out. On the front of the box a small hole is made which is no bigger than a pinhole. A piece of black insulating tape is then placed over the pinhole. Inside the box an empty film spool is mounted to one side and a full film spool is placed on the opposite side to this. The beginning of the unused film is then wrapped around the empty spool, as is the way with most non-digital cameras of today. Paddy would pull back the small piece of black tape that covered the pinhole, count to ten and then replace the tape over the hole and he then had a photograph taken.

Paddy Coffey basically served his photographic apprenticeship by going around some of the various studios in Dublin and befriending the professional photographers who were only too delighted to share their knowledge of the trade with such a keen and eager young boy. They would invite him into their studio darkroom and explain the process of film development, explain the workings of different styles of cameras and give him some hands-on experience using their chemicals. Paddy then set up his own darkroom in the basement of a rundown tenement building where he also stored bottles of leftover chemicals that the studio photographers had given him. With his brain working overtime and a camera in his hand Paddy Coffey set out to record the life and times of the environment in which he lived. He is possibly the only person from that area to have done so and the photographic legacy that he has left for us to enjoy today and for future generation to enjoy, is beyond price.

Once Paddy Coffey became proficient with his Pinhole Camera and proved himself a dedicated member of the photographic profession he upgraded his camera to a Kodak Brownie Box Camera. This was to be the very camera with which he took the vast majority of his photographs. In his early teens Paddy joined the crew of a ship in Dublin Port and sailed around the world. He was shipwrecked on three different occasions and each time he made sure to save his camera.

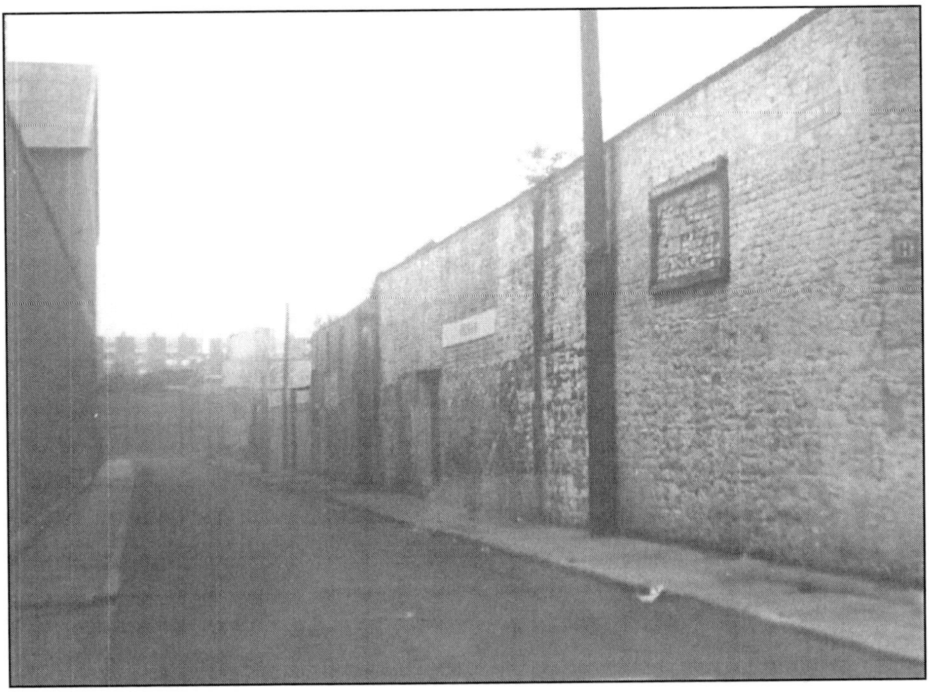

***Beaver Street, Dublin.***

On the 15th January 1905 Paddy Coffey was born in number 4 Beaver Street, the eldest of nine children. He was christened in the nearby Pro Cathedral and was named William Patrick Coffey. His grandmother Margaret Doyle owned the house in which he was born. His father Billy Coffey was 19 years old and his mother Chrissie Doyle was 18 years old. The house was let out into one-room flats and it was in one of these rooms on the ground floor that Paddy Coffey was born. He was the first grandchild of James and Margaret Doyle, so there was sure to be great celebrations when he arrived on the scene. Almost directly across from this house was a small laneway leading into a cul-de-sac called Crumline Court and it was here that Paddy's Granny Doyle had her *'Dry Farm'* consisting of pigs, a couple of cows, a horse, geese and chickens.

Paddy Coffey spoke of a family who lived in nearby Corporation Street being evicted for not paying their rent and who ended up living in a Pig Sty that they had nearby, thus evicting the pigs. Times were very hard for many families back then with no financial help from the Government and people in need relying on the charity of others. Many families in this area lived in the old tenement houses with one or maybe two families to a single room and no electricity or running water available. In recent times the remains of horse stables were found at the back of the old Varian Brush Factory that once operated out of Beaver Street.

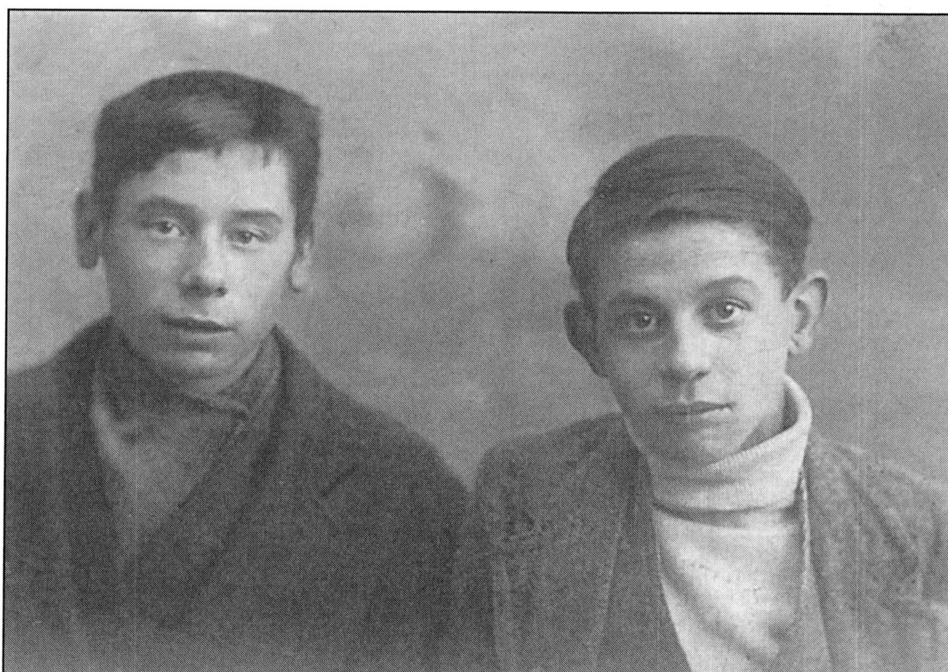

***Paddy Coffey on the left with one of his childhood pals.***

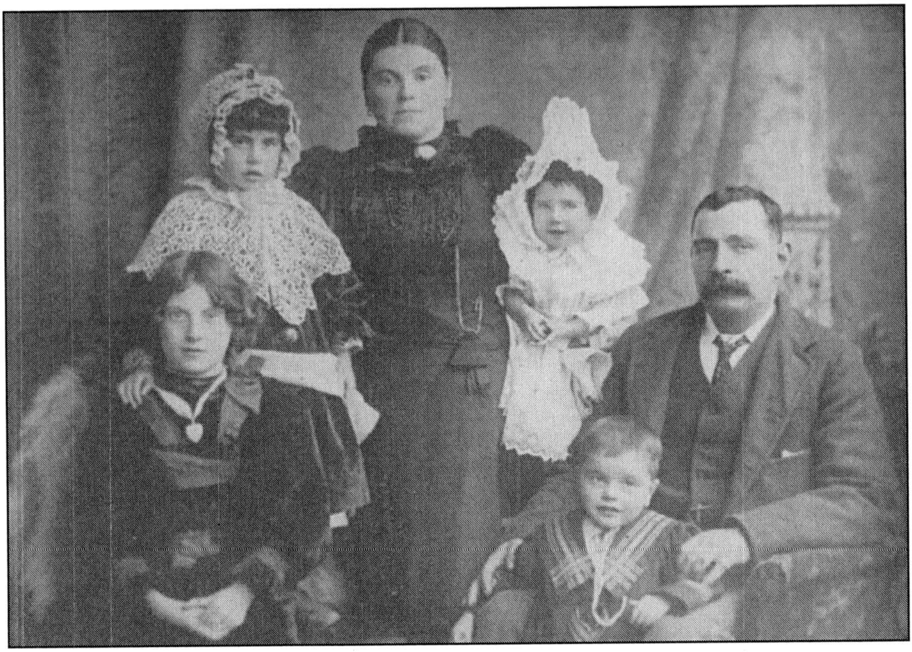

***A photographic studio shot of Paddy Coffey's mother, Christina seated on the left, his aunt Catherine (Katie), his grandmother Margaret Clyne, his aunt Mary Anne, his granddad James Doyle and his uncle, James 'Sonny' Doyle. Photo taken in Dublin, circa 1896.***

Margaret Doyle was imprisoned in Grangegorman Female Penitentiary in 1888 on a charge of running a Shebeen, an illegal drinking house. When she finally came up against the judge, or so the story goes, he looked down at the Charge Sheet and saw her address. He then looked up at her and threw the case out. She was sure that he was a regular visitor to the Monto and to her Shebeen. At this time Margaret Doyle was 25 years old, 5 foot and 1 inch in height, she had brown eyes and brown hair and had a sallow complexion. She gave her address as number 50 Purdon Street. She was born in Mullingar in 1861. James Doyle was born in Mecklinburgh Street, Dublin in 1861 to Cornelius Doyle and Anna Melia and christened in the nearby Pro Cathedral. This means that the Doyle family are living continuously in this area for at least one hundred and fifty four years.

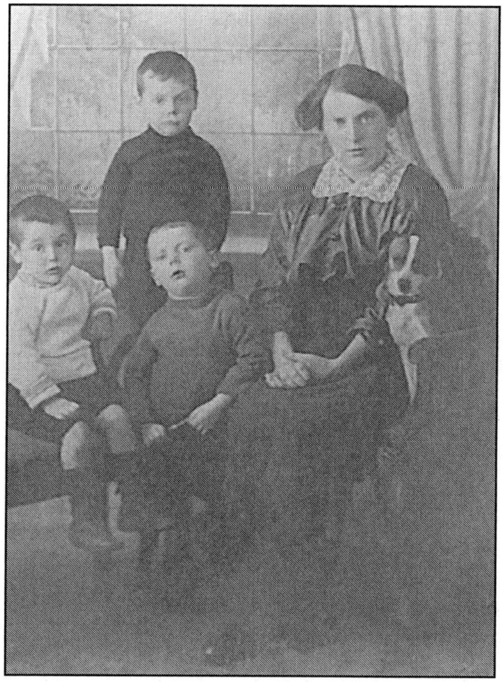

***A photographic studio photo of Paddy Coffey's mother Christina Doyle with her son Bernard (seated) and her twin boys Tommy at the back and Jimmy standing at front.***

This photograph was taken in about 1916. The dog was not a part of the family but had followed the three young boys from the Monto into the studio where the photographer suggested that they use him as a prop. Christina Coffey died in 1917 from heart failure. Her son Jimmy was killed in 1920 at ten years of age while scutting on the back of a horse and cart. He caught one of his legs in the wheel of the cart and was hurled to the ground dying instantly from major head injuries. It is told that at Christina's funeral her mother Margaret Doyle cried out that she would join her daughter within the week and sure enough the following week she too died. With Christina's husband away at war these two events were a terrible tragedy to befall such young children. After her death family, neighbours and friends looked after the children. This was done in order to prevent the authorities placing them in State Care. A young childless couple named Jack and Molly Enright took Bernard in and dressed him in a green velvet suit for Saint Patrick's Day.

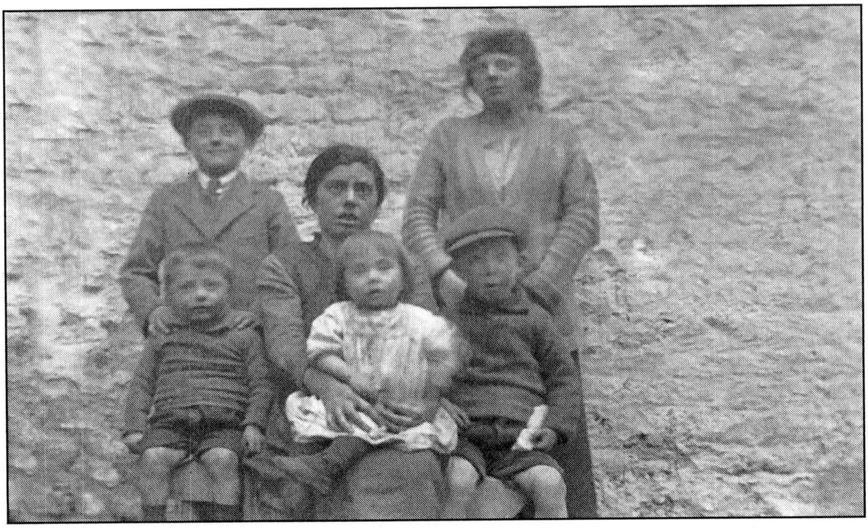

***L-R: Paddy's youngest brother Bernard (Archie) Coffey with cap, his sister Biddy Coffey standing, his young cousins Paddy and Bridie Fagan and Paddy Foran on the right, a neighbour's child. The lady in the photograph is his aunt Catherine (Katie) Doyle who first married William Barter and secondly Nicholas Fagan.***

This photograph was taken in Purdon Street that once ran parallel to present day Foley Street. Behind the wall stood the Flats complex of Corporation Buildings. Katie Doyle's first husband, William Barter worked as a Carter, which would be very similar today to a van and driver for hire. He stabled his horse in Frenchman's Lane that runs from Gardiner Street into Store Street. On the evening of the 26th April 1916 William Barter had settled his horse down for the night. William was tired, hungry and looking forward to going home to a hot meal. As he stepped out of the laneway onto Gardiner Street he heard the voices of some British Soldiers stationed on the overhead railway bridge. William ignored them and continued walking towards his home.

As he reached the corner of Talbot Street and Gardiner Street a single rifle shot rang out. William let out a cry as a bullet ripped into his leg and he fell to the ground in agony. Unknown to William the bullet had severed an artery in his leg and he was bleeding to death. The British Army would later claim that he was out on the street after the 8pm -8am curfew. When he failed to arrive home that night his wife was not too worried thinking that maybe he had gone to visit his parents or stayed overnight with some family member. The following morning however some of his neighbours found William lying dead in the doorway of Guiney's clothing shop in nearby Talbot Street. He was twenty-three years old and was buried in an unmarked grave in Glasnevin Cemetery. His son Billser would later join the British Army and end up as a Japanese prisoner of war for five years. In the early 1920's when the feared British Black and Tans became involved in a gunfight with local rebels in this area, Katie Doyle gave shelter to one of the '*Tans*'. He hid under her bed and in the early hours of the following morning when the coast was clear he made good his escape. In later years he returned to Dublin to thank Katie for saving his life.

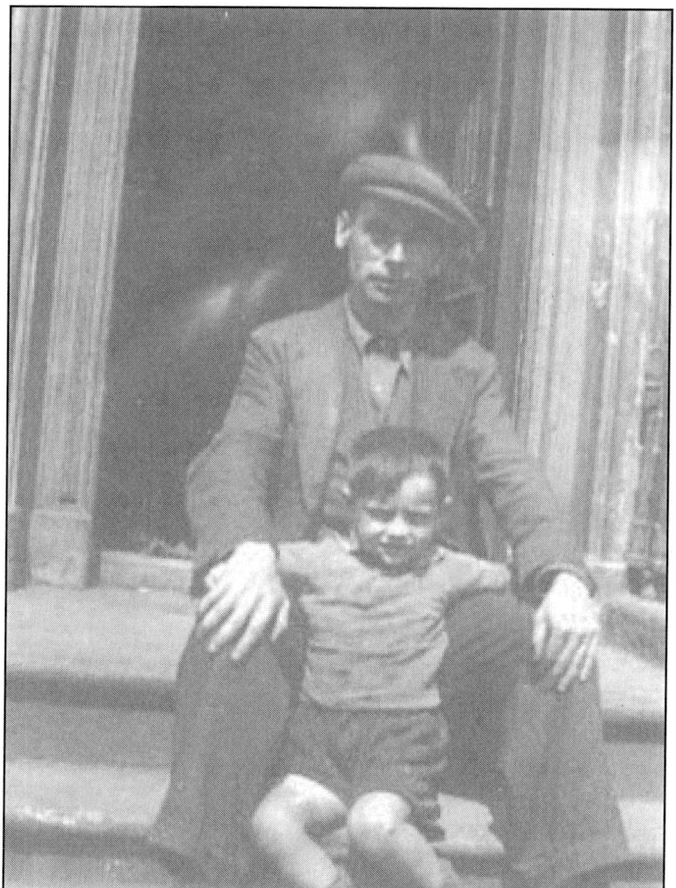

***Paddy Coffey with his nephew Barney Doyle.***

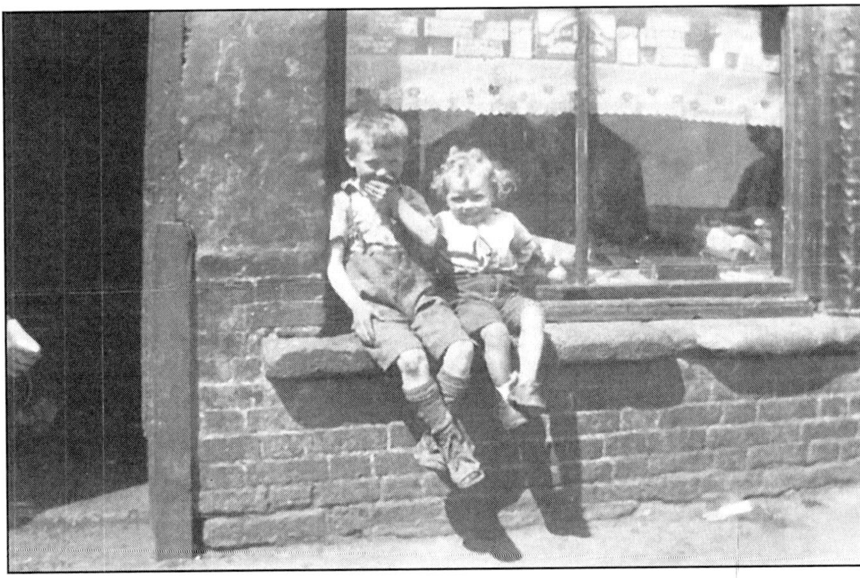

***Paddy Coffey's cousins Jack and Willie Gorman sitting on Meehan's shop window in Railway Street.***

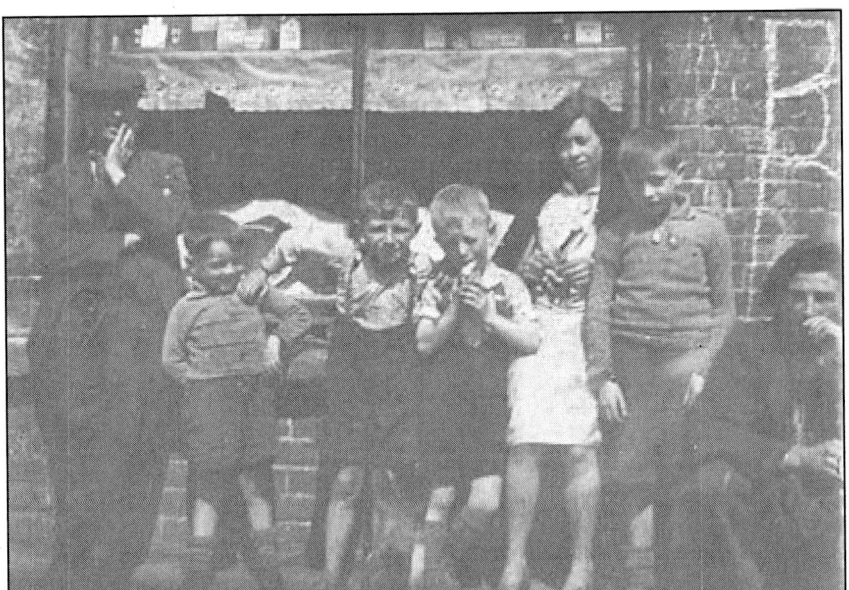

***Jack McKeever, Barney Doyle, Mousie Meehan, Murrayer Meehan, Bessy McKeever, Blacker Doyle and Johnnie Marney***

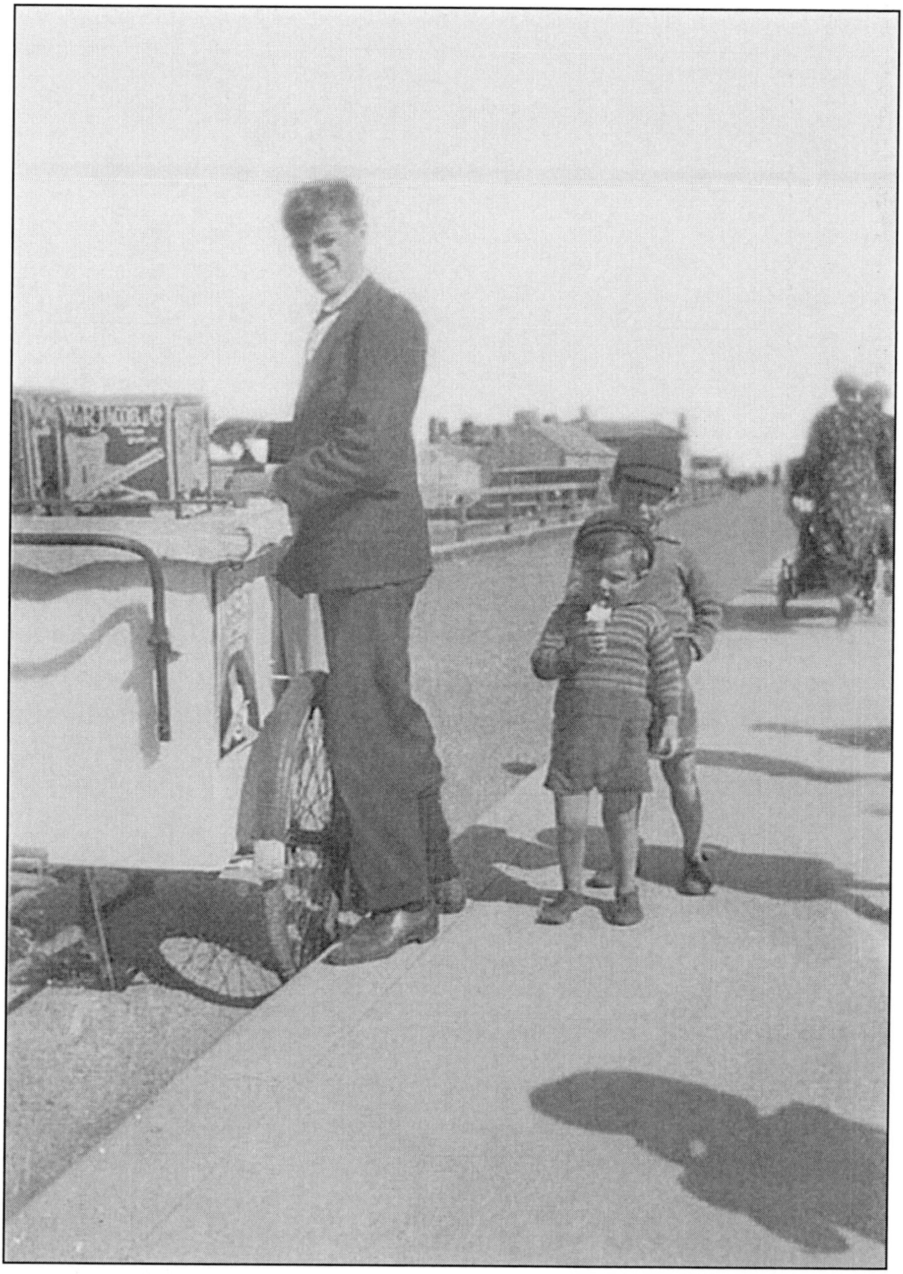

***The Doyle brothers, Barney and Blacker***

***standing on the old wooden bridge in Dollymount.***

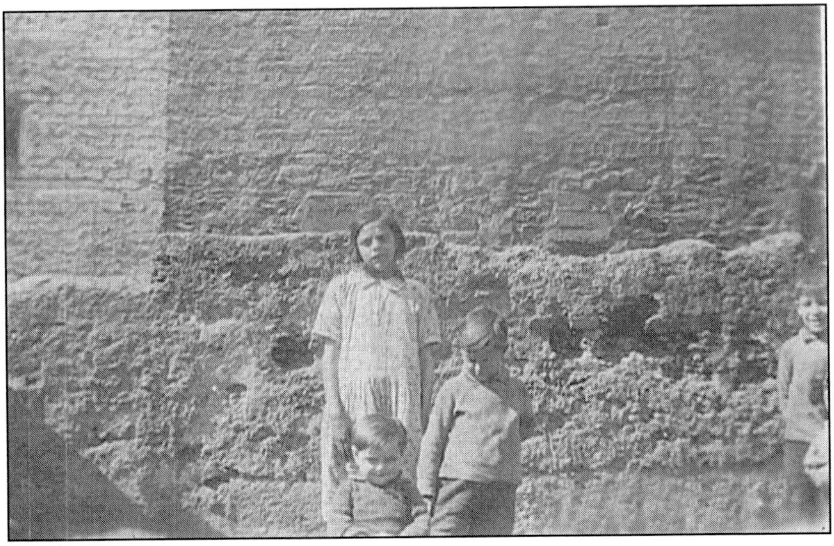

***Chrissie Doyle with two of her brothers, Barney and Dennis.***

Some of the decayed and neglected tenement houses in Dublin collapsed under their own weight. Two tenement houses collapsed in Church Street, Dublin in 1913. Fifteen people were trapped in the rubble and seven were killed with many more being seriously injured. Dublin Corporation hired professional photographers to go into the Monto area and photograph the worse scenes they could find so that the Corporation could justify the demolition of the area to the City Fathers. These vacant sites would become the playground for many of the young children in the area. In a relatively short period of time Dublin Corporation demolished a neighbourhood of dwellings and streets that resulted in a whole new landscape of Corporation Flats.

*'It was tough for the Grown-Ups to live in those hard times but it was magic for us. We knew nothing about money or anything like that. Bath time on Saturday night was in front of the fire in a big zinc bath. After we were washed we looked like Lobsters sitting on my Mam's "Home Sweet Home" fender. We were eagerly waiting for Mam to wash the floor with the bath water, water was never wasted in our house. She would make us a drink of hot Cocoa and give us a biscuit as well. I always loved that. I'm sure there were times when she was sad because our Dad, who was a sailor, was away at sea for most of the time. Looking back now I remember her favourite song was called "Together". It was about her lonely sailor and the longing for his return.'* **Rosie Kane Tormey**

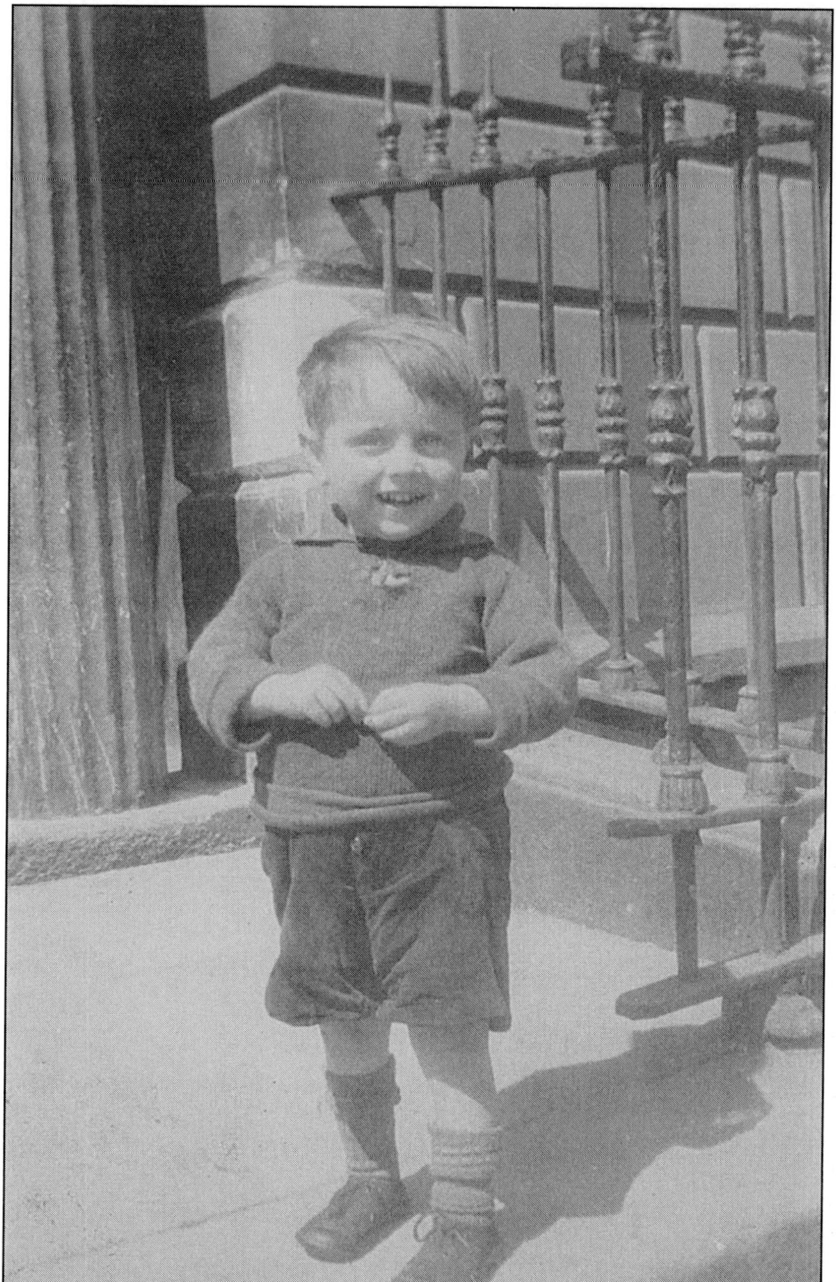

*Bernard 'Barney' Doyle.*

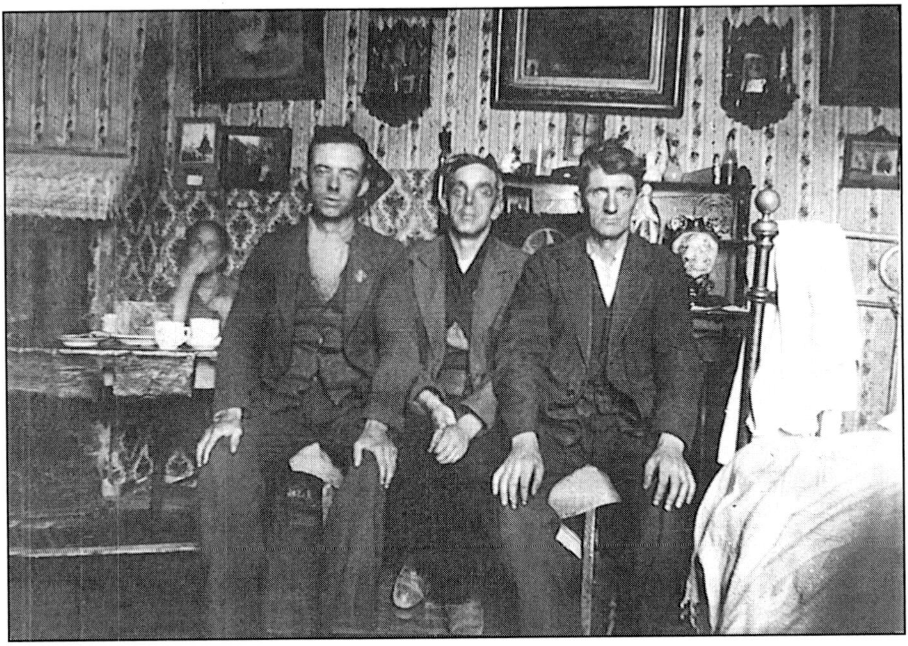

***May and Sonny Doyle (Centre) with friends.***

This photograph gives us a rare glimpse into an original tenement room situated in Railway Street, Dublin in the very early 1930's. The large framed photograph to the left of this picture is one of the Doyle's eldest daughters Chrissie as a young child. The large picture in the middle is possibly one of the Sacred Heart that adorned most rooms in the tenements of that period. The two other main pieces on the wall are pieces of wooden fretwork made by Sonny Doyle to house a holy statue and family relics. One of these relics was a small statue of The Blessed Virgin Mary that Denis Farrell, who was married to Sonny's sister Mary Anne had brought home from WWI France where he had fought in the British Army.

Denis and his troop came under enemy fire and sought shelter in a bombed out church where Dennis saw the little statue as it lay amongst the rubble. He put the statue in his army satchel for safekeeping and brought it home with him to Dublin. Sonny made a little altarpiece to especially house the statue which then took pride of place on their wall because of its historic connection to the family. In later years it would end up on the wall of Paddy Coffey's bedroom when he lived in Sean McDermot Street. Sonny Doyle taught himself how to play the piano, the mouth organ and the accordion. He was gifted with his hands and often made his own Crystal Radios. During WWII he was able to listen in to the BBC Home Service and keep up to date on what was happening. He hid his radio in a hole in the wall of his tenement room and covered it over with a Holy Picture. The wire at the back of the picture frame acted as an aerial for the radio. Sonny was offered a job working with Philips Radio Manufacturers. Before he could take up the position however he met with an accident whereby he lost his balance while joking with his friend and his hand went through the window of their tenement room resulting in major damage to his hand and as a result of which he was unable to take up the offer of a job in the radio factory.

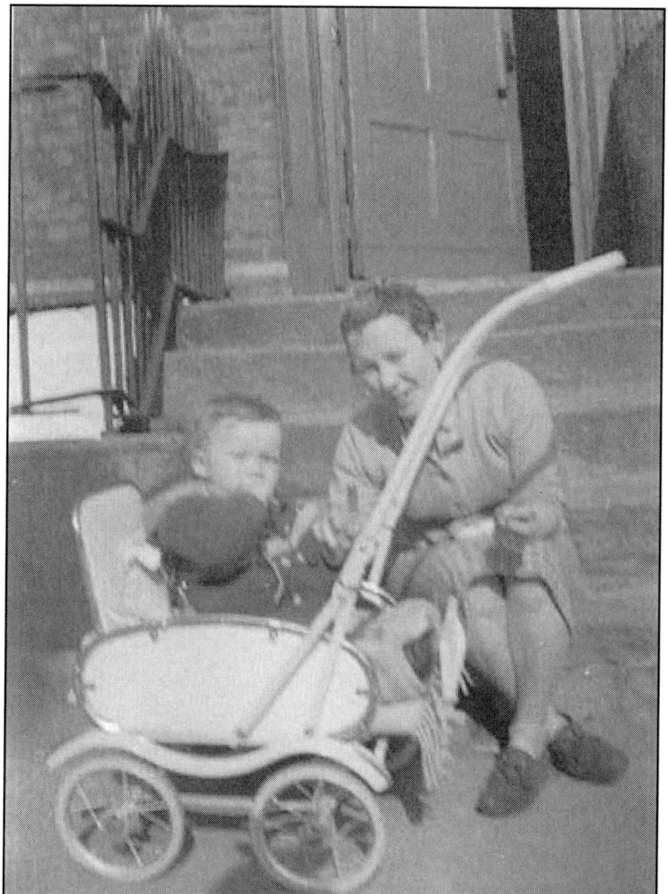

***Chrissie Dillon with her son Al on the steps of a tenement house.***

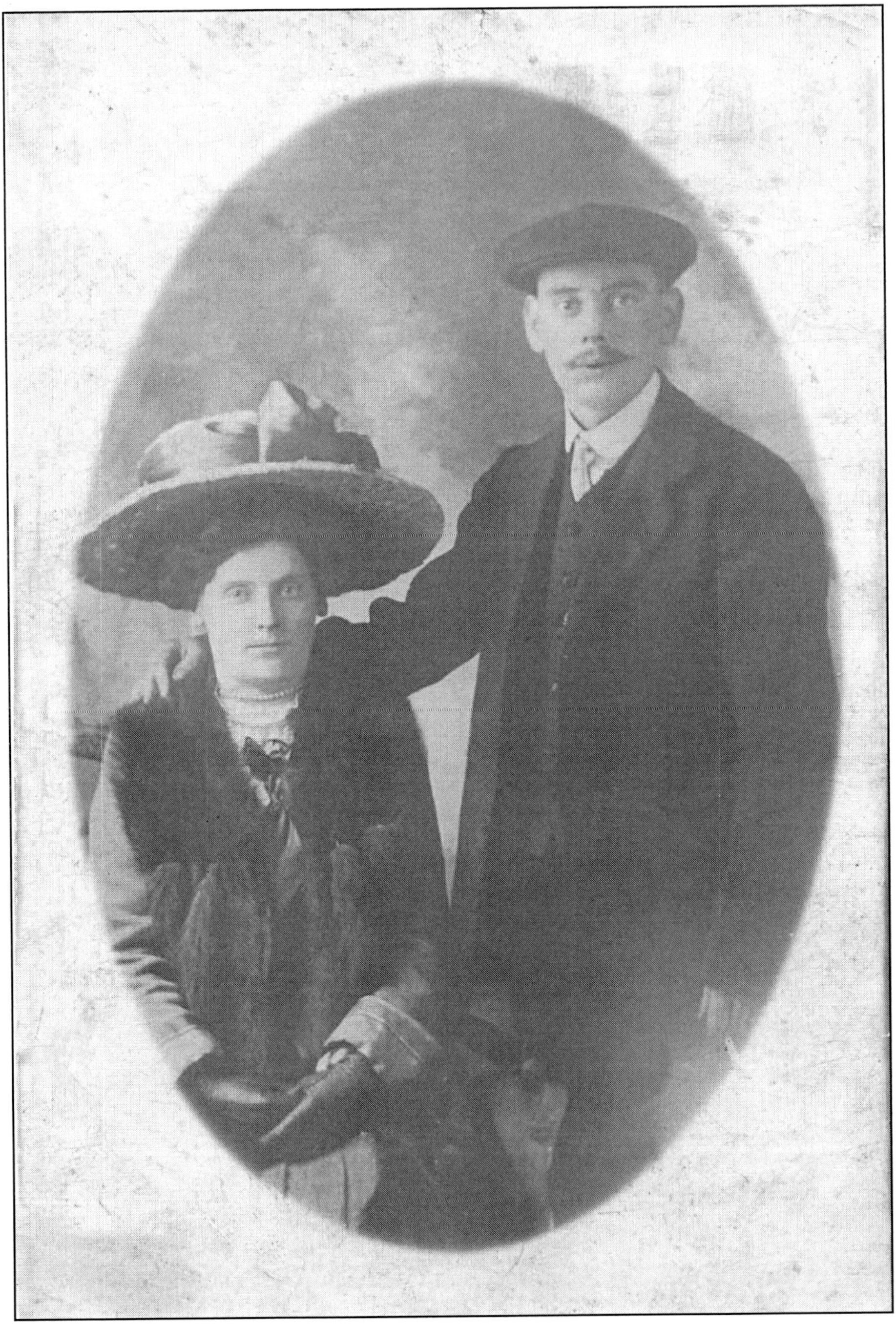

*Christina Doyle and William Coffey.*

This is Chrissie Doyle and Billy Coffey on their wedding day in 1904; they were married in the Pro Cathedral, Dublin. Chrissie was born on Christmas Eve in 1885 in the South Dublin Union Workhouse (James's Hospital). Billy was born in 69 Mabbott Street 1884. Billy Coffey brewed his own beer, which he sold in a Shebeen. He also forged his own money and passed it off to drunken customers, especially if they were British Soldiers. He had an underground bunker where he stashed his illegal booze; this was in the backyard of one of the tenement houses owned by his mother-in-law Margaret Doyle.

One night, or so the story goes Billy was serving up his home made booze to a group of soldiers from a Scottish Regiment. What he failed to realise was that one of these soldiers was a non-drinker and sadly for Billy he slipped some of his fake coins to this soldier. When the soldier realised the scam he quickly informed his pals who not only wrecked poor Billy Coffey but also wrecked his mother in law's Shebeen. Shebeens, prostitutes, stolen goods and prison sentences became a part of everyday life for many individuals and families throughout Ireland in the late 19$^{th}$ and early 20$^{th}$ centuries. Every village, town and city had its share of people living under the poverty line that felt they had no other alternative but to turn to these occupations in order to provide for themselves and their families.

*'I remember as a little one and my father was working down the docks. He'd come home of a Friday with his two trouser pockets bulging with loose tea and he'd say to my mother "I'll have the rent in the morning". He'd sell one pocket of loose tea to the neighbours and he'd keep the other one for ourselves. I often remember him walking up the street with a bundle of sticks under his arm and especially in the wintertime. They'd be for lighting the fire you see and my mother would be delighted because then she could cook our dinner over the fire.*

*We'd be all freezing sitting around the room without a fire and sometimes my mother would get into the bed with all her clothes on and have us get in beside her to keep us all warm. I used to love that because then she'd start telling us stories about when she was a little girl. You see, her mother was a countrywoman and they had very hard times as well, more so than a lot of people living in Dublin'...* ***Kathleen Burke.***

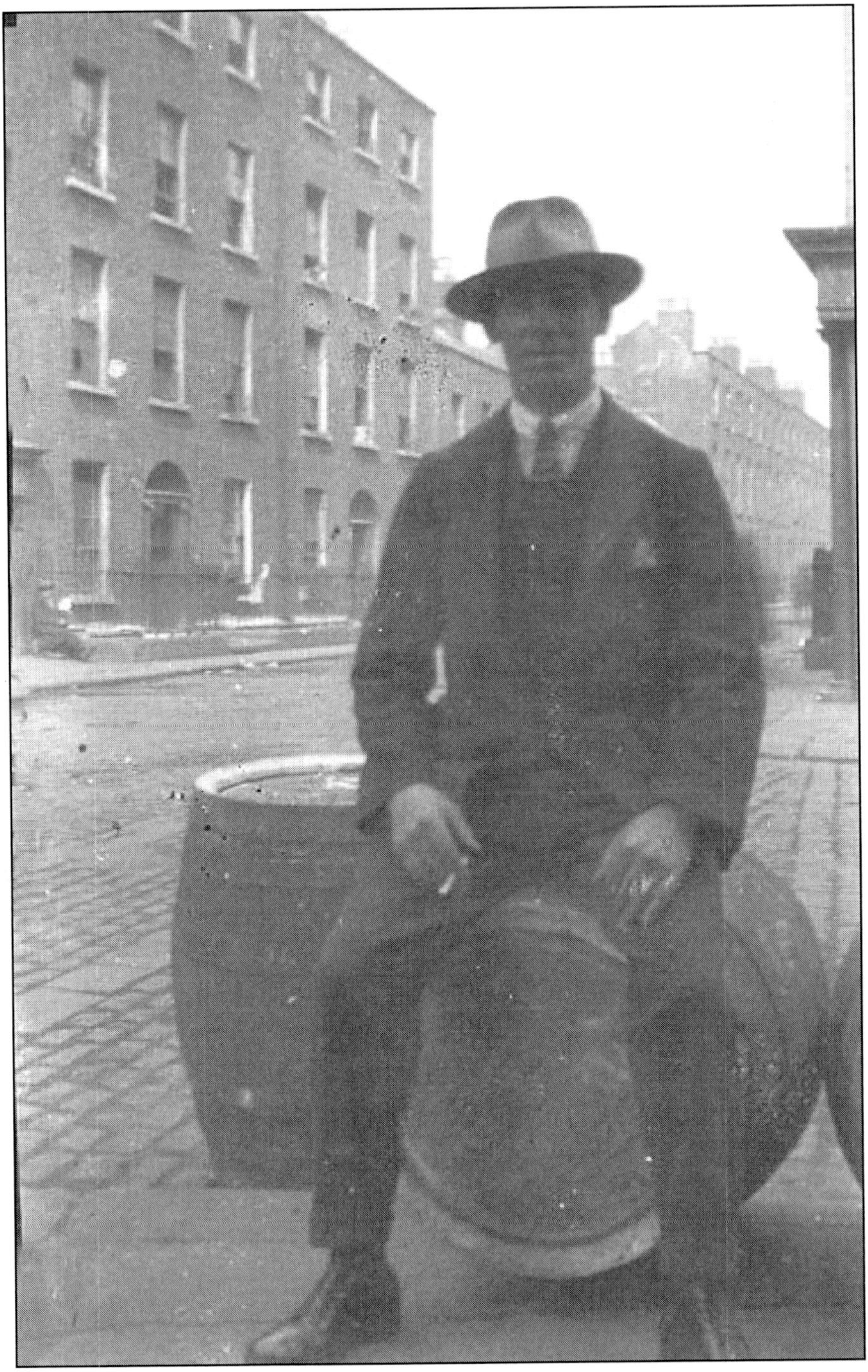

***Denis Farrell.***

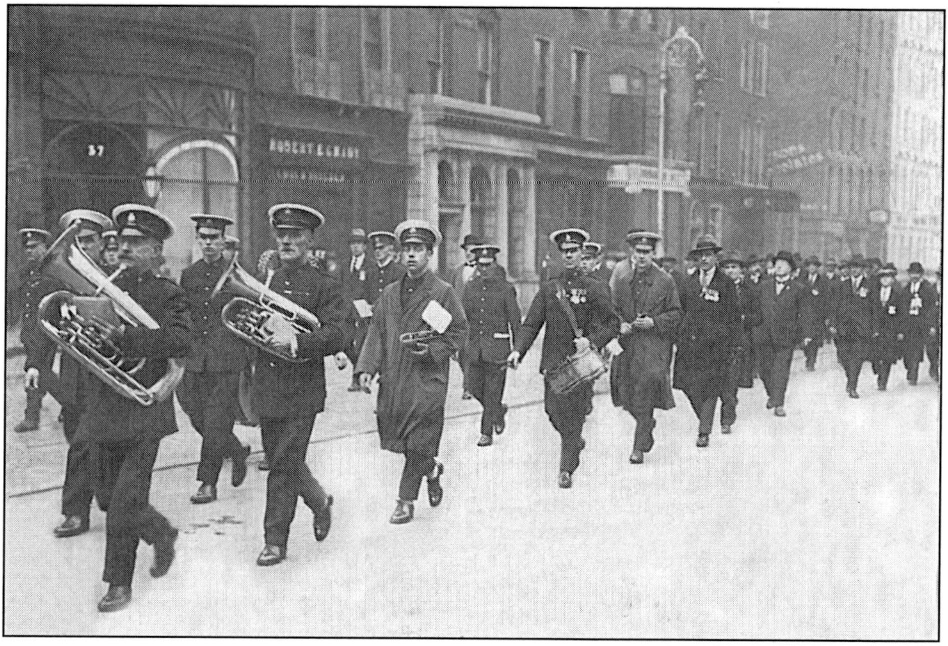

***Denis Farrell, drummer with the Ex Servicemen's Band marching along Bachelors Walk in Dublin.***

According to his army records Denis Farrell joined the British Army on the 11th March 1910 when he was eighteen years old. He was five feet and five and a quarter inches in height with grey eyes and brown hair. His army number is 9430. He travelled by train from Dublin to Belfast to sign up. His next of kin at the time were his mother Margaret and his brother James who lived in 57 Mabbott Street, Dublin. His last place of employment is stated as a farm, he had worked for Gouldings Fertilisers. Denis was assigned to the Royal Barracks in Dublin. On the 11th December 1912 his regiment was shipped out to India where Denis spent two years serving in Kamptee. In October 1914 he returned to Dublin and a month later his regiment was once again shipped overseas to France with the British Expeditionary Force where Denis saw action for another year. While serving in France he was assigned as a sniper in the Trenches where his job was to harass the enemy by shooting any soldier who appeared within his rifle sights. It was while he was serving in France that his regiment came under a heavy shelling attack from the Germans guns and Dennis found himself undercover in the ruins of a bombed out Catholic Church.

At the outbreak of WWII Denis Farrell had signed up to the Royal Ulster Rifles. After three months the Army told him he was too old to serve in a full-time regiment and sent him home. During WWI Denis was a drummer in his original regiment and was part of a front line band of musicians who led their troops into battle while playing their instruments. Denis also played in the James Larkin Drum and Fife Band in Dublin. Denis Farrell died in the South Dublin Union Hospital on the 14th April 1937. Denis was a quiet man who liked to have his pint and his pipe. While away in England he would always send money home to his wife Mary Anne and include a note to her asking that she give something of the money to her niece and namesake Mary Anne Doyle now known as Gracie Neary.

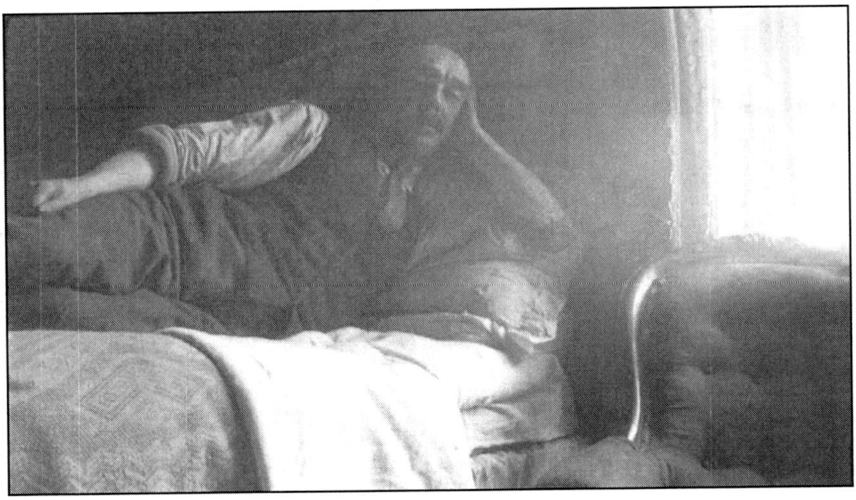

***Billy Coffey.***

This is Paddy Coffey's father lying on his bed in 18 Lower Gardiner Street, Dublin. In his right hand he is holding a string that Paddy had connected to his camera that allowed his father to take a photograph of himself. When Billy Coffey returned home from fighting in WWI he was assigned as a driver to the British Vice Regal in the Phoenix Park. When the Free State government took over the running of the country he was sacked from this position and told he would never again work in Ireland because of his association with the British Army. He later opened up his own garage and workshop but it too was closed down on government orders. He then attempted to start up his own plumbing business and again that was closed down. He never worked again in Ireland.

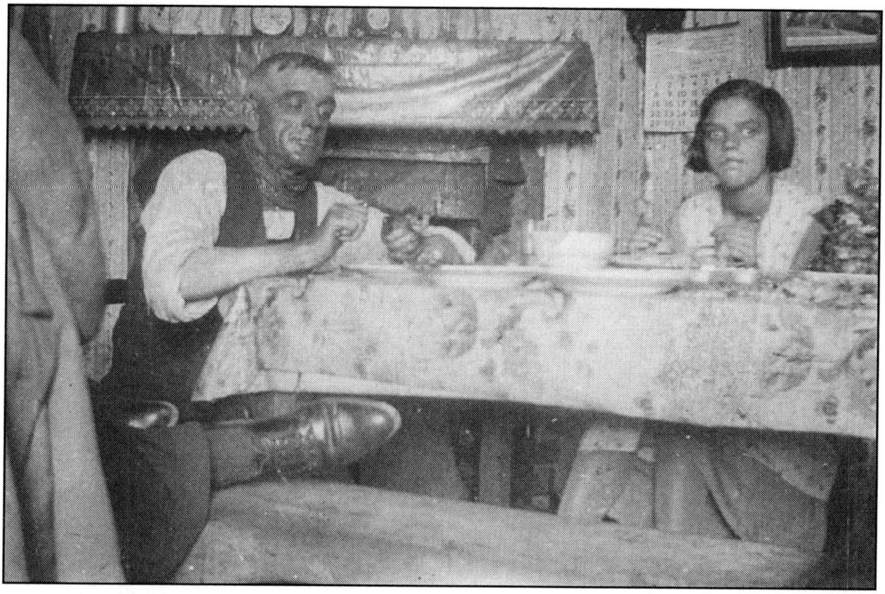

***Sonny Doyle*** and his daughter ***Chrissie*** or *'Glaxo'* as she was sometimes called, sitting down eating their dinner. This is another photograph that gives us a great insight into how the Doyle's tenement room looked in the early 1930's, a few old chairs and a long wooden stool to sit on, the cloth draped over the mantel piece to keep it clean, various ornaments, statues, an old calendar and framed pictures hanging on the wall.

There was a neighbour of Sonny Doyle's that was looked on by the rest of the neighbours as being a bit suspicious; he was seen as being too friendly with the police. He would often ask Sonny to let him listen in to the radio that Sonny had rigged up in his tenement room. Sonny wasn't too keen on him as he thought he might report Sonny for not having a radio licence. So one day Sonny decided to teach him a lesson. Sonny rigged up his microphone to the radio and then invited this man in to listen to Lord Haw Haw supposedly calling from Germany; it was in fact Sonny himself speaking into the microphone.

Some of the neighbours were also invited in to witness the scene that Sonny was setting up. As the man was listening in to the radio Sonny's voice came on and spoke out the name of this man and asked if he was listening in to the programme. The man of course thought it was Lord Haw Haw from Germany speaking directly to him and ran out of the room with fright never to come back again.

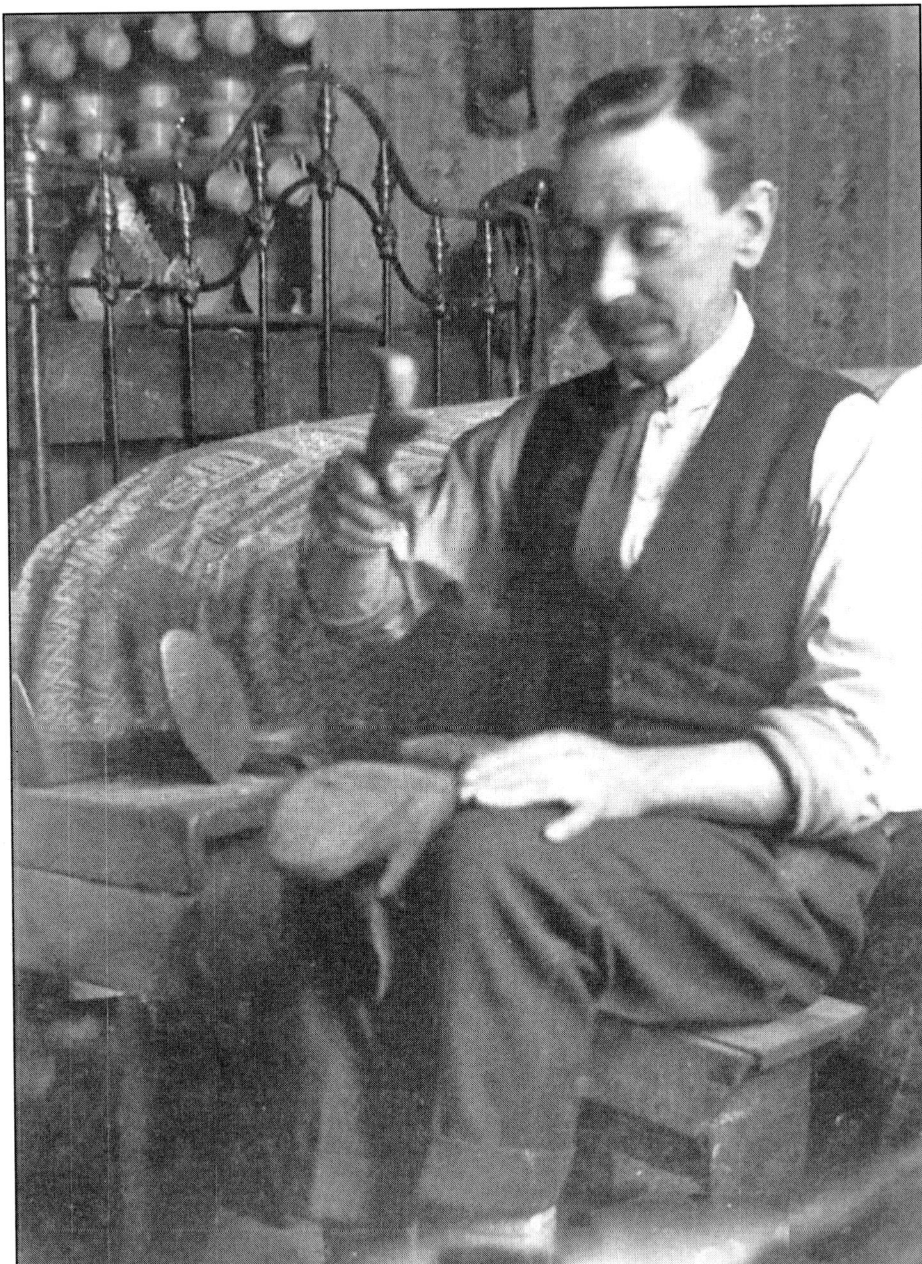

*Billy Coffey (1884 – 1941) repairing his army boots in number 18 Lower Gardiner Street.*

As a young boy growing up in Dublin's Monto Billy Coffey played a role in the business life of the area. Sometimes when a prostitute had a client up in her room and they wanted drink and cigarettes they would have a young boy standing in the street down below waiting to run and fetch for them. This is what Billy Coffey did as a young boy. The prostitute would lower a basket, containing money, on a rope down to the young boy waiting below. She would then shout to the boy and tell him what he was to buy for her. When the boy returned with the goods he would place them into the basket and shout up to the prostitute. She would then pull up the rope and the basket. The young boy, like Billy Coffey would never put any money left over from the shopping trip into the basket, it always went into his pocket and of course it wasn't the prostitute that had paid for the goods it was always her client every time.

Sometimes when a prostitute was expecting a customer she might send over to one of her neighbours who had young children and ask that one of the children be sent over to her for the day. The young child would be instructed by the prostitute to lie on the bed and pretend to be asleep when her customer arrived. He would become irate over the child being on the bed. The prostitute would then suggest that they take the child for a walk around the nearby shops. The customer would then be *'stung'* to buy something for the child, perhaps a new coat, a nice dress or perhaps a little doll. On their return to the room the child would once again climb onto the bed. This would very often result in the customer putting his hat and coat on and heading out the door but not before the prostitute would demand her money and of course she had the boyfriend standing outside the door with a lead pipe in his hand, just in case.

*'My Granny Doyle got a steel door put on the front of the Shebeen in Railway Street to stop the police from bursting in and raiding the place. Sometimes you'd see this Toff going in one door on that side of the street and coming out the door on the other side. They had tunnels under the road going from one place to the other. If there was a tip off that there was going to be a raid they'd all make for the basement and the tunnel. Some of the places had a panel in the wall that moved like a secret door that led down to the tunnels'.* ***Paddy Coffey***

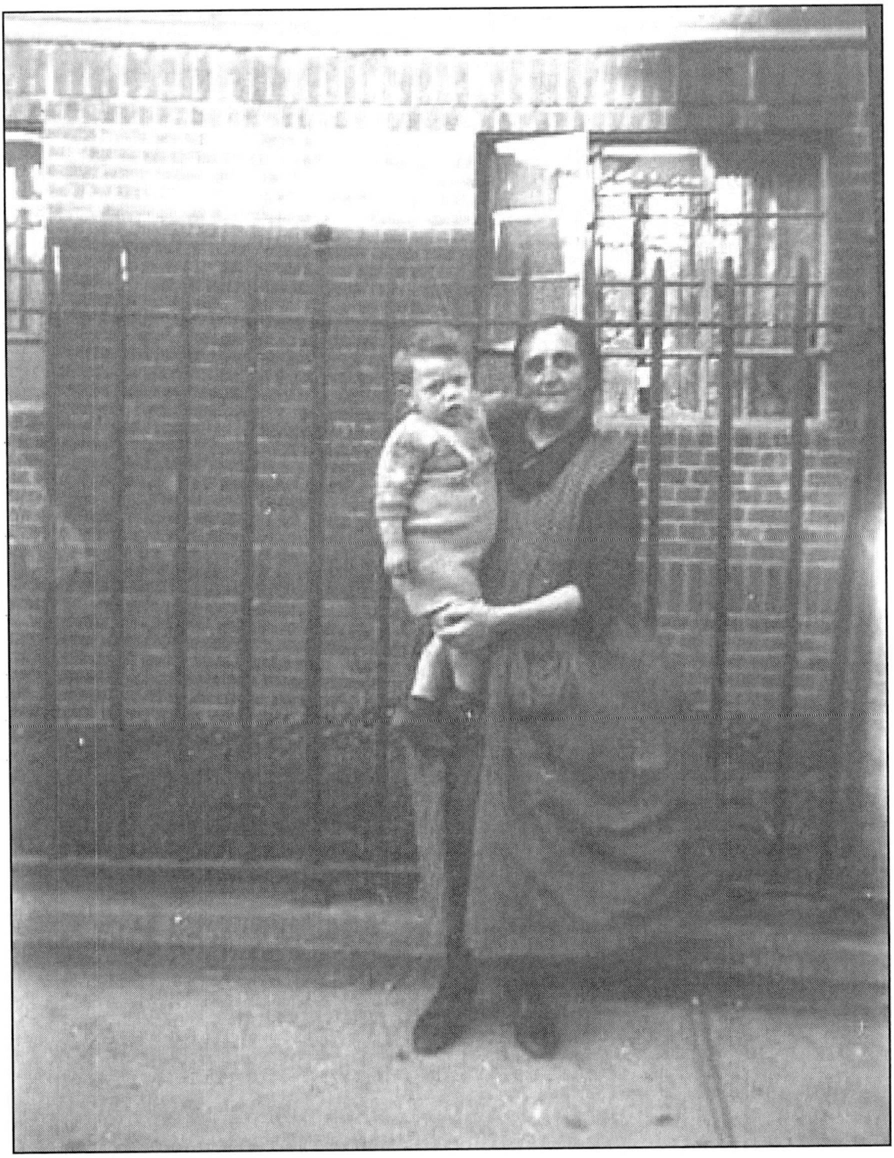

***May Doyle and young Denis Doyle in Railway Street.***

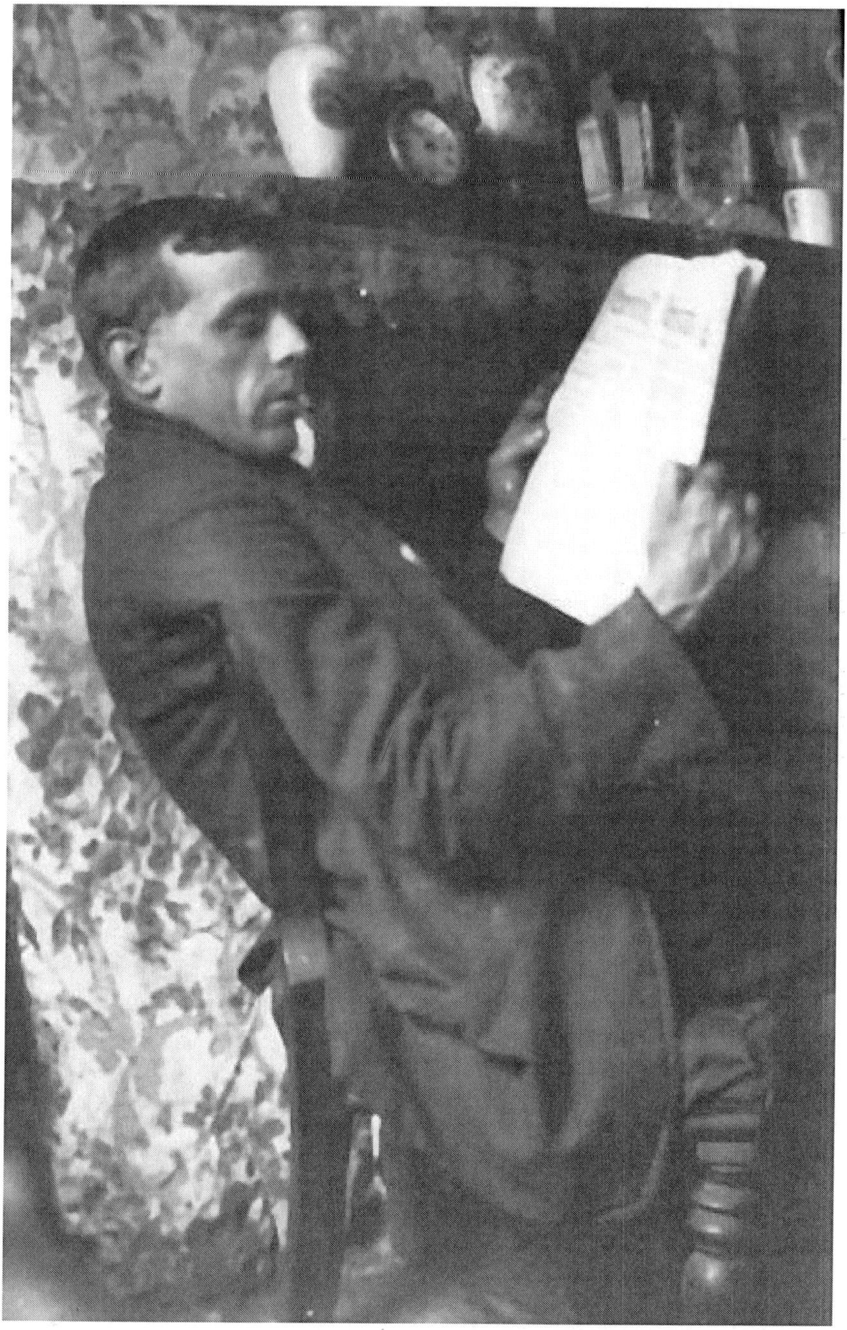

*James 'Sonny' Doyle.*

*'I remember one Christmas time in Liberty House and I don't know whether we were being bold or what but my father had his radio on and we were there listening to it. Now he was in the bedroom and we thought he was asleep. All of a sudden it came on the radio about Santy Clause. The voice said "Oh yes, this is Santy, is Gracie Doyle listening..." Well I can tell you that I didn't know what to say. I looked at my mother and it came on again. "...now Gracie I believe you want a Fairy Doll for Christmas. Well you must be very, very good..." And I'm asking my mother "How did he know." "...now if you're good you never know, you might get your Fairy Doll." And it was him in the bedroom with a microphone rigged up to his radio and we didn't know.'* ***Gracie Doyle Neary***

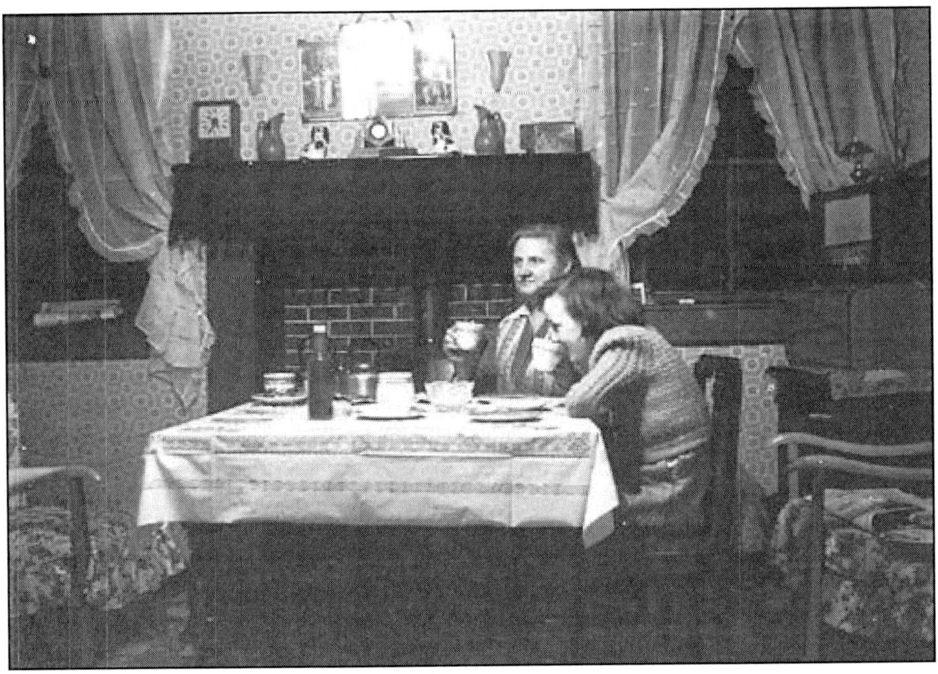

***Biddy Coffey and Angela Kane.***

This is a 1950's photograph of a tenement room in Sean McDermot Street, Dublin where Biddy Coffey lived. Paddy Coffey lived here when he would return home from being away at sea. This was a small two bedroomed tenement dwelling situated at the top of the house.

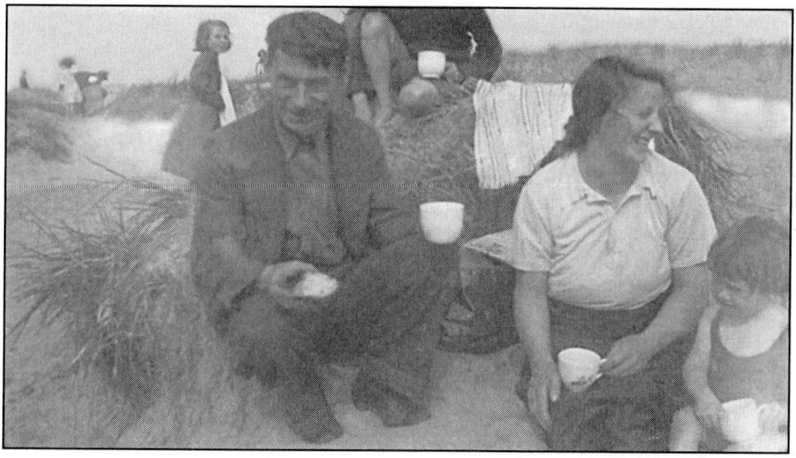

***Brother and sister, Paddy and Biddy Coffey on the beach in Dollymount.***

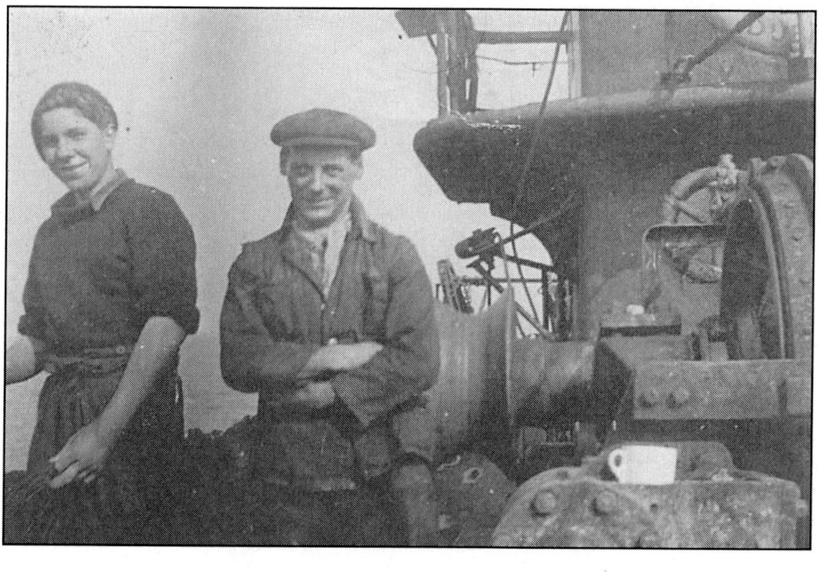

***Tommy Coffey sailing on a Trawler out of Ringsend.***

As a young boy Paddy Coffey and his brother Tommy decided to go to sea. They both boarded their first vessels in Ringsend, Paddy on a merchant ship and Tommy on a fishing trawler. Tommy would sometimes bring home several bottles of fresh Cod Liver Oil for his family to use on sick children. At one time Ringsend was the main port into Dublin for goods and passengers.

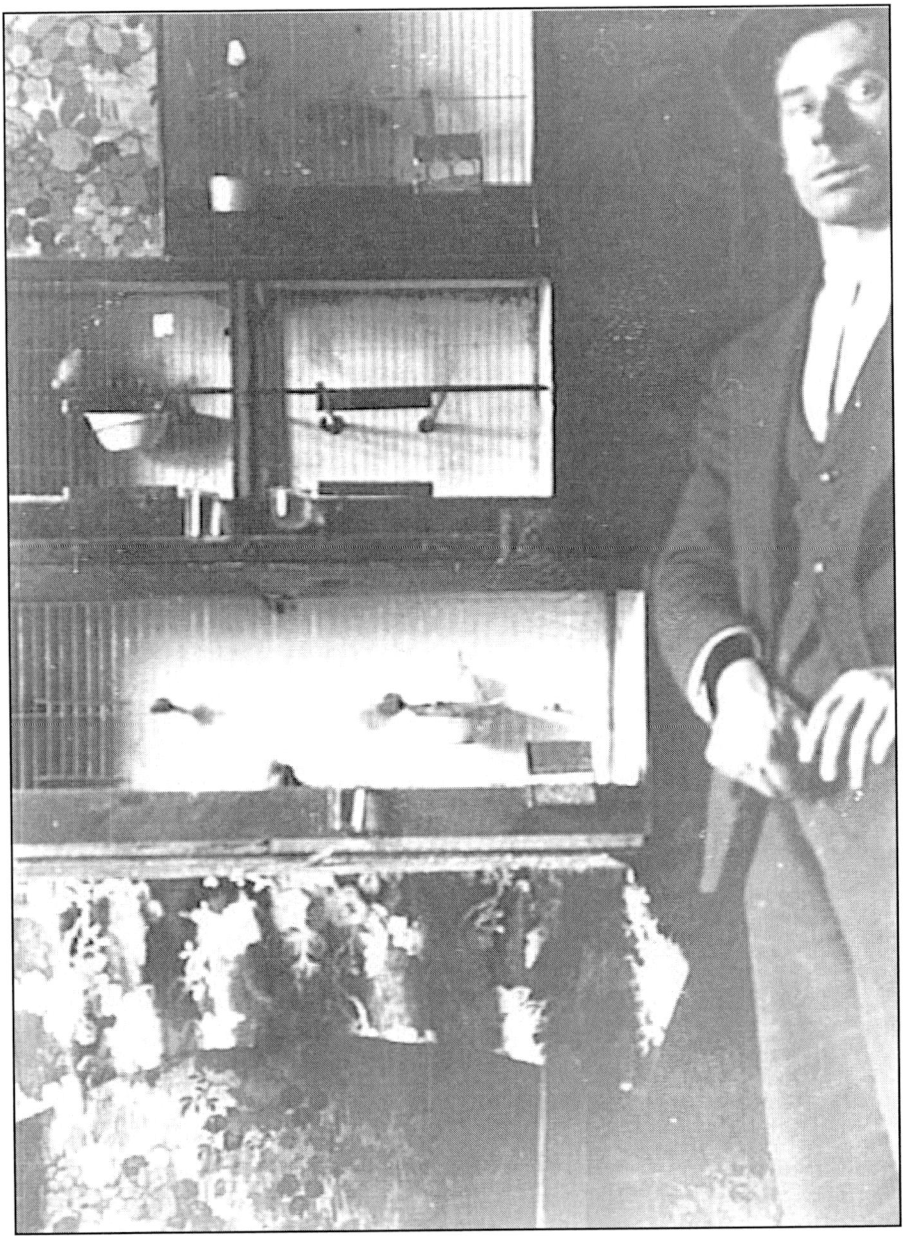

***Paddy Coffey and the tenement aviary.***

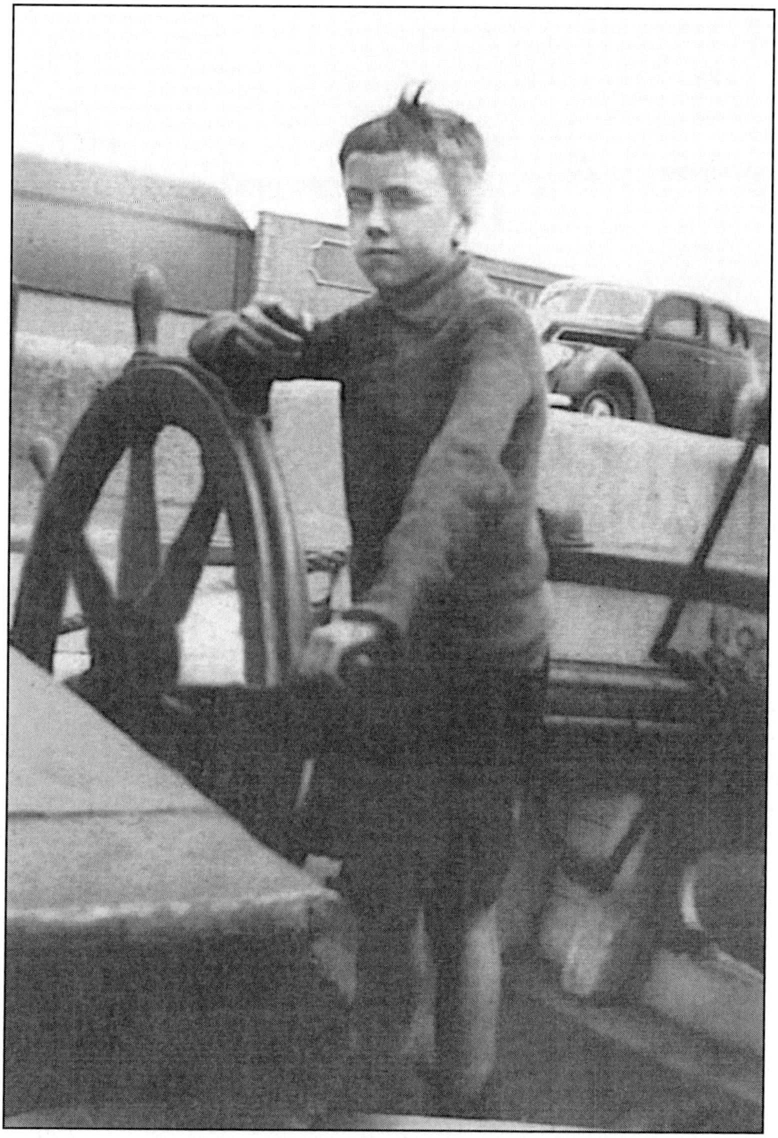

***Denis Doyle on board the Squirrel.***

Paddy Coffey would often take his nephew Denis Doyle or one of his brothers on a boat trip across to Liverpool and back. Denis was sometimes allowed to take the helm under the supervision of Paddy's watchful eye. They sailed out of City Quay carrying scrap iron to a foundry in Liverpool and would sometimes return to Dublin with a consignment of red bricks that were made in Chester.

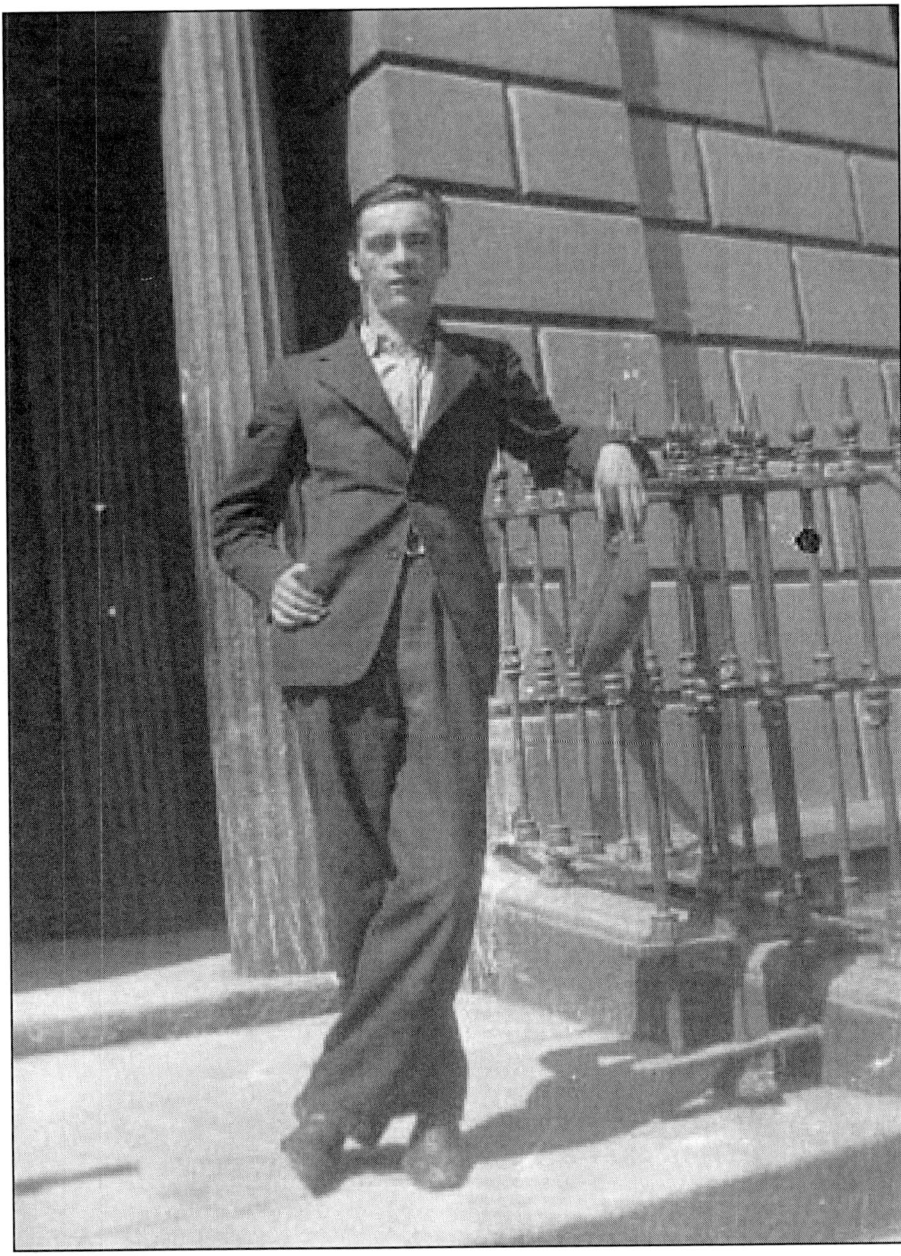

***Billser Barter Junior.***

Before the outbreak of WWII Billser Barter had joined the British Army on the advice of his cousin Bernard Coffey, who at that time was serving with the British Army in Malta. Billser became a Gunner with the 9th Coast Regiment, Royal Artillery and was stationed in Singapore. The British had begun building a naval base at Singapore in 1923, partly in response to Japan's increasing naval power. A major component of the base was completed in March 1938, when the King George VI Graving Dock was opened; more than 300 meters in length, it was the largest dry dock in the world at the time. The base was completed in 1941 and defended by artillery, searchlights, and the newly built nearby Tengah Airfield.

On the 15 January 1942 after intense fighting and with the loss of many lives Singapore fell to the Japanese Imperial Army. The Japanese registered each Allied Prisoner of War and had their name and home address printed onto index cards as part of a filing system. When Billser Barter stood before the Japanese Officer he was asked his name. When he gave his name the officer immediately recognised his accent and said *'You are from Dublin in Ireland'*. Billser answered that that was correct. The officer stepped forward and punched Billser in the face and knocking him to the ground said *'This is not your war'*. He told Billser that he had been educated in Trinity College, Dublin and recognised Billser's accent. However, the officer did arrange for Billser to be put working in the vegetable garden area of the prison camp and that made his life as a POW a little more bearable in Singapore. Billser was later transported by sea and rail to work on the Burma Railway. When Japan eventually surrendered the Japanese Officer came to Billser and shook his hand after which Billser hit him a punch and said *'Now we're quits'*. Billser was then placed under arrest by his own sergeant for striking an officer.

Billser Barter spent five years as a Japanese Prisoner of War. He was part of a forced Labour Camp situated on the banks of the River Kwai that later became famous as a Hollywood blockbuster movie *'The Bridge on the River Kwai'*. In October 1942, six hundred men from the Royal Artillery were loaded onto a former coal ship in Singapore docks. Conditions on board were horrendous. They were crammed below in the hold, without food, water, ventilation, or any sanitary arrangements, suffering from heat exhaustion, dehydration, and dysentery. During the voyage Japanese troops entertained themselves by pouring buckets of urine through the hatches onto the POW's below. Billser Barter and the Gunners were destined for the Solomon Islands but eighty-two men were disembarked at Rabaul, on 6 November 1942. Rabaul is a township in East New Britain province, on the island of New Britain, in the country of Papua New Guinea.

The Gunner POW's included Private William Barter from Dublin, Lance Bombardier Patrick Ahern, from Fermoy, County Cork, and Lance Sergeant Patrick (Nobby) Nolan from Wexford. They were put to work unloading cargo from a Japanese ship. One of the gunners had a wound on his back that broke open. Regardless, he was ordered to continue carrying sacks of rice. When he objected, he was tied to a tree and tortured. The Japanese soldiers tried to make him drink urine. When he refused they beat him and poured a bucket of urine over his head. Then they stripped him, rubbed animal manure over his genitals, and left him (tied to the tree) to be tormented by hordes of tropical biting insects. The following morning he was taken away and murdered***...(The Emperor's Irish Slaves by Robert Widders).***

In a later statement made by Billser Barter as a POW survivor he wrote that *'While unloading oil and petrol from the railway I punched holes in the drums with a Jack Knife and brick. Also bombs were being unloaded from the train and detonators; I threw a lot of them into the jungle. In Singapore I filed down the striking pin of the Jap's rifles while cleaning them. Gunners McCann, Jefferies and Hunter, these three Gunners escaped from Changi P.O.W. camp, was caught by the Japs in Singapore and was brought back to Changi and shot which was witnessed by Lt Col. Heath, D.S.P. Company, 9th Coast Regiment, R.A, Changi'.* These three young soldiers were a part of Billser's gun team.

In 1941 Billser Barter arrived at Ban Pong station in Thailand and from there was despatched north to the railway via Kanchanaburi to his destination of Kin Saiyok, a jungle camp to the north of Hellfire Pass. In July 1943, according to his report, he was sent back down to Chungkai Camp that was then a large and growing hospital camp on the outskirts of Kanchanaburi. It would appear that Billser may have remained in Chungkai (or perhaps nearby) until early 1945 when he was sent off with a large number of other prisoners to Nakhon Nayok Camp in central Thailand, well away from the railway and its main camps. Unfortunately he was then included in a party of some 600 men who were then sent on a long march/walk of some 630 kilometres over the next 3 or 4 months, repairing minor roads and bridges for the Japanese in preparation for the defence or retreat for their troops upon the anticipated invasion by the Allied Army in Thailand. Less than half of these 600 men survived this terrible ordeal.

When Billser Barter eventually arrived back home in Dublin after the war every little detail of the horrors he had endured, the endless beatings and the cruelties inflicted on him and his fellow soldiers were deeply embedded into his memory. He would never forget what he had witnessed as a Japanese Prisoner of War. But Ireland being Ireland at that time Billser mostly kept his memories of those years to himself, nobody was interested in listening to a former British Soldier and his tales of what he did in the War.

One story tells us that in later years Billser was making his way home from his local pub, very drunk when two Policemen approached him. In the strange world in which Billser lived he believed they were two Japanese soldiers coming to torture him. Because of this he attacked the two Policemen who in turn beat him senseless. The result of this beating left Billser worse than ever. He died on the 12th September 1991 and is buried in an unmarked grave in Glasnevin Cemetery, Dublin.

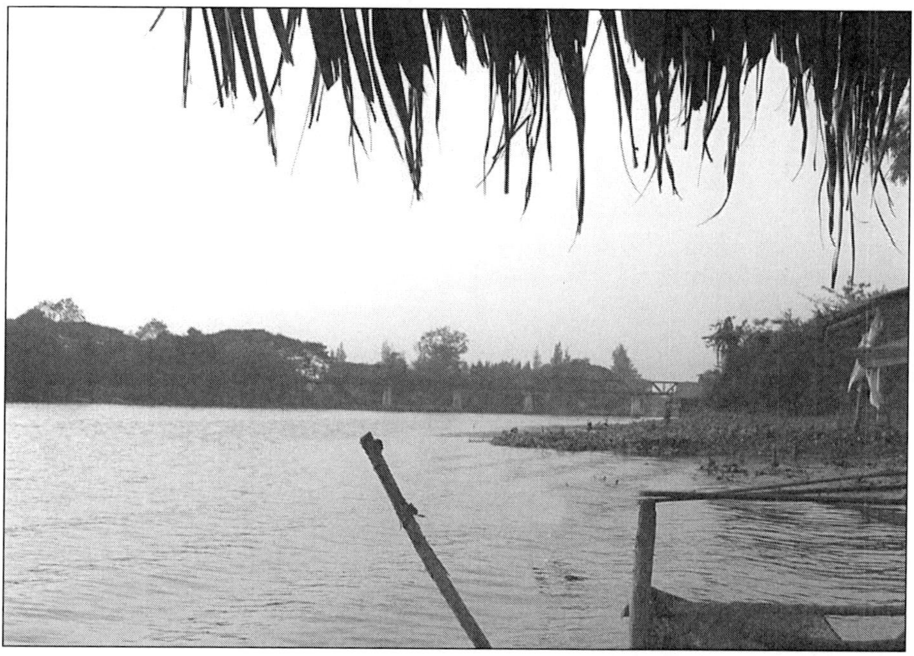

***The Bridge on the River Kwai.***

***(Photo by Martin Coffey)***

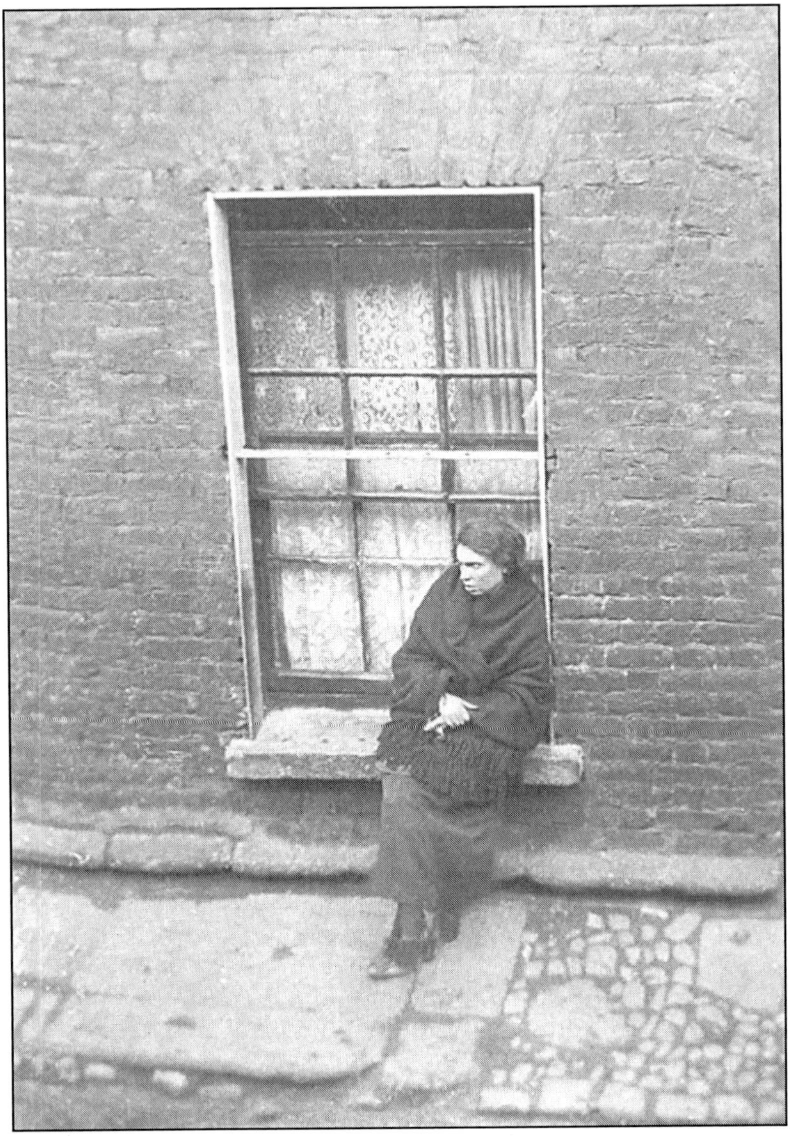

***Maggie Gorman***

In this photograph, Paddy Coffey's aunt Maggie Gorman is seated on the ledge of her parlour room window in Railway Street. The rooms on the ground floor located at the front of the tenement houses were always referred to as the 'Front Parlour'. Those at the back of the house were known as the 'Back Parlour'. The rent for the rooms at the front of the house were always more expensive than those at the back.

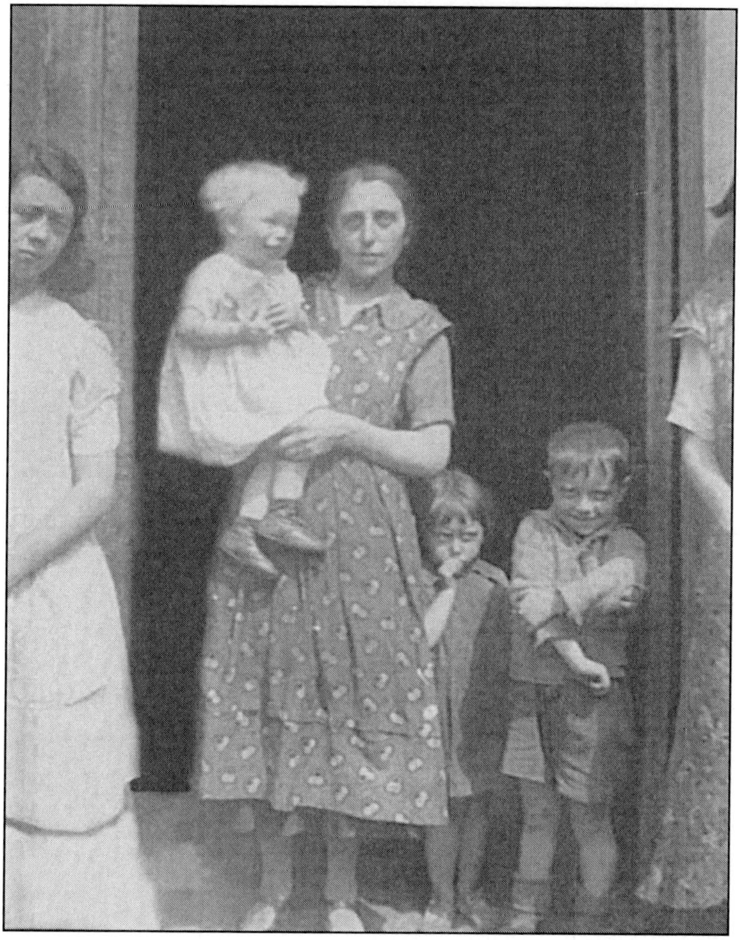

***May Doyle is holding Willie Gorman in her arms. The little girl is her daughter Mary Anne (Gracie) and the boy is her son Bernard (Barney). The girl on the left is Bessie McKeever. The girl standing on the right is Chrissie Doyle.***

By all accounts, May Doyle was known as a woman who never refused a helping hand to family, neighbour or stranger. May had a sister named Lucy who was living on the North Strand area of Dublin in 1941 when German Planes bombed the area and killed twenty-eight people. Prior to her marriage to Sonny Doyle May lived in a room with her parents at number 6 Elliott Place. After their marriage May and Sonny then lived across the road in a room in number 10 Elliott Place that was owned by Sonny's mother.

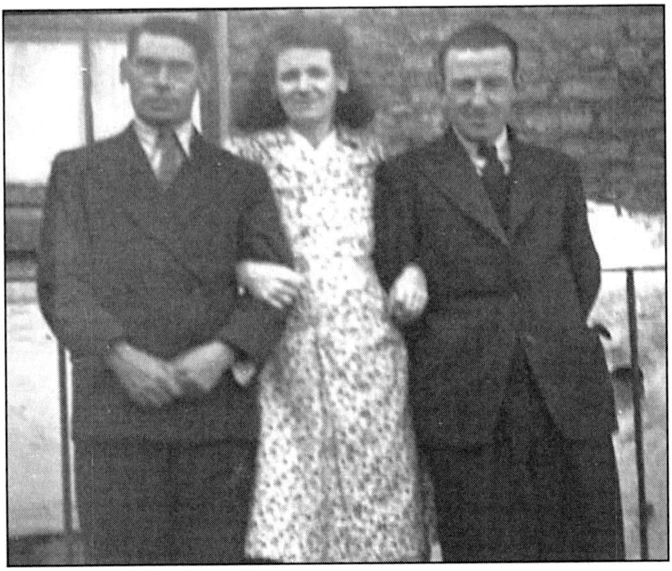

***Paddy Coffey with his sister Rooie and her husband Alfie Kane.***

Alfie Kane was a Merchant Seaman all his working life. He was a quiet man and not given to complaining or boasting about where he had travelled to or what he had to endure while away at sea. He was born and reared in the North Inner City of Dublin where things were never easy or comfortable for his family and neighbours. Like so many men from this area who lived close to the River Liffey Alfie took to the sea and a life on the ocean waves. He was often away from home for months at a time. The most famous ship that he ever served on was known in seafaring circles as *'The Bitch'*. In 1941 Sean Lemass was Minister for Industry, Commerce and Supplies. He was also the driving force behind Irelands search for ships. In peace time, ships from other countries had brought vital supplies into Ireland but with the threat from German U Boats who had formed a blockade across the Atlantic those vital supplies had now been cut off and Ireland was in a state of panic. The nation was in need of food as its pre-war reserves of wheat were quickly dwindling. Ireland was badly in need of a merchant fleet and Lemass was assigned the job of putting one together.

Most of the ships available at that time were no better than recycled tin cans. One ship in particular that had come into the hands of the Irish Government was a 2,000 ton rusty sea-scarred tramp named 'The Cetvrti', a Yugoslavian ship that had been part bombed by German fighter planes and eventually ended up in Irish waters. It was renamed 'The Beech' and on its black hull had 'Eire' painted in 6 foot high letters. To those that knew better she was always referred to as 'The Bitch'. Its navigational lights were just oil lamps. In May of 1941 Lemass decided that the 'Bitch' would set sail as part of a convoy from Dublin and head off to Canada in search of food to feed the nation. As she headed out into the Atlantic Ocean a telephone cable fouled her anchor and the convoy had to sail without her. Five days later she eventually sailed with a convoy of nearly 40 merchantmen. Within a short period of time 'The Bitch' sprung one of many leaks that would trouble her for the entire journey. An explosion shook the engine room when a piston on a dynamo broke in two. An iron bar flew through the air and struck Stoker Alfie Kane on the head, there was no doctor on board and the First Officer stitched the wound. Alfie Kane was unconscious for three days. Alfie survived the journey to Canada where the Canadians couldn't believe that 'The Bitch' had sailed all the way from Ireland in its sad condition.

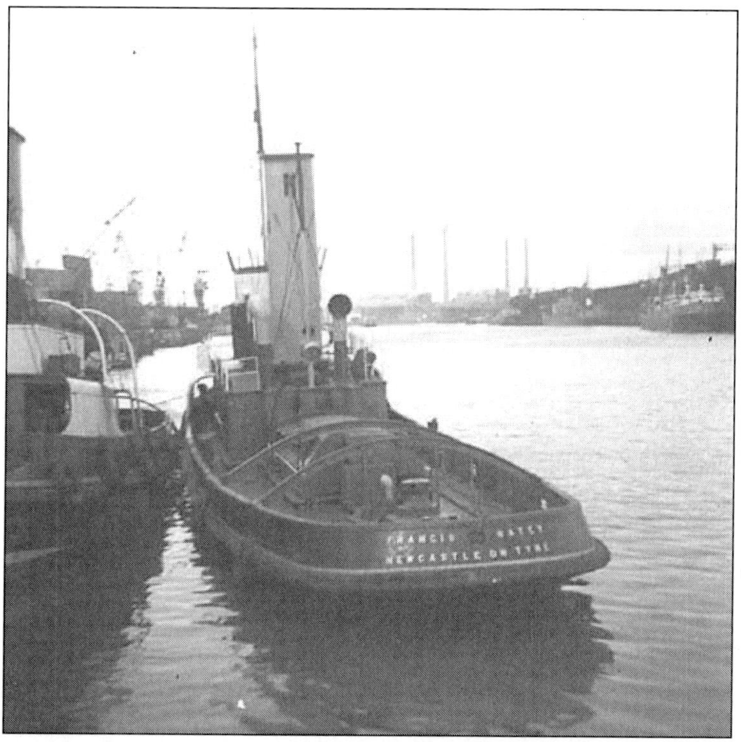

***The Francis Batey on the Tyne River, Newcastle.***

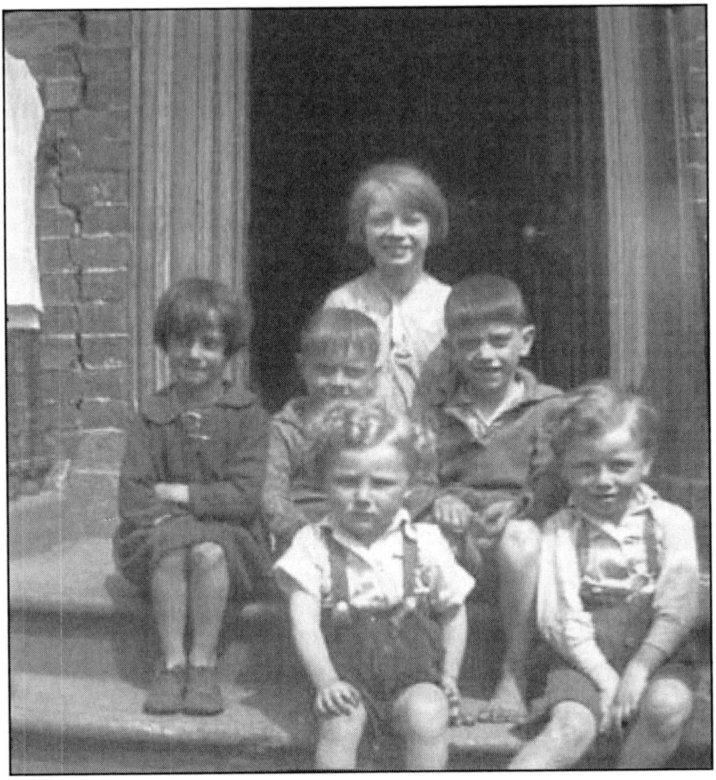

***Eileen Meehan, Barney Doyle, Mary Bridget McKeever and Blacker Doyle with Willie and Jack Gorman.***

The two Doyle brothers and the two Gorman Brothers are first cousins to each other; they are also first cousins to Paddy Coffey. The two girls are neighbours children from the same area. Blacker Doyle is barefooted which was not unusual for that time. Many young boys and girls played around the streets of Dublin with no shoes on. This photograph was taken on the steps of a tenement house in Railway Street, Dublin in the 1930's. The trousers worn by the Gorman brothers have all the appearance of being hand sewn by their mother from the remnant of some old coat or blanket.

Each of these young children grew up in a world where nothing came easy to their parents. Hard work and poverty walked hand in hand around their neighbourhood. Filth, squalor and disease were ever present in their daily lives. Death was ever present in every tenement house where Wakes were a common occurrence and every child was expected to kiss the corpse to prevent it from coming back and haunting them in their dreams.

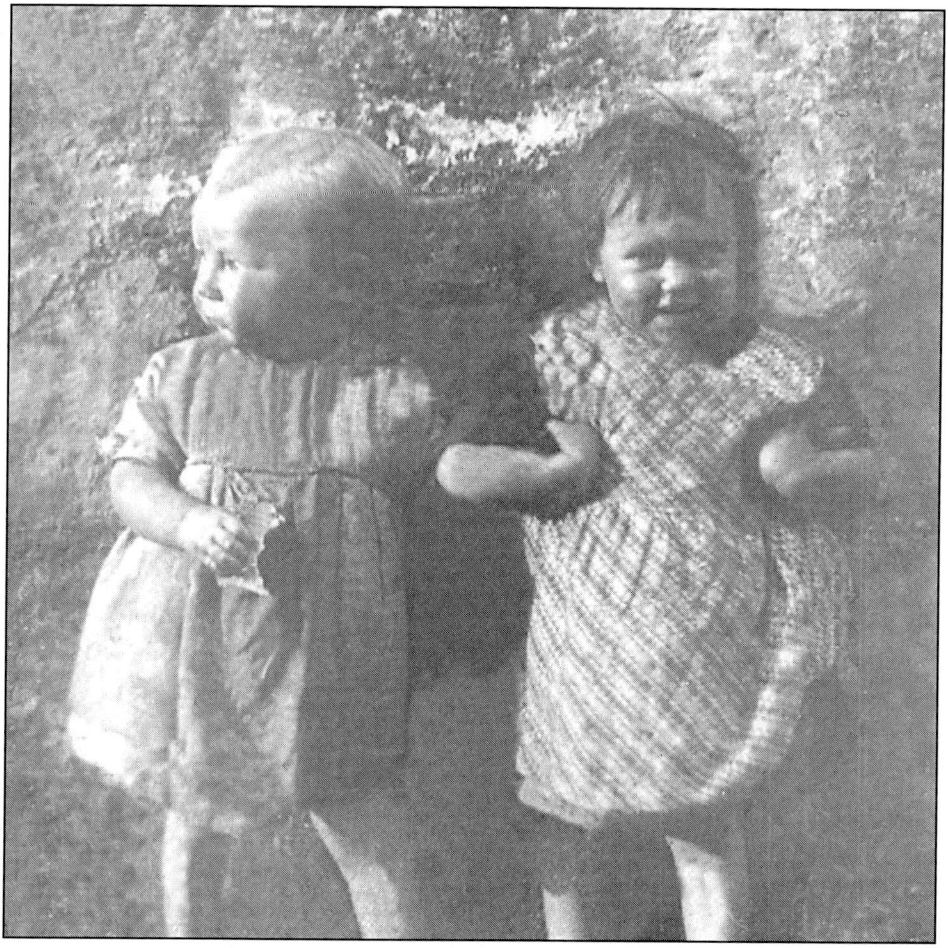

***Willie Gorman and Gracie Doyle 1936.***

One of the stories that was told by Paddy Coffey about this particular photograph concerns the Fairy Folk of Irish Myths and Legends. It was believed then and may still be believed today by some people that the Fairy Folk of long ago would sneak into the home of a family that had a newborn baby boy. They would take the human child away and leave one of their own in its place and this would be known as a 'Changeling Child'. This replacement child would grow up to be a troubled child who would get up to all kinds of mischief by bringing shame and disgrace on the family and breaking the heart of the mother who reared it. So in order to fool the Fairy Folk some mothers would dress their new little boys in the same style of clothing as a girl. In this photograph young Willie Gorman is about two years old and still being dressed like a young girl. When starting off in his early days of photography Paddy Coffey mostly used his own family members as subjects to shoot through the lens of his Box Camera. He shared these early photos with the more seasoned professional photographers who allowed him into their Studios. In this way he was gaining great experience and getting the best advice available at that time on the various ways to set up a photo shoot, how to position his subjects and where to best place them in relation to the surrounding area in which the photograph was being taken.

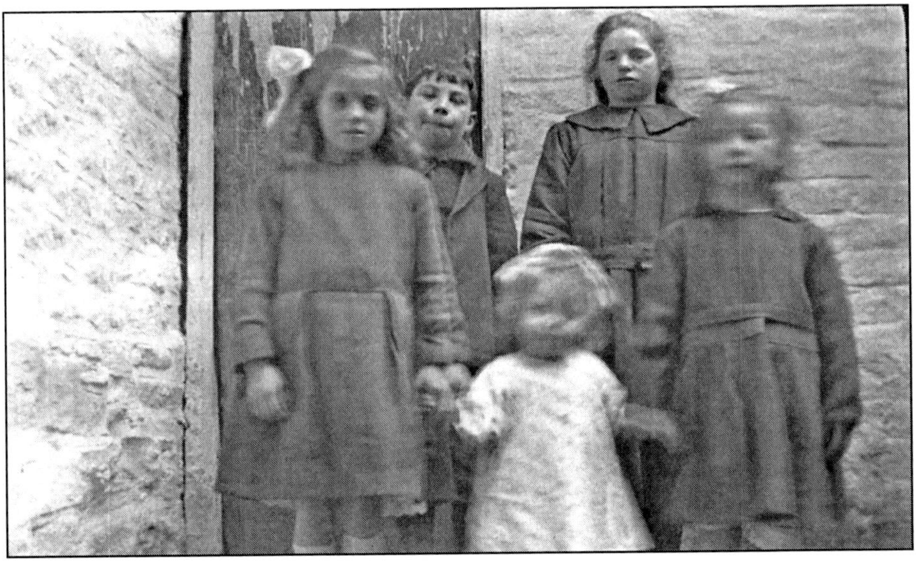

***Four young girls and a boy***

These young girls may be from some orphanage in the area as none of the local schools had girls wearing uniforms at that time. It was not unusual back then for families to *'Take in'* children who were sometime referred to as *'Monto Babies'*. These were mainly babies belonging to some of the local prostitutes who were in danger of being abandoned or sometimes they were young boys and girls with no family left to take care of them.

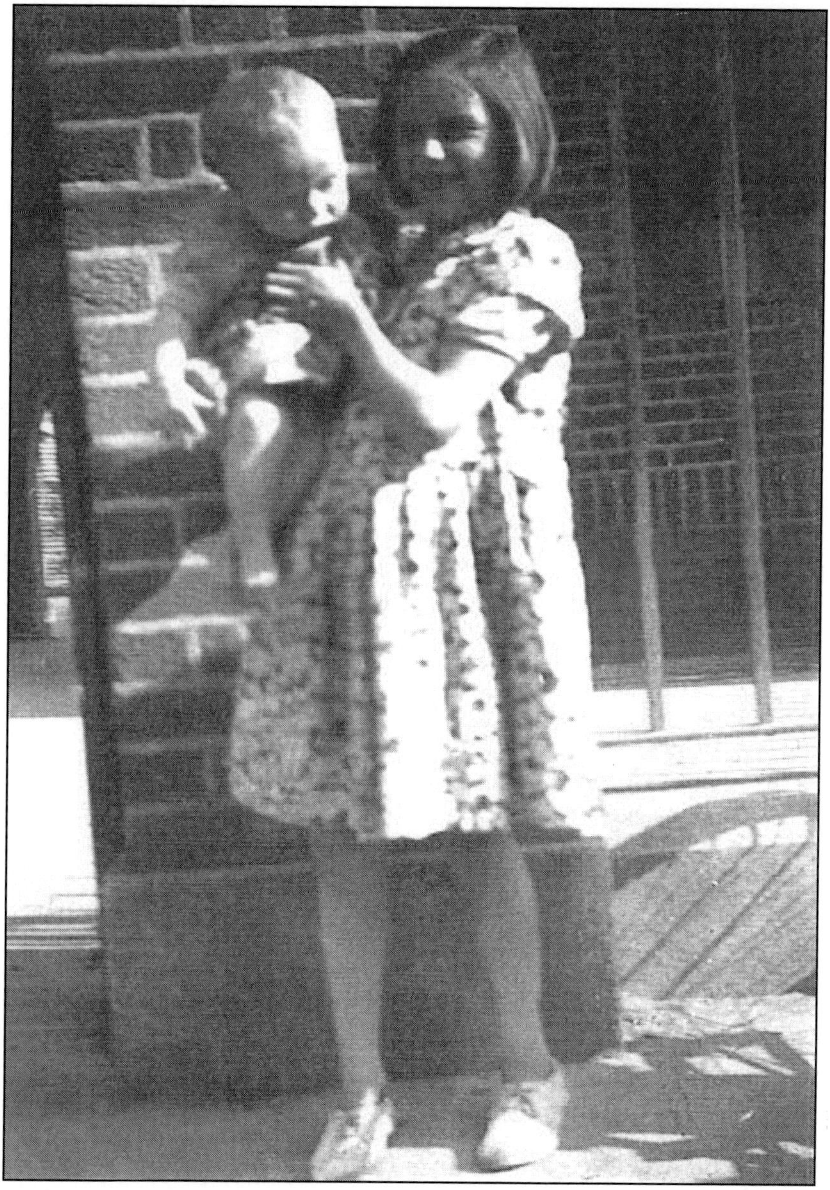

***Chrissie Doyle holding her younger sister Gracie.***

Chrissie Doyle suffered from poor eyesight all of her life. A doctor had recommended to her parents that Chrissie should be fed on plenty of Glaxo Powder. From that moment on Chrissie Doyle became known to everyone in her neighbourhood as '*Glaxo*'.

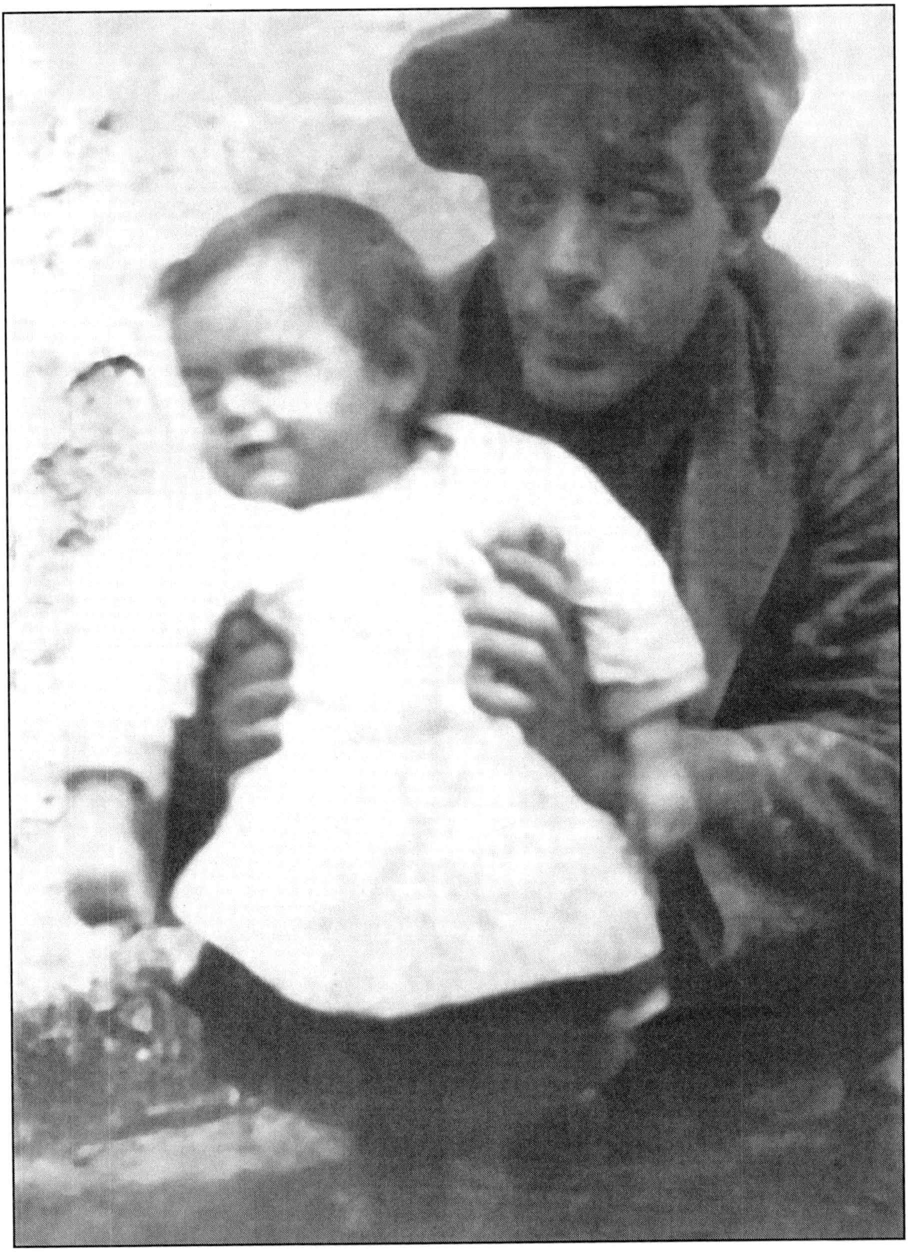

***Sonny Doyle with his daughter Chrissie 1924.***

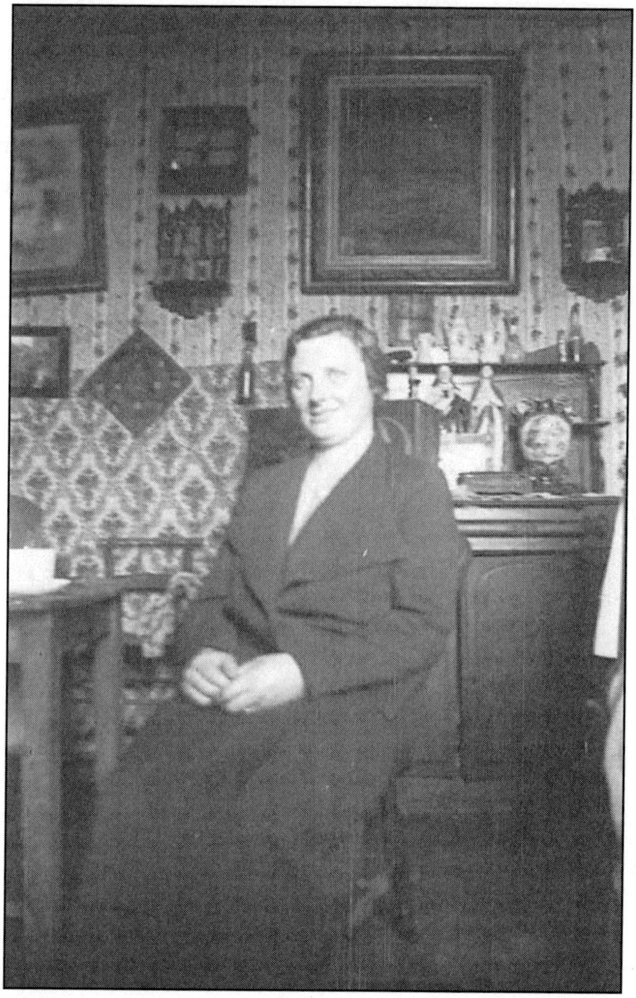

***Biddy Coffey in May Doyle's tenement room.***

This photograph with Biddy Coffey gives us a clearer view of some more of the contents of May Doyle's tenement room and especially those on her wall. Near the top of the picture there is a birdcage with a small bird inside. Sonny Doyle often laid traps to capture birds so that he could study their behaviour and listen to them whistle and sing.

The old style Ringboard is quite clearly seen. Both adults and children would have taken part in a game of *'Rings'*. To the right of the Ringboard there is a Stout Bottle with a teat on it. This would have been used by May Doyle to feed milk to her baby with.

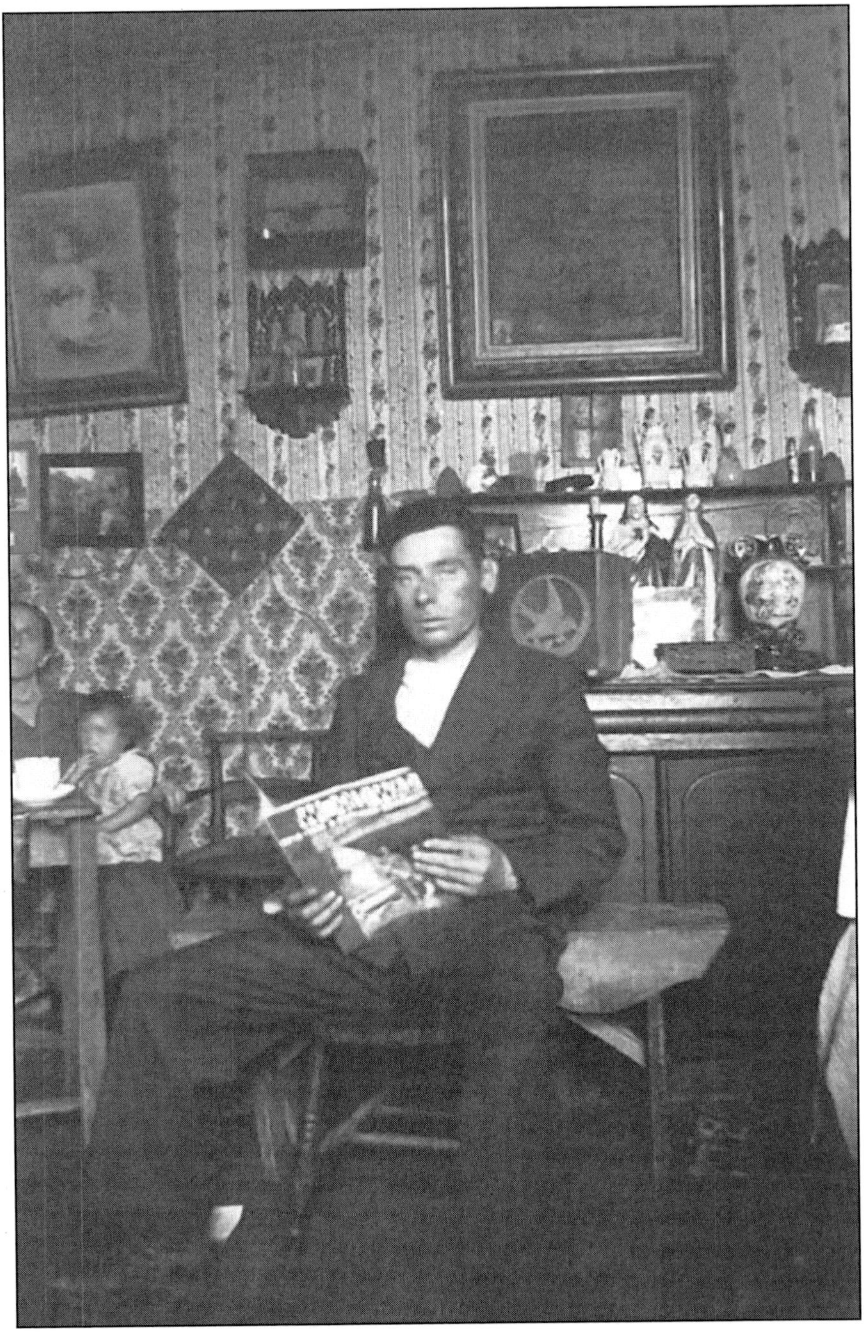

***Paddy Coffey reading a War Magazine in 1936.***

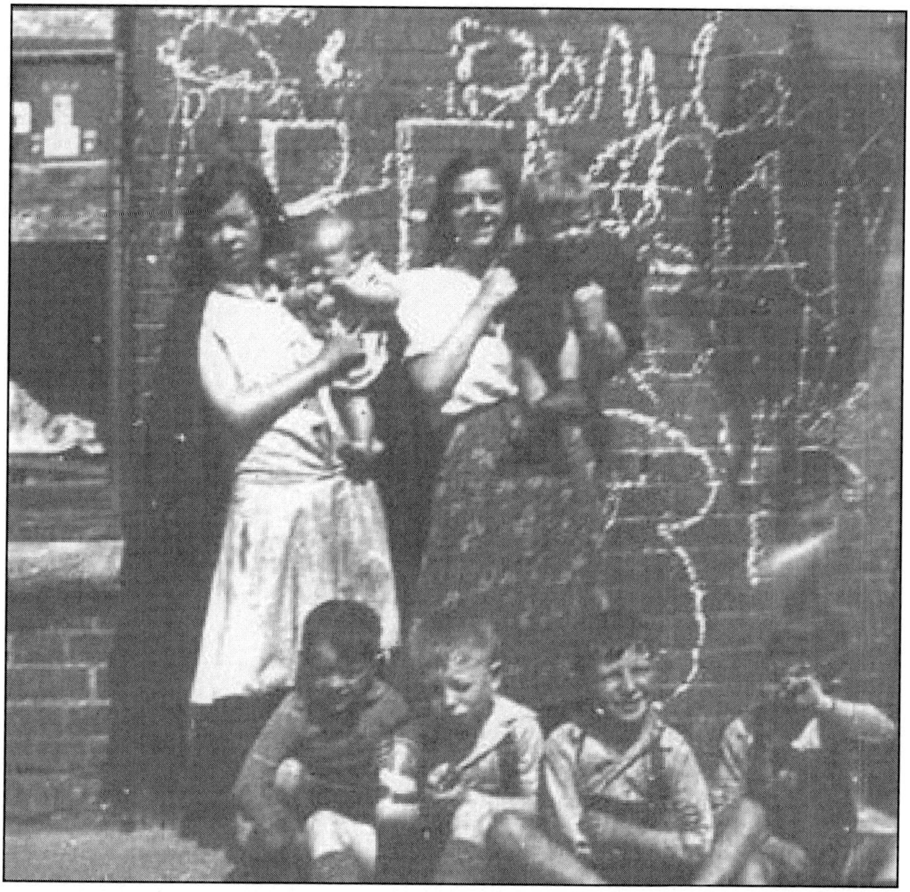

***Bessie McKeever with Chrissie Doyle holding her younger sister Gracie. Barney Doyle is sitting on the left; the other boys may be Murrayer and Mousie Meehan. There is no name for the boy on the right. Notice the name 'DOYLE' written in chalk on the wall.***

'We were all pals and we hung around with each other. We only played on a few streets back then because you had to stay where your mother could see you or you'd be grounded. You only went off your street if you were going for a message for your mother or father. Now sometimes if I asked my mother could I go around to say Beaver Street or Foley Street to play with someone she'd tell me to be home by such and such a time or if my pal was going for a message for his mother you might be let go with him and that.'... **Barney Doyle**

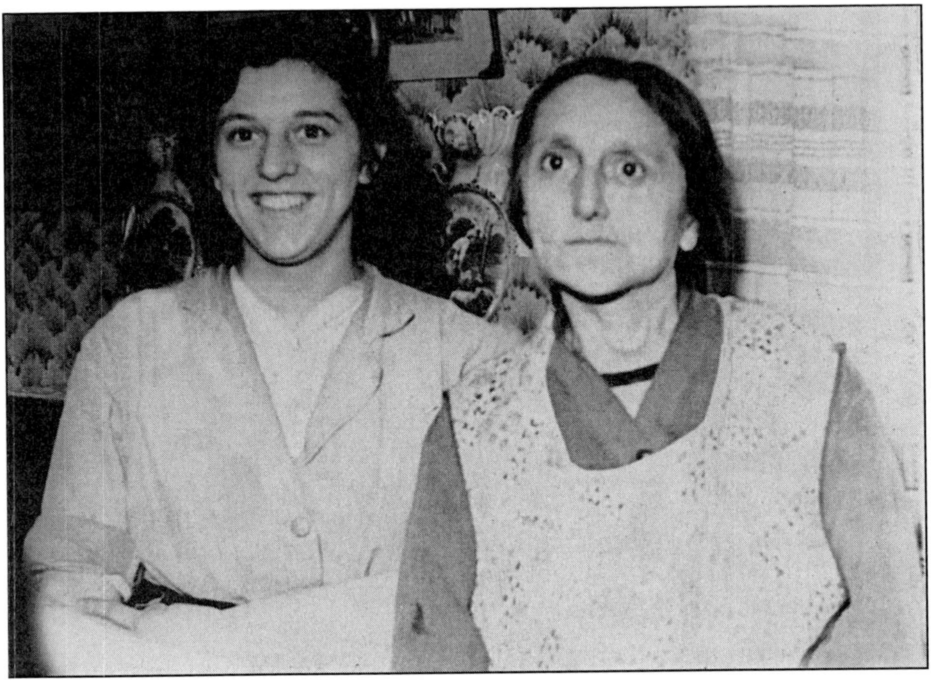

***Gracie Doyle with her mother May.***

Paddy Coffey's mother died from heart failure in 1917. His father was away fighting in France and Iraq during WWI and shortly after his return from the war he remarried. The new stepmother to his six young children decided she did not want the trouble of rearing his children and told her husband to make arrangements to have the four boys sent away to Artane Industrial School and to put the two girls into service with the nuns. Word of this plot quickly reached the ears of their aunt, May Doyle. She instructed her husband Sonny to take the children away from their stepmother and to bring them home to her and that she would look after them. And so May and Sonny Doyle took over the parental role of five of these young children. The other child, Tommy Coffey went to stay with Mary Farrell and her husband Otto Larsen who lived on Summerhill. May and Sonny Doyle already had a young family of their own and they all lived in one room in their tenement house.

In later years when Paddy Coffey's youngest sister Rooie started dating a young sailor lad from the area by the name of Alfie Kane she asked May Doyle if she could bring Alfie up to meet her and Sonny because she said that herself and Alfie were 'Getting Serious'. At that time May Doyle earned some extra money with her sewing machine. She would take up curtains or the odd hem on a skirt or trousers for people in her neighbourhood. She also made aprons with big pockets on them for some of the street dealers who lived in the area. She also sewed up little white smocks for the orphan children in North William Street orphanage/school. So on the evening that Alfie Kane was due to visit their tenement room May Doyle decided to put a set of curtains belonging to her neighbour up on her own window to impress Alfie. When it came time for him to leave the curtains were taken down.

Sonny and May Doyle set a great example to all of the children in their care. They were good living parents and neither one of them ever touched a drop of alcohol. They were decent and hardworking people who struggled like most of their neighbours in an area of extreme poverty.

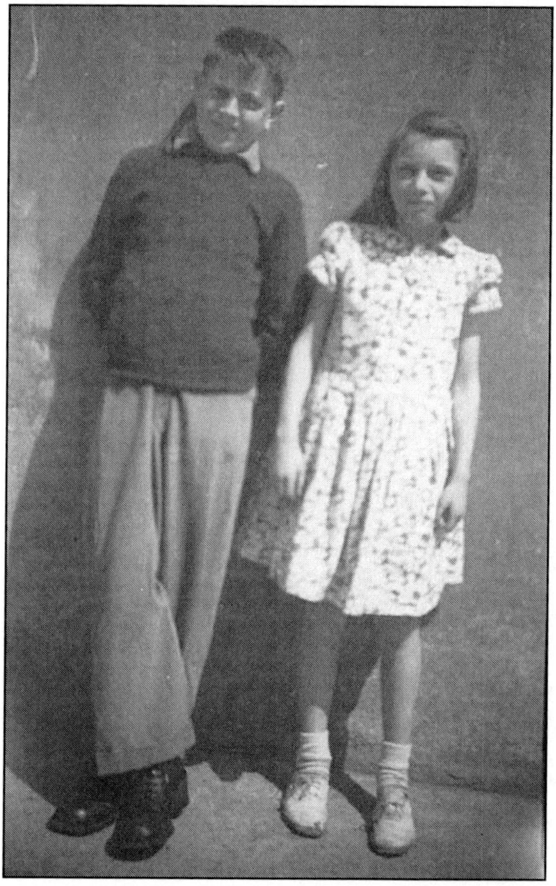

***Barney and Maggie Doyle.***

# Chapter 2

## Neighbours and Friends

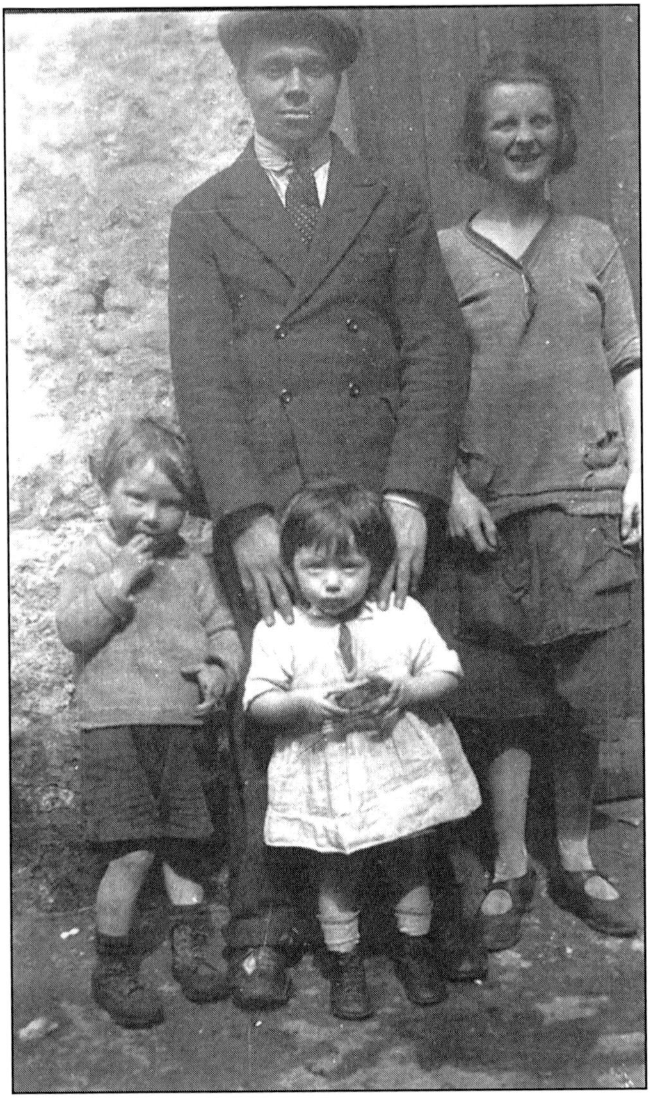

***Charlie Jameson with his wife Maggie McLoughlin. There are no names for the two children; one of whom it is believed is a 'Monto Baby.' Charlie Jameson was a great friend with Sonny Doyle.***

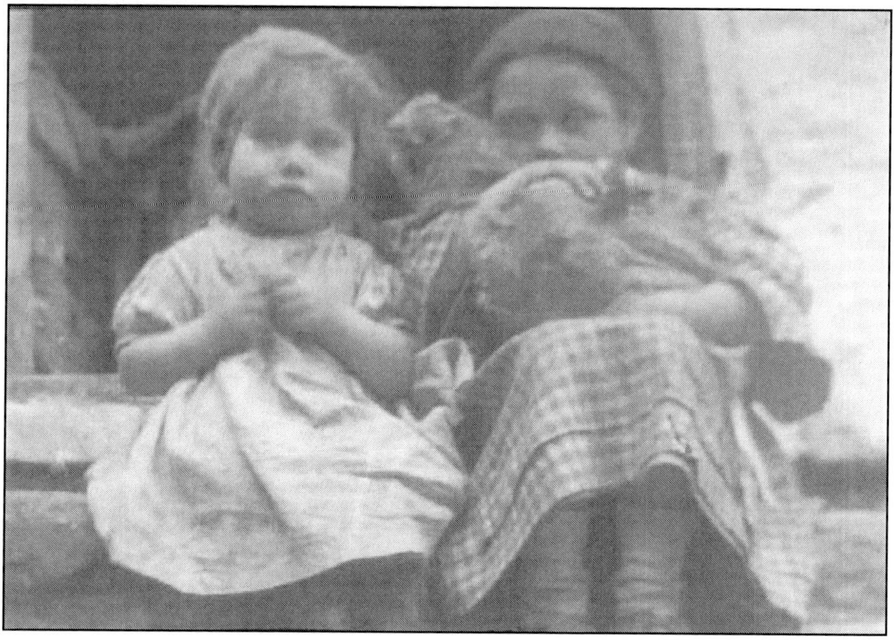

*Two young girls and their pet hen.*

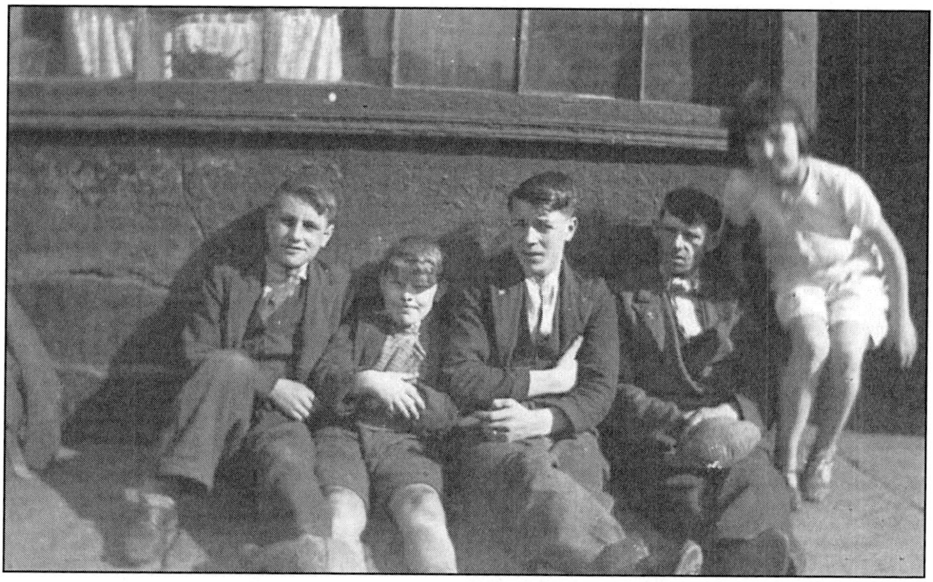

*Monto neighbours in Foley Street.*

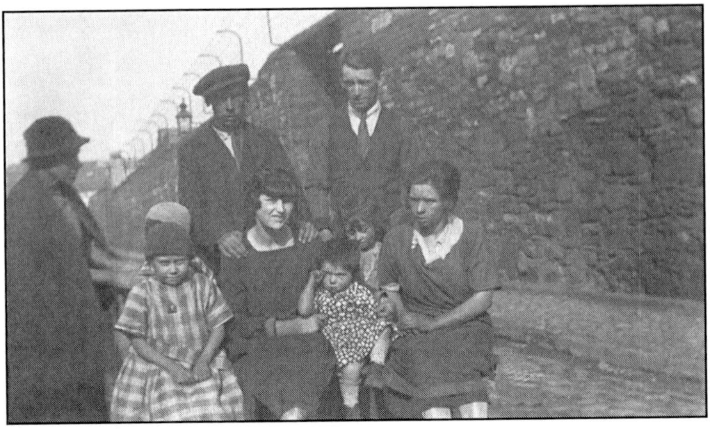

**Paddy Coffey** wearing his cap as he poses for a photograph with some of his neighbours and friends from the Monto. Seated on the right is ***Bridget Brown***, wife of ***John Darcy*** who is standing behind her. The lady on the left is wearing what appears to be a man's hat and a shawl. There is no name available for the lady in the middle or for any of the children. As with Paddy Coffey the children all look very dark skinned and tanned. The photograph was taken in Beaver Street about 1925. There once stood an old steel mill and iron works behind the wall on the right. The site was later cleared to make way for the building of Liberty House flats complex.

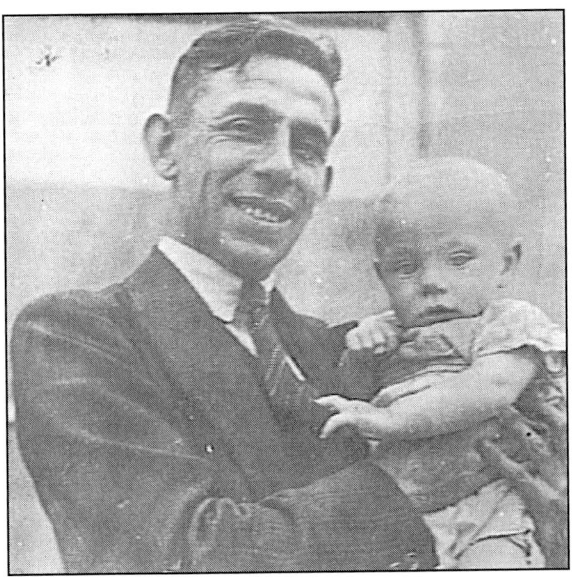

***Walter 'Wattie' Meehan and baby.***

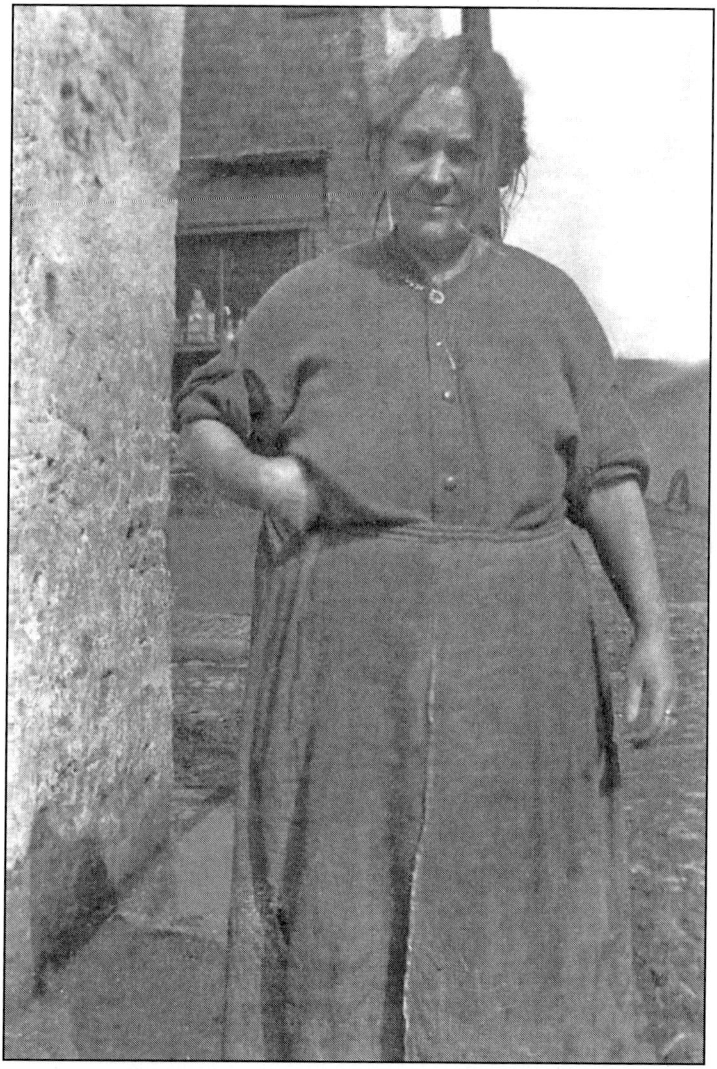

**Julia Farrell, a sister to Denis Farrell.**

*'A relation of Denis and Julia Farrell became widowed at a young age and was left with three young children. Unable to cope with her situation she went to speak with her parish priest. He suggested that she should allow the nuns to take care of her children until she felt more able to cope. He also offered her a job as his housekeeper. After a short while she decided to take the advice of the priest and allowed him to make the necessary arrangements for her children, two boys and a girl to go into short term*

*care. A little over a year later this young mother told the priest that she had met a man whom she wanted to marry.*

*The priest insisted on meeting her new man and spoke to him about the three young children in care. After the wedding ceremony the new couple and the priest paid a visit to the nuns. When the priest explained the situation to the Mother Superior she asked him to wait while she checked her records. After waiting almost one full hour two young nuns came along with two of the original children. They told the priest that the Mother Superior said he must have made a mistake because they only had two children, a boy and a girl on their records for that mother. The priest told them that there must be some mistake and asked to speak to the Mother Superior. He was told that she was too busy to speak to him. The poor young mother was heartbroken and never really came to terms with the loss of her little boy who was never to be seen again'.*

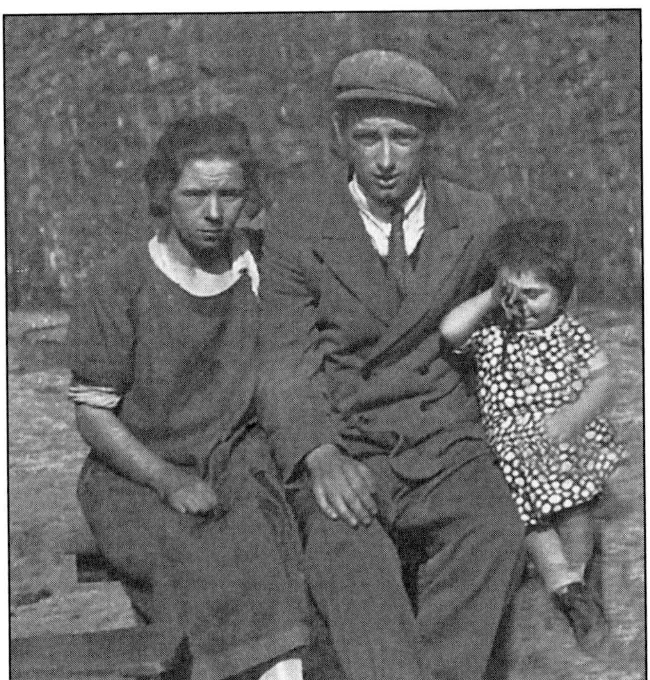

***John Darcy and his wife Bridget Brown, girl unknown.***

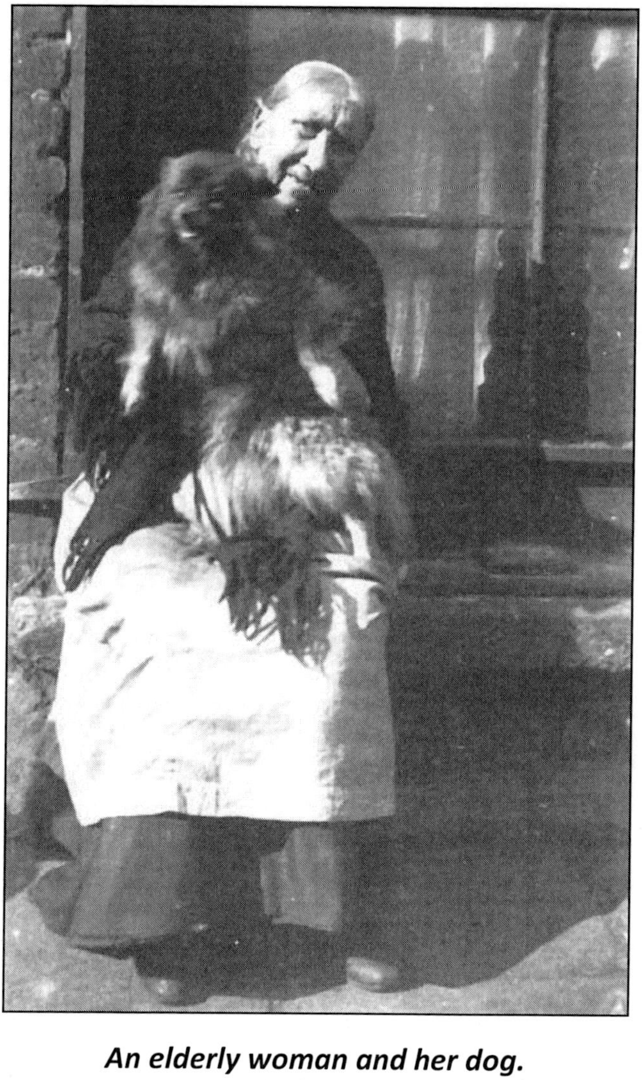

***An elderly woman and her dog.***

Sitting on the ledge of a front parlour window of a tenement house was a great way to pass the time of day and especially if the sun was shining in the right direction. There was always plenty of opportunity to stop a passing neighbour and catch up with the latest news or gossip. Many of these tenement houses were as tall as four stories or higher and in such narrow streets as were found in the Monto area not too much sunshine would find its way onto these dark and dreary streets. So sunshine was always a welcome visitor in the Monto.

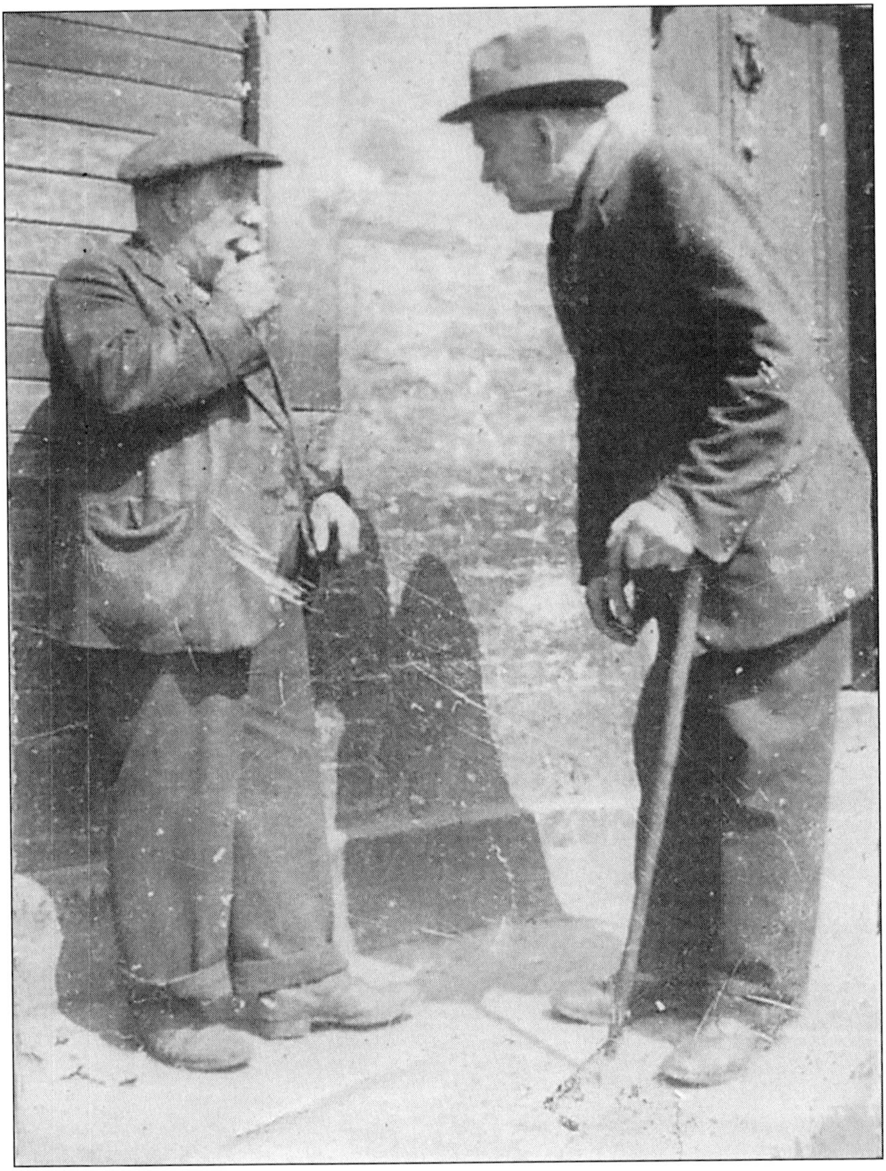

***Two old Dubliners having a chat... Harry McGinn on the left.***

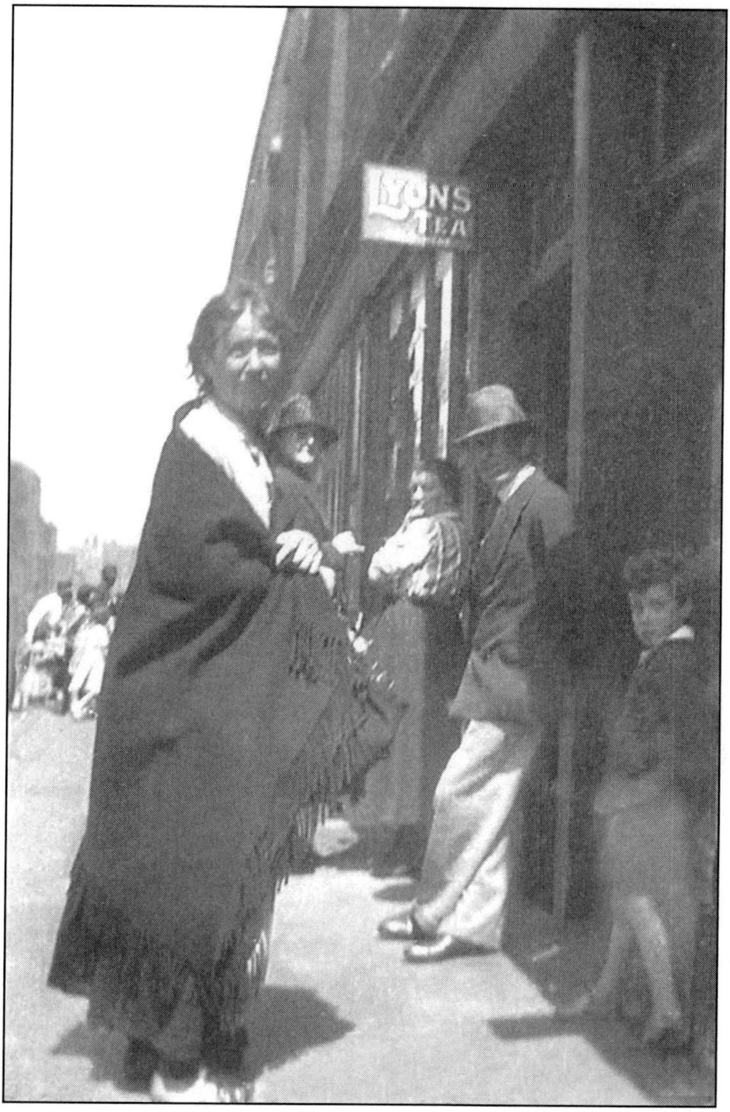


***Woman with a Shawl.***

In times gone by a lot of Dublin women wore shawls similar to the one this lady in the photograph is wearing. It was probably a fashion that had been handed down through generations of Irish women before coats came into fashion. A woman carrying a baby would sometimes keep it tucked in under the shawl out of the cold. In times of political unrest it was also a way of carrying concealed guns or other such weapons when taking them to rebel forces around the city or neighbourhood.

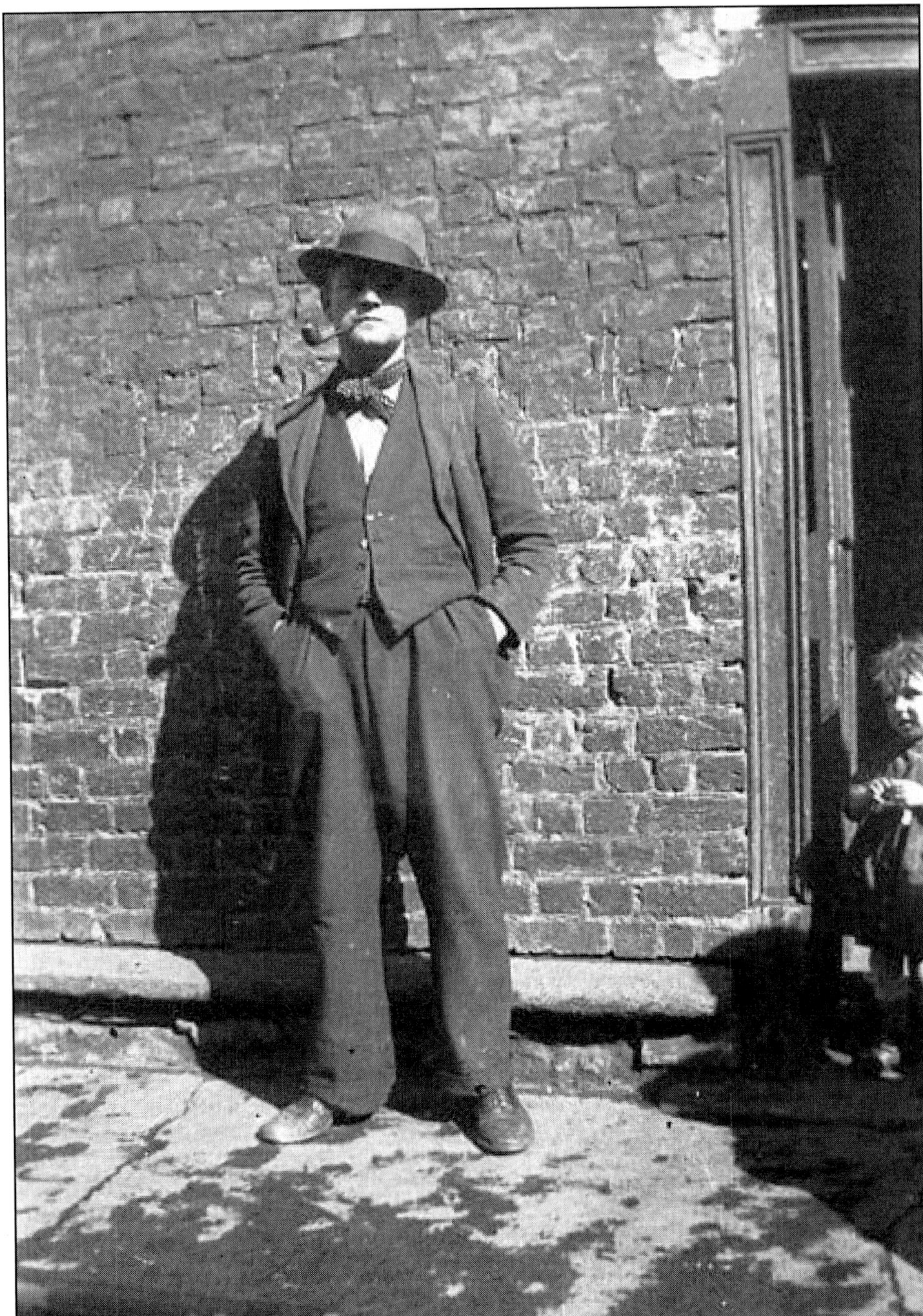

***A man and his pipe.***

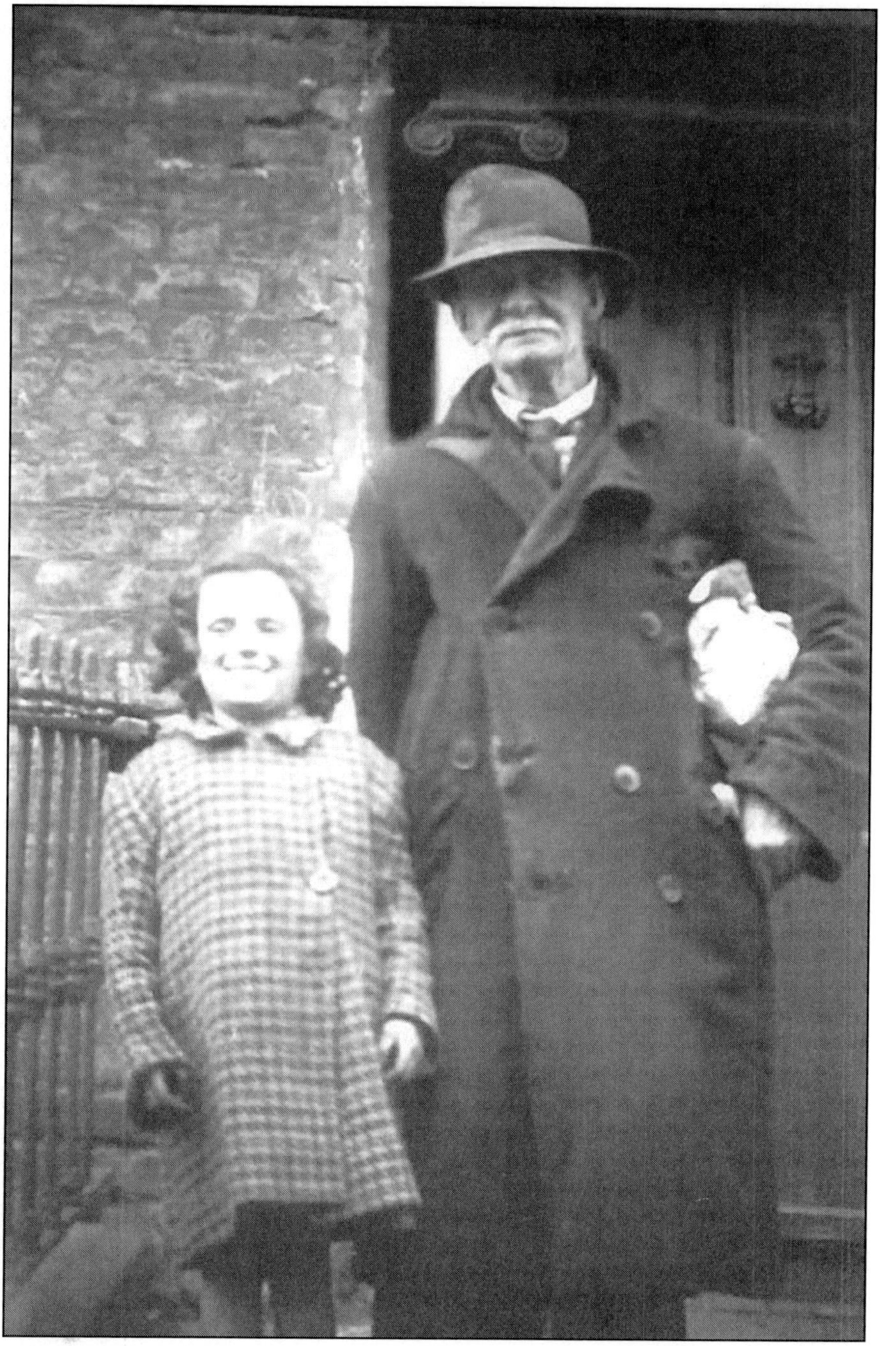

***An elderly gentleman with a young girl.***

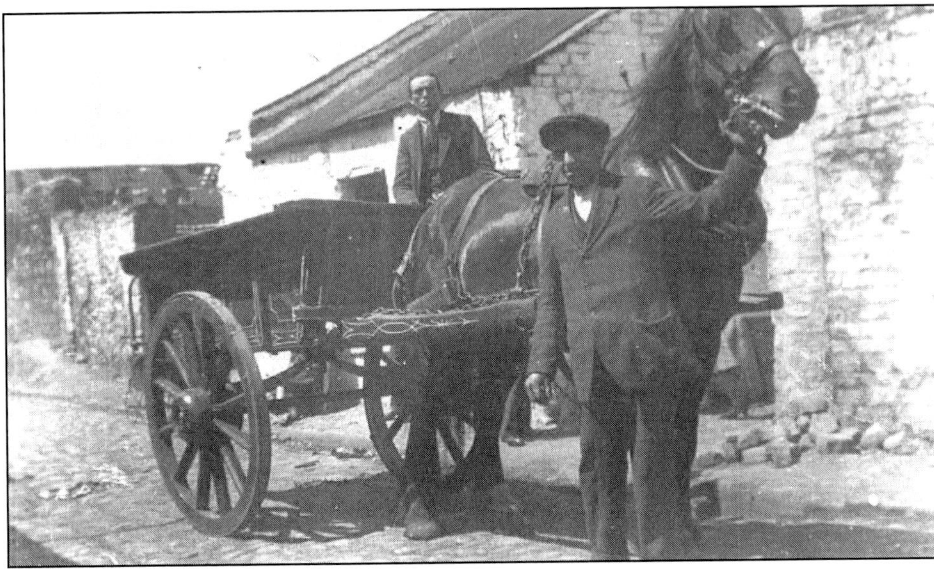

***Whacker Costigan with his horse and cart.***

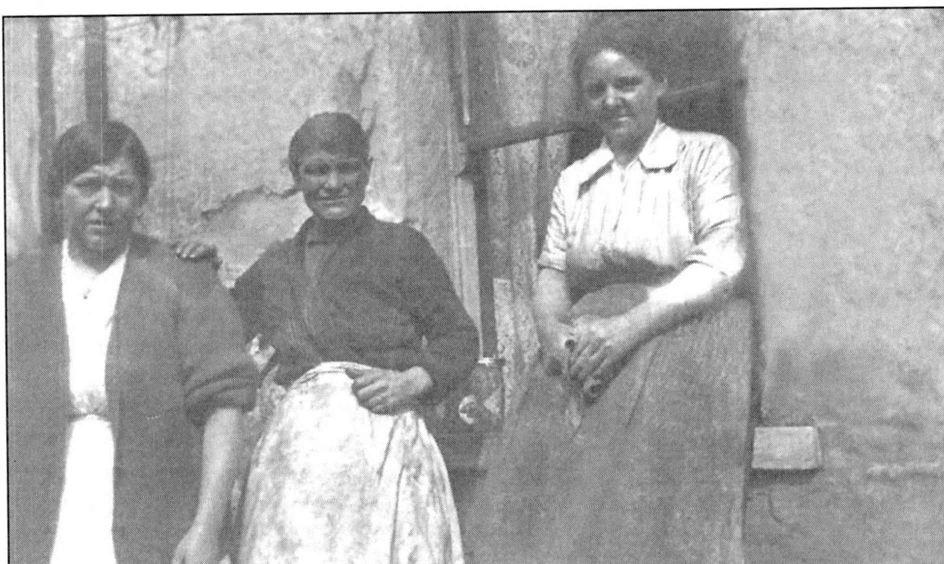

***Three women from the Monto area posing for the camera. Each of these women have hard work and a hard life etched into their faces.***

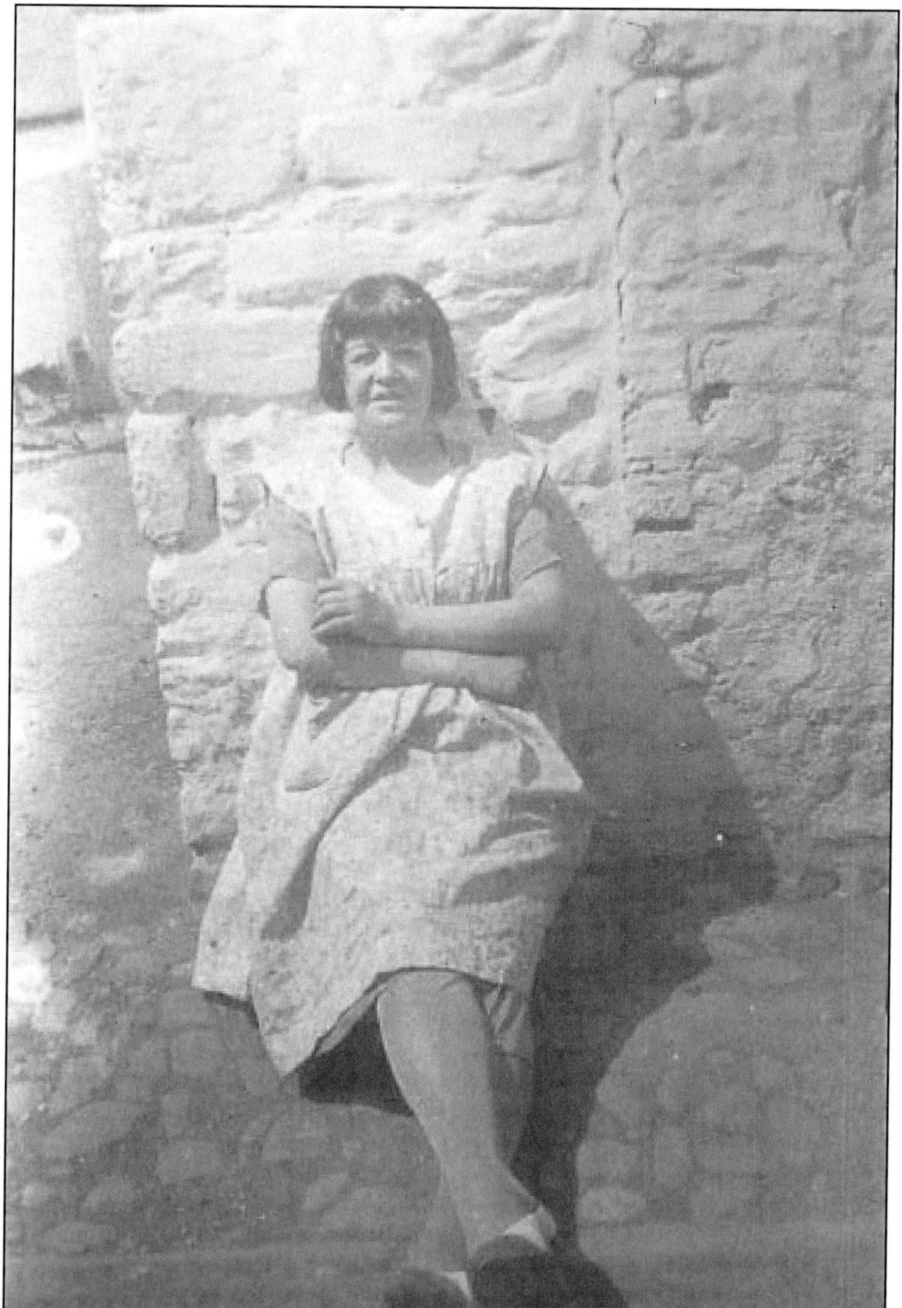

***Enjoying a quiet moment in Purdon Street.***

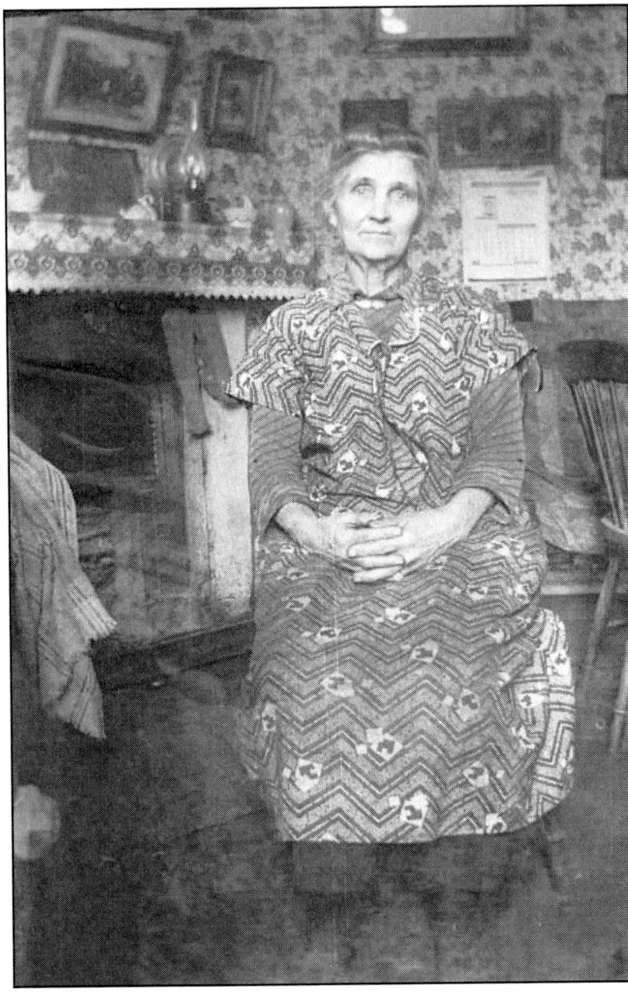

***Tenement Lady.***

Here is another photograph showing the inside of a tenement room where this elderly lady lived. She has beautiful flowered wallpaper on the wall and a lovely mantel cover adorns the fireplace. There is also an oil lamp on the mantelpiece because at that time there was no electricity or gas in the tenement houses and most families' cooked over an open fire. She has at least two chairs with some type of small settee against the back wall. Paddy Coffey gives us no name or indication as to who this lady is or why he was in her tenement room but she appears to be very relaxed and at ease in front of the camera.

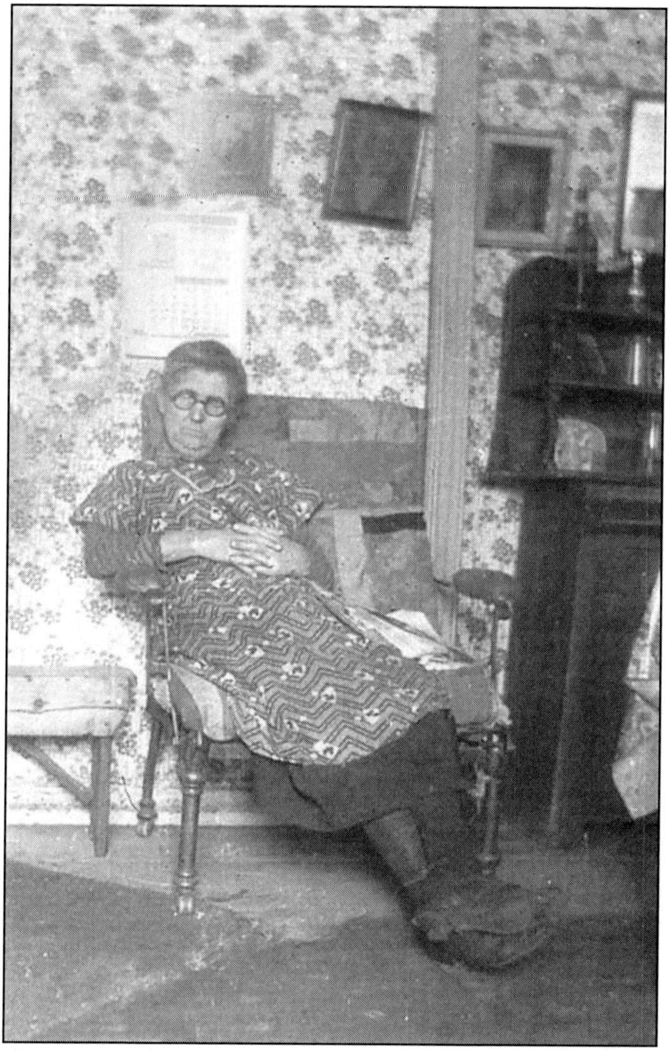

***In quiet repose.***

Paddy Coffey was never one to miss an opportunity when it came to taking a good photograph. This poor neighbour probably fell asleep while Paddy was rambling on about one of his seafaring adventures around the world. This photograph gives us a bit more insight into the layout of this tenement room. It almost appears as if it was once two rooms that were made into one complete unit. It seems to be one of the larger rooms in the house. The door of the room is to the left of the photograph and her bed is positioned on the far right of the room.

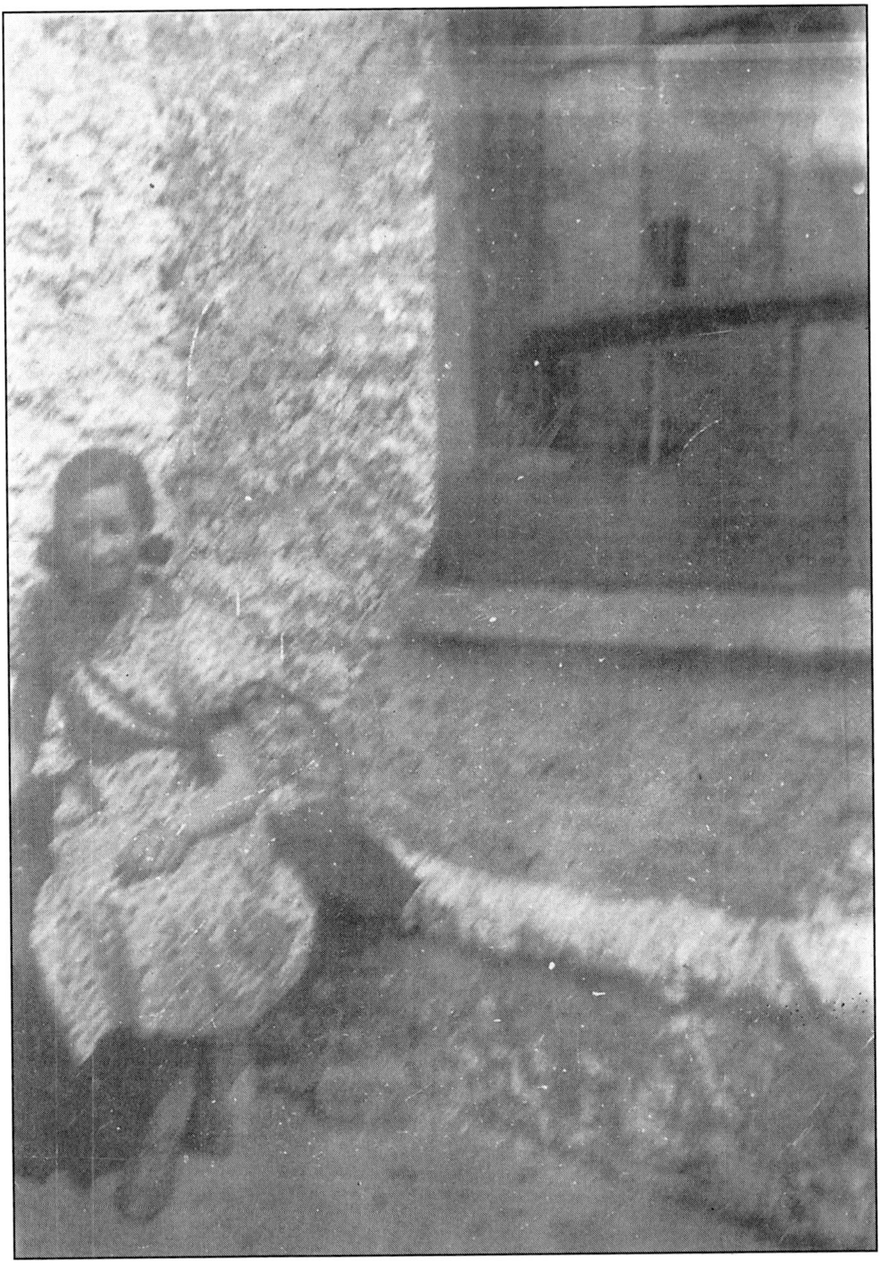

***Pamela Byrne in the backyard of her tenement house.***

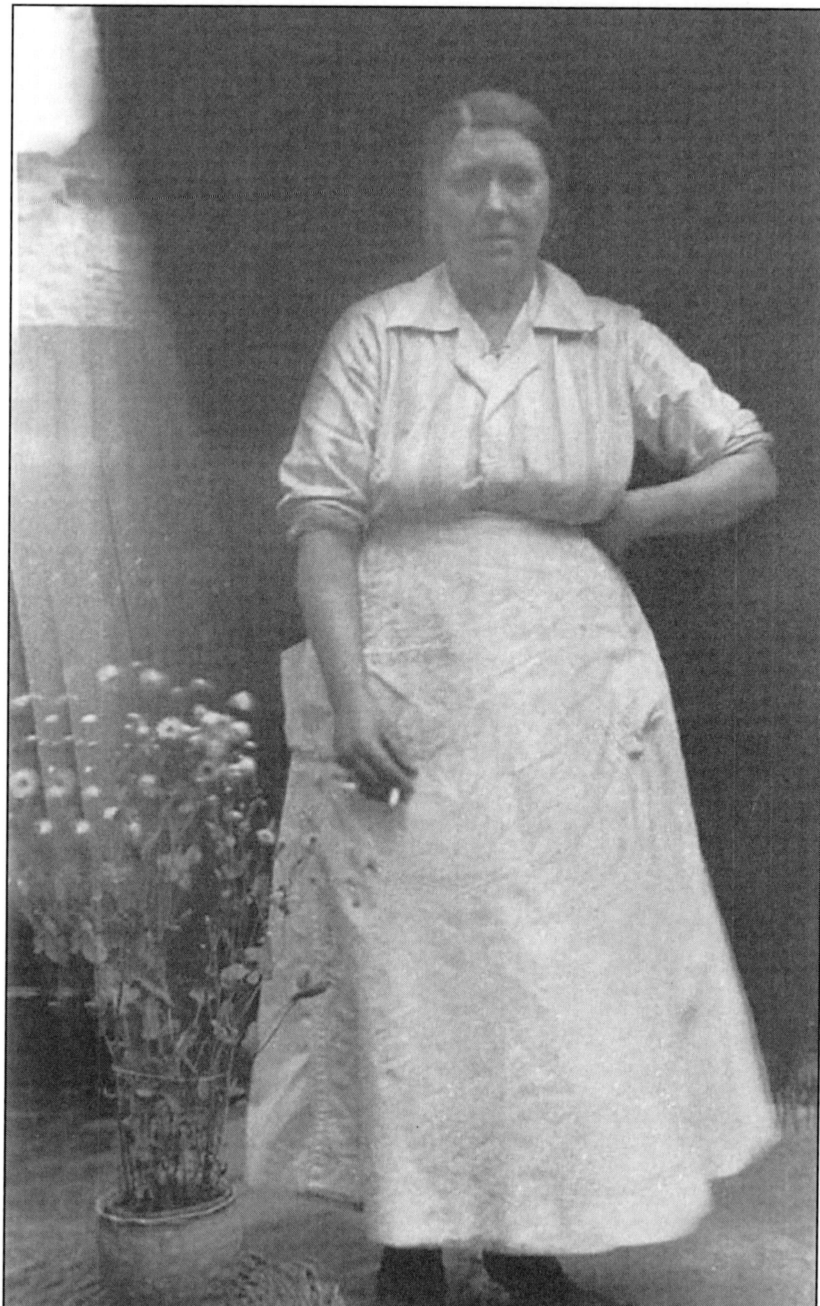

***Enjoying her cigarette.***

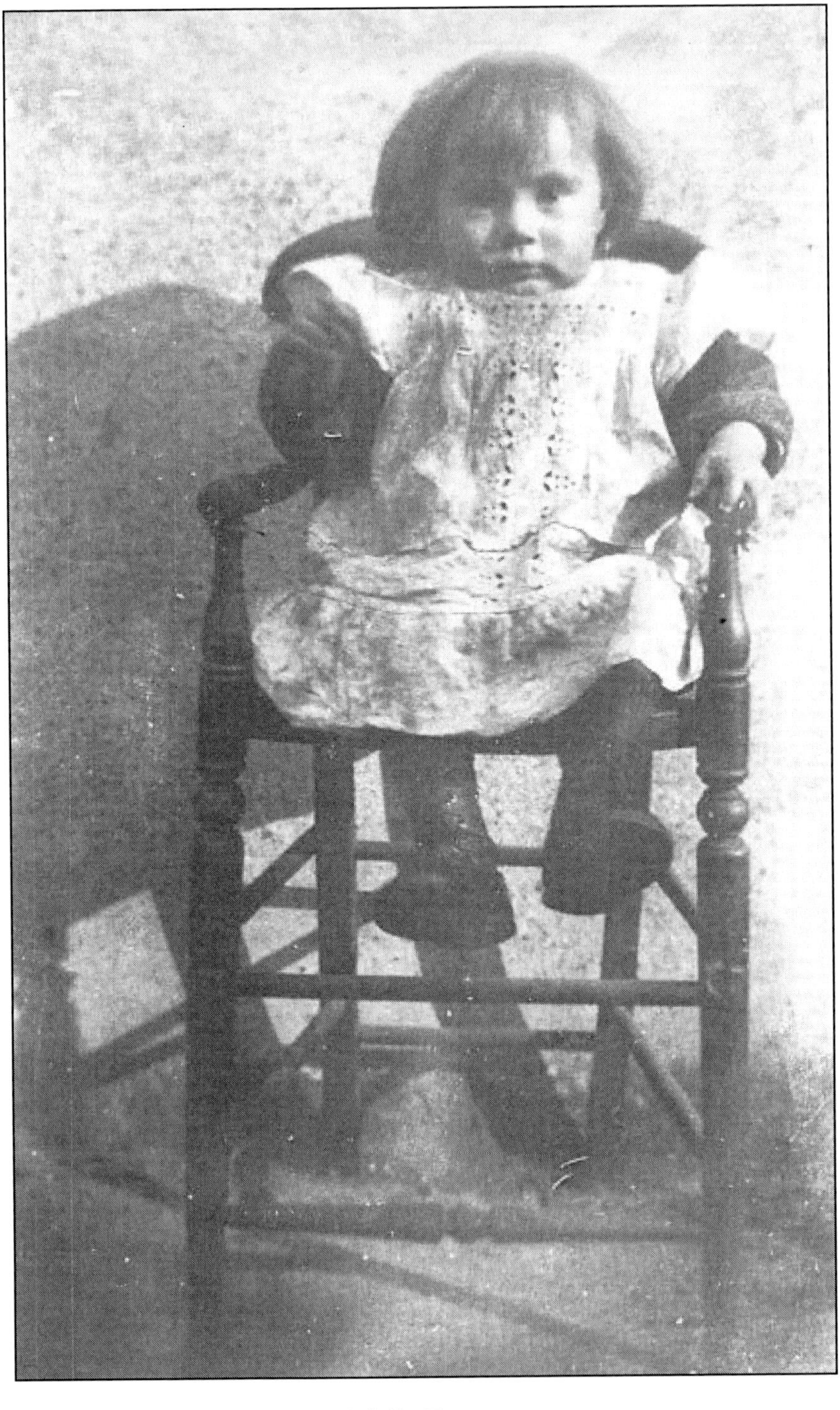

***Bridie Fagan.***

Young children, without a care in the world were allowed the freedom of playing out on the streets and laneways of this neighbourhood. If a young mother died it was not unusual for her neighbours to take her children into their home and rear them as their own.

There is a big difference between a 'Monto Child' and a 'Monto Baby'. A 'Monto Child' lived with its family whereas a 'Monto Baby' usually referred to a child that was abandoned by its mother who was very possibly a prostitute. These abandoned children were in some cases left in a tenement hallway or if they were old enough to walk were very often left wandering around the streets. Families from the area, if they could manage it would take these children into their homes and keep them as one of their own. Other unfortunate children ended up in state care or were handed into a Convent where the nuns would look after their welfare.

*'I remember one time when I was about ten years old I was asked to mind a neighbours child, there was me and me pal. So we decided to walk out to Dollymount and we brought a bottle of water with us. It was a lovely day and we took our time getting there. We spent the whole day there running up and down the beach and into the water and that. But didn't we forget about the baby being in the sun all the time. The poor child was as red as a tomato and we poured some of the water over her to cool her down.*

*By the time we got home to Railway Street it was about teatime. Well the child's mother was in a panic because we had been out all day and the child hadn't been fed or anything. When the mother saw the state of the poor child from the sun she made a go at me and I ran into me mother screaming. Well me Auntie Mary came running out and grabbed your one and told her to leave me alone and not to lay a hand on me. The woman was screaming about the state of her child and Mary told her she should be ashamed of herself for letting a child mind her baby. I never took that child for a walk again'...* ***Aggie Coffey***

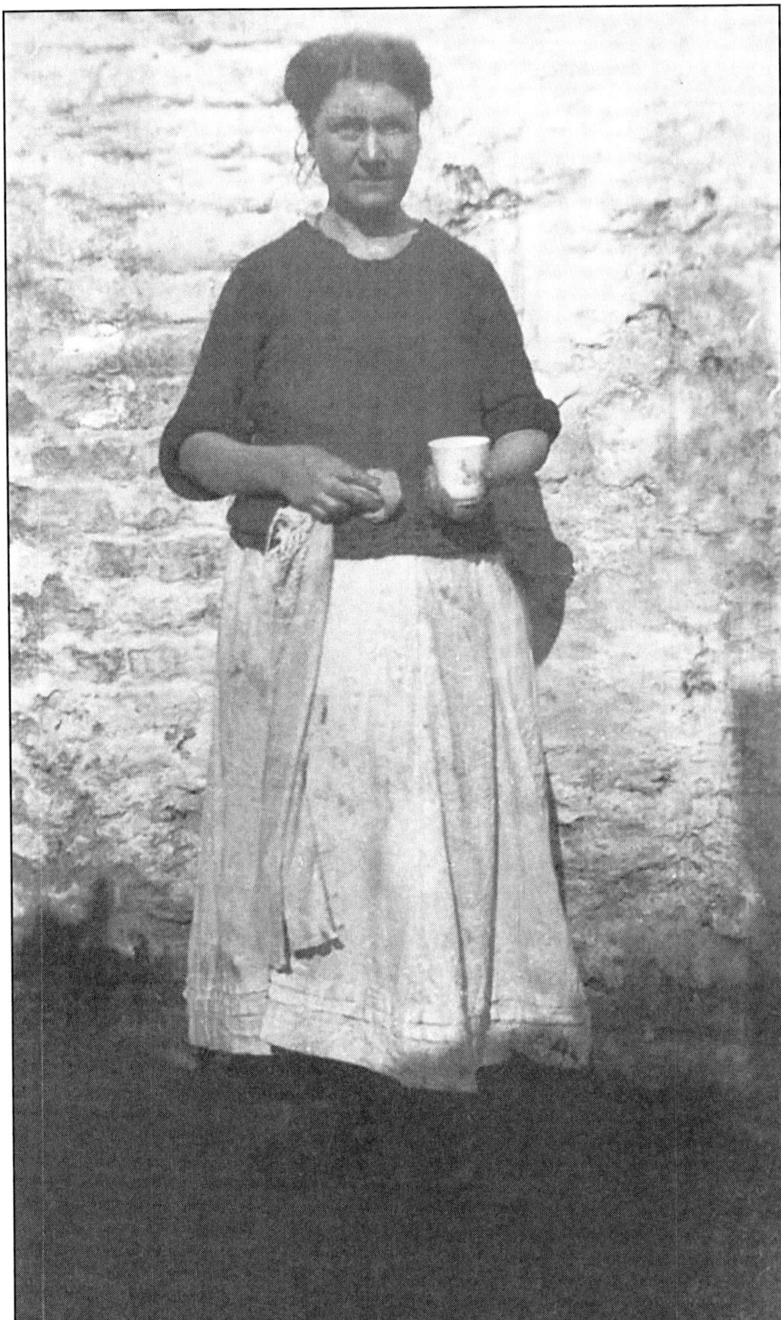

***Lady cleaning her cup.***

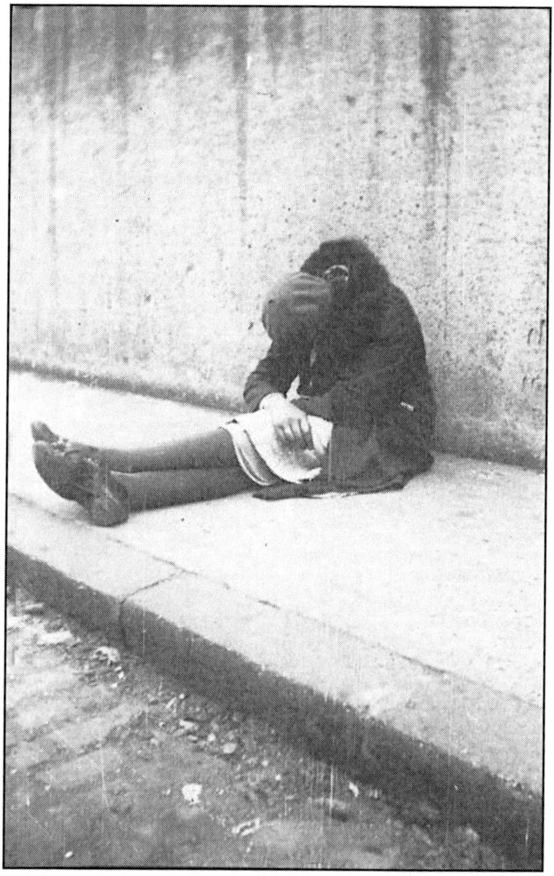

***A woman asleep in Purdon Street.***

This young woman is sitting upright while asleep on the footpath in Purdon Street during daylight hours. Paddy Coffey was very much aware of some of the tragedies that befell a lot of the women in his neighbourhood. One infamous place in this particular area was known as *'The Man-Trap'* that is not too far away from where this poor unfortunate woman is sleeping. It was a small lane situated at the back of Jack Meagher's pub off Purdon Street. It was into this trap that some poor unfortunate punter would be led by a prostitute where she would encourage him to take off his coat and to drop his trousers. While his trousers were halfway down she would grab his coat, which hopefully had his money in it and run through a doorway at the back of the pub. Inside this door there was a small hallway with three more doors, one of which the prostitute would have disappeared through.

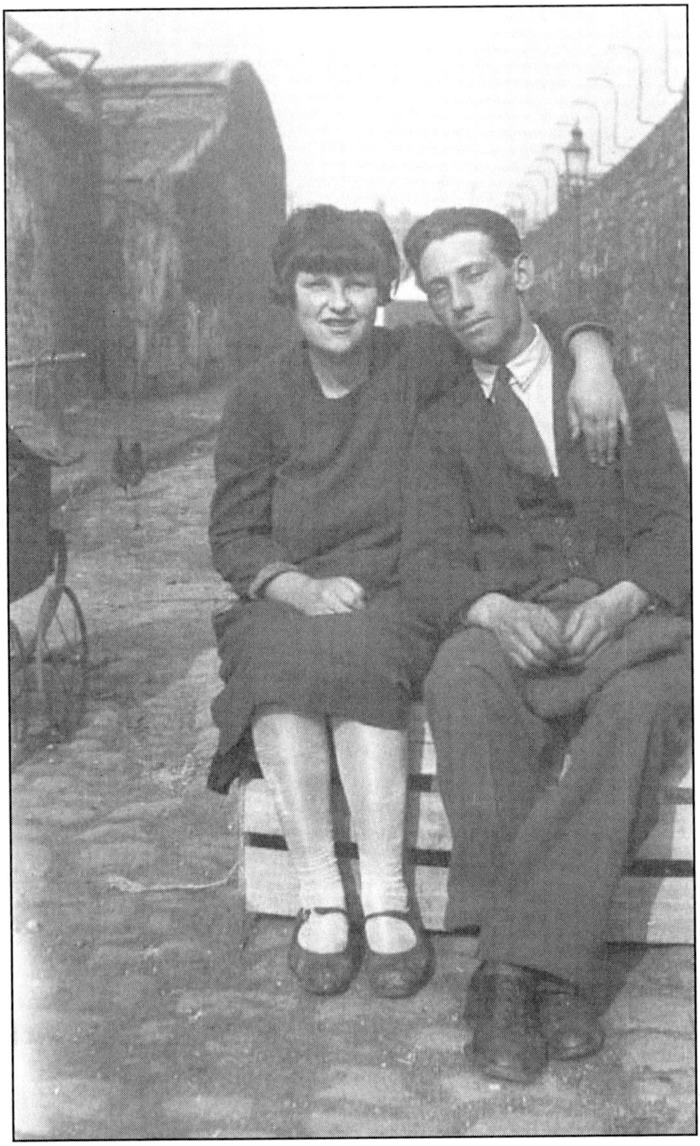

***Posing Couple in Beaver Street.***

This handsome couple are sitting on a wooden crate in Beaver Street. This street runs from present day Foley Street to Railway Street. There is no wedding ring on the young girl's finger and no indication is given as to their relationship. To the left of the photographer however is a child pram that may or may not belong to this couple. Strutting up the street in the background is a hen.

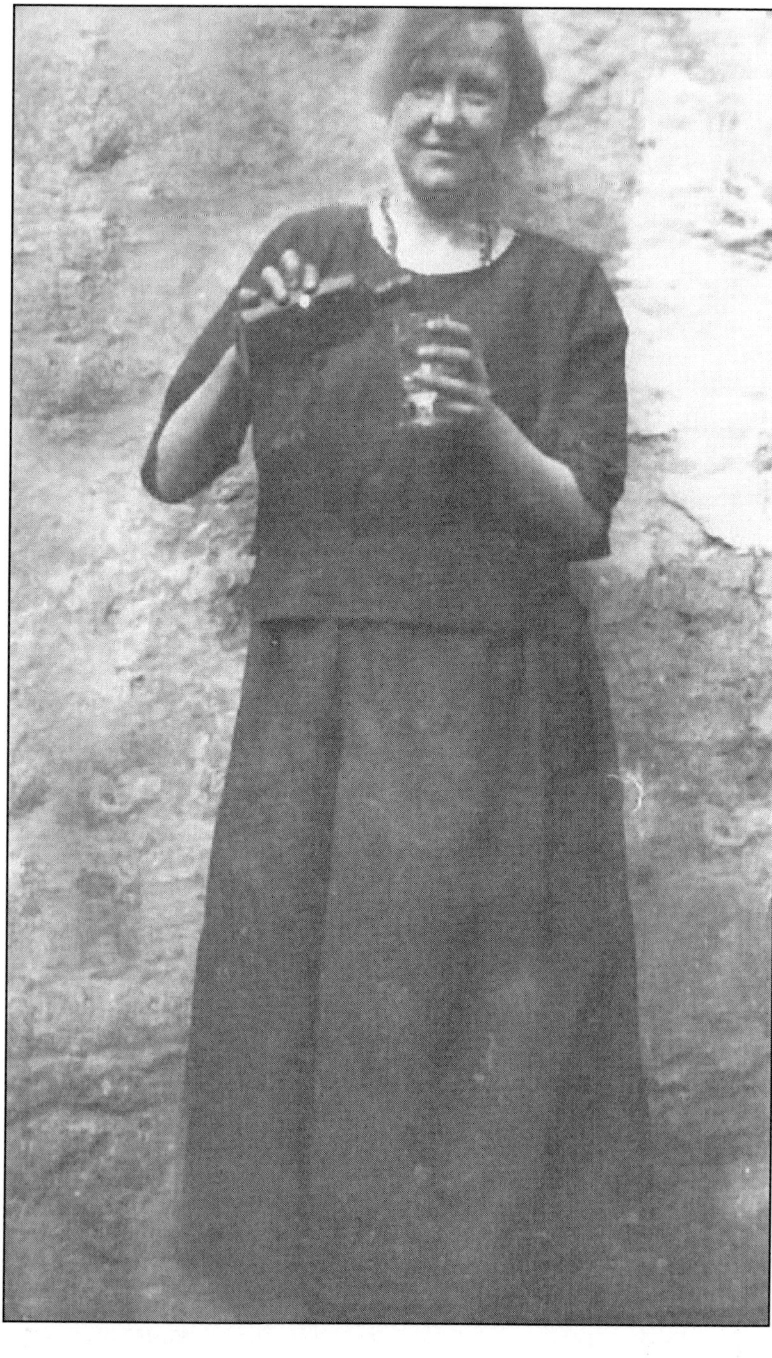

***A Monto woman about to enjoy a quiet drink.***

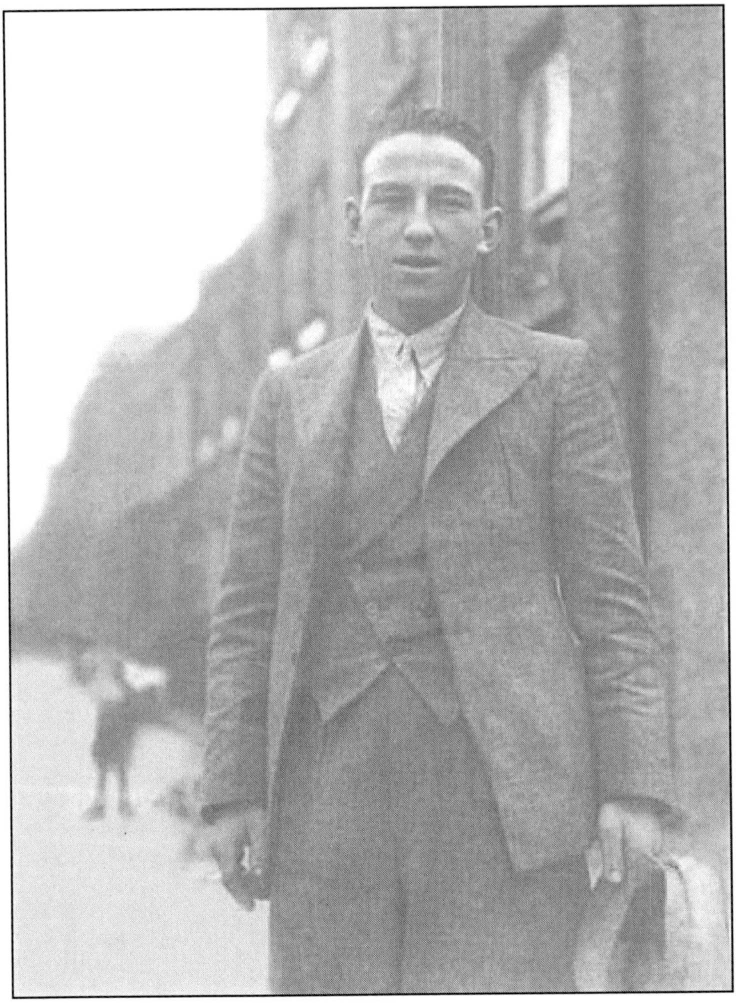

***Alfie Kane.***

Alfie Kane was born in 1911; his family lived in number 13 Gloucester Place, Dublin. Alfie spent all of his working life at sea. His father Thomas was born in Malta and died in Dublin in the 1920's. Alfie's mother, Mary Farrell was born in County Meath in 1882 and remarried Otto Larsen, a ships cook from Copenhagen, Denmark in 1925. They had a daughter named Annie who married Tommy Coffey. In years gone by it was a custom in some Nordic countries to use a man's first given name as a child's surname and so Annie Larsen became known as Annie Otto. Alfie had a sister Rose Kane who lived in London.

☞ NOTICE TO OWNERS OR AGENTS.—An Allotment of Wages under this Note may be remitted from Port to Port, free of Expense, by means of Seamen's Money Orders, to be obtained at the Mercantile Marine Offices.

# No. ______ Seaman's Allotment Note.

The Allotment can only be in favour of the Seaman's Wife, Father, Mother, Grandfather, Grandmother, Child, Grandchild, Brother, or Sister, or in favour of a Savings Bank.

(L*)

**A. Ship in which Seaman has engaged.**

| Name, Port of Registry and Official No. of Ship. |
|---|
| IRISH Beech. 154839 |

**B. Name, &c., of Seaman by whom Allotment is made.**

| Christian Name of Seaman. | Surname. |
|---|---|
| Alfred | Kane. |
| Rank or Rating | |
| Fireman | |

ISSUED BY THE DEPARTMENT OF INDUSTRY AND COMMERCE.

**C. Relation(1) or Bank in whose favour this Allotment Note is given.**

| Name and Address, or Name of Bank. | Degree of Relationship. |
|---|---|
| Johannah Kane. | Wife |

**D. Amount and Particulars of Allotment.**

| | Pounds. | Shillings. | Pence. | Date when first Payment is to be made. | Intervals at which* Payment is to be made. |
|---|---|---|---|---|---|
| Figures | 5 | = | — | 4 Nov. 41 | ½ Monthly |
| Words | Five | — | — | | |

(C.5170) Wt. 5047—1218—P55—Gp. 27—100 Bks.—8/31—M.P.W (P)

The Seaman named in division B above, having entered into an Agreement to serve in the Ship named in division A above, and having required that a stipulation be inserted in the Agreement for the allotment of part of his wages by means of an allotment note, and such stipulation having been inserted pursuant to Section 61 of the Merchant Shipping Act, 1906, I, the undersigned, being the Master (2) of the said Ship, give this Allotment Note for the amount named in division D above in favour of the relative or bank named in division C above, to the intent that the said relative or bank shall be entitled to recover the sum so allotted in accordance with the provisions of Section 143 of the Merchant Shipping Act, 1894.

Payable by Palgrave Murphy, 17 Eden Quay, Dublin

H. Wilson ........ Master.(2)

Alfred Kane ........ Seaman.

[illegible] ........ Witness.(3)

MERCANTILE MARINE OFFICE 14 OCT 1941 DUB

1 In case of a Wife the Marriage Certificate must be produced, if required, when payment is demanded. 2 If the Owner or Agent give the note, this must be altered accordingly. 3 This should be the Superintendent of a Mercantile Marine Office, a British Consul, or an Official Shipping Master in a British Possession. It should be marked with the Office Stamp to show the date and place of issue.

* If only one payment is to be made, insert " One payment only " in this space.

OFFICE STAMP.

*Alfie Kane's 'Seaman's Allotment Note' 1941.*

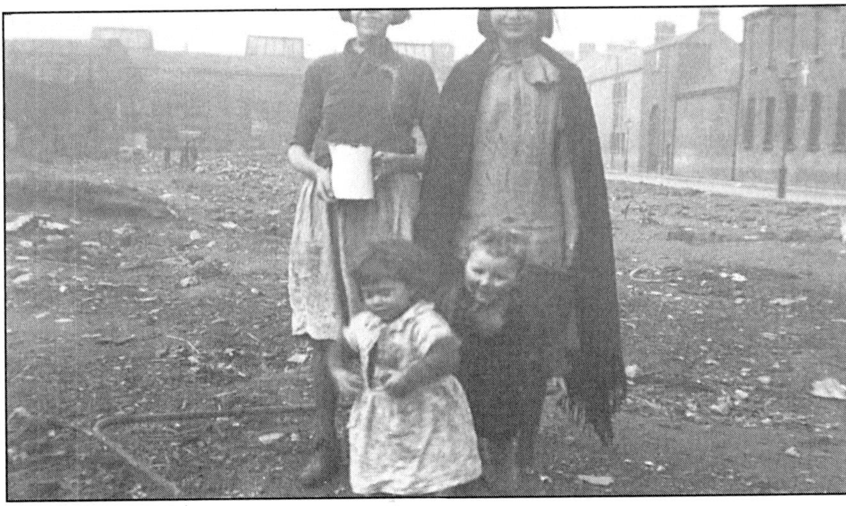

This photograph is taken on the site where Liberty House stands today. A Steel Mill once operated from this site. To the right of the photograph is the back gate into the Magdalene Laundry and Convent situated on Sean McDermot Street. The two white crosses on the wall are still in evidence today. There are no names given for the two girls and the two children in the photograph

*'There was plenty of Hooleys. It would go like this, maybe someone would come in and maybe you'd go down and get a few bottles and then there'd be more come in. There was great Hooleys. Or I'll tell you what they used to do, facing where we lived in the Pub there was what we used to call "The Hut", it was big and every now and then they'd have a dance go on in that. There'd be crowds there and they'd be out on the street and all dancing. Of a summer evening I'll tell you what they often done, the kid's would be gone up to bed and the men would be playing cards and the women would be out skipping. Maybe the men would be turning the rope and the women would be skipping. Jemmy West would come down with his ould melodeon and he'd start playing that. Somebody else would play the mouth organ or maybe somebody would play on a comb. The next you'd look out, and we could see from our window, you see we had three windows on that side, three big windows in the front room.*

*We could look out and see them all dancing on the corner because it was a big corner. They'd be all out dancing and singing there down in Railway Street. The path came out and it was a big path. There was no traffic really so they'd be out on the road and on the path. And they wouldn't have a*

*drink maybe at that time, they'd do it just for the crack and you'd have them all out there. Every now and then, there was a fella who was married to one of the Meehan's, if he had a few bottles at all he'd be handing them around to people, you know. He was a great man for the kids, he'd play races with them, and he'd give them sweets if they'd win the race and all. Maybe Ginger Beer, that time you'd get a big thing of Ginger Beer for a penny. He'd give Ginger Beer out amongst the kids and all, getting them to sit around, the windowsills were only about that height and you'd sit on them. He'd have them all singing songs and everything. Then there was what's his name? Stephen Fox, he was a big man but a beautiful Step Dancer. He'd get up and start dancing with the kids. There was great enjoyment in the summer evenings and that'...***Aggie Coffey.***

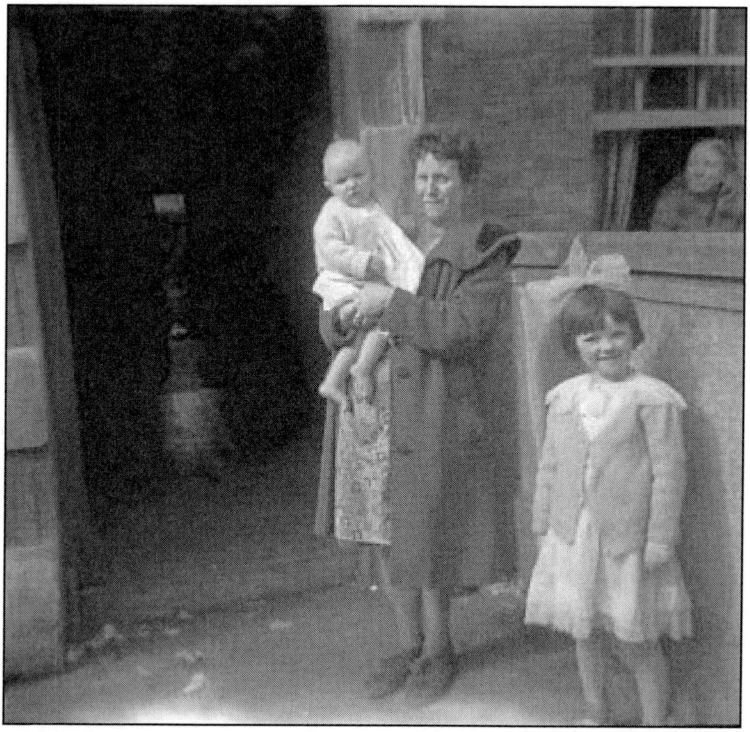

**Mrs Rose Mahon** and her baby daughter **Bridge**t posing for a photograph outside number 43 Sean McDermott Street. The young girl, **Mary Arkins** is showing off her big bright ribbon as **Mrs Harte** looks out of her window at the scene outside.

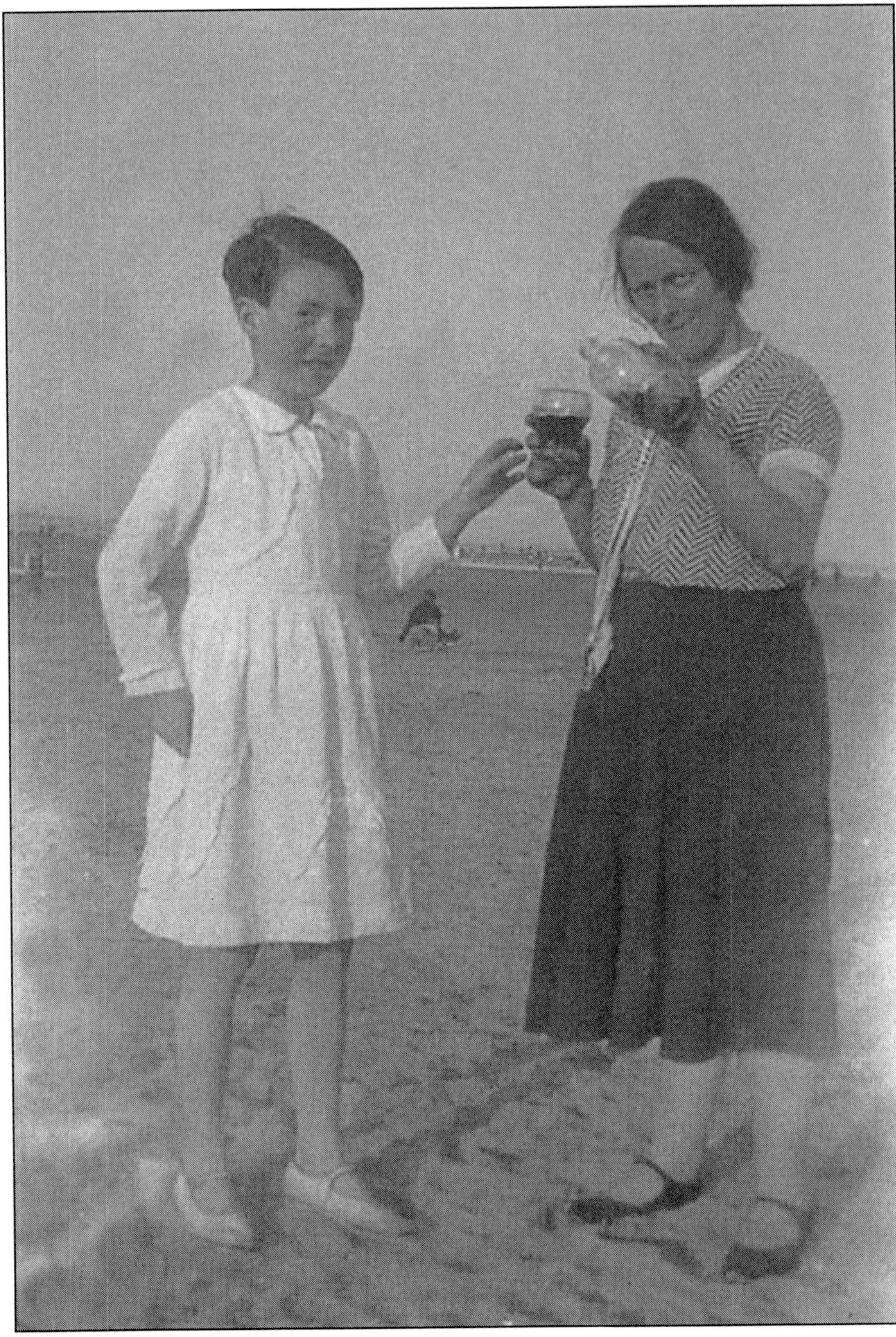

***Kathleen Boyle and her mother.***

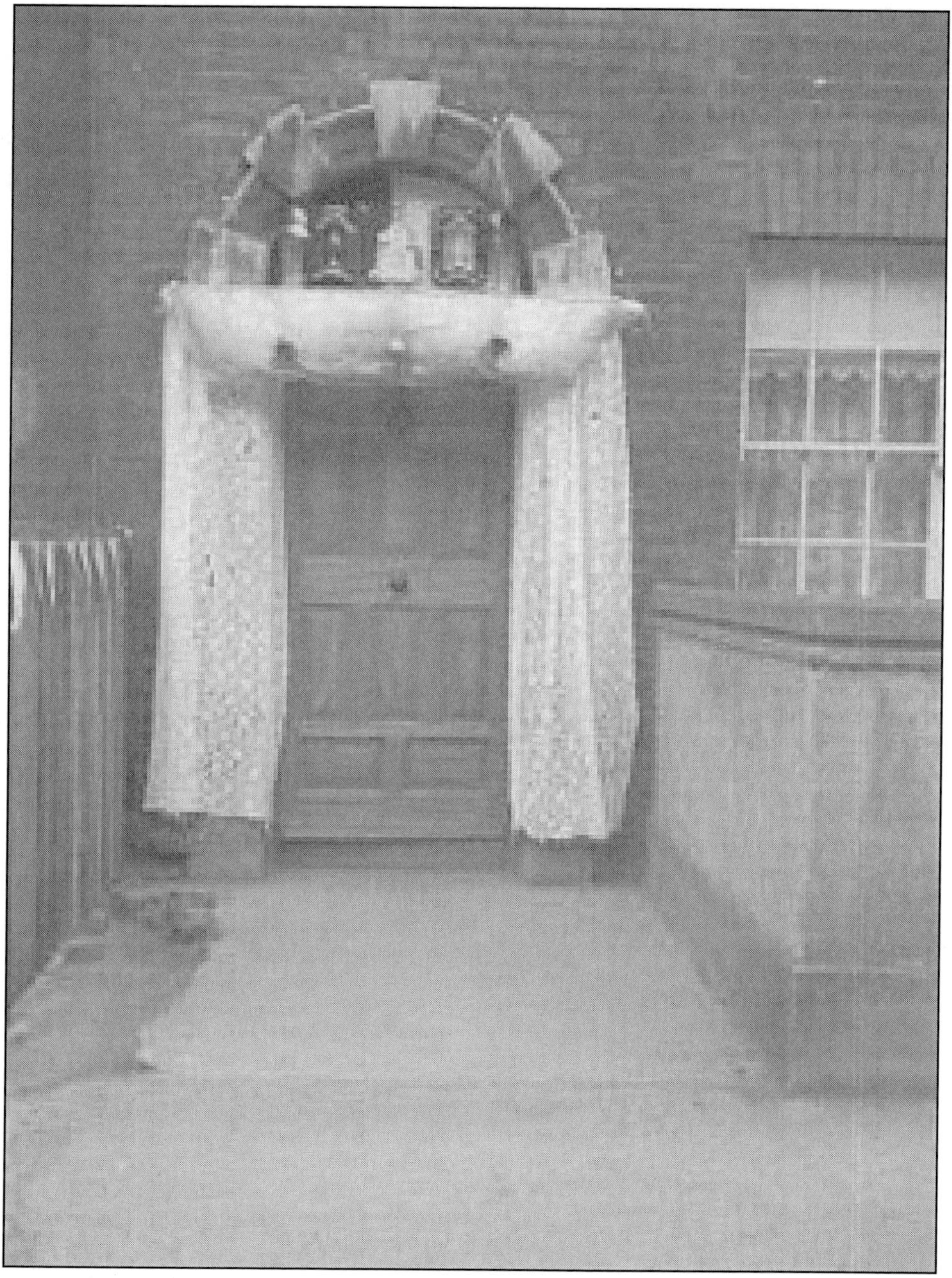

***Sean McDermott Street.***

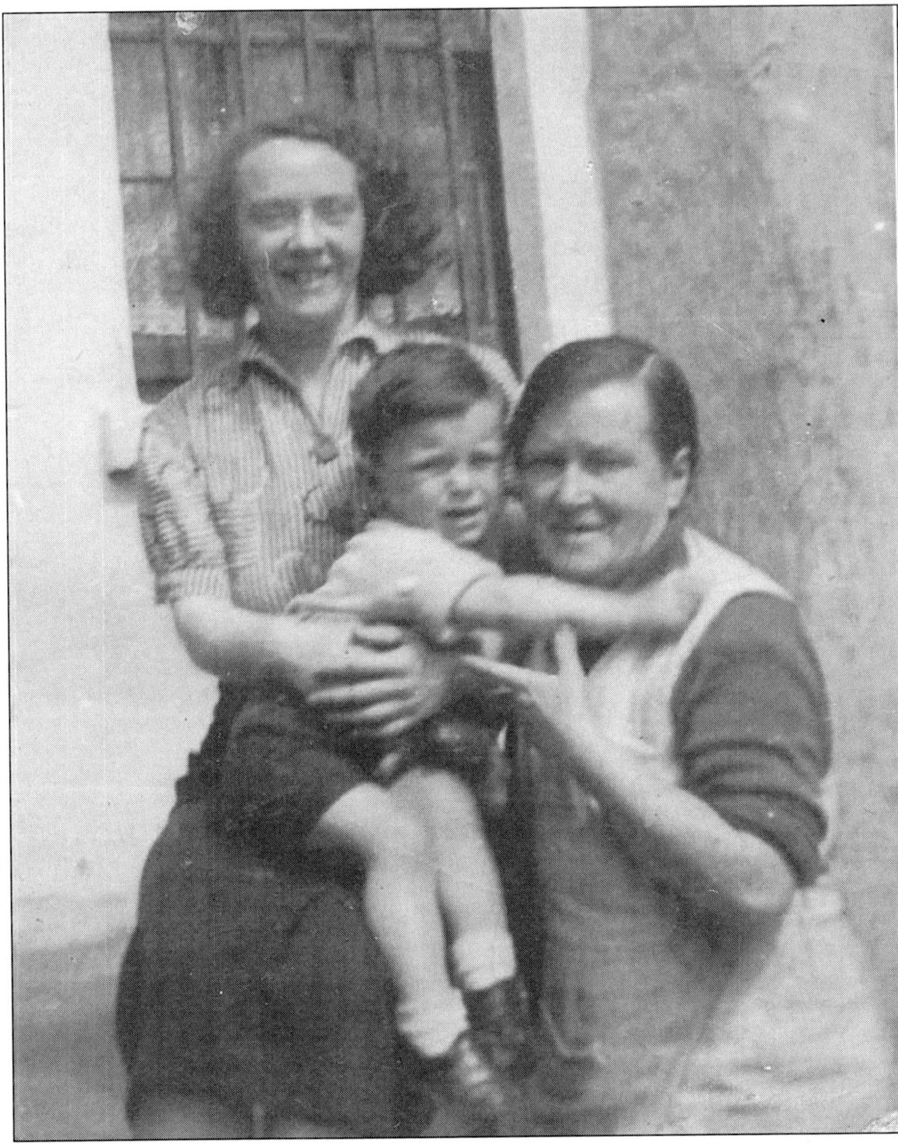

***Three generations?***

It was not unusual for three generations of a family to live in the one room in a tenement house. The grandparents sometimes played as much a role in the upbringing and training of young children as did their parents. According to the 1901 and 1911 census many of the married women from the Monto area put '*Domestic*' down as their occupation thus signifying that they may have worked outside of the home.

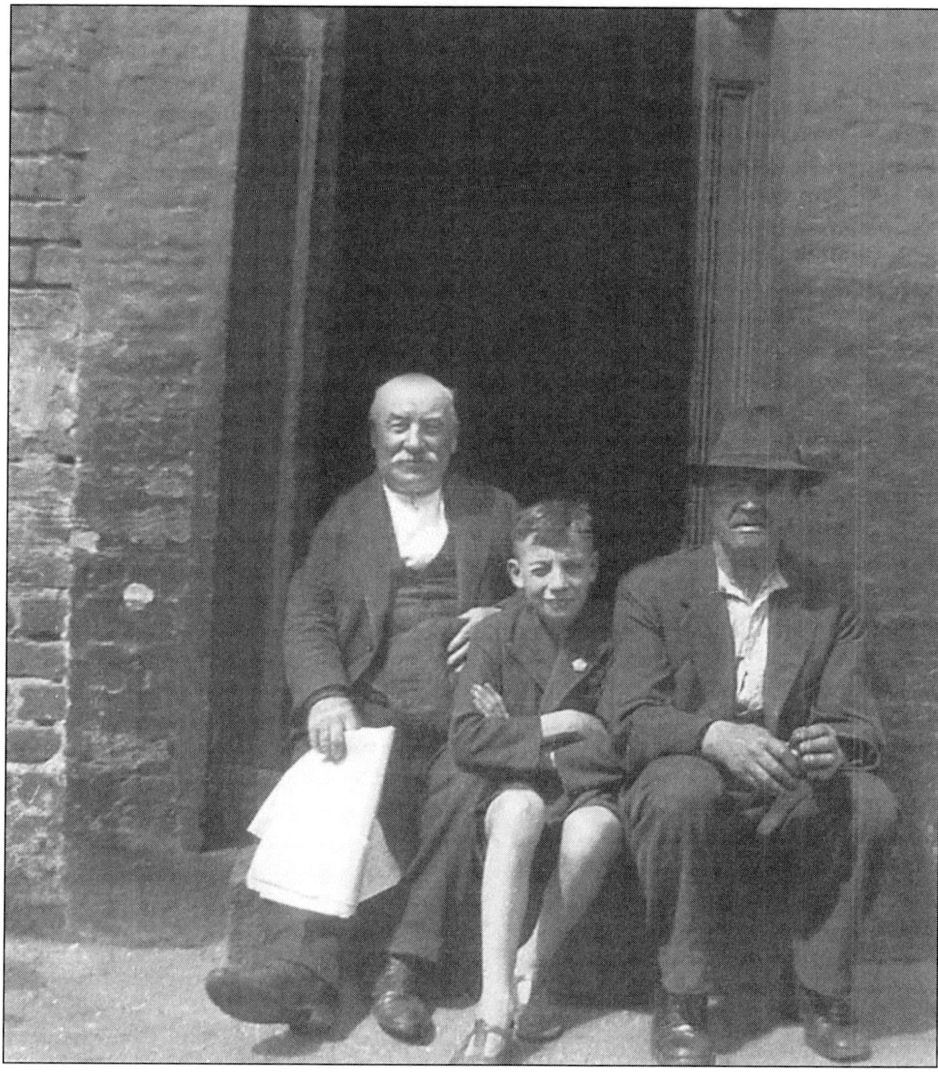

***Two men and a boy.***

These are some of the everyday faces of the people that lived in Dublin in the early 1900's. At a casual glance they may not appear to be anyone special or famous but in their own way each of them had a story to tell of the life that they had lived. These are some of the people who witnessed the scenes of the 1916 Irish Rebellion, listened to the stories of the horrors of WWI, perhaps took part in the fight against the Black and Tans or lived through the Civil War. These are the everyday people of Dublin.

# Chapter 3

## Around the Monto area

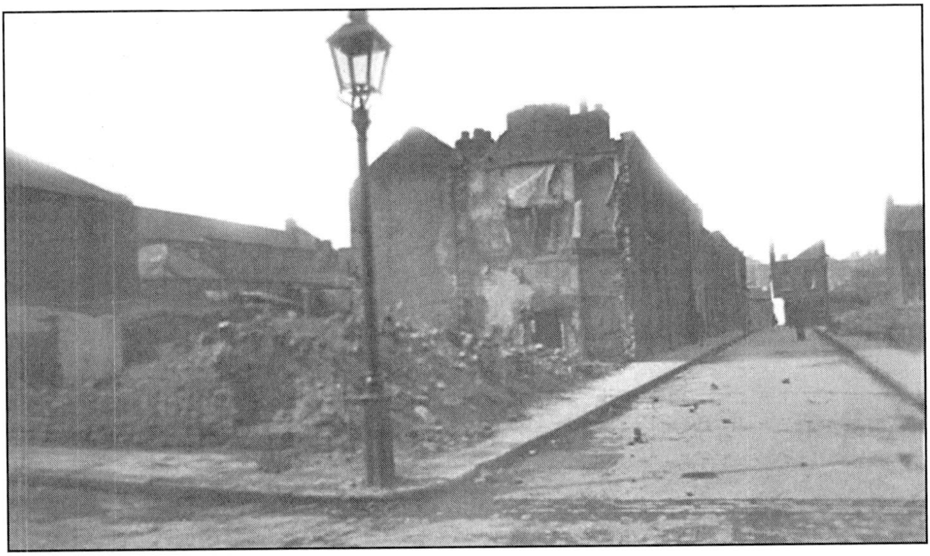

***The corner of Elliott Place and Purdon Street, looking towards Railway Street.***

The house that once stood on the corner of Elliott Place and Purdon Street belonged to Paddy Coffey's grandmother Margaret Doyle. Each room in the house was rented out to either a family or individual. One of these families was that of John Burke and his wife Annie, they had four young children. They lived upstairs in the front room. A prostitute named Ginger Kate lived and slept on the landing at the top of the stairs next to the door of the Burke family. John and Annie Burke invited Ginger Kate to move into the room with them. She lived under their small kitchen table. During the day Ginger Kate looked after the young Burke children while the parents went out to work. At nighttime she plied her trade in the street below where she stood beside the street lamp in the above photograph.

Sometime later on the police raided the area looking for illegal alcohol and stolen goods. Ginger Kate had a few bottles of the illegal stuff hidden underneath the bed belonging to John Burke who was of course unaware of their existence. When the bottles were later discovered by John's wife

Annie Burke, Ginger Kate was asked to move out of the room. With so many Shebeens and illegal drinking houses in the area the police were always raiding some premises or other and Annie Burke was afraid of getting into trouble with the law.

Margaret Doyle and her husband lived in number 14 Elliott Place. Paddy Coffey remembered being in this house as a young boy. He spoke of a dining table that was laid out with silver cutlery and a beautiful lace tablecloth. On the wall overlooking the table hung an oil painting of his grandmother Margaret Doyle. After her death her husband sold the painting and quite a few of her houses. He drank most of the money and gambled the rest away. The building at the end of this street and situated on Railway Street was known locally as *'The Hut'*, local people used it as a Dance Hall.

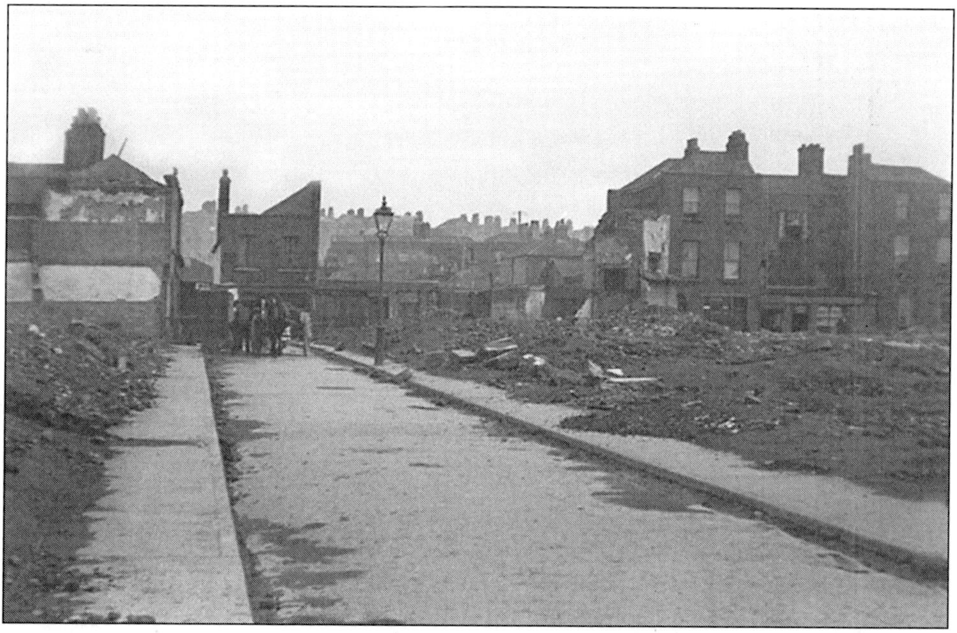

***Elliott Place showing Joe O'Reilly's pub on the left next to 'The Hut'. The shop on the right possibly belongs to the Meehan family.***

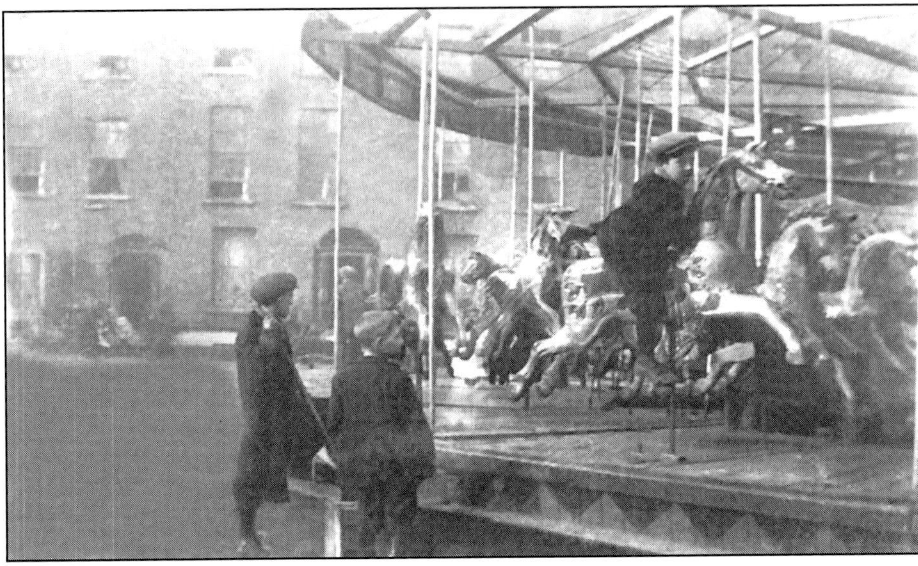

## *Fairground in Dublin?*

This is most likely one of the very earliest photographs of Dublin life that was captured on camera by Paddy Coffey and may be dated to 1917 – 1920 period. The three young boys are dressed in the fashion of that time. They appear to be well dressed and have shoes or boots on their feet. The young boy on the Hobby Horse is probably jumping on for a free ride. There are tenement houses in the background with people sitting on the steps. It is difficult to know where the location of this photograph is or what the occasion was.

*'I remember one time a man coming around with a thing that looked like an accordion with a handle on the side that he would wind it up with. He had a little purse on the front of it for people to put money in, like begging but I don't ever remember anyone ever giving him money. My mother would get him to sit on the end of the stairs in our hall and she'd give him a cup of tea or something. The kids would be all running around him when he was going down the street making his music. It was great fun and that.*

***Jimmy Burke***

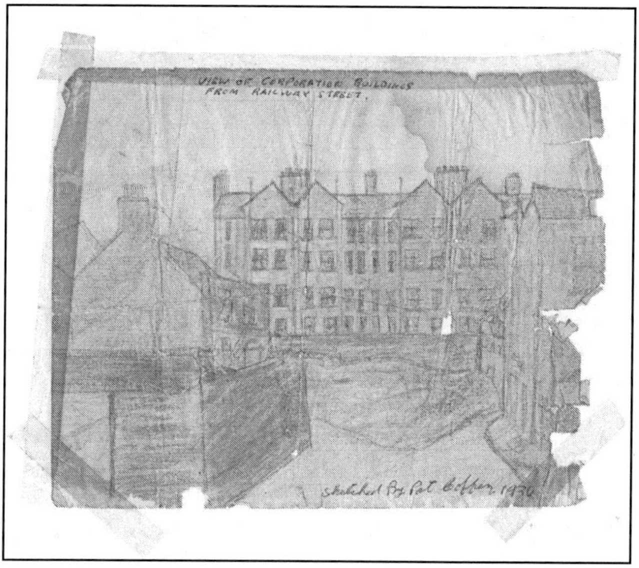


***A pencil sketch of the scene below by Paddy Coffey***

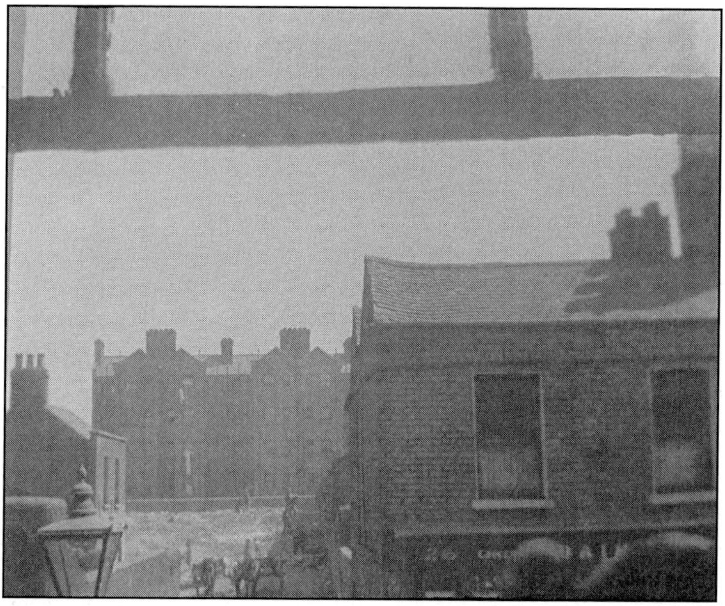

***Faithful Place.***

Looking out the window of a tenement flat in Railway Street, Paddy Coffey captures a scene from the aftermath of the demolition of Faithful Place. Carters are brought in to help clear the site and young children are seen playing amongst the rubble. In the background is the wall that ran along

Purdon Street, from Corporation Street to Beaver Street. Also in the background is Corporation Buildings, a complex of what at that time was considered modern flats. In the corner of the sketch Paddy Coffey places this event to 1930.

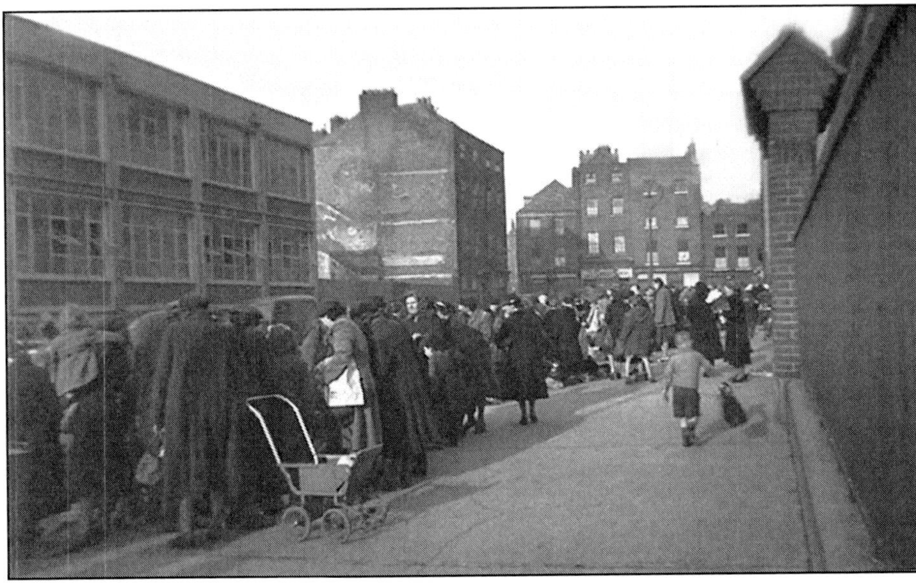

***Cumberland Street, Dublin 1930's.***

Cumberland Street, *'The Hill or The Tuggers'* as it is sometimes known is one of the many street markets where Dublin people went in search of a bargain in second-hand clothes, shoes and furniture. The Dealers would often have their stalls set up and ready for business by six o'clock every Saturday morning. Many of the women in these two photographs appear to be dressed in black and that may indicate they are widowed.

This was a time when coats were thrown on the bed to keep the family warm at night in their cold and draughty tenement room. In some of the smaller tenement rooms there was barely enough space for a single bed that was often shared by all of the family including parents and children. Paddy Coffey once had to sleep in a tea chest at night in which the coal was stored in during the day. There was nowhere else for him to sleep in the room where he lived with his father, younger siblings and his stepmother.

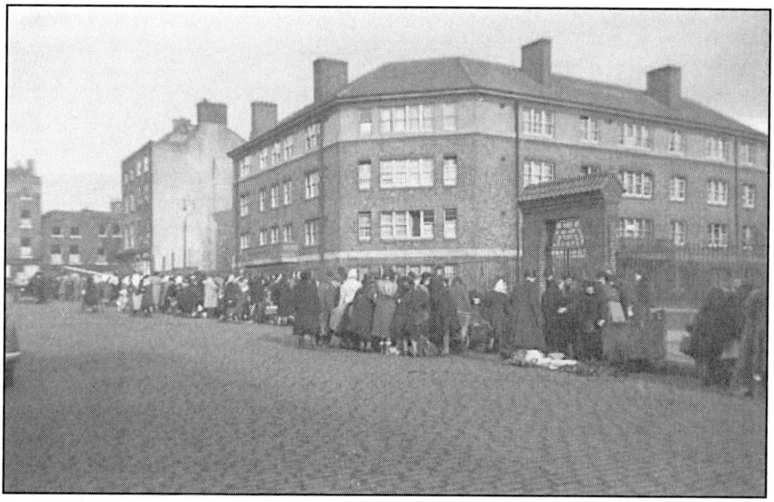

***Cumberland Street, Dublin in the 1930's***

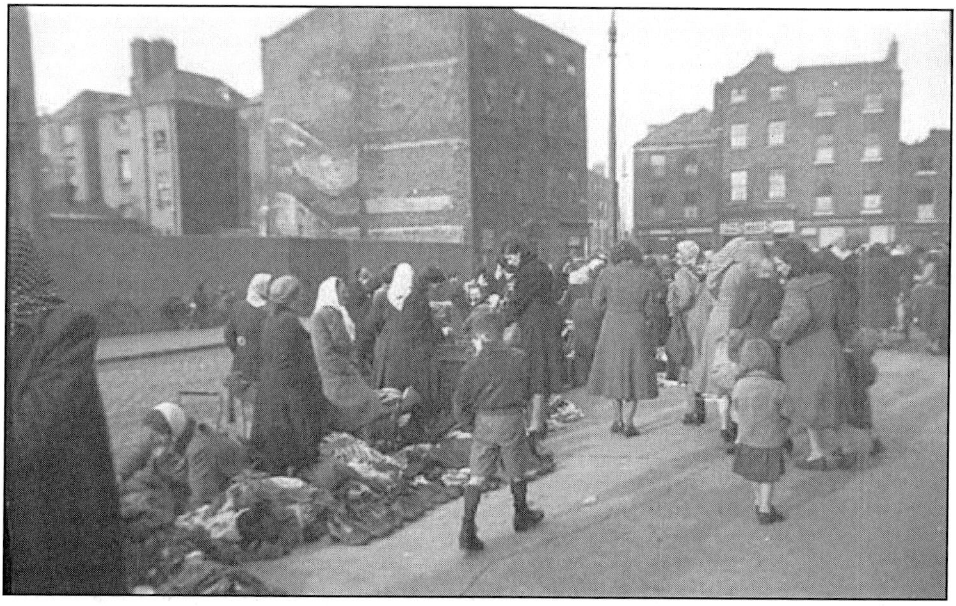

***Something for all the family.***

While Ireland struggled to raise itself up off its knees as a new nation so too did its people. Almost every family nationwide lived in dread of *'Lady Poverty'* knocking on their door. Thousands had already lost loved ones to mass emigration, some of whom were never seen or heard from once they left Irelands green shores. In Dublin, jobs were as scarce as the proverbial *'Hen's Teeth'* and especially for a people with little or no education. Scenes like these photograph were an almost everyday occurrence where families with little or no choice sought out a living selling off their personal and family belongings. Others in turn sought out a bargain to cloth their own in whatever they could afford to buy.

*'We never had new clothes only for our First Holy Communion or our Confirmation. My mother would borrow from the moneylender, she was a dealer and everyone borrowed from her but you see afterwards the clothes were put in the pawn and the money paid back to your one. It wasn't just us; it was everyone went to the pawnshop of a Monday morning. They'd be queuing up outside all along the wall and that. There might be your father's suit or maybe just his waistcoat that went in or his overcoat if he had one that he didn't need for the summer. In the winter it went on our bed to keep us warm'.* ***Denis Doyle***

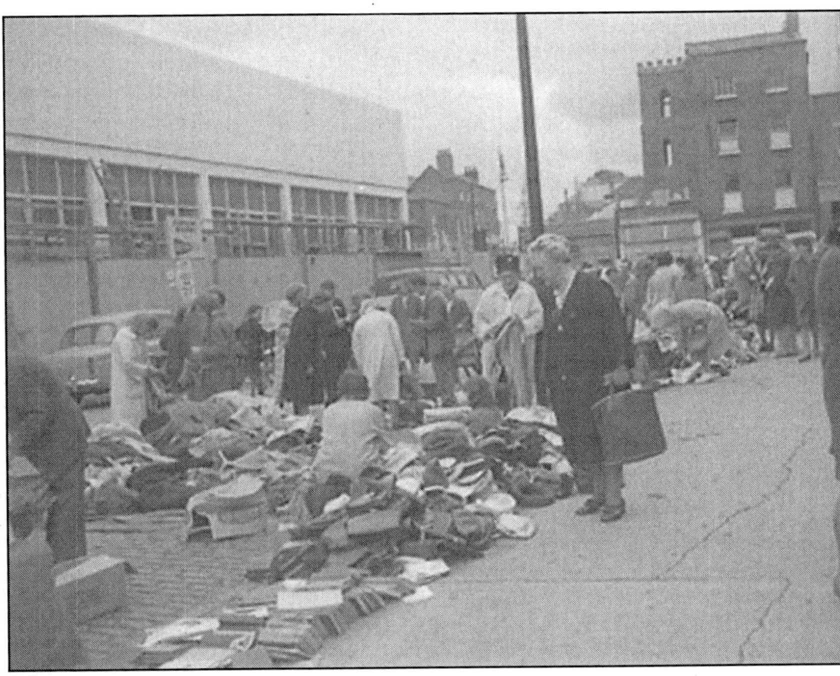

***Everything on sale from second-hand books to hats and corsets.***

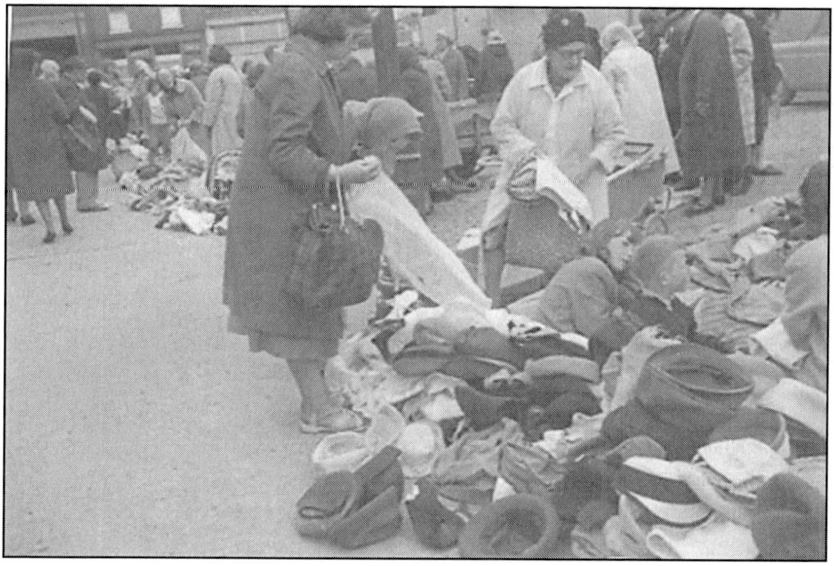

***The Hat Stall.***

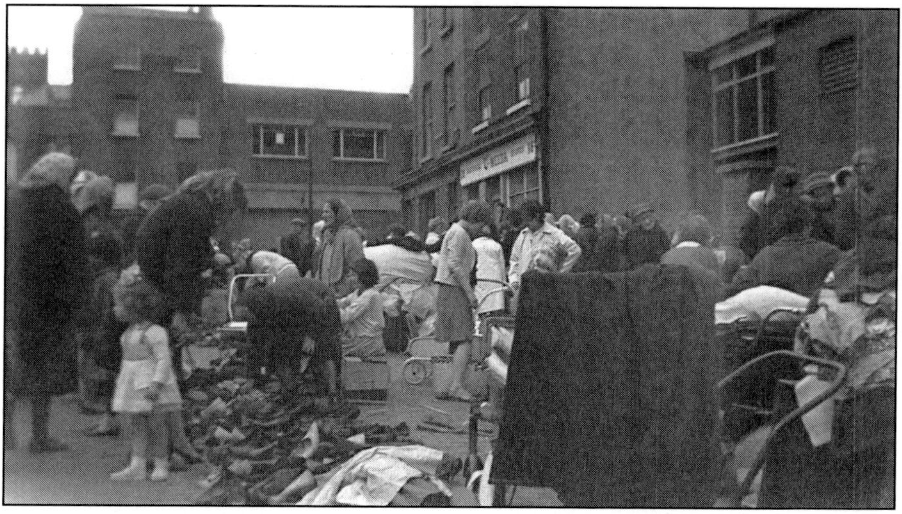

The '*Hill*' in the 1960's and of course there were certain Dealers or Traders who had their own '*Patch*' or place from which they carried on their business that no one else dare trespass on. A good spot or patch was very important, as people would then get to know where a particular stall was or where certain items could be found. If you wanted the best bargains you had to make sure to be there early.

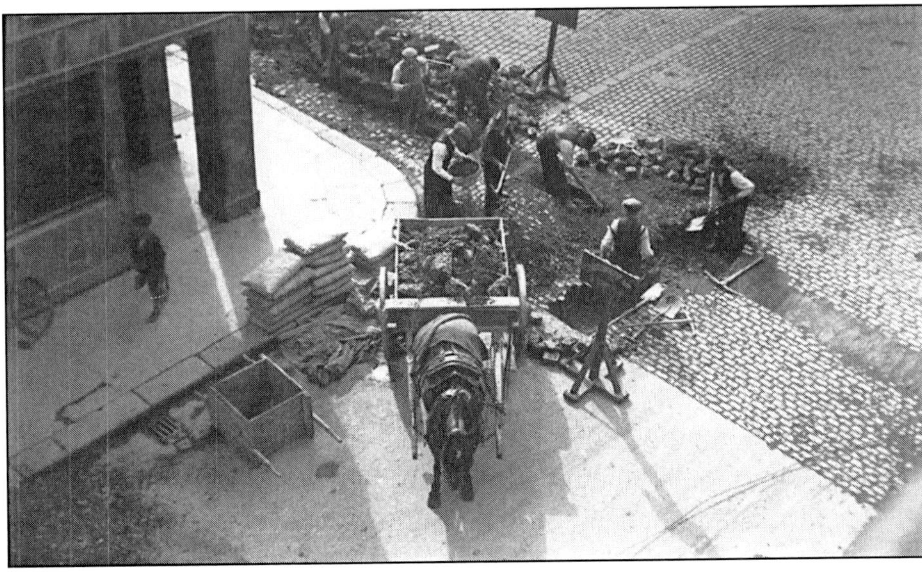

***Dublin Corporation workmen.***

This photograph was taken from the window of a tenement room overlooking the junction of Foley Street and Corporation Street. Each of the Corporation workers are wearing what appears to be white shirts, waistcoats and caps as they work on the cobblestone street below.

The pub on the corner was formally owned by Phil Shanahan who fought in the Easter Rising of 1916 and in the Irish War of Independence with Michael Collins. Shanahan and Collins had met while being held prisoners in a British Internment Camp in Wales. Phil Shanahan offered Collins the eyes and ears of the people from the Monto area in his fight against British Rule in Ireland.

Some of the prostitutes used *'Pillow Talk'* to gain important information from any young soldier that they may have had in their bed. This information was then passed on to people like Phil Shanahan who in turn passed it on to Michael Collins or one of his men. Shanahan had a secret door in his pub through which Collins and his men could pass through to make good their escape from any British soldiers who might raid the pub.

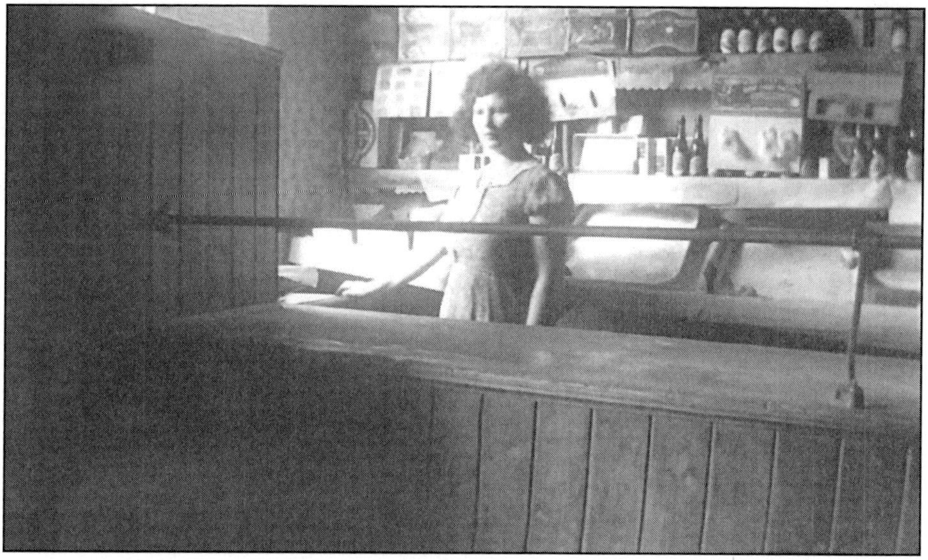

***A Monto Shop.***

This is one of those rare and unusual photographs of the inside of a shop in the Monto area of 1930's Dublin. The bread trays on the lower back shelf are empty of the bread they probably had on display. There is a whole array of items for sale on the other shelves. The bar running along the top of the counter was most likely there to stop any would-be-thief from hopping over the counter and making off with the days takings. A lot of families in the area would have bought their foodstuffs and cigarettes on the 'Slate' or the 'Book'. In other words they would purchase some items of shopping without paying for them there and then, money would change hands at a later date, perhaps when the customer's husband came home from sea.

*'Dirty Shirts was the shop that used to sell the paraffin oil and the penny drinks. He used to knock up raspberry and lemonade drinks for the kids. And we used to go to Croke Park and collect the Taylor Keith's lemonade bottles and we used to sell them in Dirty Shirt's, We used to buy these penny drinks but the one time I looked down his cellar and there was a sixpence down there and I done the old act, everybody had tried it on before. I went in crying. "Ah Dirty Shirt me mammy sent me down for to get some messages and I dropped the sixpence down the cellar". He says "Feck off, that's been down there since three weeks". It wasn't mine at all. So we had to hatch a plan on how to get that sixpence. So me and me pals went*

*into the tenement houses at the side and there was three of us. Now one of them done a number two, done a poo, a fella got a piece of string and put it through a piece of cardboard with poo on it and dropped it down onto the sixpence, the poo stuck to the sixpence and we took it up and went into Dirty Shirt's and spent it. There you are now, that's the extent of the tricks we used to have to do in them days'...* ***Matt Redmond MBE***

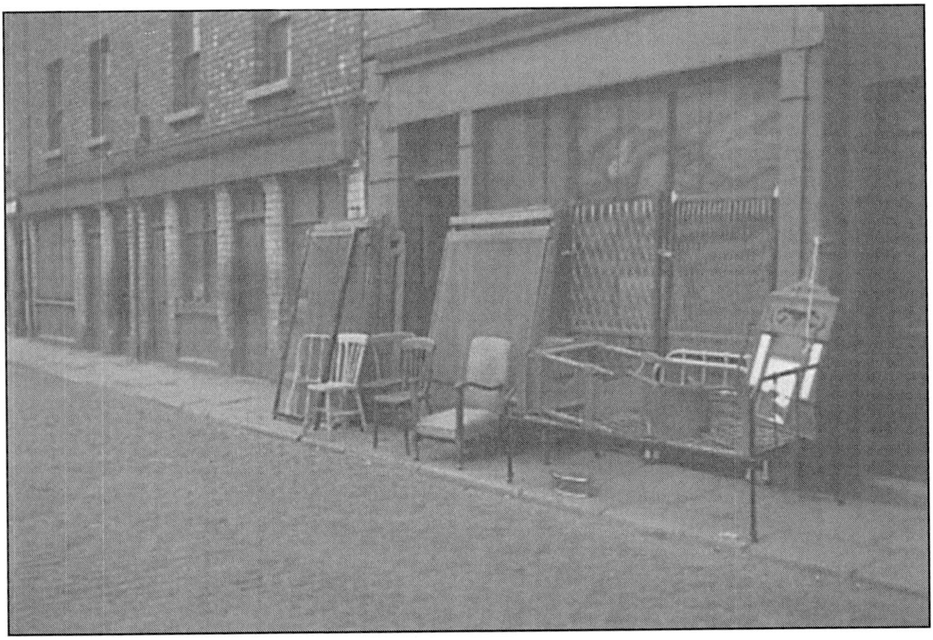

***Second-hand Furniture Shop.***

Very few people living in this area would have been in a position to buy new furniture. The various street markets and second-hand shops were very popular for this reason. On the single bed to the right in this photograph are a bedroom washstand, a chair and an Over-Mantle. The large wooden framed bedsprings standing near the door of the shop usually came with a tool that was used to wind the springs tight when they became loose over a period of time. In winter times families would often break up their furniture and burn it on their fire to keep themselves and their children warm and to cook their food on.

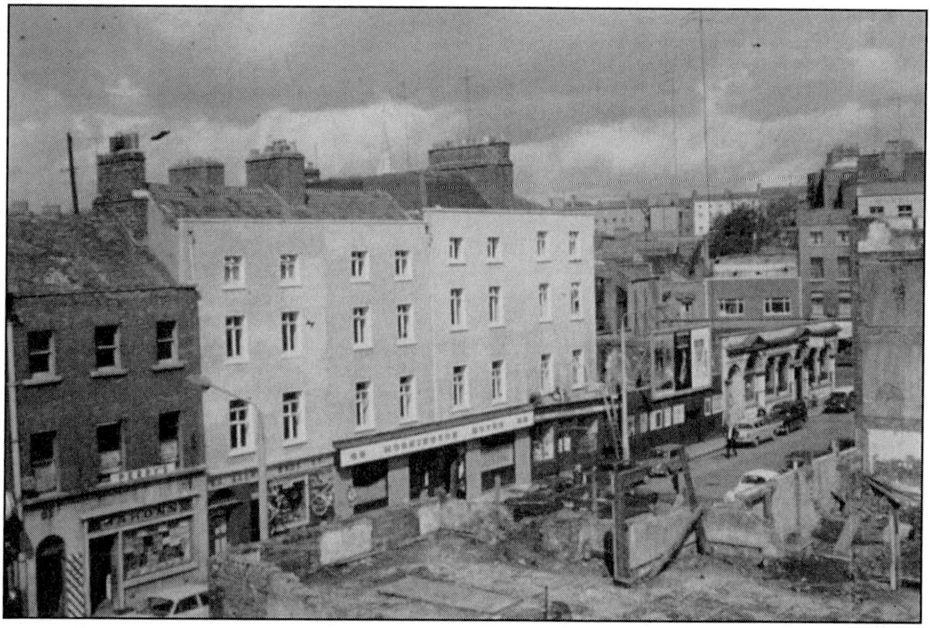

***Marlborough Street.***

Looking out from the room at the back of his tenement house in Sean McDermott Street Paddy Coffey photographs the site where the new Telephone Exchange is due to be built. In this ever-changing world and with his camera at the ready he documented the destruction of a way of life he grew up with.

Around the corner from the pub on the top left of this photograph member of the Ulster Volunteer Force detonated a car bomb in 1974. This resulted in the death of John O'Brien and his wife Anna Doyle as well as that of their two young children, Jacqueline and Anne Marie. It was the day of Anna's birthday and as a family they had strolled uptown from their tenement flat in nearby Gardiner Street. As they passed by the car housing the bomb it exploded. Anna's father is a first cousin to Paddy Coffey. Nobody was ever charged with these murders.

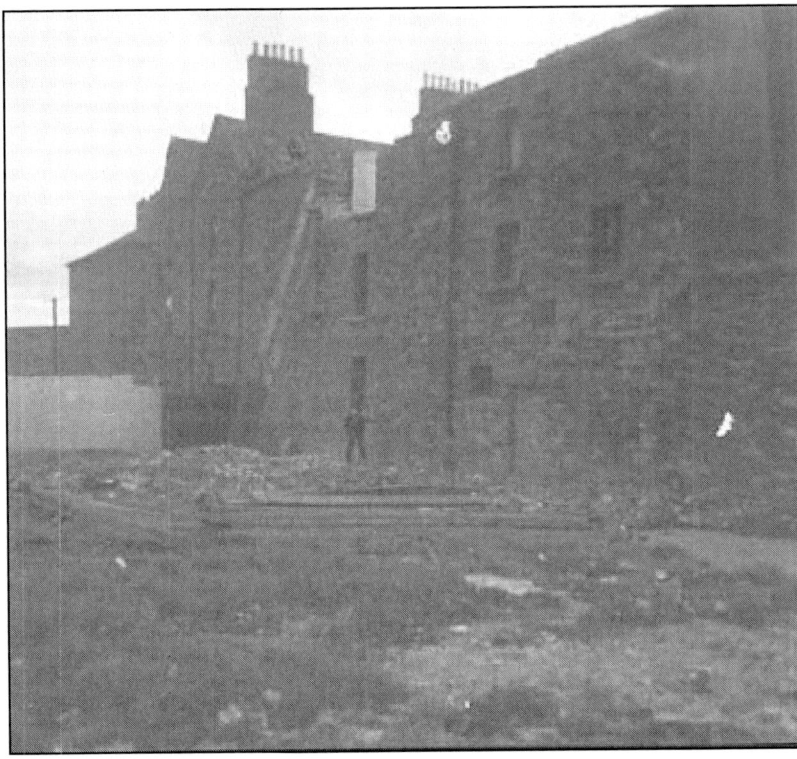

*Old buildings being demolished.*

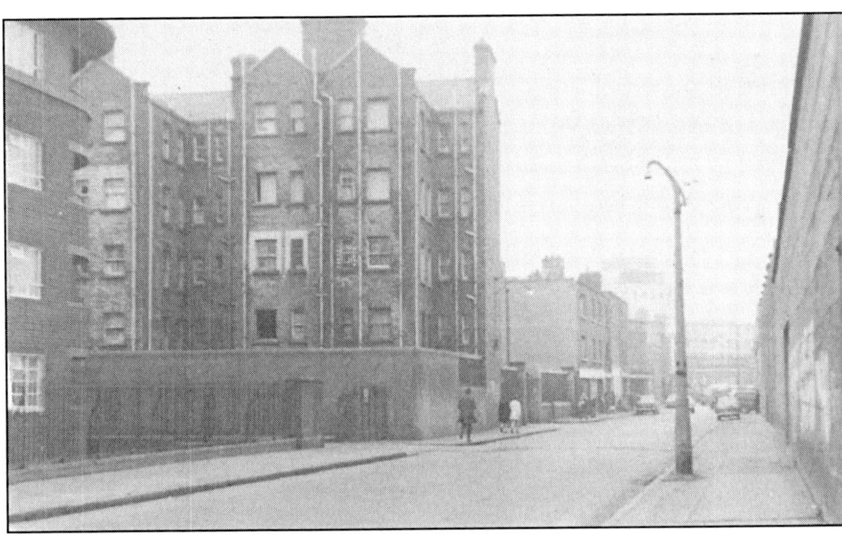

*Corporation Street, Dublin.*

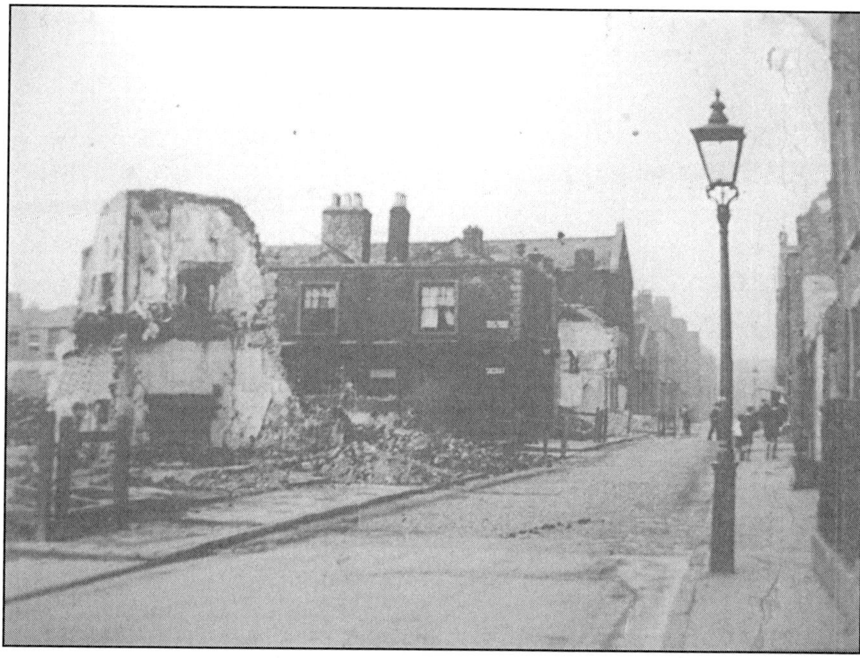

***Railway Street.***

The main building in this photograph is a pub that once belonged to Joe O'Reilly and his family. It is on the corner of Railway Street and Elliott Place. The large building behind the pub was the old National School where young children from the area attended daily. When the old school was eventually demolished shortly after this photograph was taken the children were transferred to a new school in Rutland Street. This view is looking in the direction of Corporation Street.

When Joe O'Reilly's pub was being demolished he was asked by Dublin Corporation to produce the necessary paperwork proving that he was the legal owner of the property. It seems that at some stage of his life Joe O'Reilly lost a lot of paperwork that related to both the pub and a number of tenement houses that he owned in Railway Street and because of this he never received any financial compensation for either premises or pub from Dublin Corporation. On top of Joe's pub there were what was then known in the area as two *'Love Cups'* situated on the roof at the front of the building. When the pub was demolished the two *'Cups'* were given to Joe's tenant Annie Burke who lived with her family in the flat over his pub, she had decided to move to the new housing suburb of Cabra West where she placed them in her front garden.

There is one well-known photograph that was taken from this corner looking down Elliott Place towards Purdon Street. It shows two young girls standing in the middle of the road facing the cameraman. This street photograph and its wrong name are in several publications written about this area and are also used by some Public Libraries on their web page. The name of the street accompanying the photograph is mistakenly given as *Faithful Place*; it is in fact *Elliott Place*. Paddy Coffey always considered it very important to be as precise as possible when naming people, places or locations in photographs.

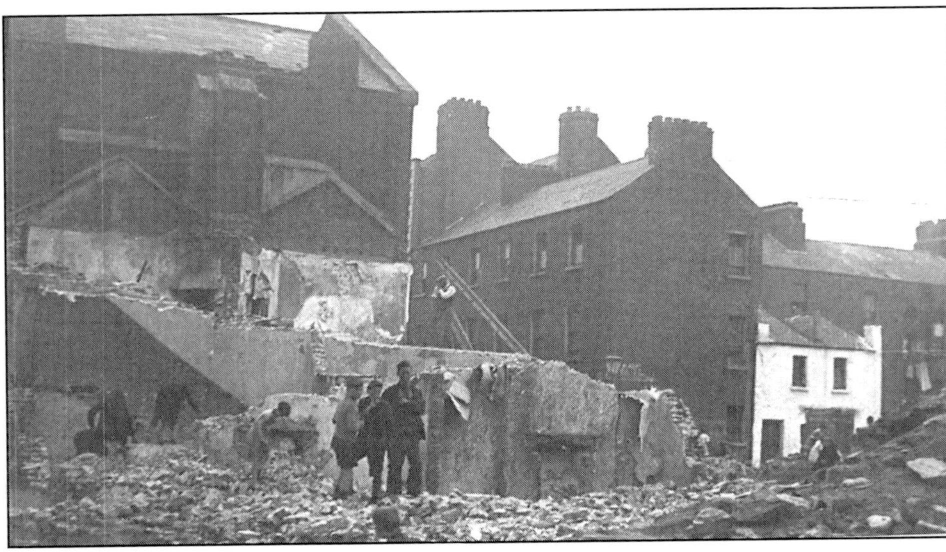

***The remains of Joe O'Rielly's Pub.***

This photograph shows the remains of Joe O'Rielly's pub which was situated on the corner of Elliott Place and Railway Street. The whitewashed house on the right of the photograph is in Gloucester Lane where young children can be seen playing amongst the rubble. The large tenement house on the corner of Railway Street and Gloucester Lane belonged to Margaret Doyle. There are three young boys and a young girl rummaging through the remains of the pub in search of anything of value. The other three young lads seem more interested in the camera. A workman can also be seen as he lights up a cigarette.

*'My mother worked for Joe O'Reilly. She looked after his wife who was living in their house out in Drumcondra. I think Mrs O'Rielly was from England. Joe O'Rielly owned the Pub down our street. We lived over the pub*

*for a good few years until they were all getting knocked down and then we moved to Cumberland Street. When my brother Johnnie started working in Joe O'Rielly's pub first he used to collect the empty stout bottles from people in the area. He would call to their tenement room and ask them for the bottles back. You see, at that time when you took your few bottles home the Publican had to go and collect them off you.*

*So Johnnie used to collect them and he'd wash them and then him and Joe O'Rielly used to bottle Stout and cork it. And then they had this barrel of wine in the hall, I don't know the name of it but we used to call it the Red Biddy, and they'd bottle that. I think you could buy a glass of that for sixpence. Johnnie was serving then behind the counter and then he got he used to be helping in the pub with ould Joe. Of course when that all closed down Johnnie went off to England. The man that owned the Pub died and young Joe had it then for a while. When they came to knock the pub down he went and looked for compensation. The O'Rielly's owned 20 and 21 Railway Street as well as the pub and then there was also 18 and 19 Elliott Place that they owned and part of the pub was around the corner as well. Well what happened was there was something about Papers, he hadn't put in some papers for a claim so they got nothing for the two houses in Elliott Place'...* **Aggie Coffey**.

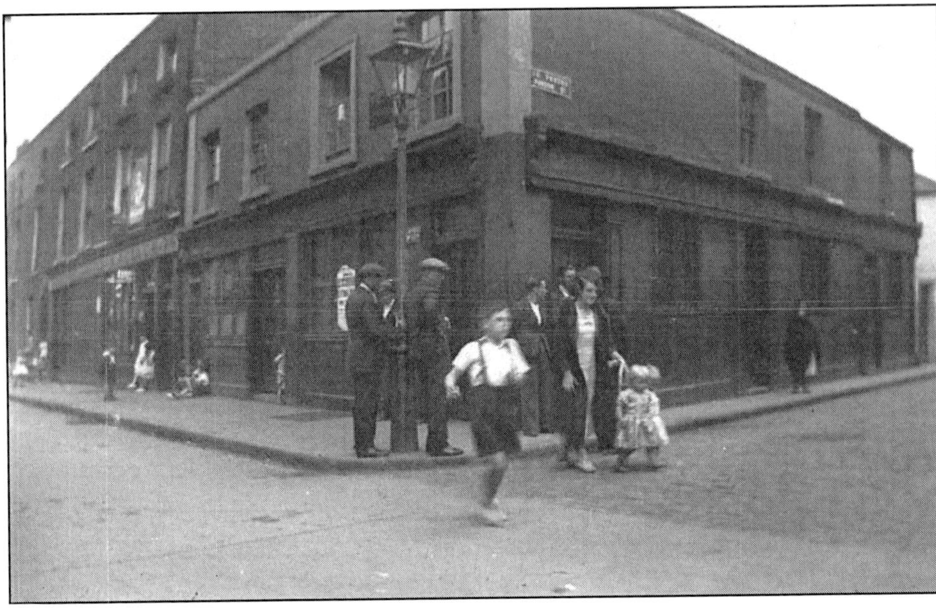

***The Dunleavy twins and Jack Meagher's Pub.***

Jack Meagher's pub was located on the corner of Corporation Street and Purdon Street, which is to the right of this photograph. A woman wearing a black shawl is seen standing in Purdon Street and appears to be watching the scene being photographed. The group of men standing on the corner are obviously waiting for the pub to open. Throughout the daytime young boys would sit on this corner waiting to be called into the pub by one of the men who would then send them off to *'Go up and tell the wife I'll be up in a few minutes for me dinner'*. The boy would sometimes get money from the man or a slice of bread and jam from his wife or maybe both if they were very lucky, for running this errand for them. The laneway off Purdon Street, at the back of this pub, where the white building is seen in this photograph was known as Byrne's Court where Paddy Coffey's grandfather lived. There are three cottages and three tenement houses recorded in this lane on the 1901 Dublin census. When the tenements and cottages were knocked down the end of the lane was closed off. The lane was later known locally as *'The Man Trap'* where sailors, soldiers and strangers alike were brought by girls of the night and robbed.

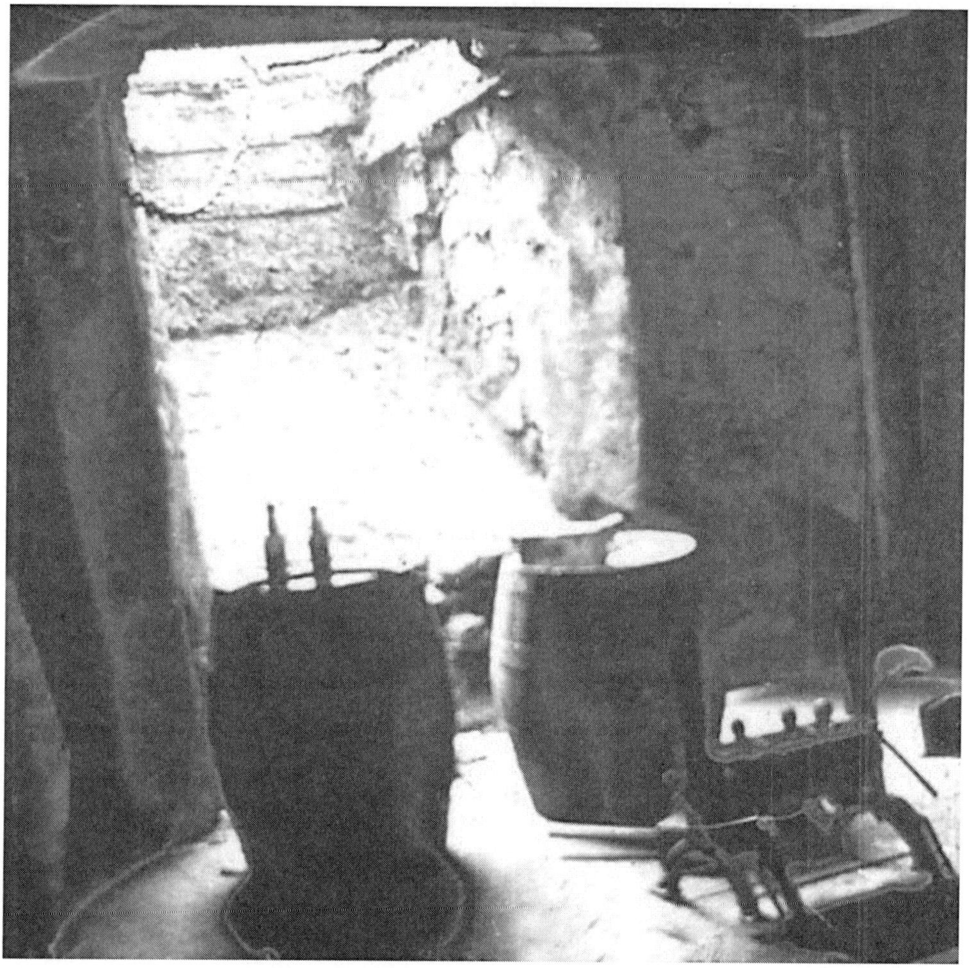

***The basement of Jack Meagher's pub.***

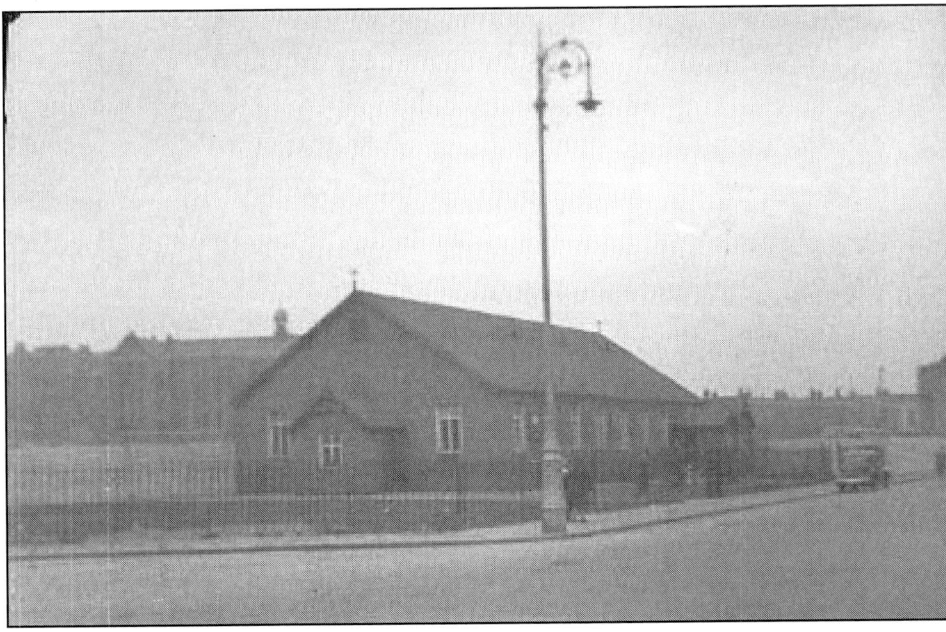

***The old Tin Church in Sean McDermot Street.***

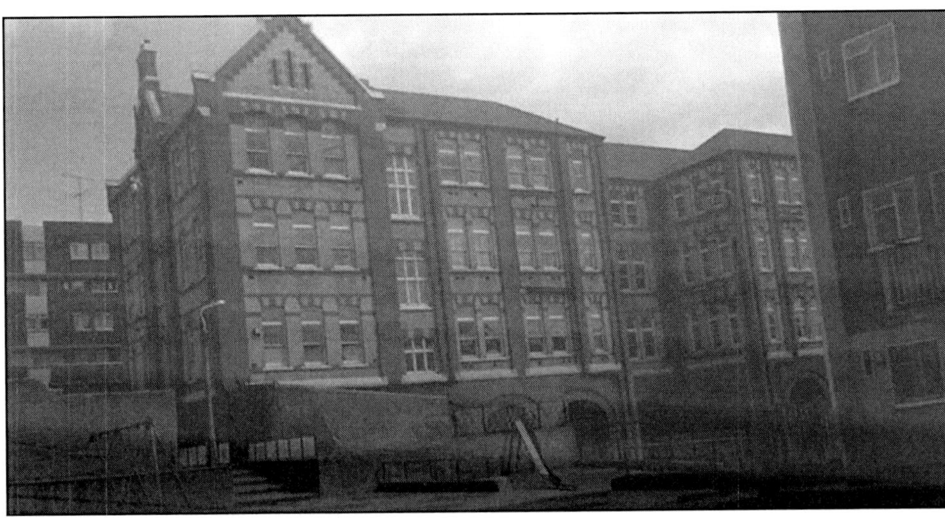

***Rutland Street School for boys and girls.***

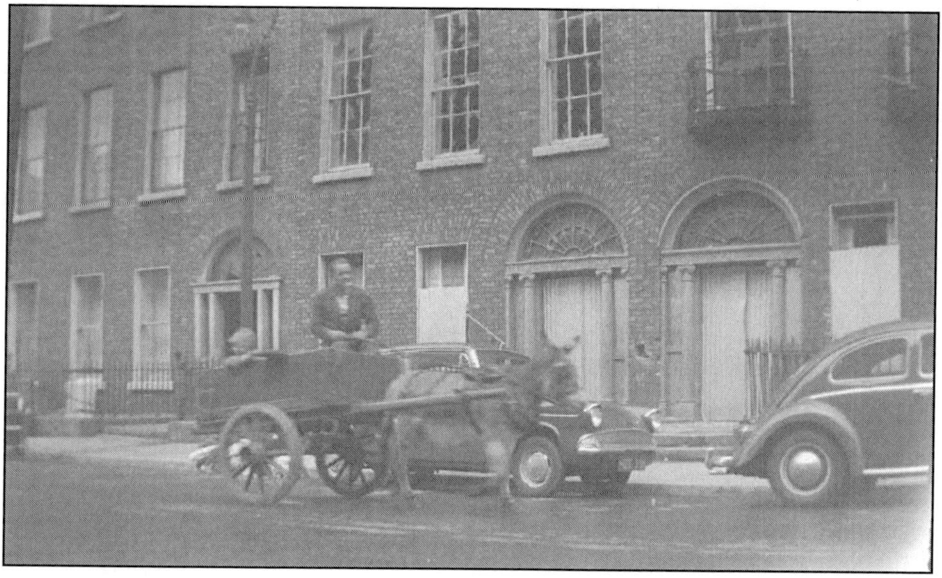

***Doolin's Ass.***

Within living memory the ass and cart were a very familiar sight in and around the streets of Dublin. Household slops, which may have consisted of old or discarded cabbage leafs, potato skins and other such food items that may have been discarded by families in the area were collected from door to door.  The owners of the numerous pig sty's that were housed in small laneways and side streets would feed the slop to their pigs. In some areas a 'Slop Collection Point' was often set up where young children would bring the slops from their own area and be given a few pennies for it. When some young children would see the ass and cart coming along they would start singing...

***'Doolin's Ass.***

***On the grass.***

***Lift his tail***

***And see his ars'.***

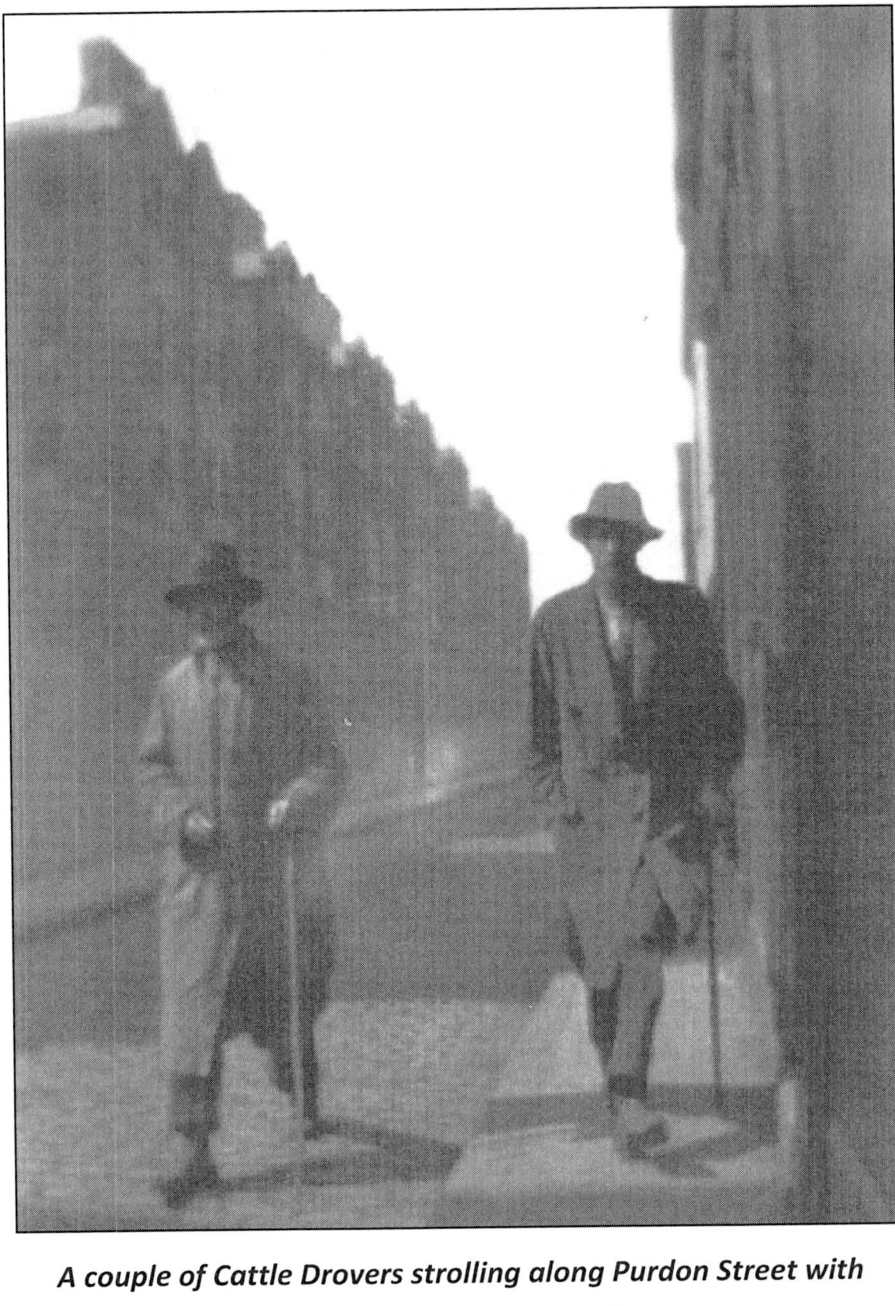

***A couple of Cattle Drovers strolling along Purdon Street with Corporation Buildings towering over the street scene.***

*'Of a Tuesday and Thursday you got a mug of stew, you know them enamel mugs? It used to be grand but we used to say at home "I'm not going over there, I wouldn't eat that dirty old stew". Sometimes if you were cute enough and quick enough you could dodge on the line, you could get your thing of stew, dodge out of the line and get on the line again and get another one. When the weather'd be very bad, if it was lashing rain or snow or anything they used to bring big churns of Cocoa over to the school and Bread and Jam, it was lovely, we used to think that was great but we used to tell our mother and she'd go "You're not going over there". My brother Johnnie would say, "I saw you, I saw you going over to the Stew House", and I'd say, "Weren't you going over too". We'd be looking for the money for the Black Babies, for the whole of Lent you'd be expected to bring in your ha'penny for the Black Babies every morning, you'd think hard of giving it. And do you know what we used to do, there used to be Doyle's at the corner of Gardiner Street and Gloucester Street, it's Sean Mc Dermot Street now, but it used to be an Off Licence then, I don't know if it was called an Off Licence then or not, but this was like an Off Licence place, and they used to sell Tea and Sugar and all, and they used to sell lovely Brown Sugar, now it used to be gorgeous and you could get a bag of that for a ha'penny, a little bag for a ha'penny'.*

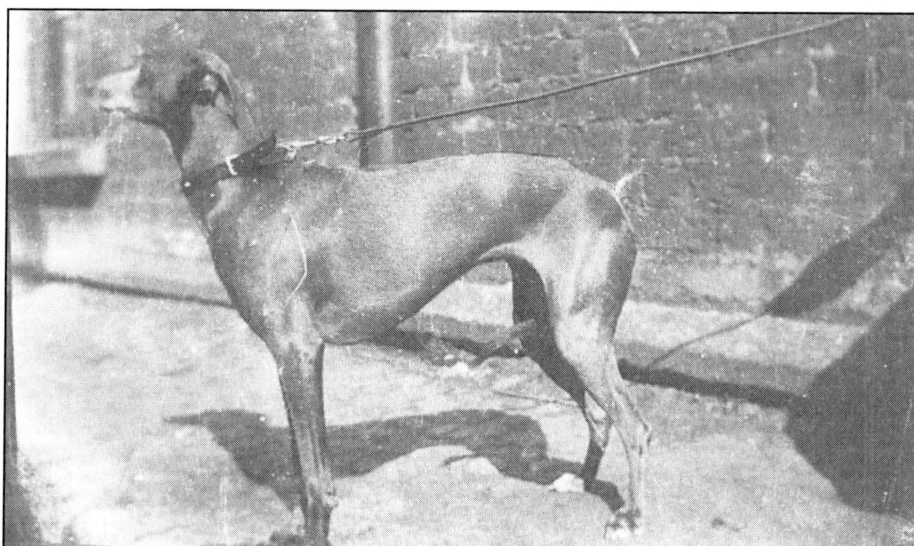

***Sonny Doyle's Lurcher.***

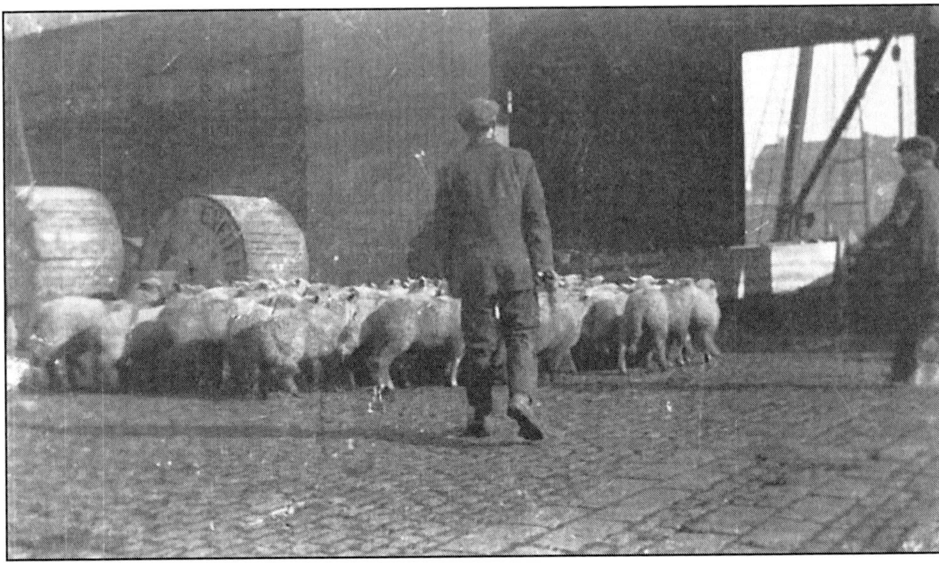

***The North Wall.***

A flock of sheep being herded into a shed on the North Wall to await transportation to England. Live cattle were also shipped overseas from this point. Cattle were very often brought from the main cattle market in Prussia Street down through Phibsborough, the North Circular Road and Seville Place where they were corralled to await shipment to England. Cattle Drovers were employed to drive the herd through the streets and ensure that they arrived at their destination safely.

*'My first job was in the Rosary Bead factory at Five Bob a week. Well it was work, you know, it was something. When I went in first I went in on the Buttons, polishing Buttons. You'd have to sort the different sizes; you know you know the 45's the 35's, the 20's. When he finished doing buttons after a few years and we went onto Crosses, Crosses of the Rosary, polishing them. When they'd be slack Paddy O'Neil said to me "Will you go into the Grinding Room", they all hated going into the Grinding Room because it was full of dust. I didn't care I'd go to the Grinding Room.*

*You see when the Cross would be cut out it might be too thick and you'd have to grind them down to the size to go on the beads. I could do that, I could grind them down, I could polish them and I could cut them out. Because I used to, when he'd ask me anything I'd say yes I'll do it. I started work when I was just gone fourteen. Then sometimes some of the things we do eh, for the middle of the bead they'd have this little heart shape* *thing or maybe it'd be a Shamrock shape, and it might be "Souvenir of Knock" or souvenir of something else and different things like that. Well they'd have to be polished and they'd have to be gilded, the lettering would be gilded. Then you had to polish them so that the Gilding would be only in the lettering because when it'd be done it'd be all over them. I could join the beads. You got that you could pick up things if you were willing to, you now. Sure I was a few years out of work and I went back to try and get Kathleen a job. He told me he'd no job for her but he'd give me one'...***Aggie Coffey***

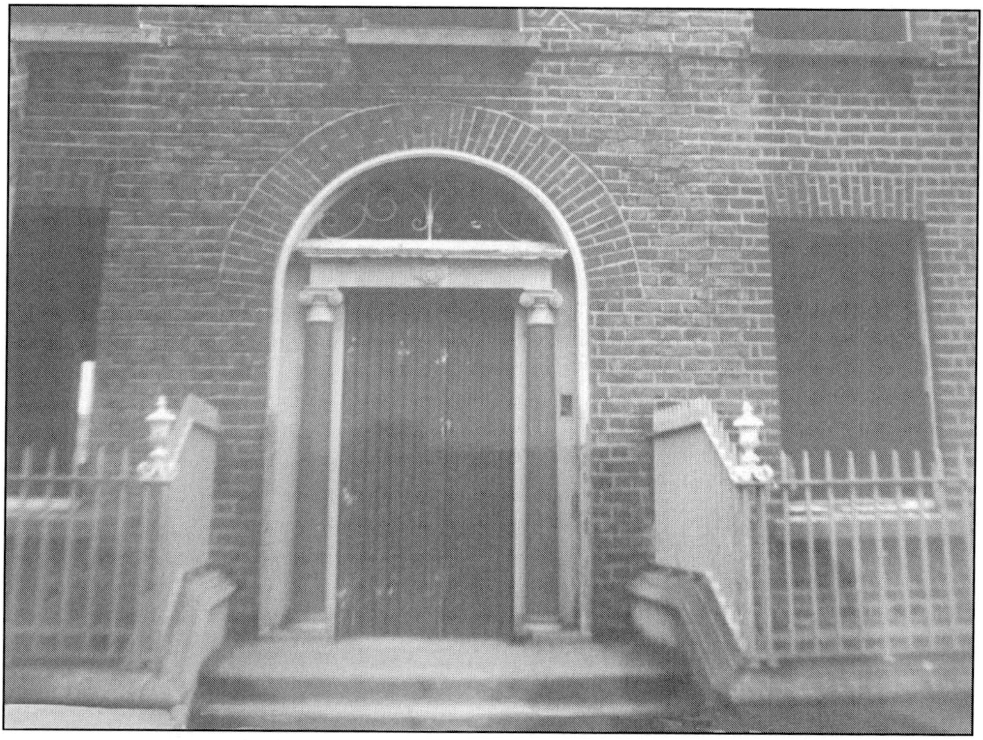

***A Georgian Doorway on a tenement house.***

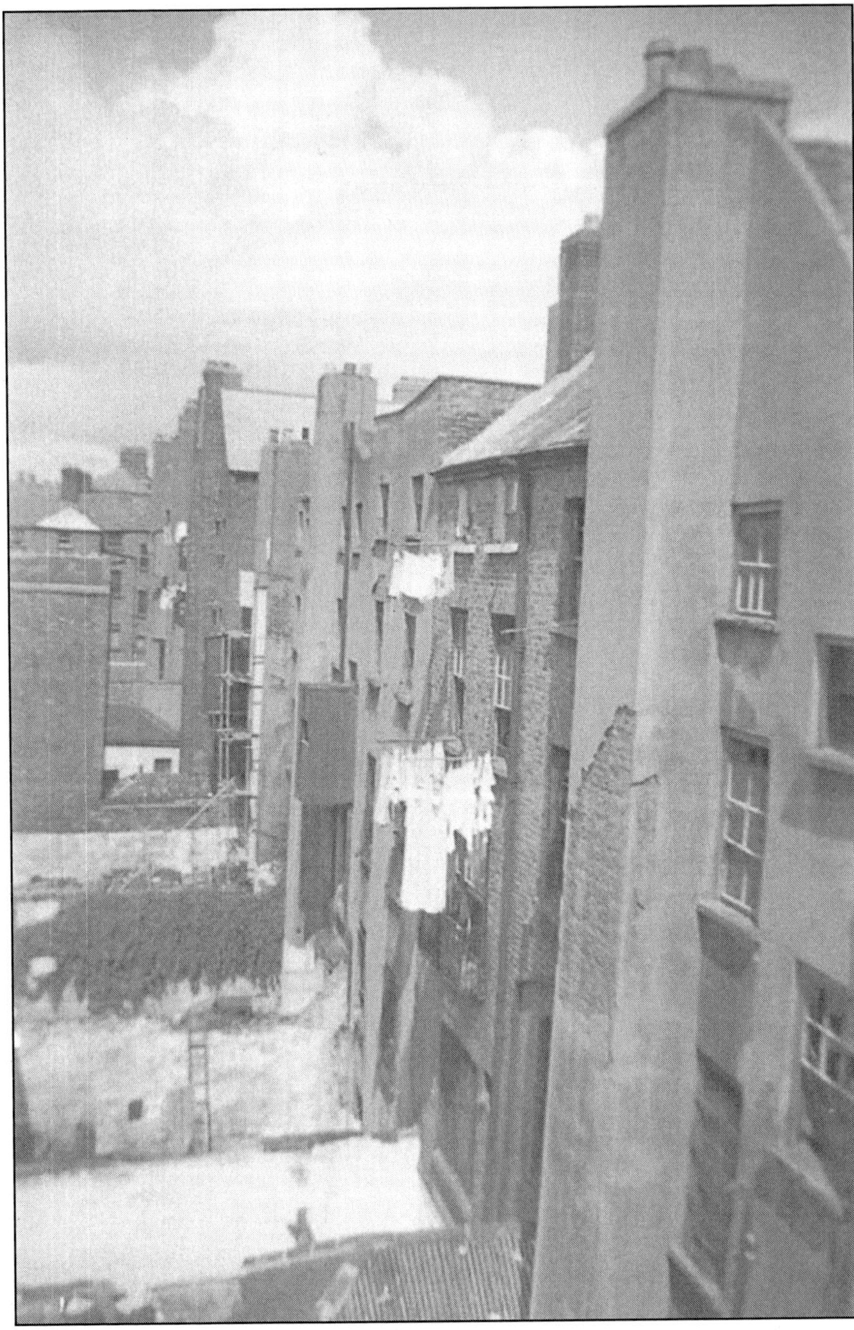

***A back view of the tenements.***

*'We lived in the Parlour in number 10 Elliott Place and that was small. Then we moved up stairs, May Doyle used to live in that room and then she moved out. She moved up to Railway Street. You'd open the door and there was the foot of the bed and the other end went up to the wall and that was the bed. Then just over in that corner was the Chair-Bed, it used to open out for my brother Johnnie, and then there was the Fireplace. She had a small Kitchen Dresser, and the table was up at the bed, they were all small rooms. People would move out of one room if they heard another room was a bit bigger, even if it was in the same house, you now that way. They moved from down in the parlour to upstairs 'cause that was a little bit bigger than the Parlour. We'd eat and sleep all in the one room; we'd just the one room. We used to keep our bucket with our slops on the Landing. We didn't have running water; you'd go down to the yard. If you came in covered in muck you were sent out to the tap to wash yourself, out to the cold tap to wash your feet and all.*

*They used to say that 20 Railway Street was haunted. They said that Teresa Carr went down, she was after emptying the slops, she had an empty slop bucket and she'd a bucket of water coming up and a figure was supposed to stop her, a figure at the top of the cellar stairs stopped her and was trying to entice her down, she could hear music down stairs and she let the buckets fall and she run out onto the road. I used to be sent down for the water and I never seen anything. My mother said that there used to be a what-do-you-call-it, a figure seen walking around the yard. She'd say to me that she'd keep talking to me, keep talking to me out of the window.*

*Davy Frame ownded two scrapyards down in Railway Street, two big things, and Barney something I think it was used to work with him, he took him to work in Hammond Lane after. There was the Big Iron Yard as we called it and the Small Iron Yard, so when they were kind of moving, it was all, ould scrap was still there to be moved. We used to play in and out of it and then when they did finally get all the stuff out of it, it was like a big waste ground, a big hill. We used to play up on that. I think it was Betty McKeever who climbed up on the wall and fell off and somebody said that it didn't make any improvement on her nose. We used to have them ould places to play.*

*Then there was Holmes' Lane, they had been old cottages and we used to go up there and we'd play shops and all, but ould Holmes now and then would come out and chase us because we shouldn't have been in there, the places were dangerous. Then they all got knocked down. We used to go up there and make shops and have all our sweets and all there, the what-do-you-call-it, the broken delph and the broken bottles for the sweets. Like you hadn't got all the things that kids have now, still you had a happy childhood.*

*There was one time my sister Kathleen had a shop, you see, and I had another one, and this young fella's sister, she came and she started because Kathleen wouldn't let out the Bench Shop she started kicking all the things down. So Kathleen hit her and her brother came and start hitting Kathleen and I went for him. Didn't he run, after me giving him a few digs he run home, and what did he do, his street overlooked the lane, their room looked out onto the yard, then across the yard was the lane, Holmes' lane as we used to call it, where we were playing, didn't he throw a piece of slate and got me there on the arm. I was so mad I run around to the house, into the room and pushed him around the room and kicked and boxed him. His mother had to get between us. Ould Mary O'Toole came along, "Oh you want to get that seen to, bring her up to the Children's Hospital" so all the kids brought me up to the hospital. I was put up on the stretcher thing in the hospital and eh the Nurse cleaned me face and the Doctor comes in and I heard the Doctor saying to her "Oh we'll need a few stitches on that".*

*He went over to attend somebody else and she went to get the things ready for my stitches and away with me down Temple Street. Mary O'Toole said "Well what did they do to you?" I said "They were going to stitch me and I'm not letting them stitch me." Do you know what she done, she got a bottle of Iodine, held me head back, poured the Iodine all on me. So I never got me stitches. I just said to Kathleen "That's over you." Of course me mother heard of it "Oh that's another of the "Vincent's" tenants for ye."*

*People wouldn't believe me when I told them that people took children in to rear them that weren't their own. There was many a one that was reared with a family that wasn't theirs down there. Everyone was your Uncle or your Aunt. Sure all the "Girls" as they used to call them, they were all my Aunts. Me Aunt Kitty, me Aunt Kathleen, Kathleen Williams was my Aunt Kathleen, Kitty Byrne was my Aunt Kitty. Molly McGinn, although she was married and had a family, she was my Aunt Molly. They were nothing to me and I mean Mary Vincent was my Aunt Mary, she was nothing to me. They were all my Aunts. Mary Oblong or Mrs Mary Roberts, she'd say as me and Kathleen would be passing, when we'd be coming back from the Lec'*

*Picture House I'd say "Kathleen, quick, are you ready, now dive past here". We'd be flying past her shop how she wouldn't see us because if she'd see us she'd say, "Come here, come in and kiss your Granny" and the woman would give us biscuits. I used to be afraid because she'd sit there with her big white apron on her and she had a big knife for cutting the meat and cutting the cheese. I used to be afraid of my life of her. The woman never done anything on me, she's in the song now as May Oblong'*

**Aggie Coffey**.

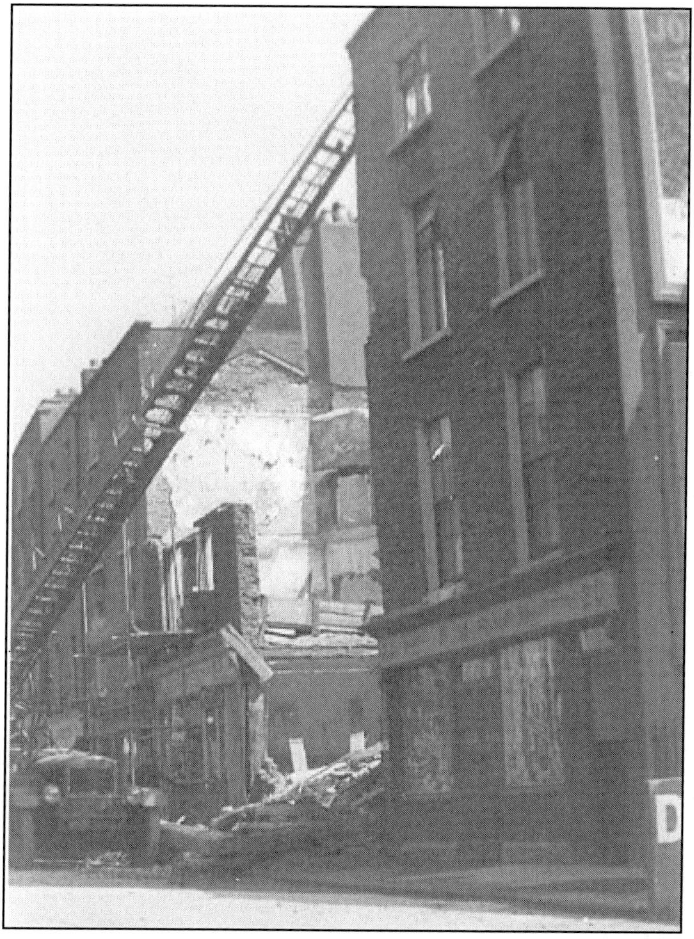

***Demolition work old buildings in Dublin.***

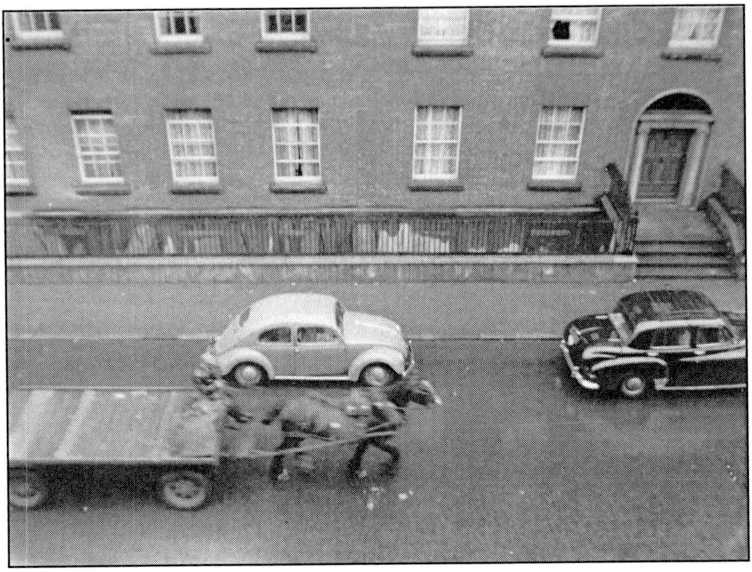

***Sean McDermot Street.***

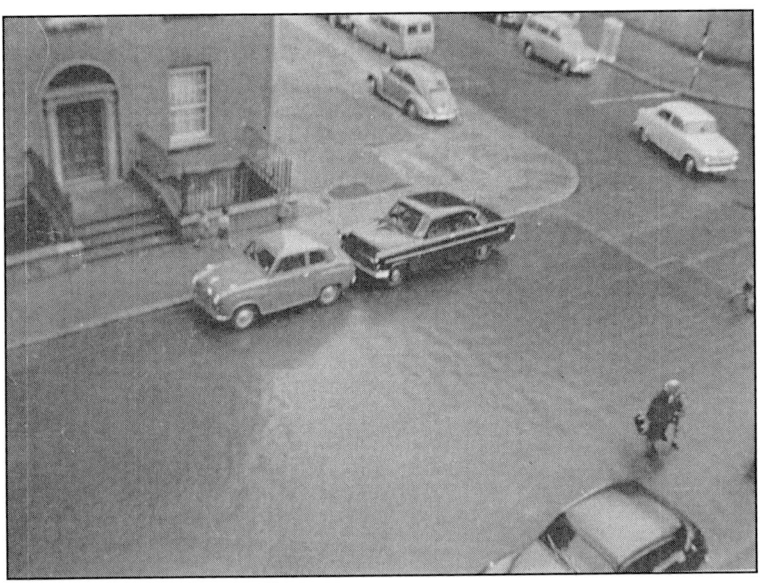

This photograph was taken from Paddy Coffey's bedroom window that was situated at the top of the tenement house where he lived near the corner of Sean McDermot Street and Marlborough Street, Dublin. Three young boys are seen passing by the beautiful Georgian doorway of the tenement house across the street.

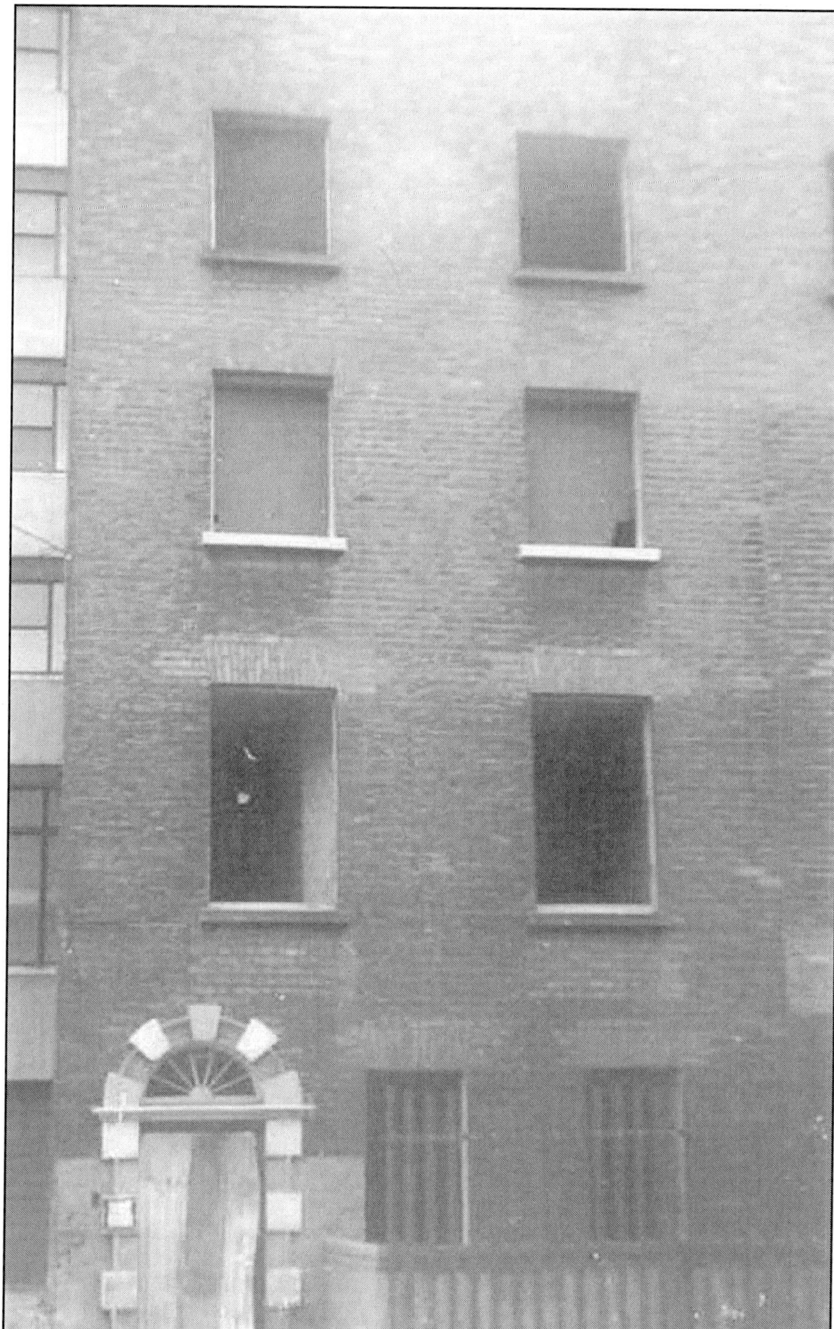

***Paddy Coffey lived with his sister in the top floor flat.***

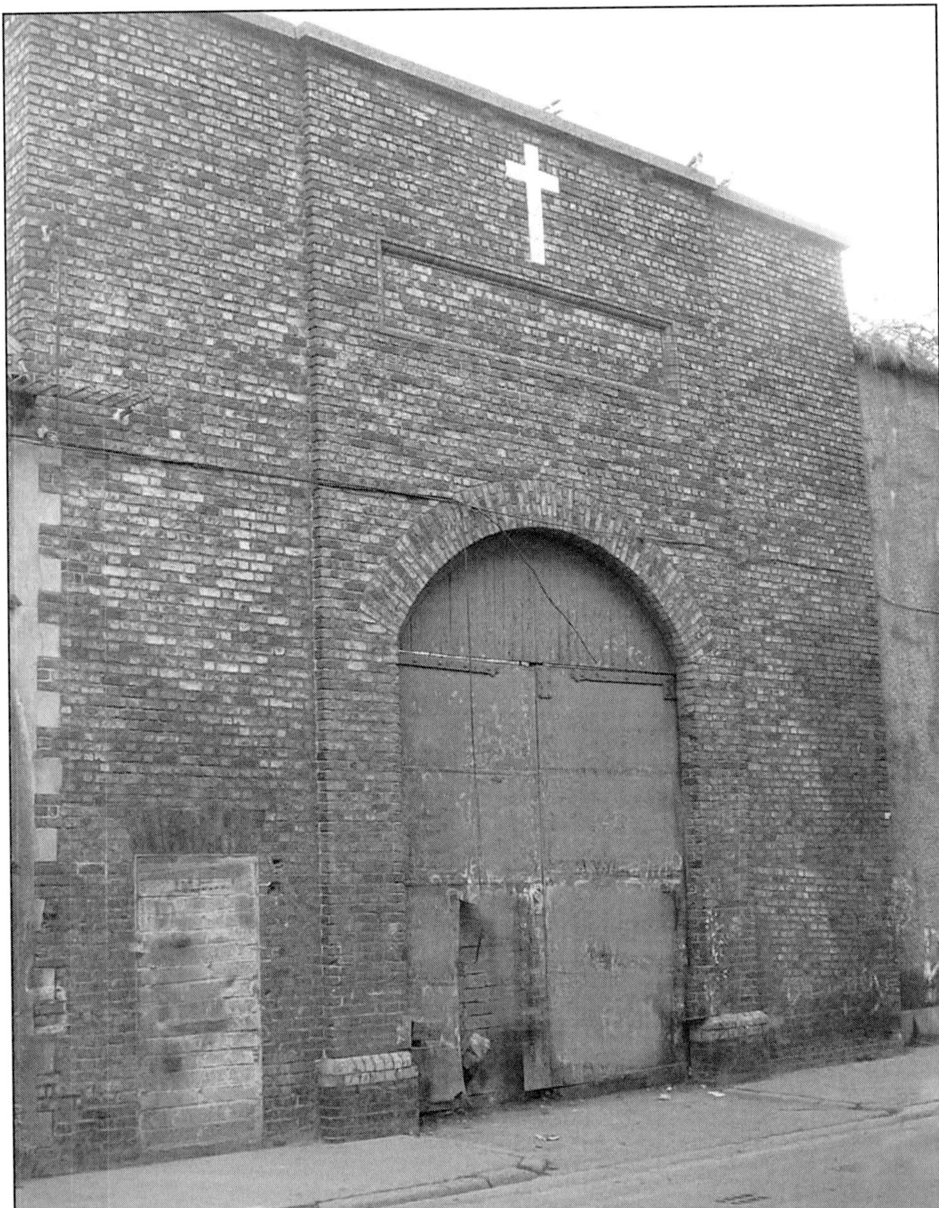

*The back gate into the Magdalene Convent on Railway Street.*

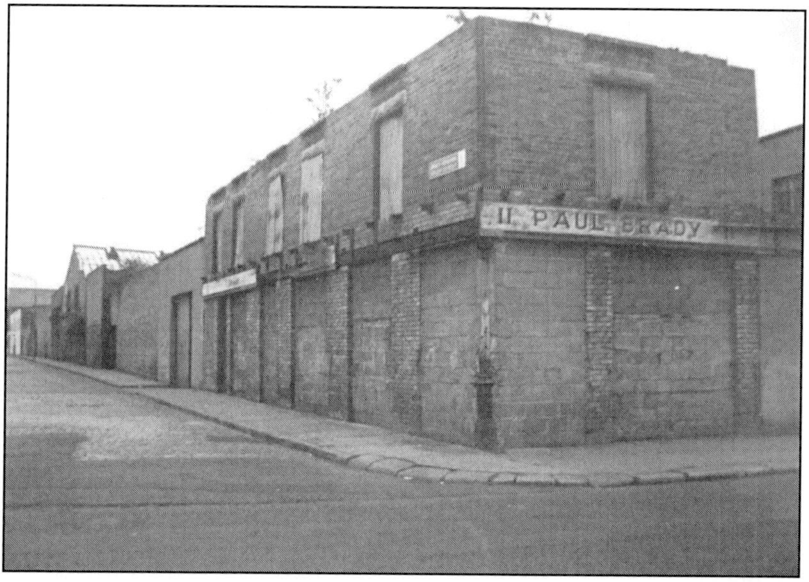


***Paul Brady's pub on the corner of Corporation Street and Foley Street.***

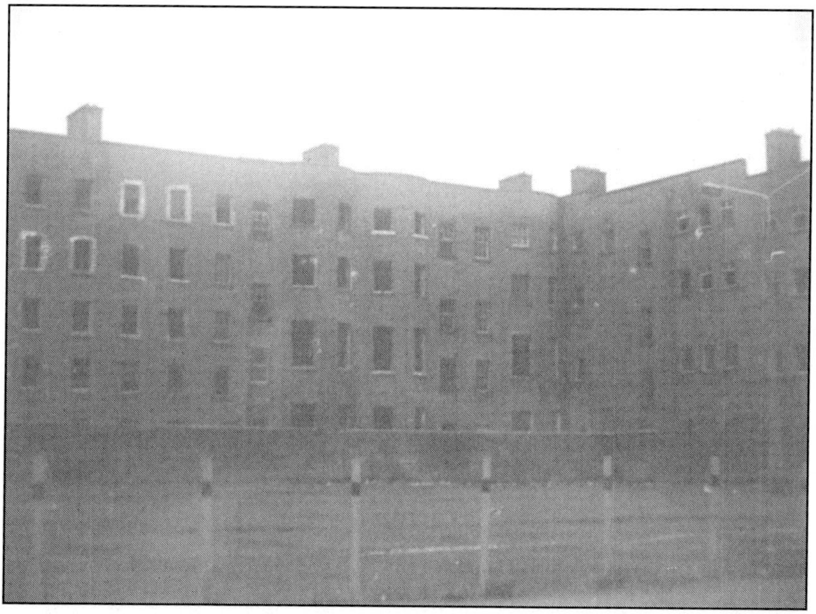

***A photograph of the tenement houses taken from Waterford Street.***

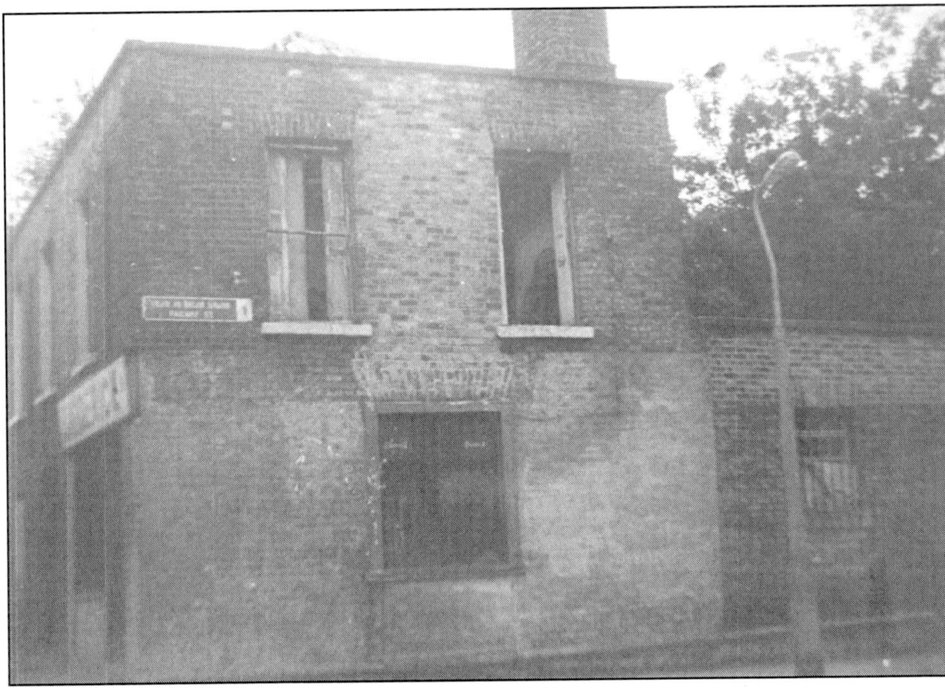

*Derelict building on Railway Street.*

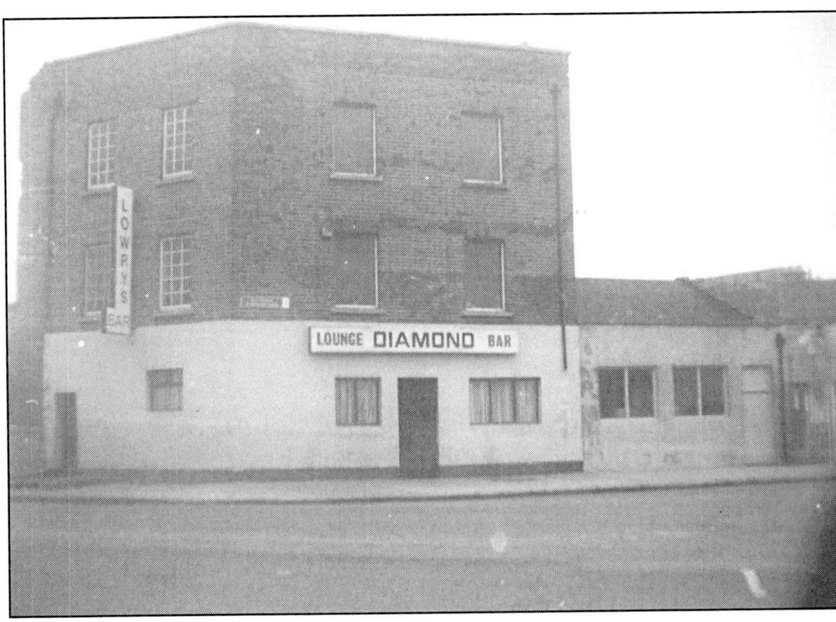


*The Gloucester Diamond pub.*

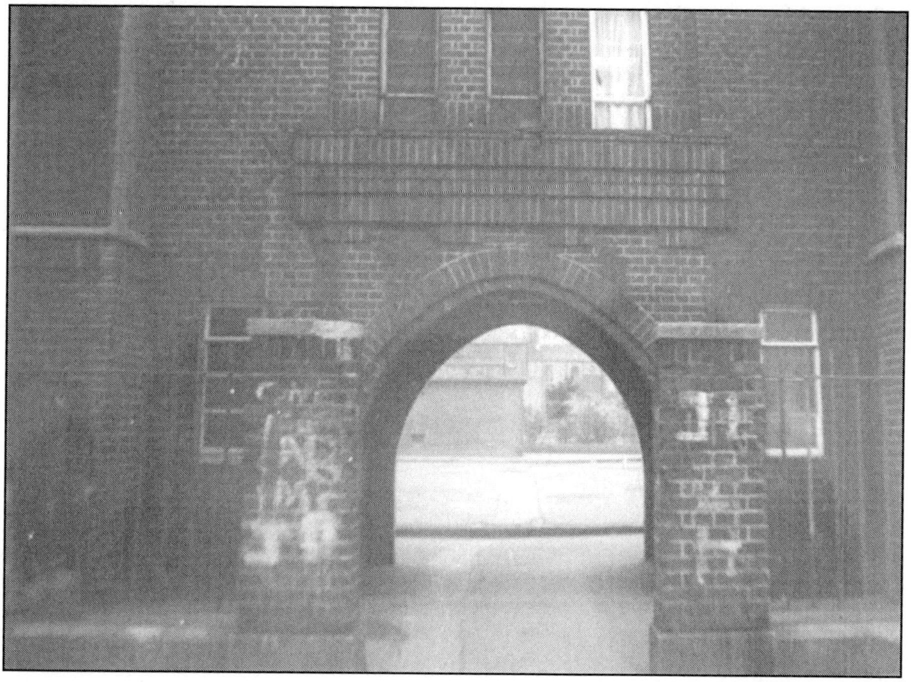

*The old archway on Railway Street leading into Liberty House.*

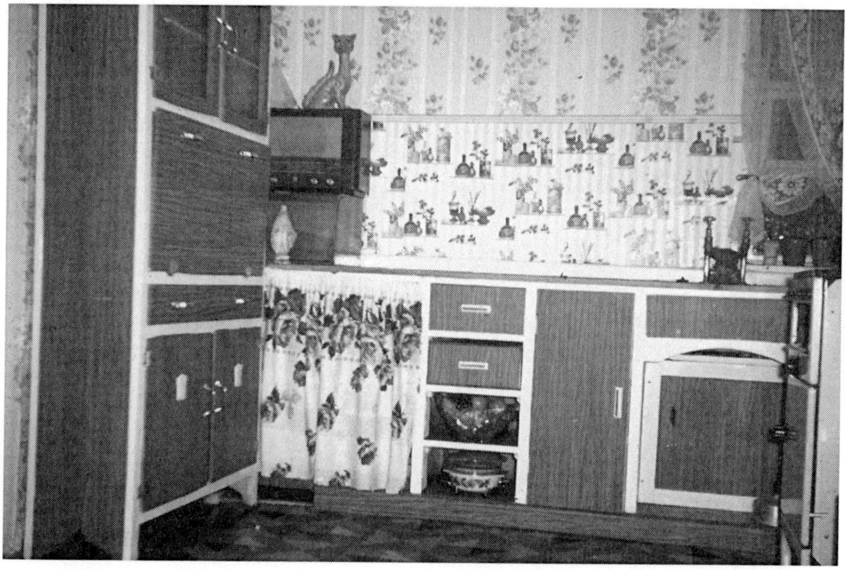

**The kitchen in Biddy Coffey's flat in Sean McDermot Street.**

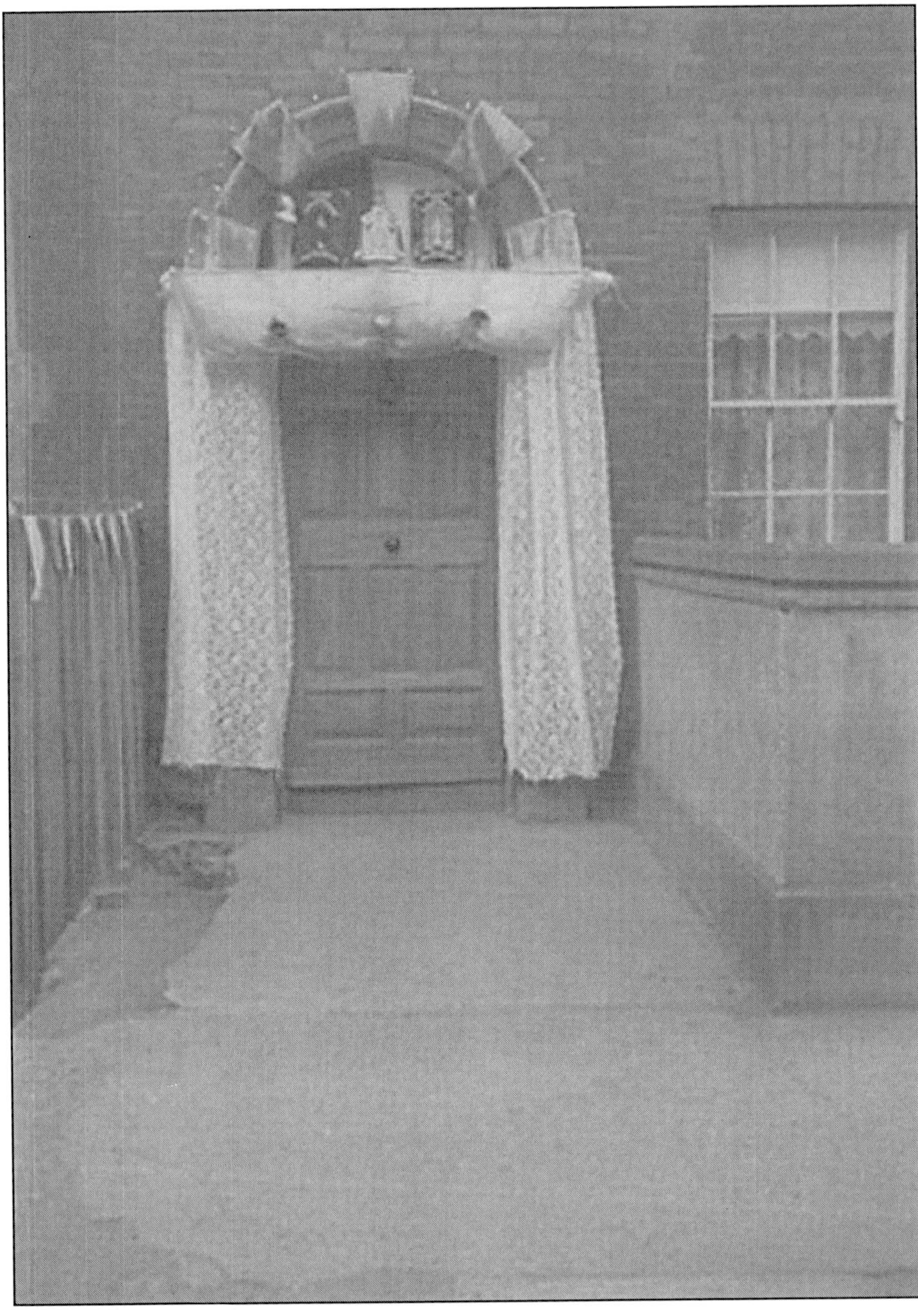

*Tenement Doorway in Sean McDermot Street, Dublin.*

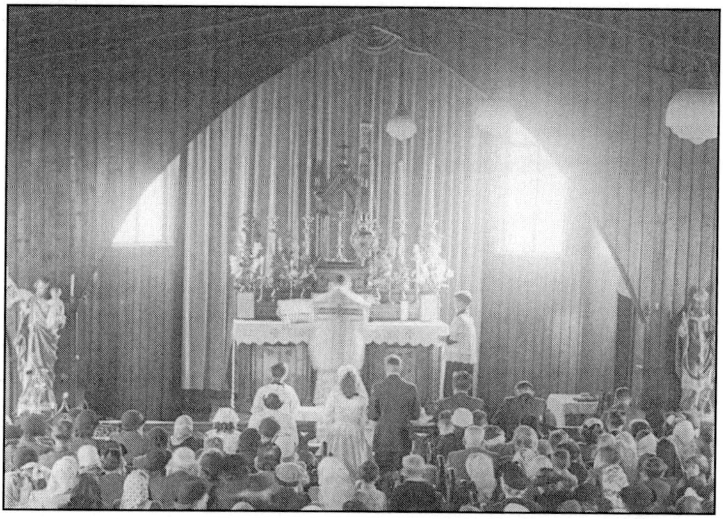

***Paddy Gorman's and Teresa Dillon's wedding in the old Tin Church.***

A rare photograph showing the inside of the Tin Church during a wedding ceremony. The wedding is that of Paddy Gorman to Teresa Dillon in 1951.

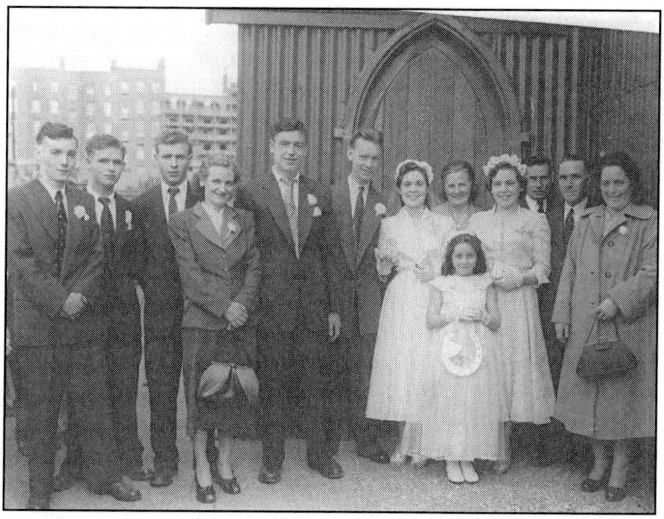

***L-R: Willie Gorman, Thomas Dillon Jr, Billy Dillon, Rooie Coffey Kane, Jack Gorman, Paddy Gorman, Teresa Dillon, Biddy Coffey, Rita Dillon, Bridesmaid ?, Paddy Coffey, Thomas Dillon Senior and Kathleen Kelly Dillon.***

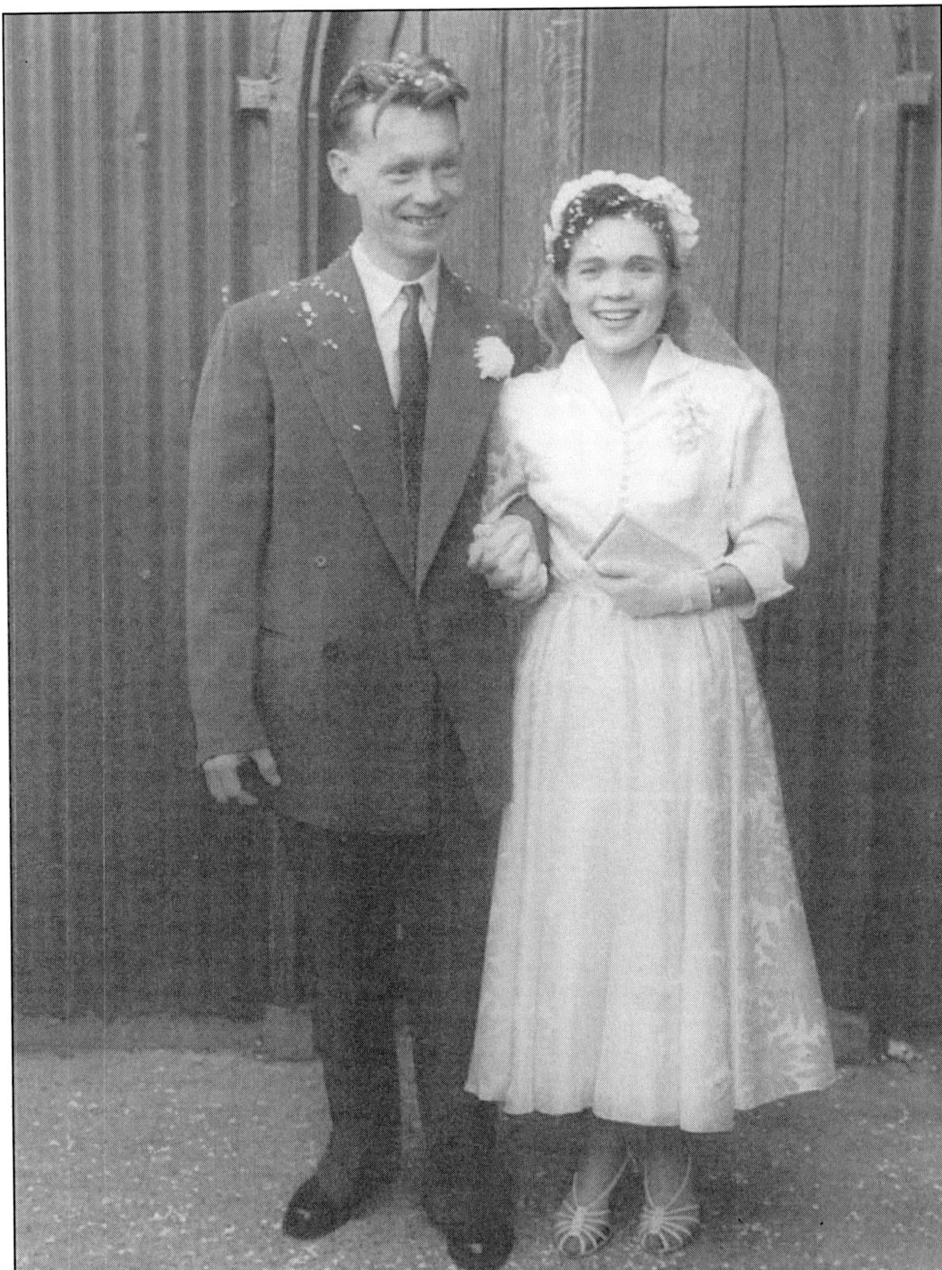

***Paddy Gorman and Teresa Dillon 1951.***

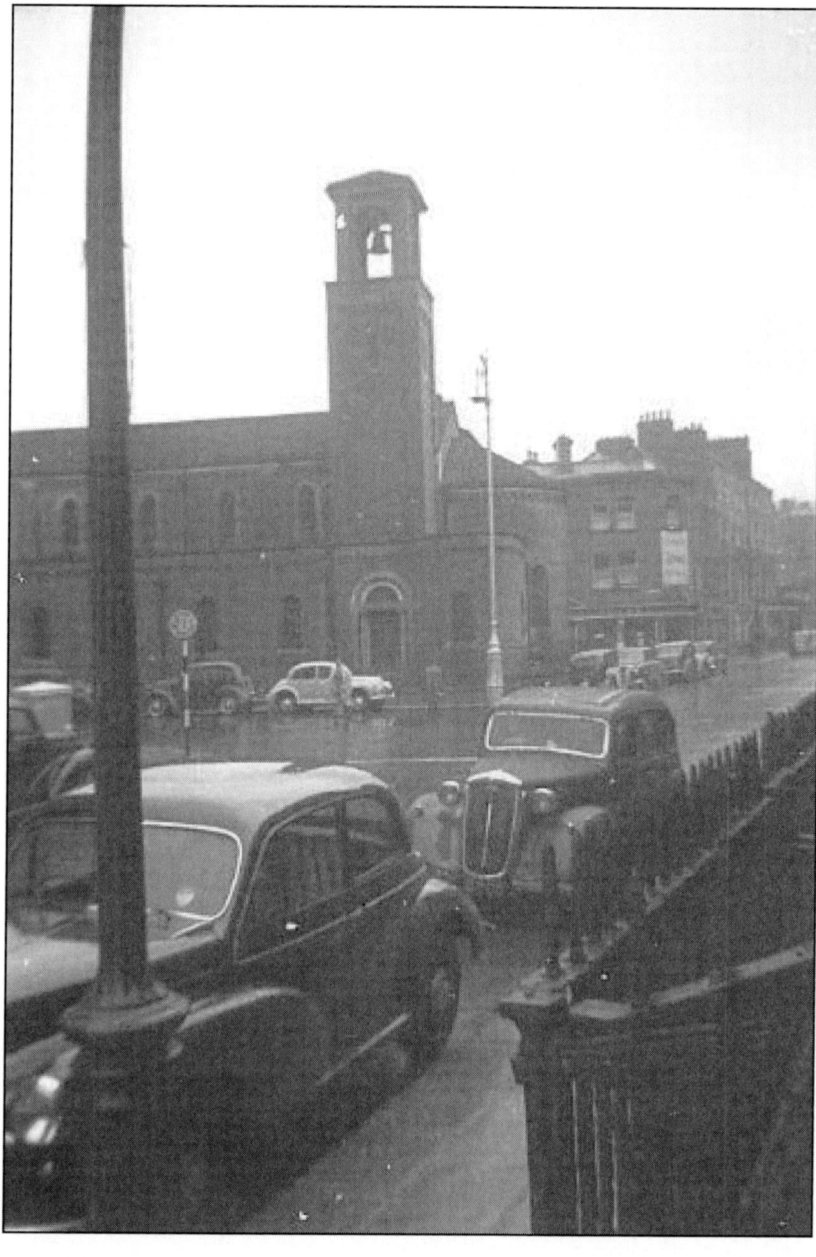

***Looking across at the old Protestant Church from the steps of the tenement house where Paddy Coffey lived in Sean McDermot Street.***

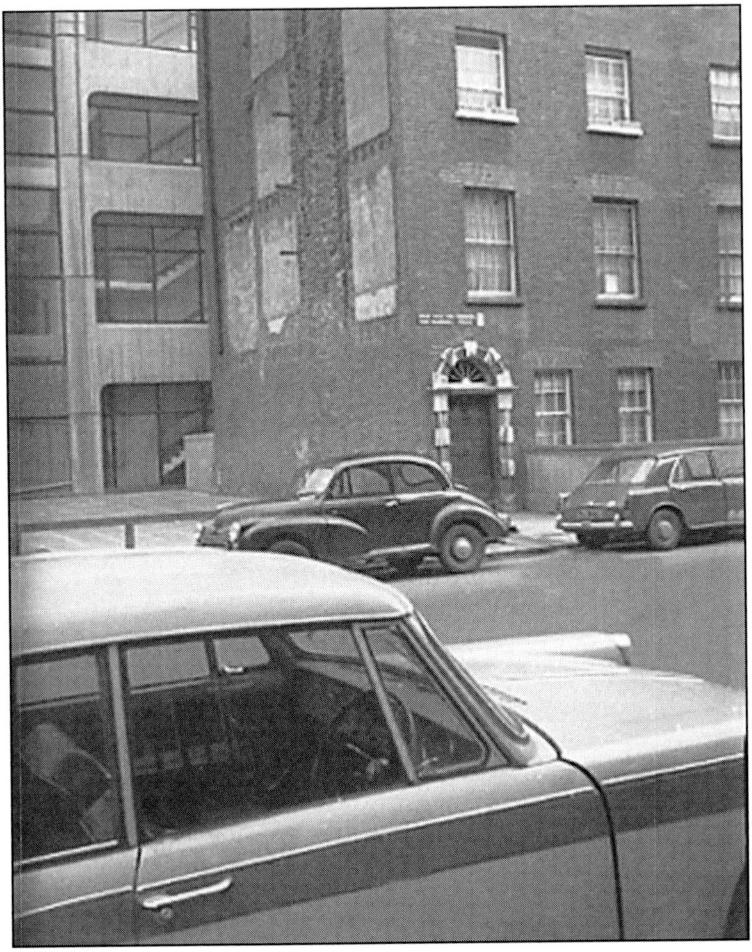

***The new Telephone Exchange and the old Tenement House.***

Looking across Sean McDermot Street at the old and the new, Paddy Coffey would fondly recall all his old neighbours and their families who lived on this street. He could tell who their parents and grandparents were, how each family was connected through marriage and relationships, who died and when. In a lot of cases many of the families in a tenement house would all be related to each other. Paddy Coffey not only photographed a lot of this area and its people, he also had a movie camera with which he recorded on cine film these now lost neighbourhoods. Much of what he filmed is unfortunately lost or missing but some of it has survived.

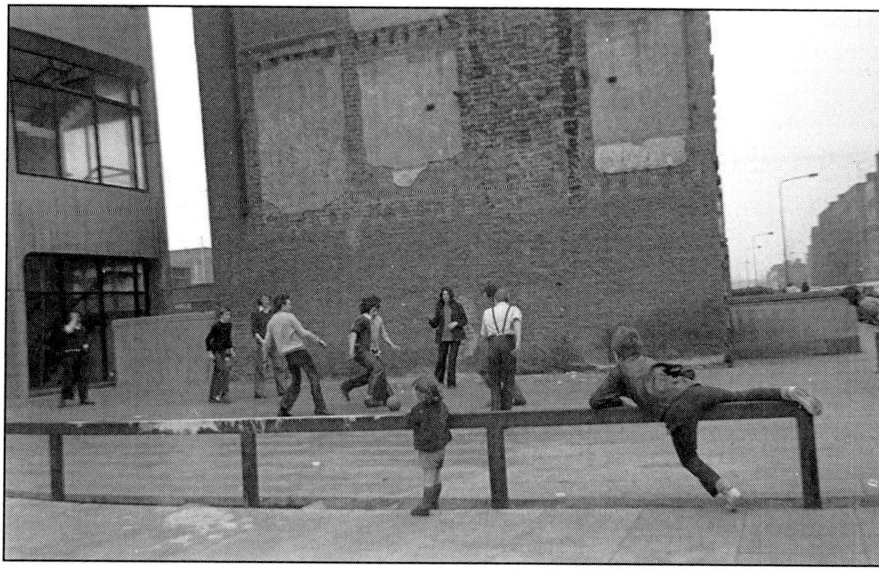

***The corner of Sean McDermot Street and Marlborough Street.***

With no green areas to play football in these young men use a sight which became a vacant area at the side of the tenement house where Paddy Coffey lived. To the left of the photograph is part of the new Telephone Exchange.

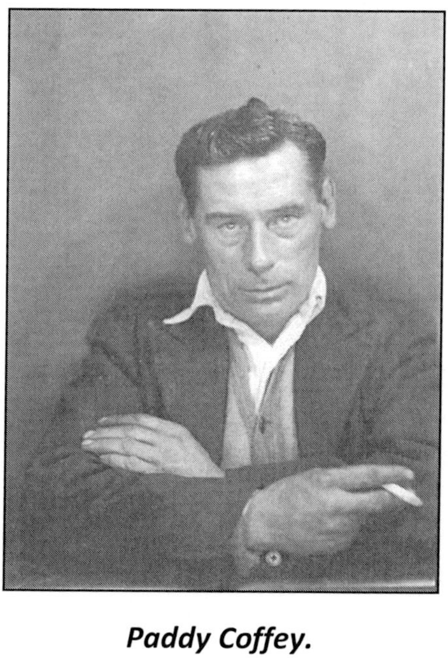

***Paddy Coffey.***

## *'The Rent Man'*

***by***

***Jimmy Burke***

***(1922 – 2014)***

*'I was born in one room in a tenement house which measured about 14 square feet. There was no gas, electricity or water in the room. All we had in the room, like many other families in the street, was a table, some chairs and two beds. My father died in 1930. He worked as a Warehouse Man in Liffey Street where tea and coffee was stored. My mother found it hard to keep the family together after my father died. The rent for our room was three shillings a week. This was paid to a Mister Albert Siev, a rent collector for the owner of the tenement building. He called to the room every Wednesday to collect the rent.*

*I remember one particular week when my poor -mother didn't have any money to give him. You see, my mother had spent the rent money food for the table; it was starve or pay the rent. I remember her pleading with him to leave it over until next week. 'Please Mister Siev; I'll pay you on the double next week'. Well he was not too pleased about it. He called back the next week to collect his double rent and my mother handed him three shillings, one weeks rent. He looked at it and said to her, "Mrs. Burke, what about last weeks rent?". "Mister Siev could you please wait until next week? I'm finding it hard to get things together." He answered her "Ah Mrs. Burke, you don't value money they way I do." My mother had to make sure she had it for him the following week.*

*He didn't carry out any repairs to the house which was in bits. He didn't give a damn about the conditions that we had to live in. They were deplorable. I remember some of the men that lived in the house had to go out and get a big length of timber to nail it up along the stairs to stop them collapsing down around us. The rooms were full of bugs that use to come out of the walls. The plasterwork was mixed with some sort of straw that the bugs were able to survive in. The rooms were freezing in the winter with the wind blowing through the broken window and coming in under the door. We had to put all our coats on the beds to keep us warm. Our coats were usually hung on a nail on the back of the door that was our wardrobe. When we got up in the morning time we had a cup of tea and a slice of bread before heading off to school'.*

***(Extract from: 'Monto, Madams, Murder and Black Coddle' by Terry Fagan)***

## *Dirty Biddy*

***by***

***Michael Foran***

*'It was a cold day in October. My family and I were not long living in Sheriff Street. We lived on the second balcony and my mother had just given birth to my new sister Mary. She had the baby at home. There were lots of nurses and a midwife around. I was totally confused at what was going on - being only five years old at the time. My mother called me over to her side to show me my new sister. I was sitting on the side of the bed having a good look, when a knock came on the door. My father quickly answered it. I could hear voices coming through the hallway. My father entered the room walking slowly with his two arms out straight. He was carrying a large plate with two big hairy pigs' feet floating in water and there was a bedraggled looking woman walking behind him. My father, winking his eye, said to my mother, "A bit of neighbourly kindness from Biddy." I could see my mother's face dropping with horror as she stared at the hairy pigs' feet.*

*Biddy stood at the door, she had a fringe slightly over her eyes and a long dress down to her ankles. She looked and smelt like something from the Celtic period. My father walked over to the sideboard to lay down the plate. Biddy walked over and grabbed me by the scruff of the neck with her thumb and index finger. I could feel them digging into me, she then frog-marched me out the door and onto the balcony. She mumbled into my ear, "Now go on down and play on the flat like a good little boy" and the hall door slammed behind me. I cursed dirty Biddy under my breath. I was glad my mother made a face when she saw the hairy pigs trotters. I had no breakfast that morning with all the commotion. It was cold all that day and I only had a light gansey on, but I daren't cross the door of our flat.*

*At about 3 o'clock that day Biddy called my two brothers and me up to her flat. She also had a gang of kids of her own. Her husband Tom was kind and decent but very much laid back. We all walked up the stairs. I was dreading going into her flat. She made us all sit around a big table. She then walked out of the kitchen with a big pot of steaming hot jacket spuds. Her husband Tom spread a newspaper on the table and she tipped the pot in the middle. The room was full of steam. Then Tom brought out a big plate of fried sausages. We all tucked in and there was very little left on the table when we were finished. My mother's words came back to me, "Hunger is great sauce"...'*

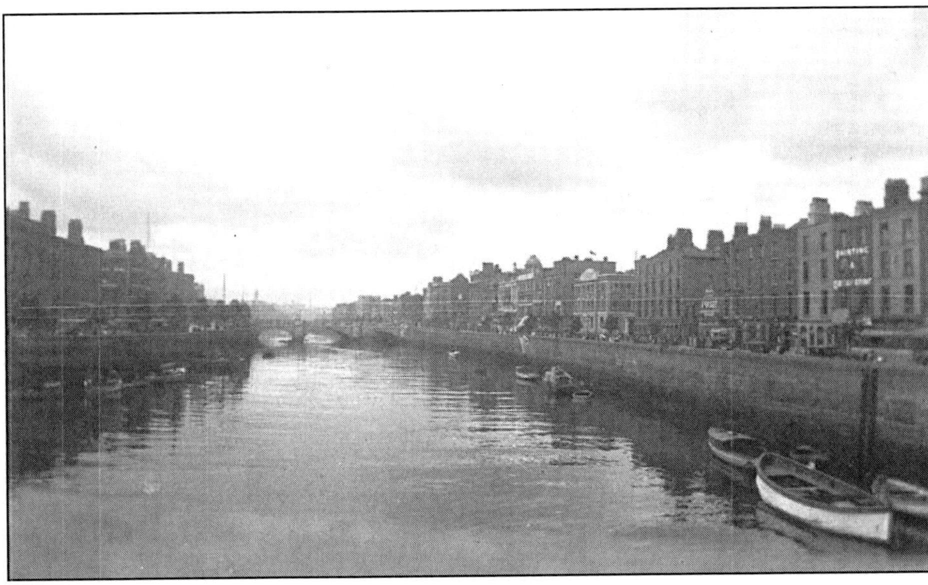

***River Liffey, Dublin.***

An unusual photograph of small craft tied up along the River Liffey. This was obviously a time when there was much more maritime traffic moving up and down the river than is seen today.

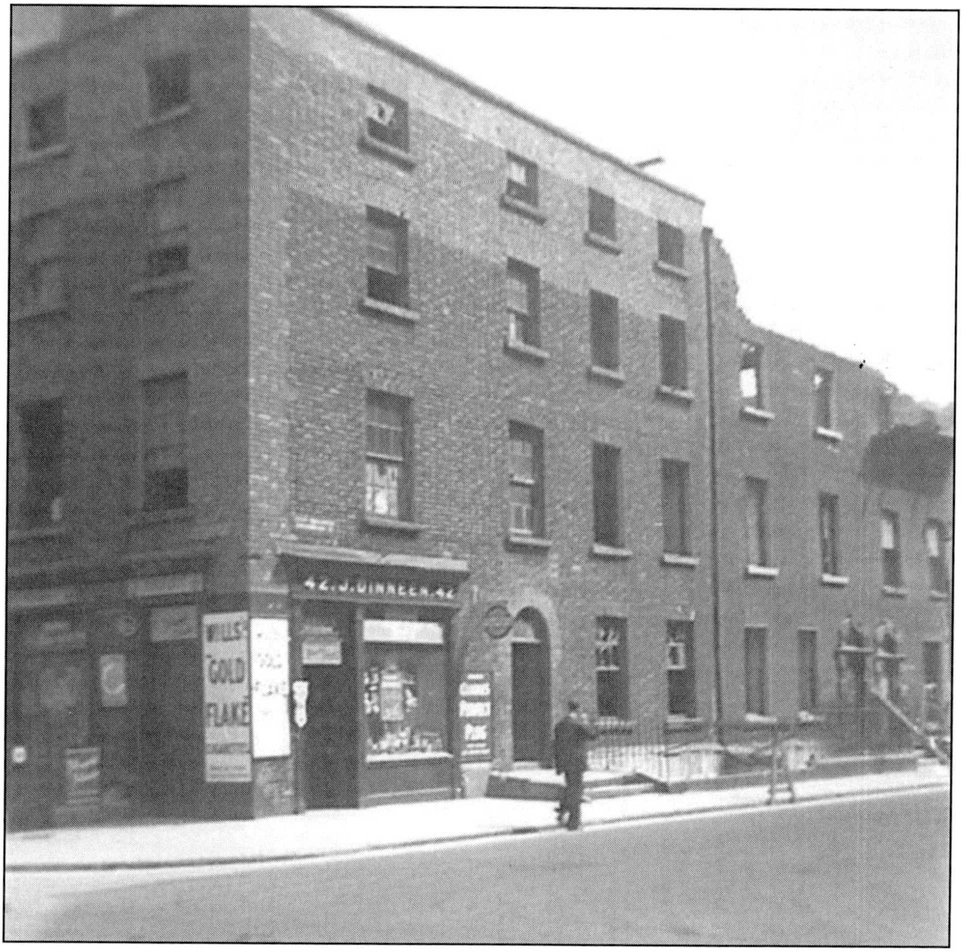


***Dineen's Corner Shop.***

## Chapter 4

## Scenes in Dublin

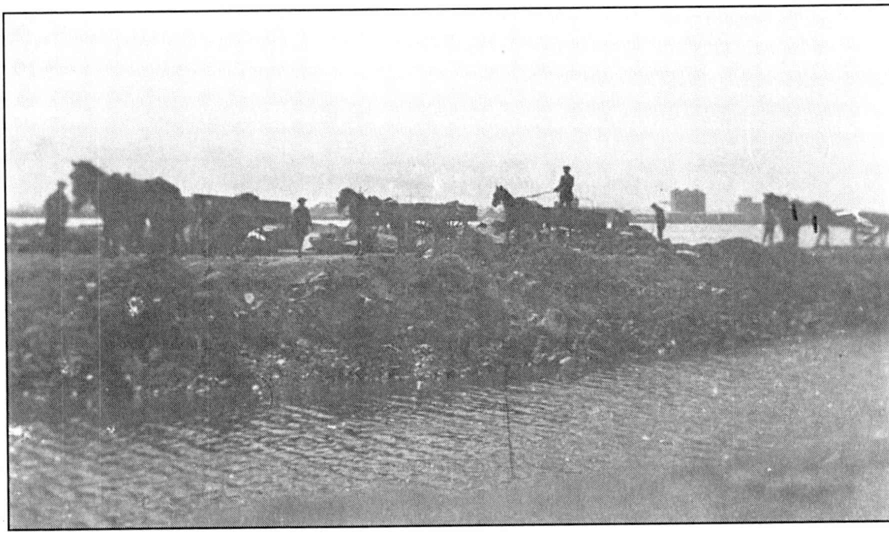

***Reclaiming land in Fairview, Dublin.***

The area known today as Fairview Park was originally a tidal mud flat, which was used for landfill in the early 1900's. Paddy Coffey tells a story of a time when he came to the rescue of a ship that ran aground here. After many unsuccessful attempts to re-float it Paddy was sent for. He checked the tides, put a sail on the ship and successfully moved it off the flats.

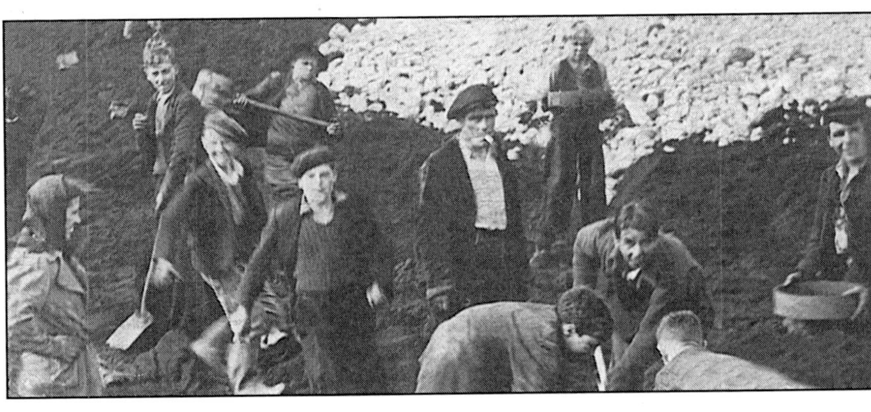

***The Slob Lands.***

The Slob Lands were situated near to present day Fairview Park and was used by the City Council as a refuse dump. Most of the household rubbish from the 'Big Houses around Dublin was dumped here. People would scour the dump for anything that could be recycled or sold on. Young boys would dig through the rubbish for Cinders, small pieces of partially burned coal that was often thrown out with the ashes from a household fire. The boys would collect as much Cinder as possible and bag it. They would then go around the tenement houses and try to sell it for a few pence a bag. People would burn it on their fire along with pieces of coal.

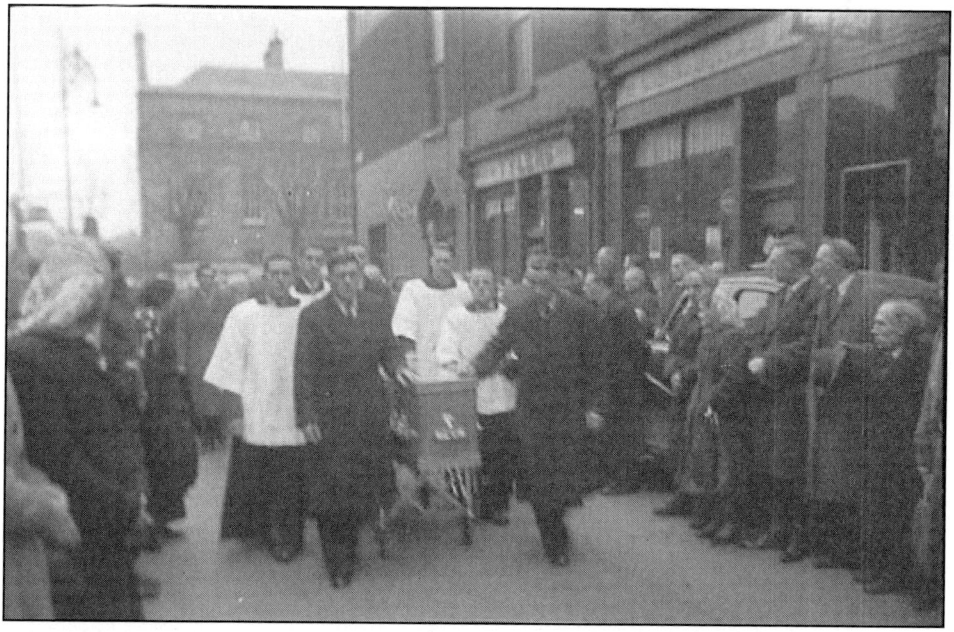

***Funeral cortege of a member of the Roman Catholic clergy being led to the underground vaults in the Pro Cathedral, Dublin.***

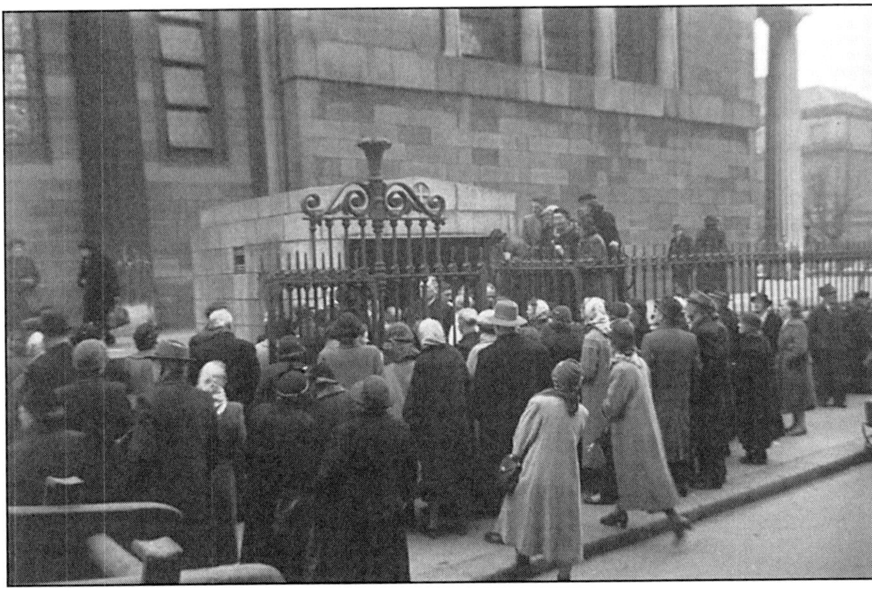

***Dublin people always love a funeral and especially if it's someone of importance. Paddy Coffey was on hand to snap the reaction and faces of the general public at this particular funeral.***

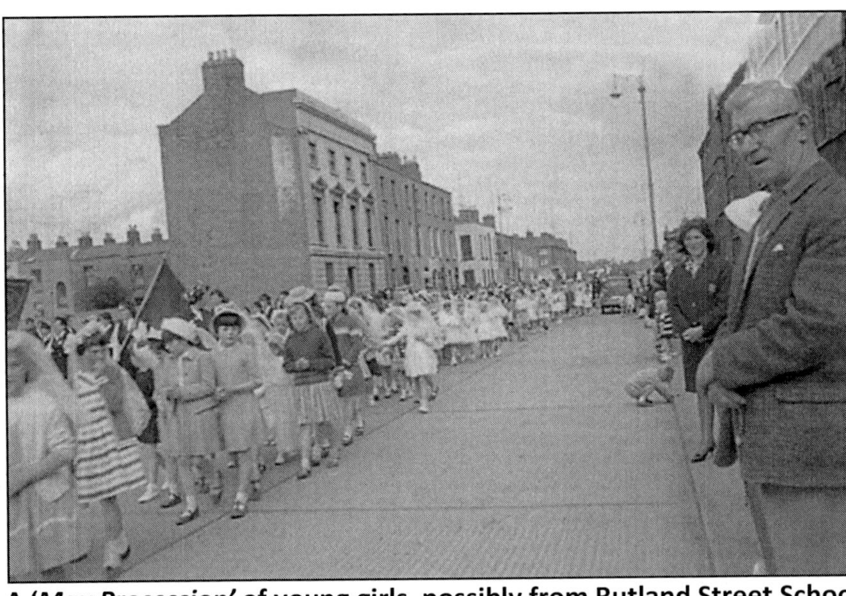

**A *'May Procession'* of young girls, possibly from Rutland Street School walking towards Our Lady of Lourdes Church in Sean McDermott Street.**

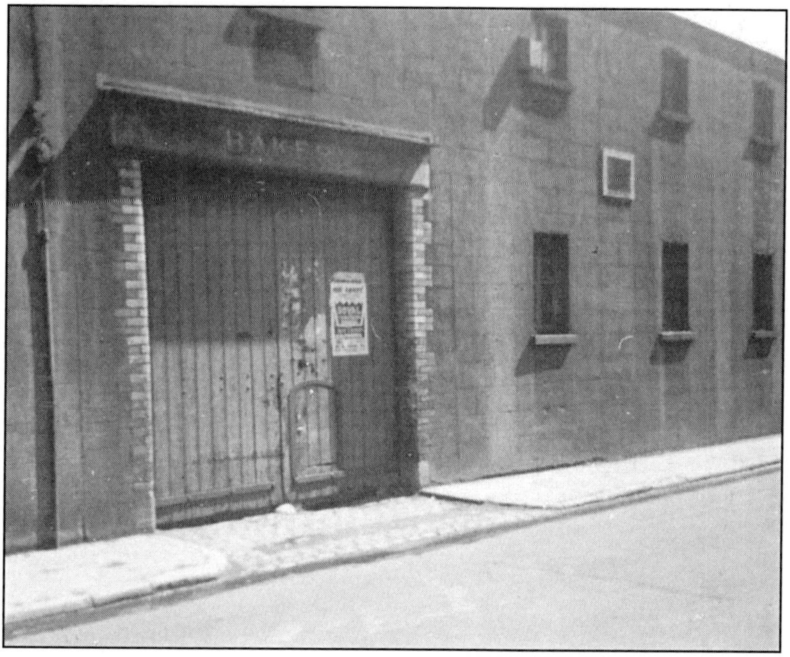

***Monk's Bakery in Church Street, Dublin.***

This is a rare photograph of the gateway into Monk's Bakery in Church Street, Dublin. One morning in September 1922 a party of volunteers from the Irish Republican Army were ordered to ambush a British Army truck that was due to arrive at Monk's bakery in Church Street to collect some bread. Their mission was to capture any weapons that the British soldiers had with them. One of the members of this group was an eighteen-year-old medical student named Kevin Barry who was studying at Belvedere College. One British Soldier was shot dead and two others later died of their wounds. During the shootout Barry's gun jammed twice so he climbed under the truck for cover.

It is said that a woman standing nearby saw Barry under the truck and let out a scream because she mistakenly thought that the truck was going to drive over him. As a result he was arrested and later held in Mountjoy Gaol. At his trial Kevin Barry refused to recognise the military court that was set up to try him for his role in the deaths of the three British soldiers. He was sentenced to death by hanging and his execution took place within the prison walls on the 1st November 1920.

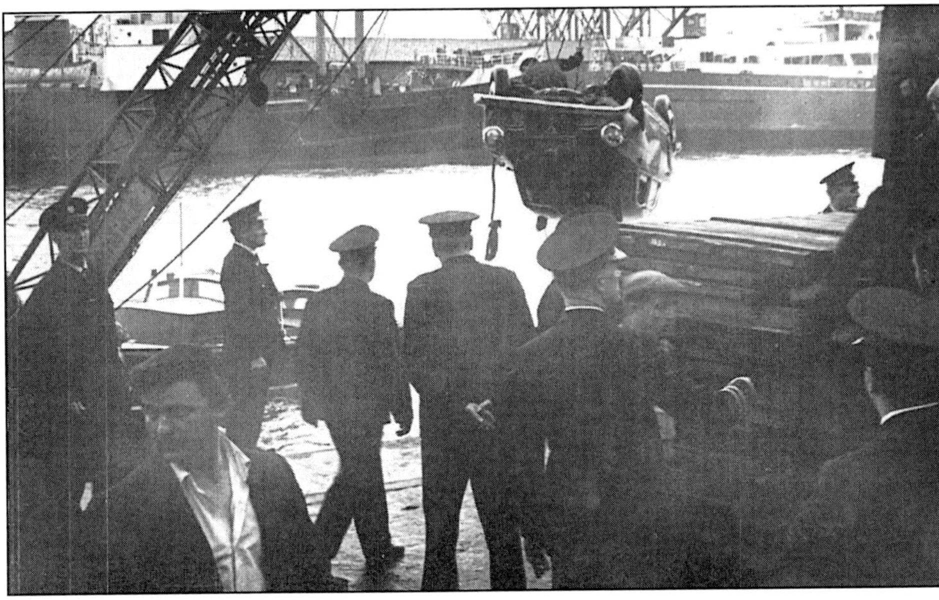

***River Liffey rescue.***

In 1951 a taxi carrying two young girls from England accidently drove into the waters of the River Liffey. The girls were on holiday in Dublin and had visited a dance hall on the south side of the city. It was a damp and foggy evening with poor visibility. The two girls hailed a taxi to take them back to their lodgings in Clontarf, on the north side of the city. The taxi driver drove down a side street from Townsend Street onto the quayside and in such poor weather conditions failed to realise how close he was to the quayside. Two young men crossing nearby Butt Bridge heard the splash and quickly came to the rescue. The taxi driver, a non- swimmer was rescued alive but it was too late to save the two young girls. The taxi driver was originally from the north Dublin suburb of Cabra West.

Young boys would often dive off Butt Bridge into the Liffey water below and especially to cool off on a hot summer day. The currents were quite strong here and sometimes the boys would have to grab onto a rope hanging from a nearby ship to stop themselves from being dragged down the river.

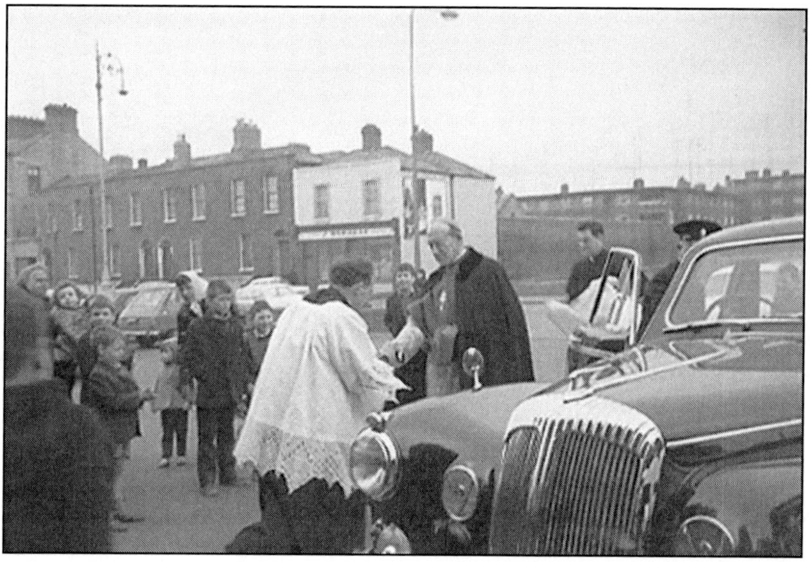

***John Charles McQuaid.***

John Charles McQuaid C.S.Sp was the Catholic Archbishop of Dublin and Primate of Ireland between December 1940 and January 1972. Here he is seen arriving at Our Lady of Lourdes Church, Sean McDermot Street with his driver Robert, and the priest on the right is Brendan Houlihan. Jack Whelan is welcoming the Bishop. This photograph was taken in 1962

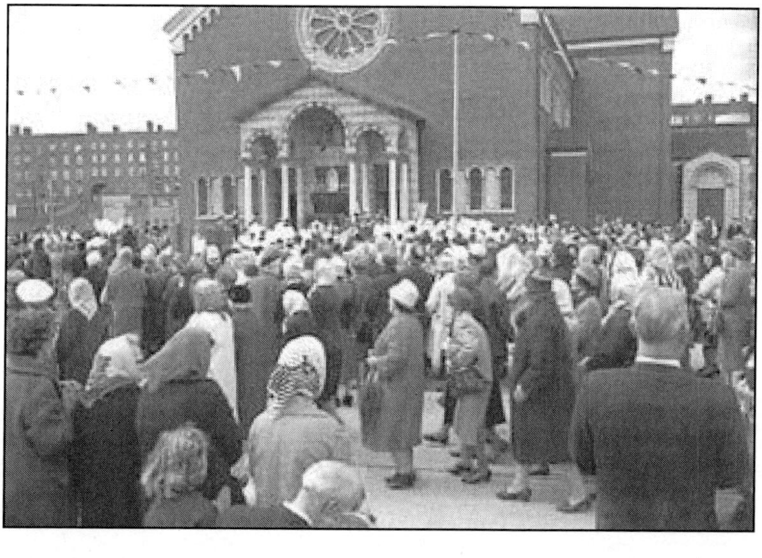

***Our Lady of Lourdes Church in Sean McDermot Street, Dublin.***

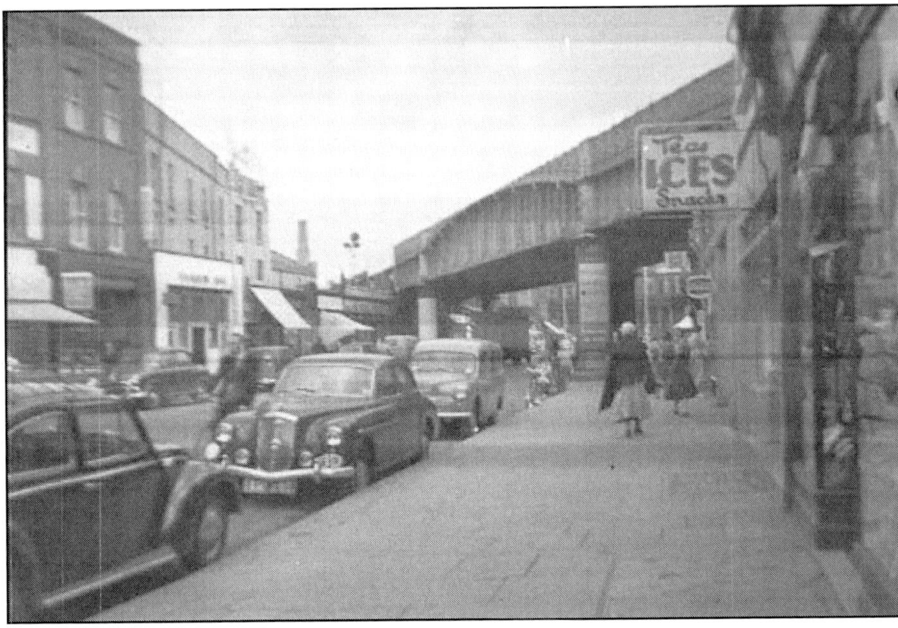


***A woman wearing a black shawl walking along Talbot Street.***

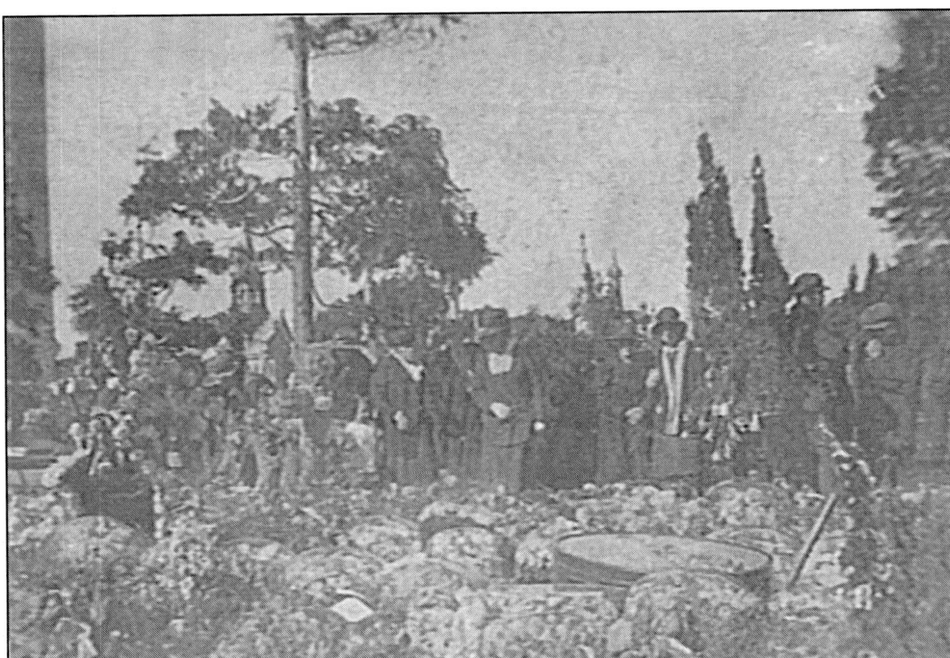

***A photograph of Michael Collin's Grave 1922.***

Michael Collins was an Irish revolutionary leader who played a major role in the fight for Irish freedom. Collins was killed in a shootout during an ambush by opposing forces in the Irish Civil War in 1922. In 1921 Michael Collins ordered members of his 'Flying Squad' to execute a known British informer from the Monto by the name of John Ryan. The shooting was ordered to take place in Phil Shanahan's pub located on the corner of Corporation Street and Foley Street.

Paddy Coffey's young brother Bernard remembered sitting outside the pub on the day the shooting occurred. He was there to run messages for the men inside. Bernard said that he remembered two or perhaps three men dressed in long coats and wearing their hats pulled down over their eyes walking quickly into the pub. He said that some of the men that had been drinking inside the pub rushed out the door and ran off. It was then he heard loud voices followed by gunfire. The gunmen then left the pub and walked rapidly away. Bernard looked in through the door of the pub and saw a man lying on the floor in a pool of blood.

John Ryan was a brother to one of the Madams who operated a brothel in the Monto. There were many 'Safe Houses' in this area for Collins and his men. Some of the local newspaper boys were used as sources of intelligence by watching and reporting on the movement of British Troops and the Auxiliaries who patrolled throughout Dublin at this time.

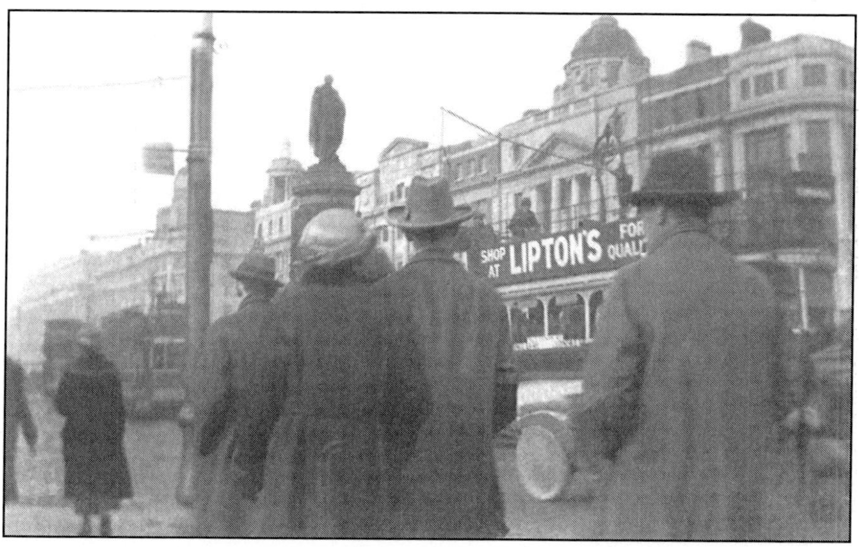


***An early Paddy Coffey photograph of O'Connell Street, Dublin.***

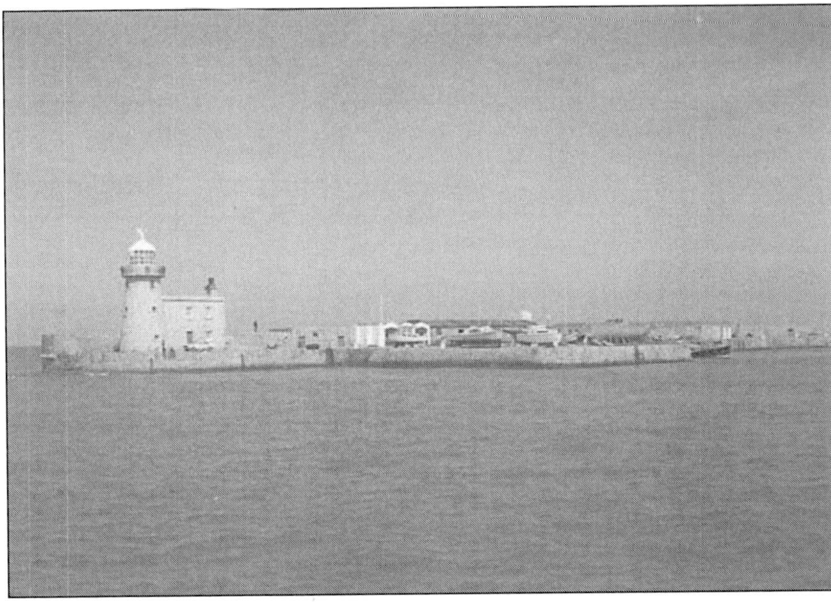

*Howth, County Dublin.*

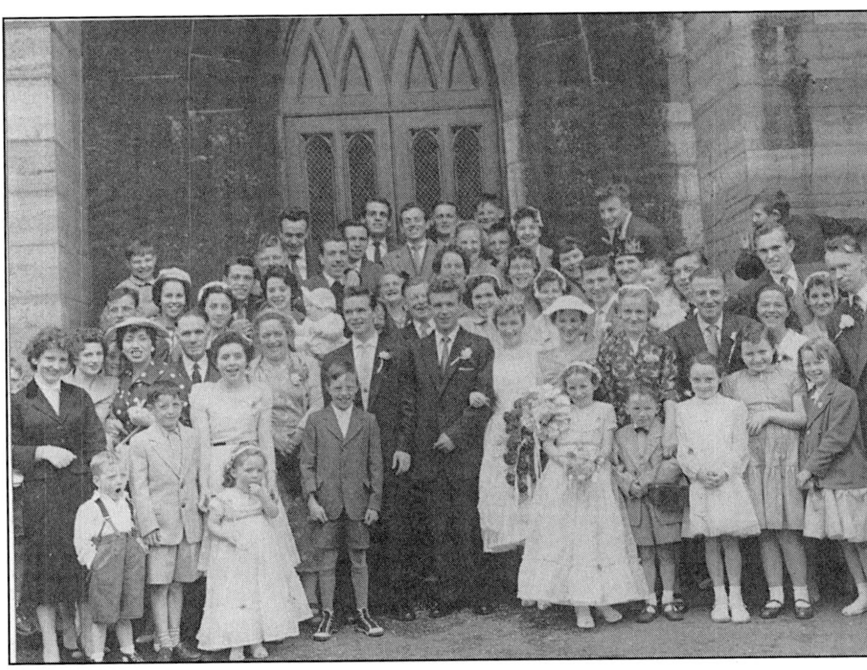

*1958 wedding of Billy Dillon and Chrissie Kane, Seville Place.*

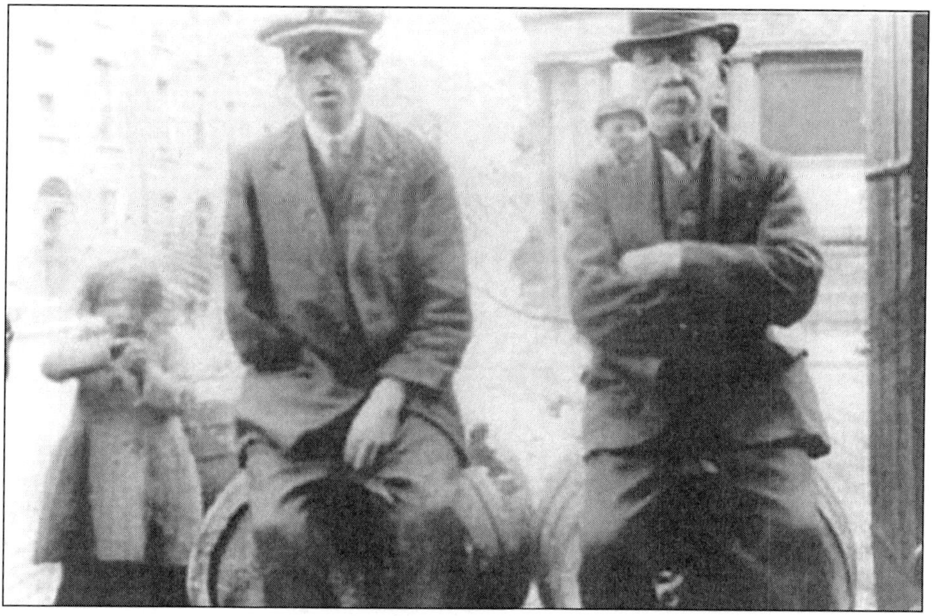

**John and Robert Laird.**

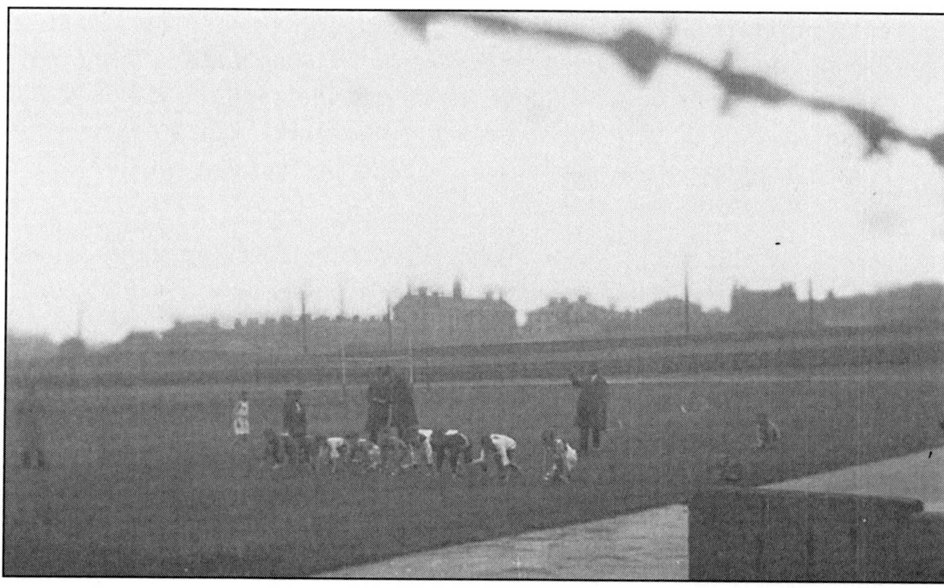

***Location Unknown.***

Many of Paddy Coffey's young school pals were sent away to Industrial Schools for committing the smallest of offences such as missing time from school or stealing an apple. The Industrial Schools were well known to be places of extreme hardship were all types of punishment was meted out to young boys for the least offence. The most feared of all in Paddy Coffey's young days was that of Artane Industrial School, the closest one to Dublin City. Some boys were sent to schools far away from home and would not see any family or friends for as long as they were committed there.

*'My mother was in an Orphanage down in Tipperary. She was working for Maher's and Ryan, a pub in Bansha. She'd go to the dances across the road and the Priest would come in and chase them with his walking stick. The difference from now and then. She said she always had long hair and she was looking over the banisters in the Orphanage and some girl caught her hair and then let it go. My mother lost her balance and went over and went down onto the marble floor and damaged her eye. It was never looked after properly and then when she came home here, the time of the Black and Tans, she had to go up to the Eye and Ear Hospital and she'd be trying to dodge them.*

*Her eye was never looked after properly. She still had her eye but she could never see anything, but still she could see you a mile away. We'd hear her calling and we'd say "See if that's me mother calling". They'd look around the corner and we knew once we got in we wouldn't get out. Once we went in for our tea we wouldn't get out. She'd say, "I saw you looking around the corner", or you'd be coming down along and you'd say "Here's me mother, come on we'll dodge here", and she'd tell you it was you. But when you'd be up near her she couldn't see so well, it was only when you were in the distance, whatever kind of sight she had. I'm not sure why she was in Tipperary.*

*The first husband, my grandfather, must have died. That time, say now, say your father dies and your mother's there on her own, now if you missed a day out of school, you were gone, your father wasn't there, see. Say if you robbed an apple outside the shop and you were caught, well you were gone. If a neighbour complained that you weren't getting looked after properly, you were taken away and put into a "Home". The parents sometimes weren't even told where they were. You had to watch yourself all the time. She told me one time that she had a brother but she never knew whatever happened to him, she said she never knew where he went. She'd never kind of tell you anything'...* ***Aggie Coffey.***

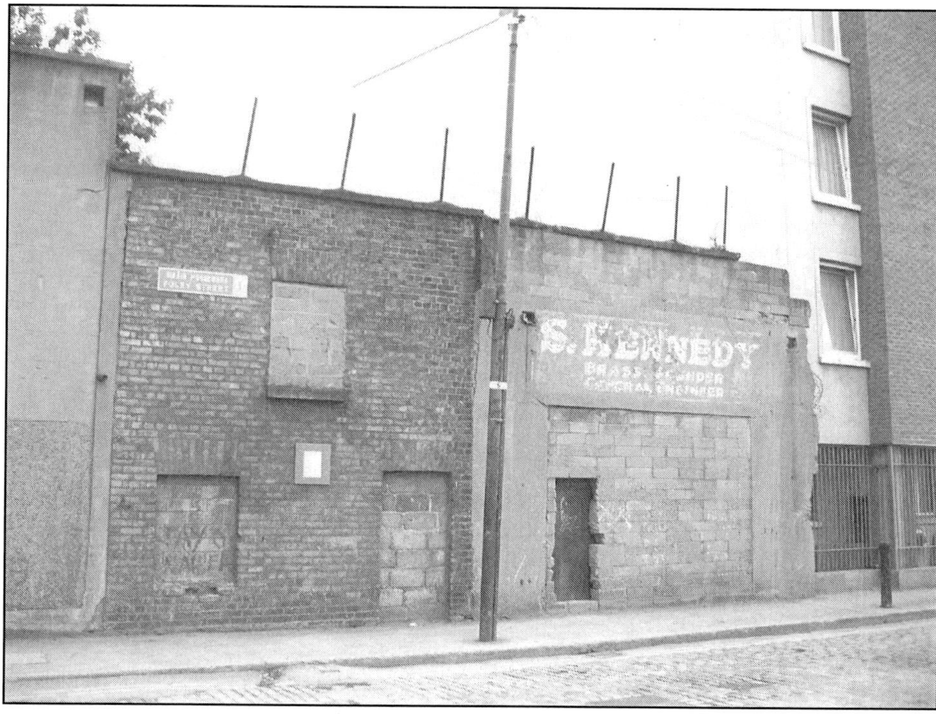


***Foley Street, Dublin.***

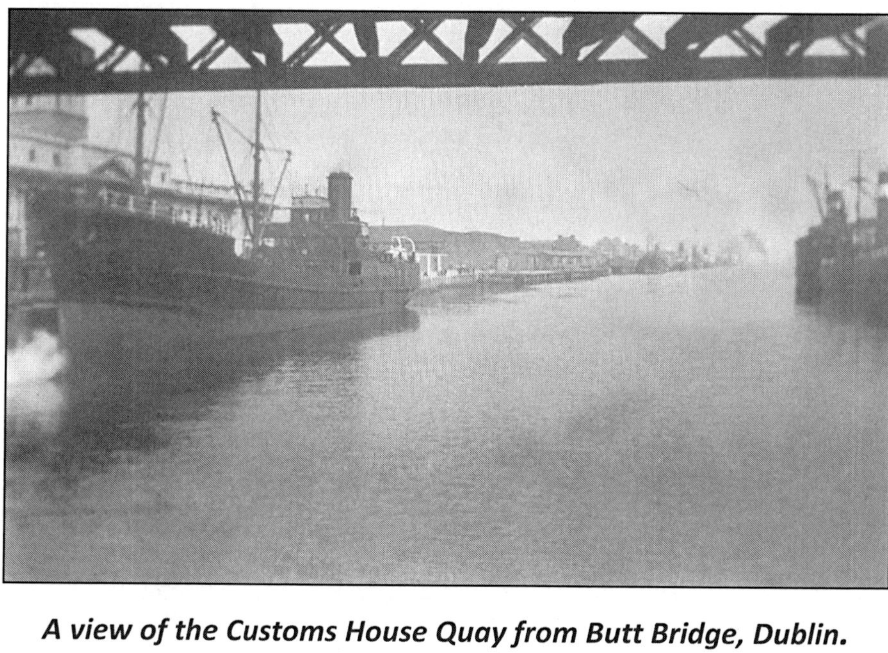

***A view of the Customs House Quay from Butt Bridge, Dublin.***

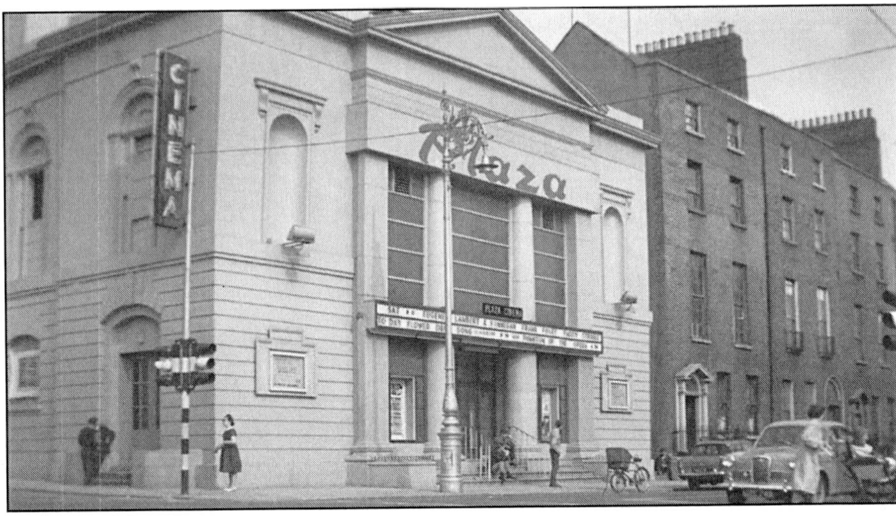


***The old Plaza Picture House.***

The Plaza Cinema was situated on the corner of Parnell Square North and Dorset Street. It was later named the Plaza Cinerama. Before becoming a Picture House this building was a church. It finally closed its doors as a cinema in 1981 and reopened as the National Wax Works Museum.

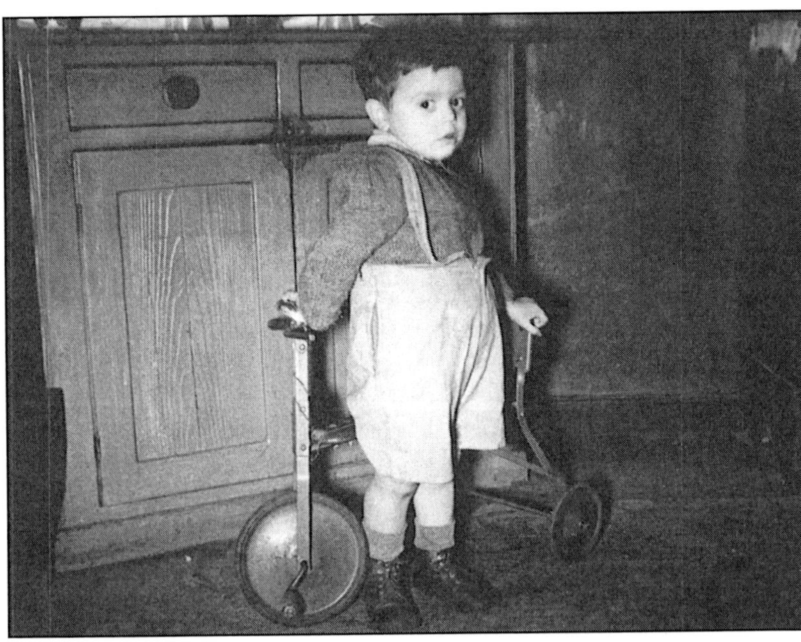

***Denis Doyle***

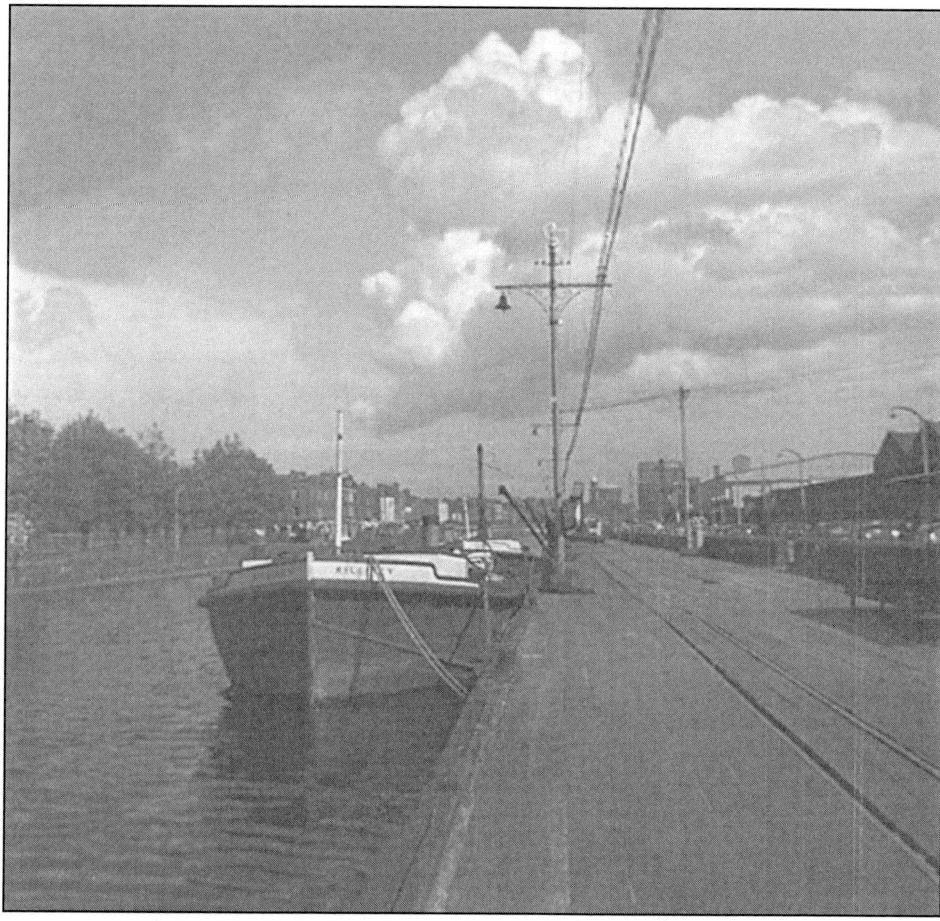

***Guinness barge 'The Killiney' built in 1927.***

In 1873 the Guinness Brewery built its own jetty on the River Liffey. They were then able to load barrels of their famous drink directly onto barges such as the Killiney and transport them to ships tied up along City Quay. Each barge had its own funnel that was hinged to allow the stack to fold down when the barge had to travel under a low bridge. The last barge to sail down the Liffey did so in 1961.

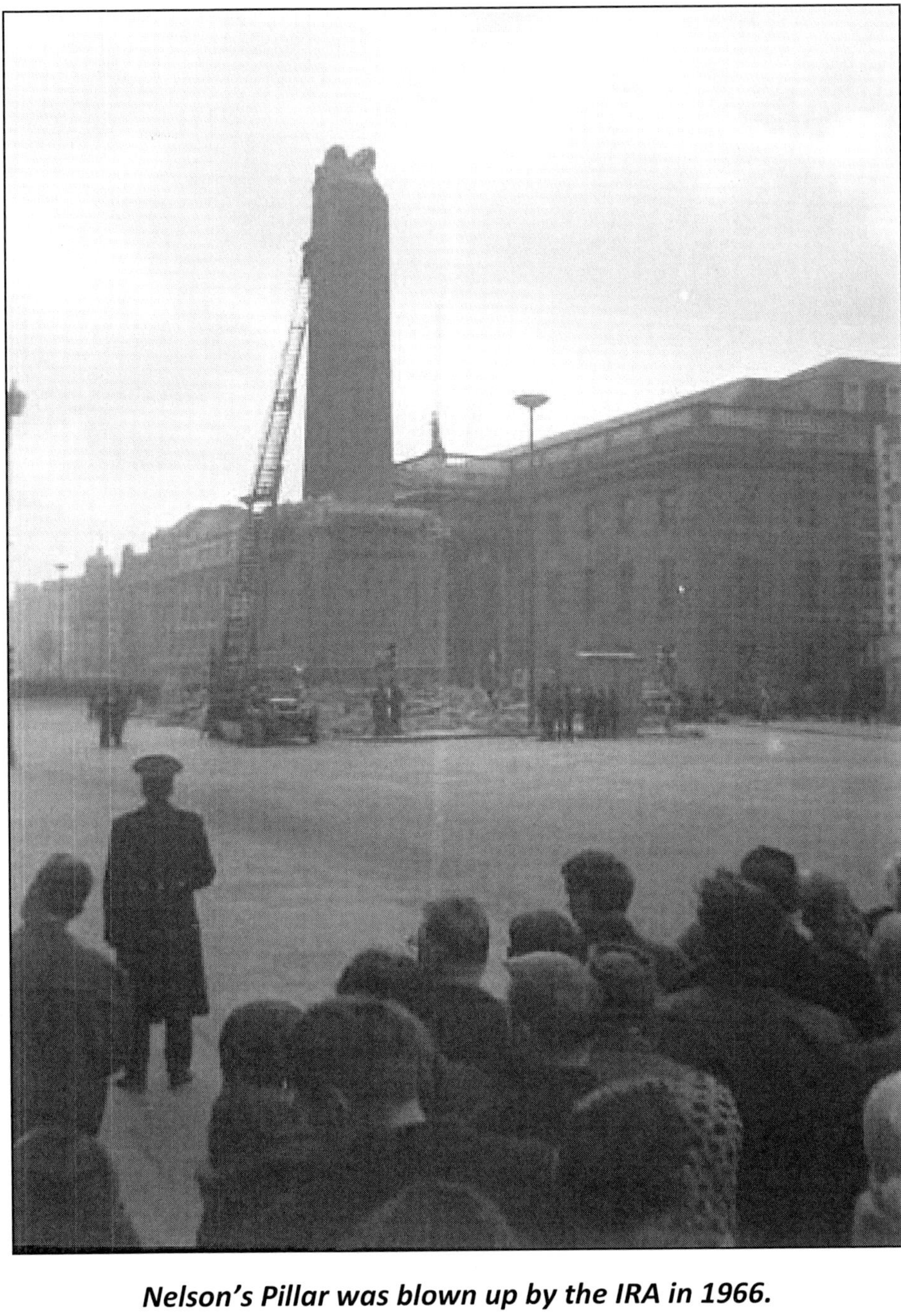

***Nelson's Pillar was blown up by the IRA in 1966.***

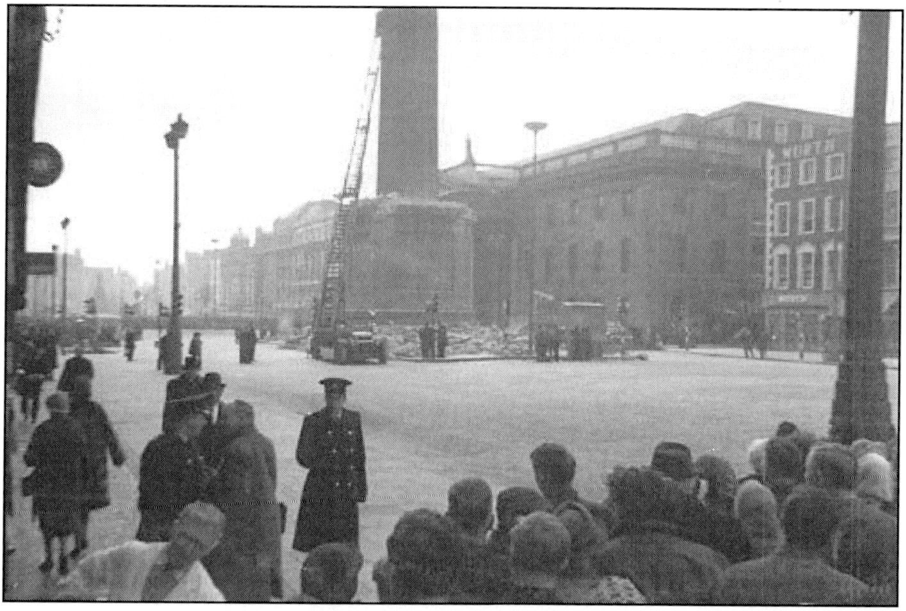

***Nelson's Pillar 1966***

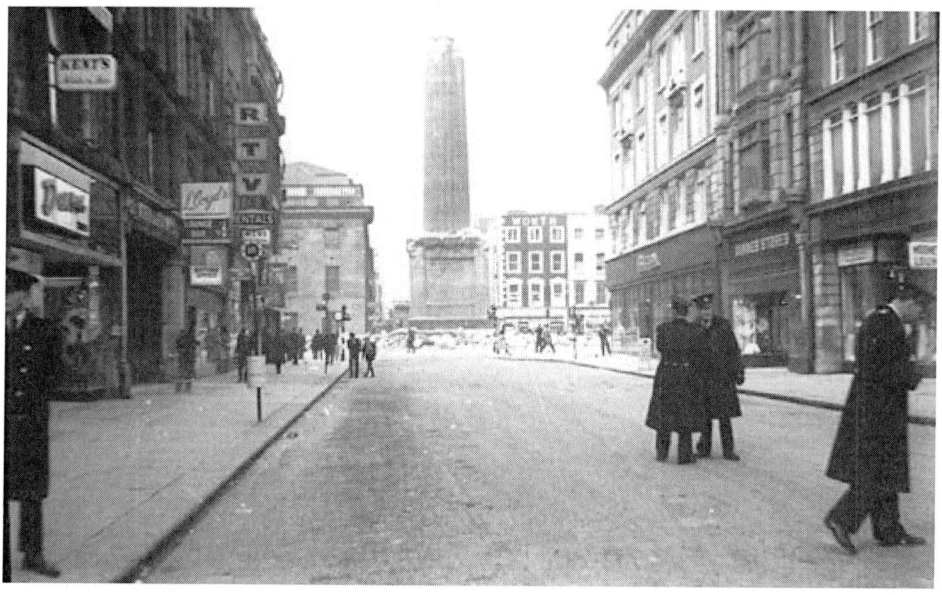

***A view of the destruction to Nelson's Pillar, taken from North Earl Street in 1966.***

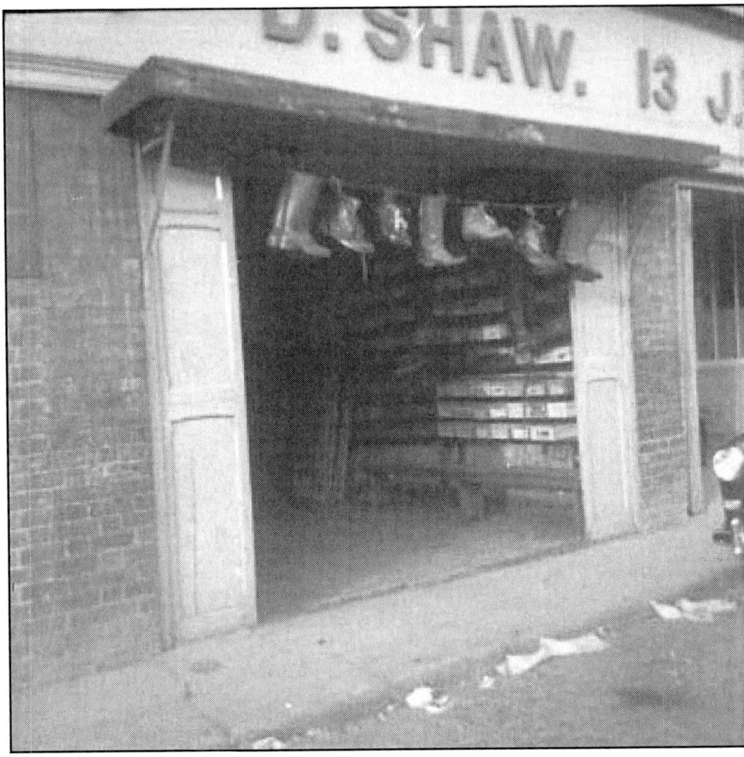


*Boots and Shoes for Sale.*

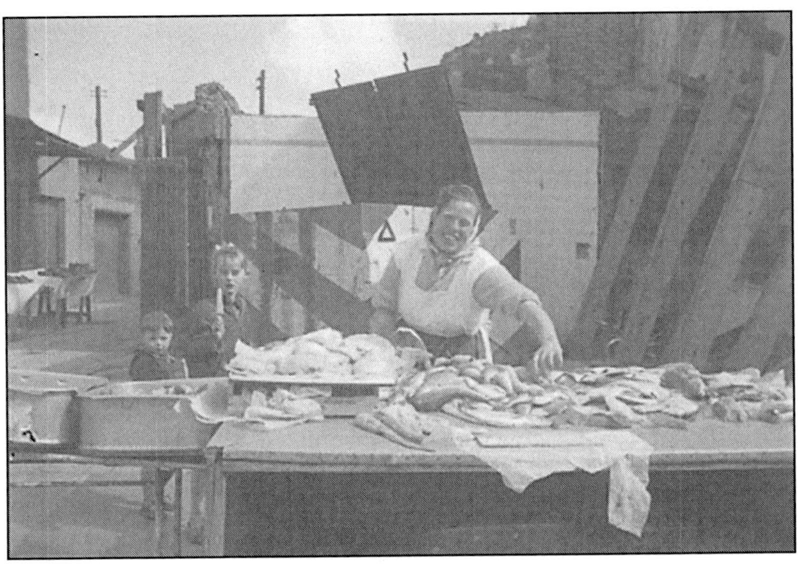

*A Dublin Fish Woman.*

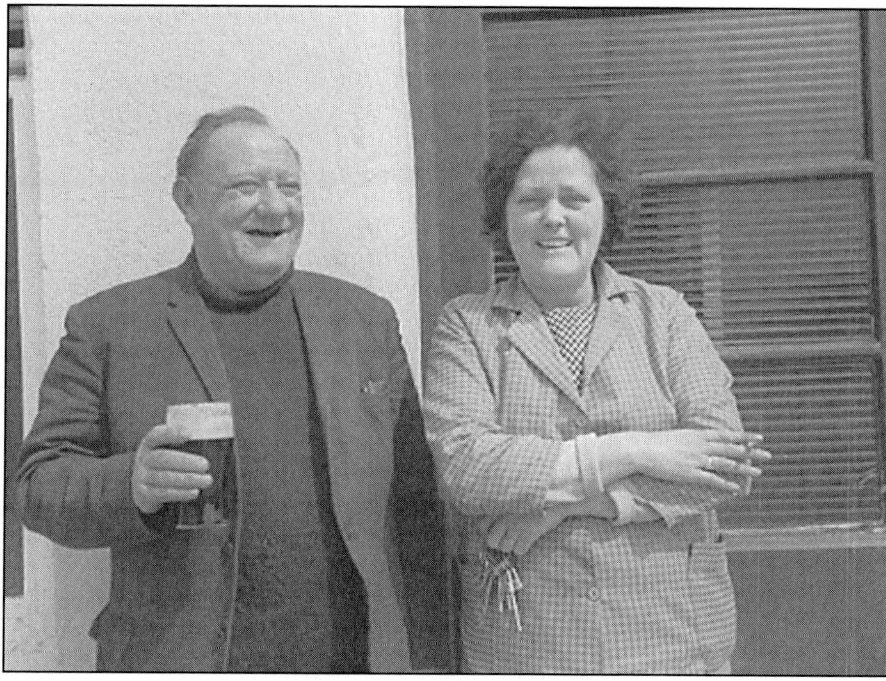

***Dinny and Mrs Kelly.***

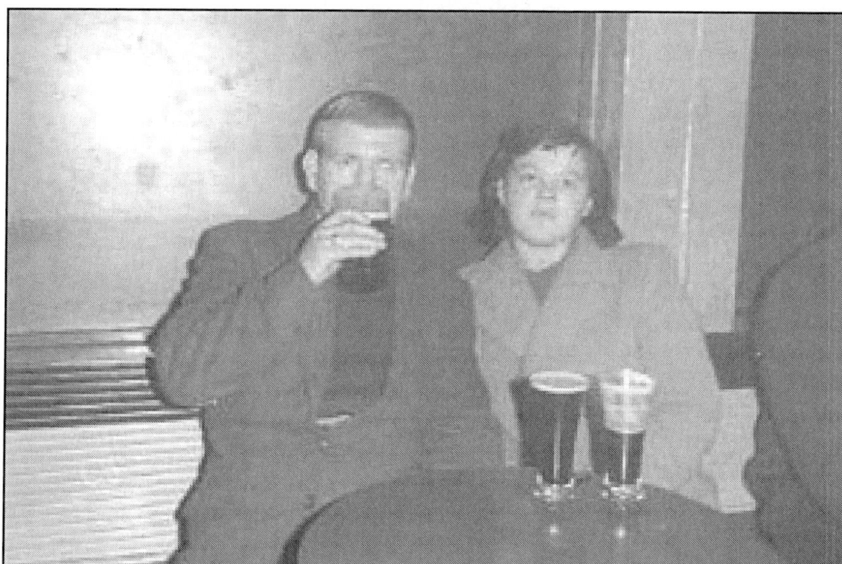

***Couple having a quiet drink together.***

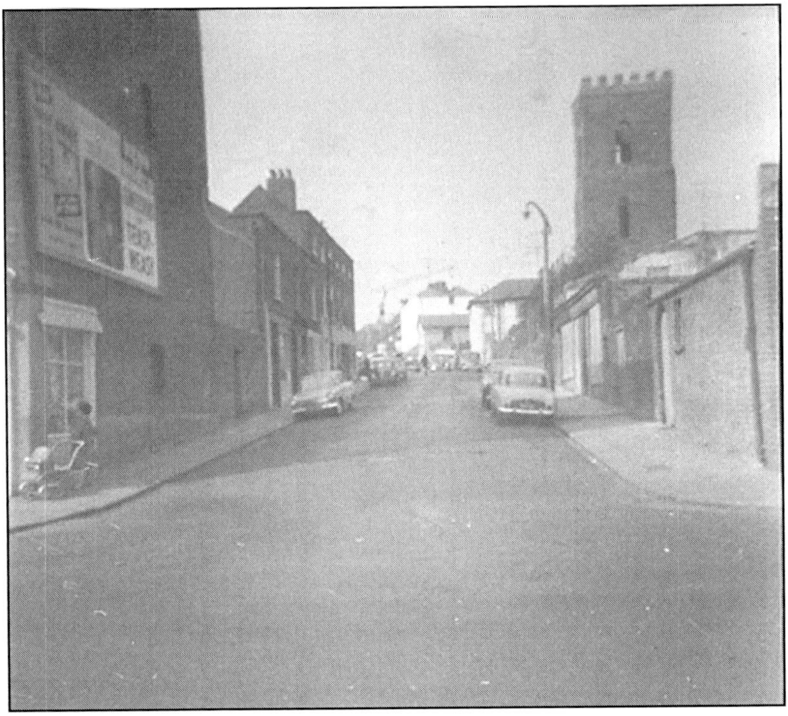

***Hill Street, Dublin.***

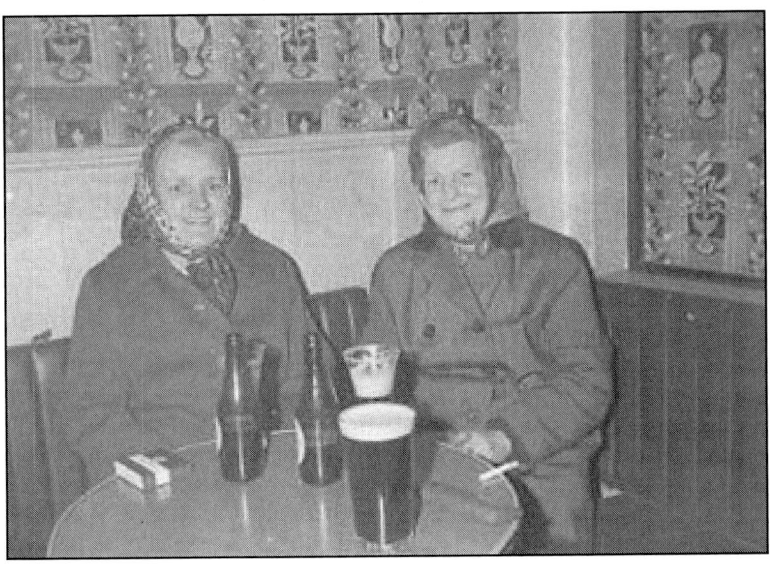

***Rooie Kane and Bella Keating in Mulvihill's Pub.***

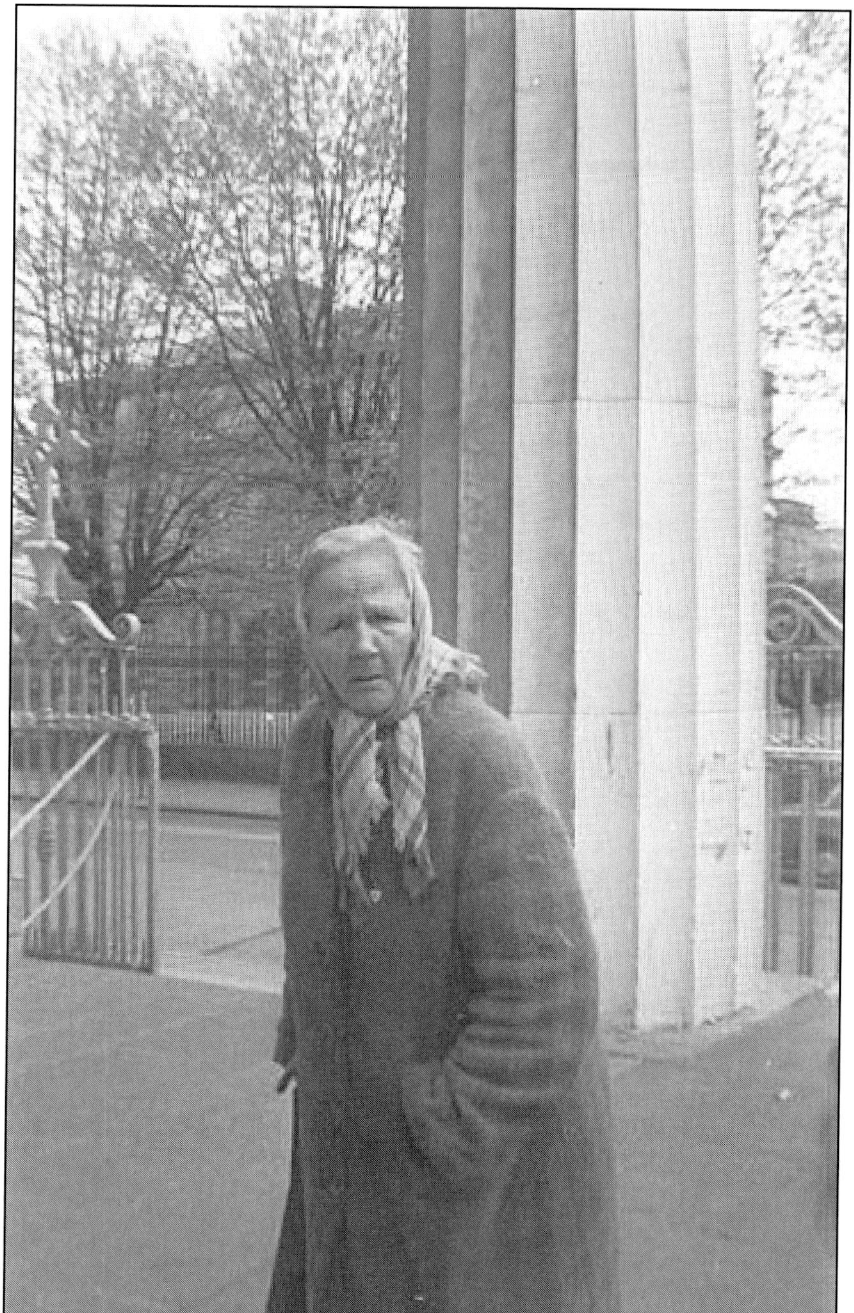

***Going to Mass in the Pro Cathedral while wearing her Pioneer Pin.***

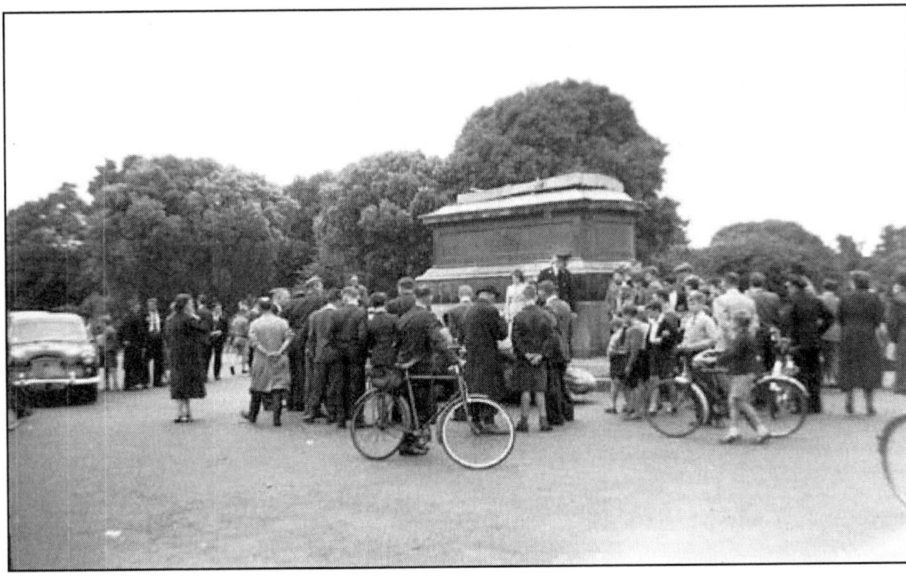

***The Lord Gough statue blown off its pedestal in the Phoenix Park on the 3rd July 1957.***

In 1880 Dublin Corporation were undecided as to where to place a statue of Field-Marshall Lord Gough and his horse. Several sites, including O'Connell Bridge were recommended. Eventually it was agreed to place it in the Phoenix Park. On Christmas Eve 1944 the rider was beheaded and his sword removed and 1956 the right hind leg of the horse was blown off. In 1957 the whole statue was blasted from its base by a huge explosion set off by Irish Republicans. For the next twenty-nine years the original base remained in place.

What was left of the statue was kept in storage by Dublin Corporation because they didn't know what else to do with it. In 1986 the statue was taken out of storage and sold to Robert Guinness, a member of the famous brewing family. It was then passed on to a distant relative of Lord Gough who had it restored and re-erected in the grounds of Chillingham Castle, Northumberland, England.

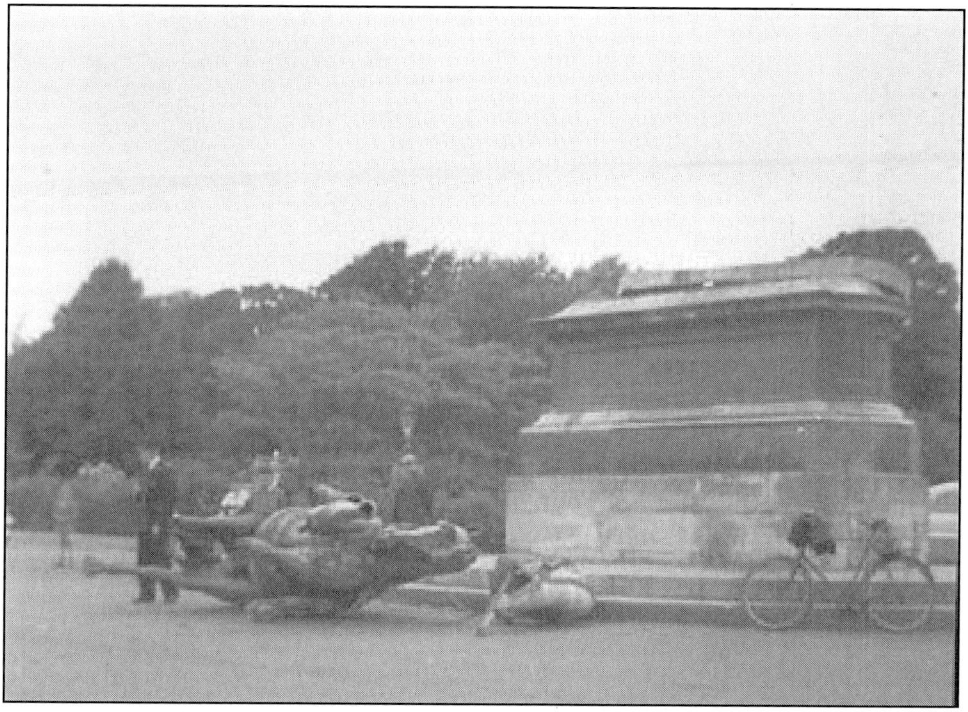

***Lord Gough's horse in the Phoenix Park 1957.***

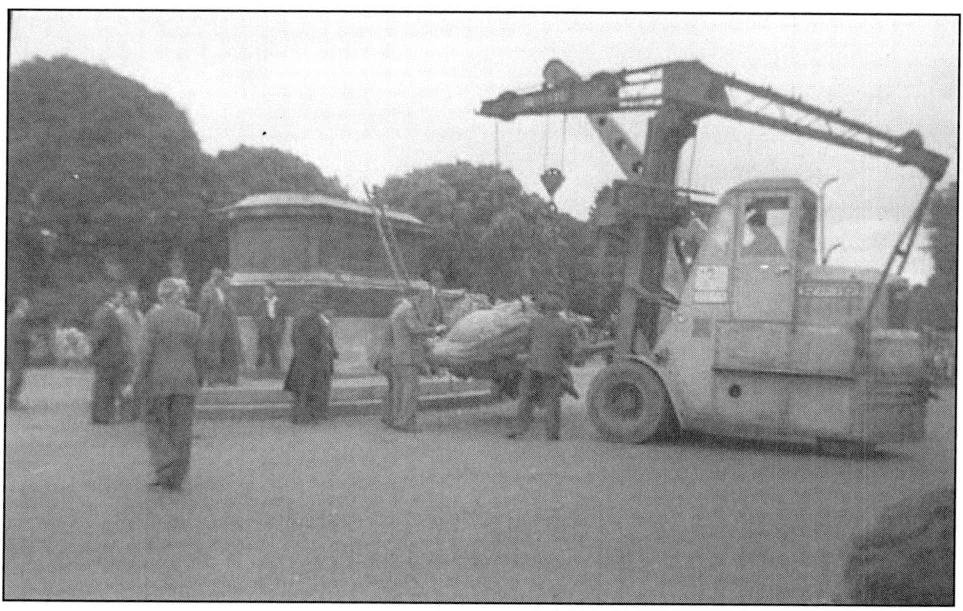

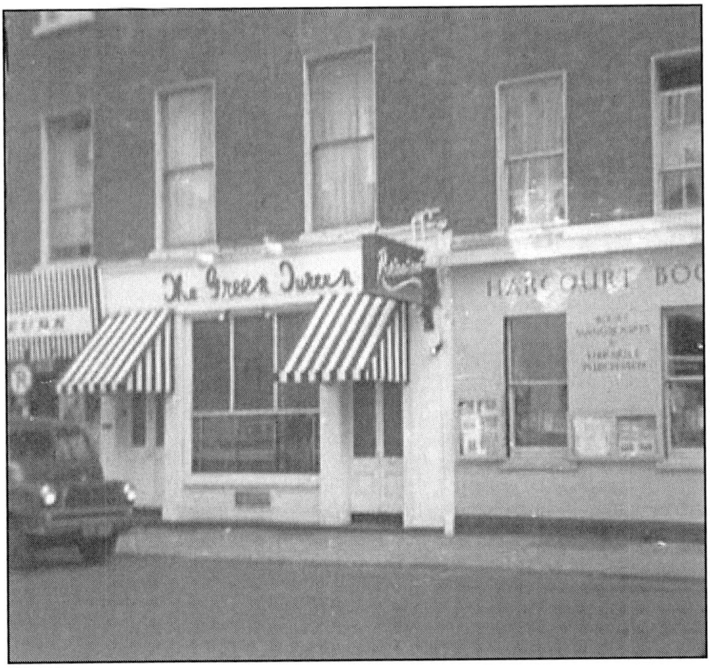


***The Green Tureen.***

In 1964 Shan Mohangi was a twenty two year old medical student who, in a jealous rage strangled to death a sixteen year old girl. He had subjected the young girl to a horrific ordeal before finally ending her life. He then dismembered her body and tried to destroy the remains through incineration in the oven of the Green Tureen restaurant kitchen where he had worked. Mohangi was caught boiling up her remains when a woman complained about the awful smell of smoke coming into the overhead flat where she lived.

Mohangi had originally been sentenced to death for murder but his conviction was reduced to manslaughter and his sentence reduced to seven years on appeal. After serving only four years of his original sentence he was release and deported to his home country of South Africa where he eventually entered politics.

In 2009 he had been living the life of a politician when his past crime was revealed to a newspaper journalist. For 15 years he had served as a politician and all that time managed to conceal his past from fellow members of his party and the government.

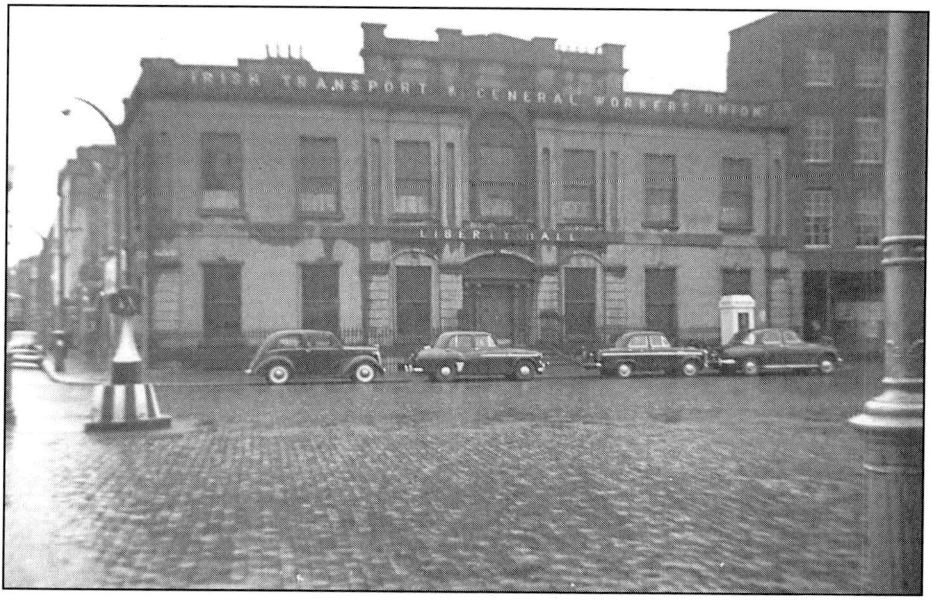


***Liberty Hall.***

In 1916 Liberty Hall, once a hotel was the headquarters of the Irish Citizen Army. It was outside this building in 1916 that the leaders of the rebellion assembled before marching to the General Post Office in O'Connell Street. When the rebel forces engaged with British Troops from the GPO, British gunboats sailed up the River Liffey and chose Liberty Hall as its first target to shell believing that it was sheltering more rebels. In the run-up to the rebellion it had been used as a munitions factory by the Irish leaders. However for the week of the uprising it was unused by the rebels. The gunboats however, completely levelled the building. In the years following the rebellion the building was restored.

In the late 1950's the building was declared unsafe and was once again demolished. It was replaced by a sixteen storey building and was viewed by many Dubliners to be as tall as any skyscraper found in New York City in America. It took almost five years to build the new structure whose foundations are built on solid rock. Liberty Hall later became the headquarters of SIPTU, a workers union. In 2006 they sought and were granted permission to demolish the 1960's building and to erect a new headquarters on the same site. In 2012 however, planning permission was

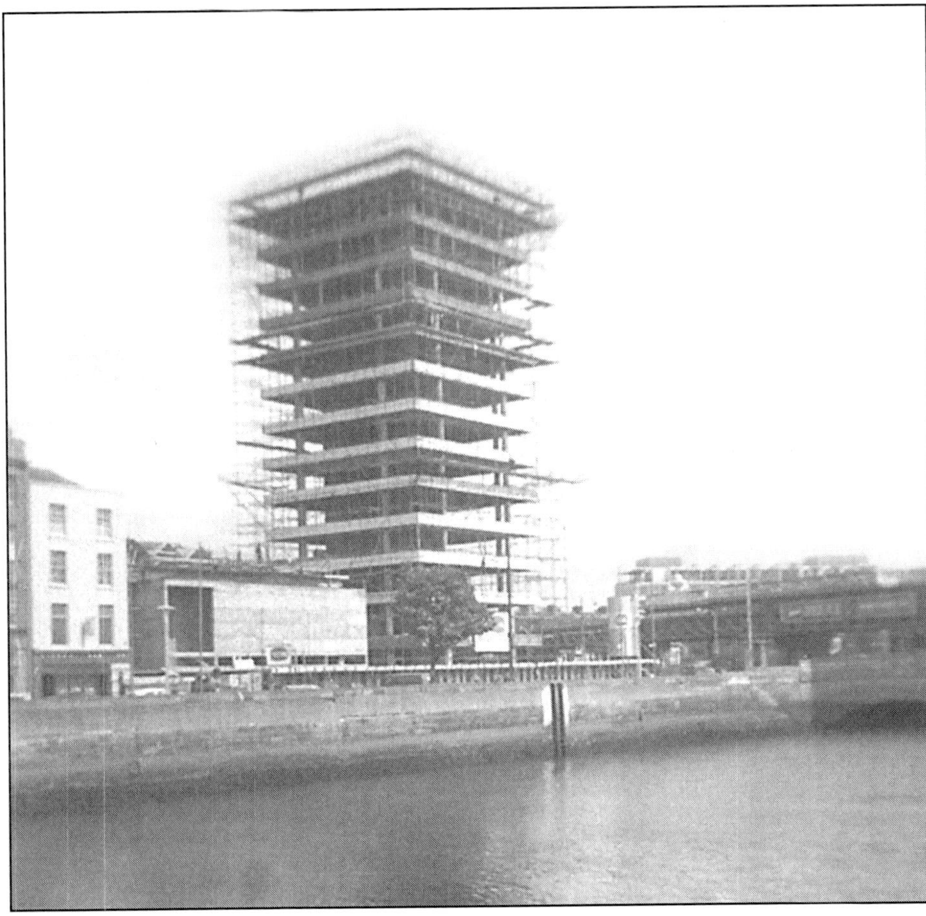

***The building of Liberty Hall 1960-1965.***

.

overturned on the grounds that the new building would be *'Unacceptably dominant in the city'*

The foundations for Liberty Hall are built on solid bedrock as are the foundations for the overhead railway line across the road as seen in this photograph. On the odd occasion visitors are allowed up onto the viewing gallery situated on the top floor. From here the visitor can see Dublin in all direction and in particular a superb view along the banks of the River Liffey to the east.

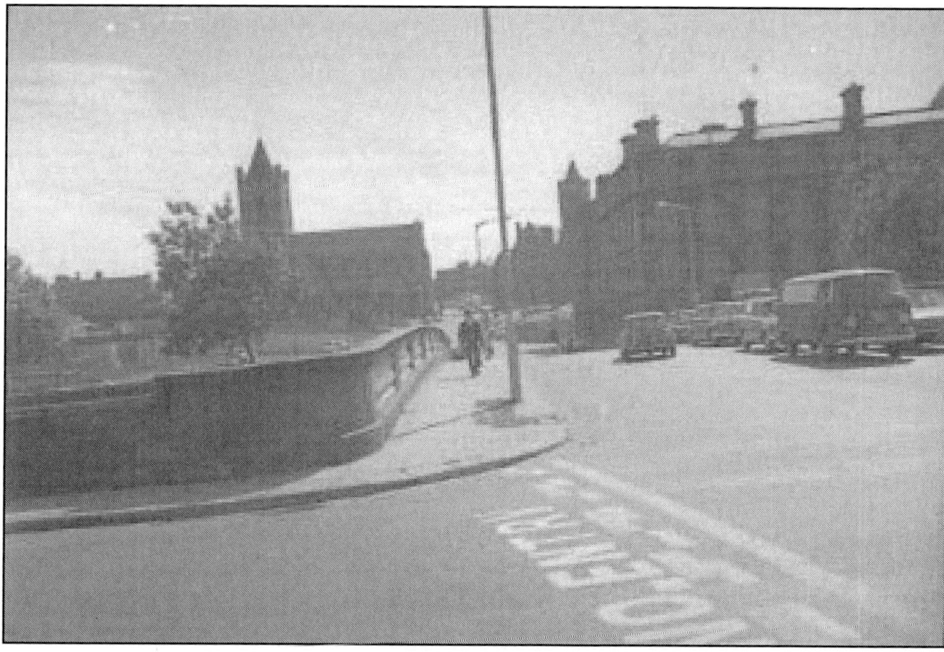

*A view of Christchurch Cathedral across the River Liffey.*

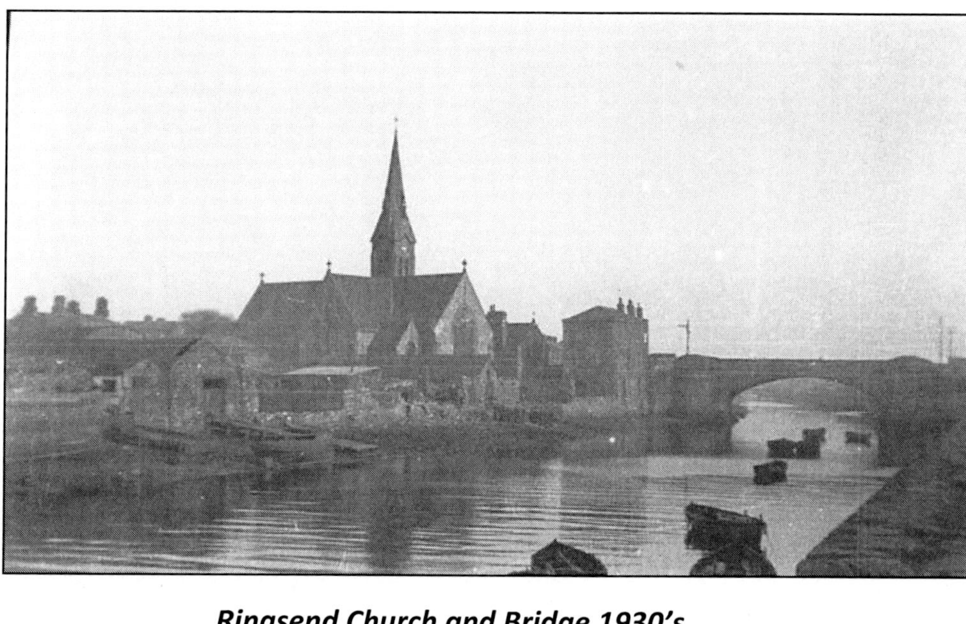

*Ringsend Church and Bridge 1930's.*

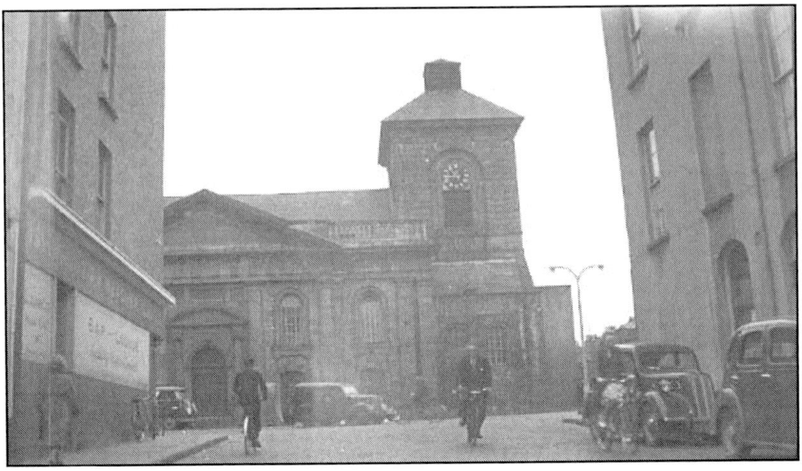

***St. Catherine's Church, Dublin.***

In 1803 the Irish rebel Robert Emmett was executed by hanging from a scaffold set up in front of Saint Catherine's Church in Thomas Street, Dublin. Paddy Coffey captured this scene of the area in the 1930's. The tall building to the right of the photograph is now long demolished to allow for the street to be widened. The pub on the opposite corner is still there today as is the church.

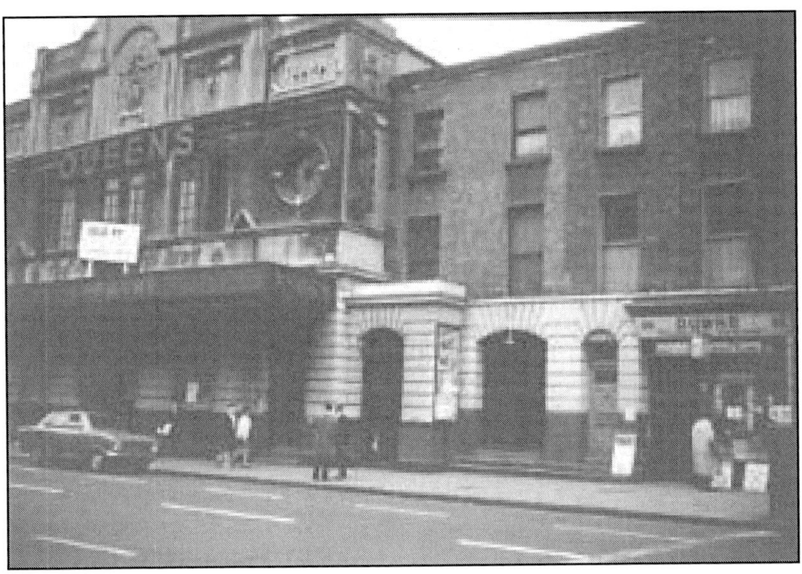


***The Queen's Theatre in Pearse Street.***

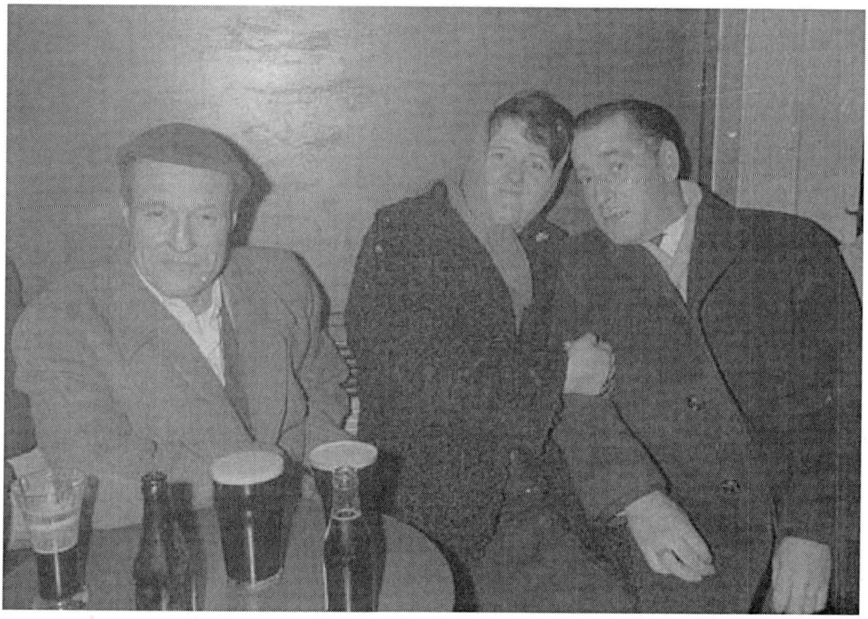

***A quiet drink together.***

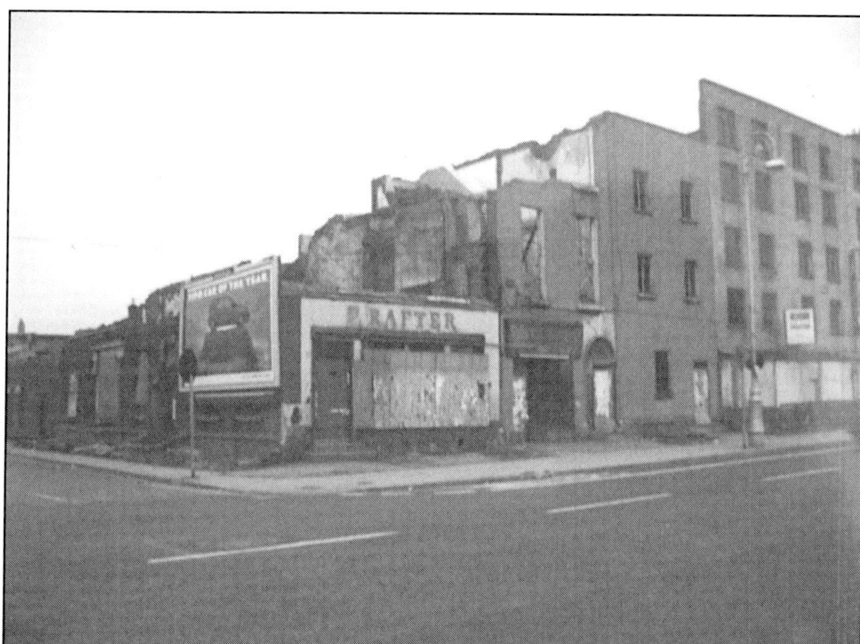


***Rafter's pawn shop in Gardiner Street.***

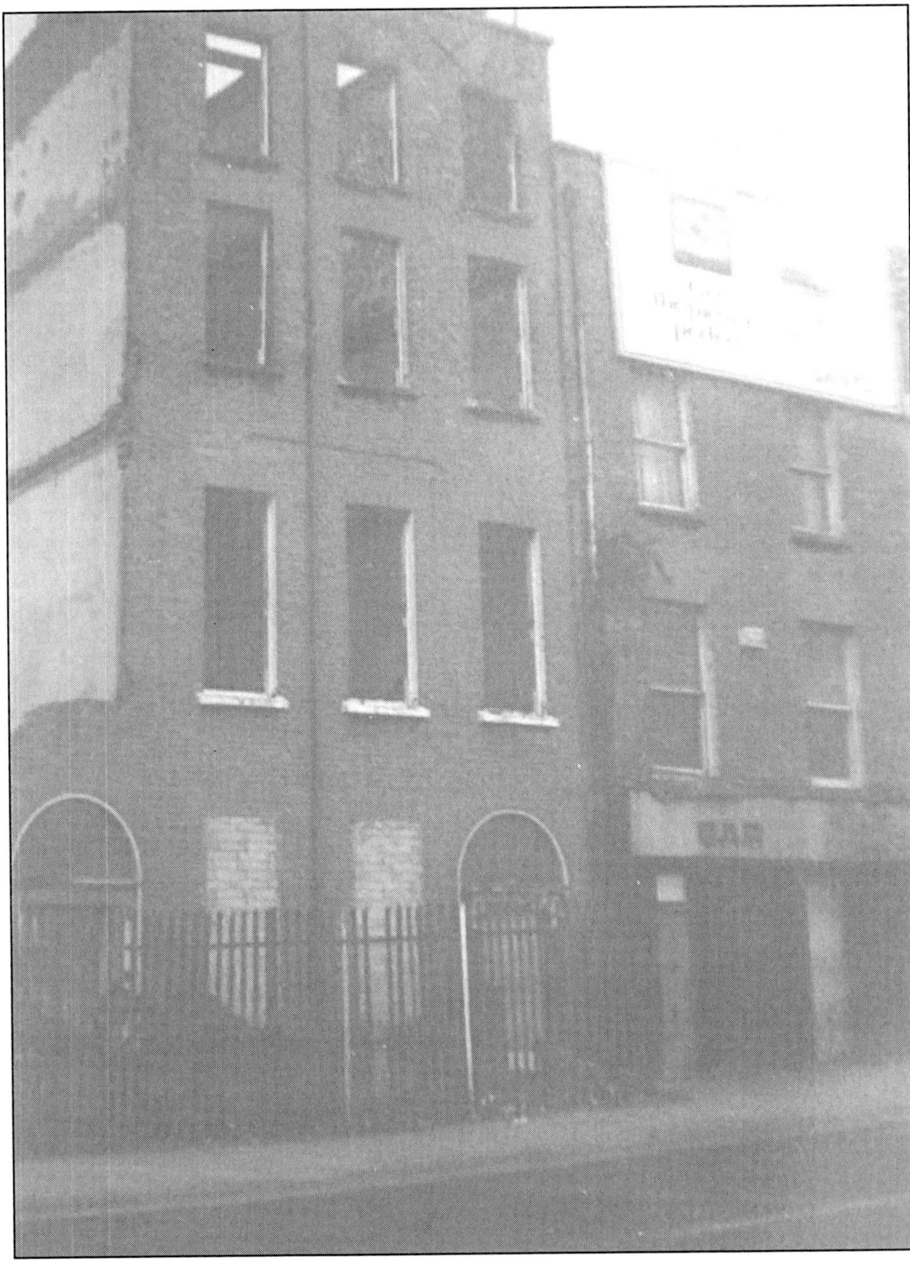

***Gardiner Street.***

*'We lived in the top flat of the house next to the Honey Pot pub on Gardiner Street. When the men in the pub wanted to go to the toilet they went into a small yard at the back of the pub. But when the women had to go they came out of the pub and into the hallway of the tenement house to go. They went in behind the hall door and did their business. I had to come down four flights of stairs every morning carrying a bucket of scolding water to try and wash away the smell, it was all over the house. When I was about ten years old my job was to go down to the back yard every night and fill up a bucket with water for my father's tea in the morning. I had to walk down the stairs with my back to the wall because there was always rats running up and down the stairs in the dark'...***Aggie Coffey***

*'I remember one time when we lived in Elliott Place the man who lived upstairs had just died and my mother got his flat. It was number 10 Elliott Place owned by the Doyle's. The thing was that the man that lived in the front room upstairs had died and my mother had put in for that room. Now it wasn't much bigger than the one we had in the back of the house but she wanted one at the front because she could look out and see what was going on. Well this day my mother had us up town and it was raining so we didn't stay out too long. When we got to our front door my mother and my Auntie Mary were trying to lift our pram up the stairs with all the messages and the baby in it. So my mother took out the door key to the room and gave it to my sister Aggie and told her to go on up and open the door. Well she did and all of a sudden didn't Aggie let out an unmerciful scream all over the house. I remember I jumped with the fright and let out a scream as well. When we got up the stairs with the pram there she was just standing at the door of the room and screaming. My mother had to practically sit on top of her to stop her screaming. She told my mother that when she opened the door to our room she saw the man that had died standing in the middle of the room. Now Aggie was like that, she used to see things and that'...***Kathleen Burke***

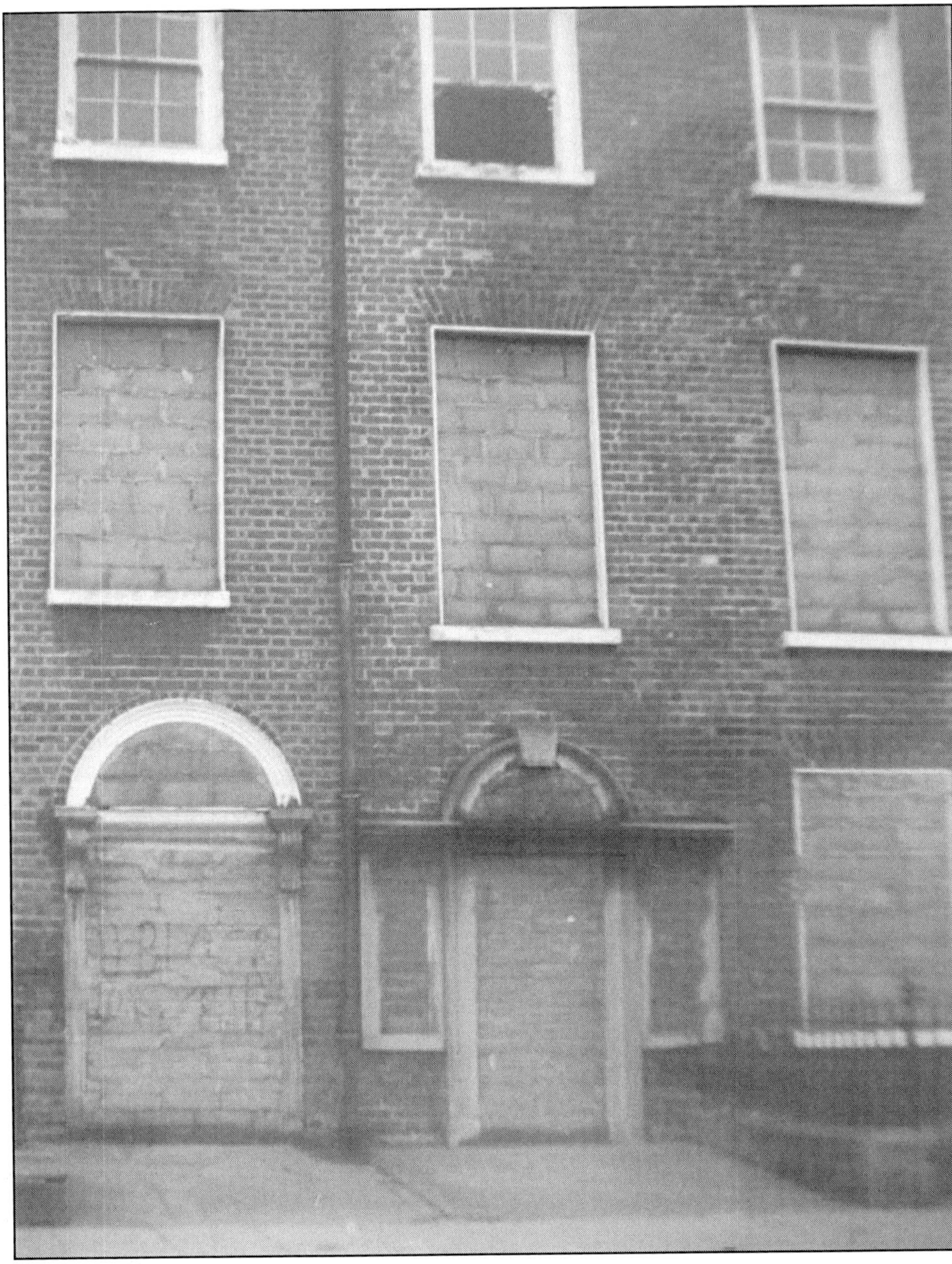

***Premises of the old Belvedere Newsboys' Club in Marlborough Street.***

In 1918 Doctor William Lombard Murphy, a past pupil of Belvedere College and Victor Plunkett were instrumental in founding the Belvedere Social Service Club that later became the Belvedere Newsboys' Club. Doctor Murphy had studied medicine in Cambridge University, England. Some years later on his return to Dublin he set up a practise in Merrion Square. On the death of his father he became chairman of Independent Newspapers. Doctor Murphy became involved with the Dublin Boys' Club that was founded by a then well-known Probation Offer, Miss Gargan.

Through this club Doctor Murphy became aware that the many young boys who sold his newspapers on the streets of Dublin, did so in their bare feet, few if any of them could actually read or write and they mainly came from very poor and deprived families. It wasn't too long before there were 120 young boys on the attendance roll. In recent years the name of the old club was changed to the Belvedere Youth Club and now has a mixed membership of both boys and girls. The present club is situated in Buckingham Street. It is very possibly the longest continuous running youth club in Europe. **('How' ya Doc'? by Gerry Walsh KSG)**

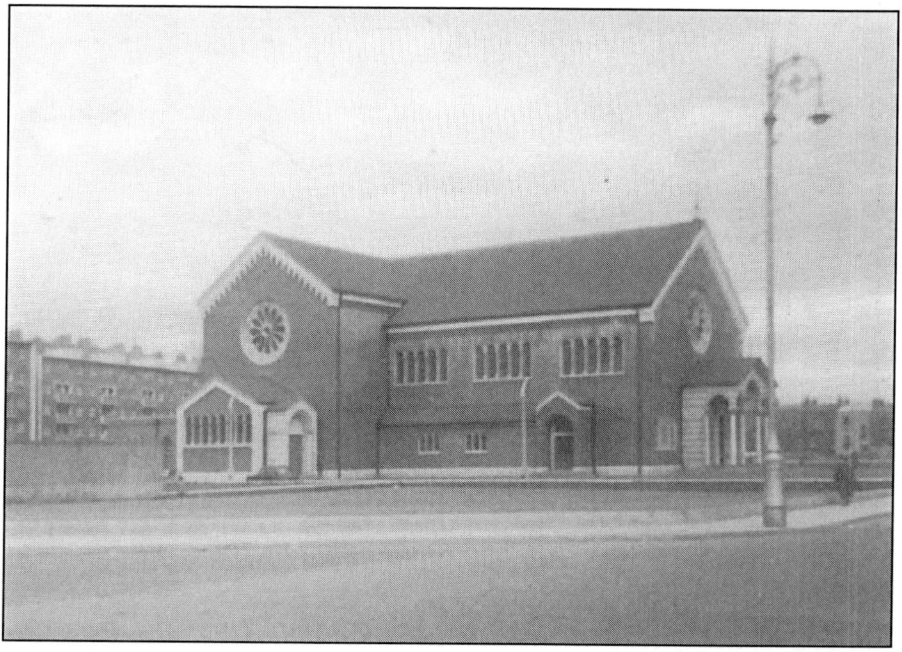

***Our Lady of Lourdes Church, Sean McDermot Street.***

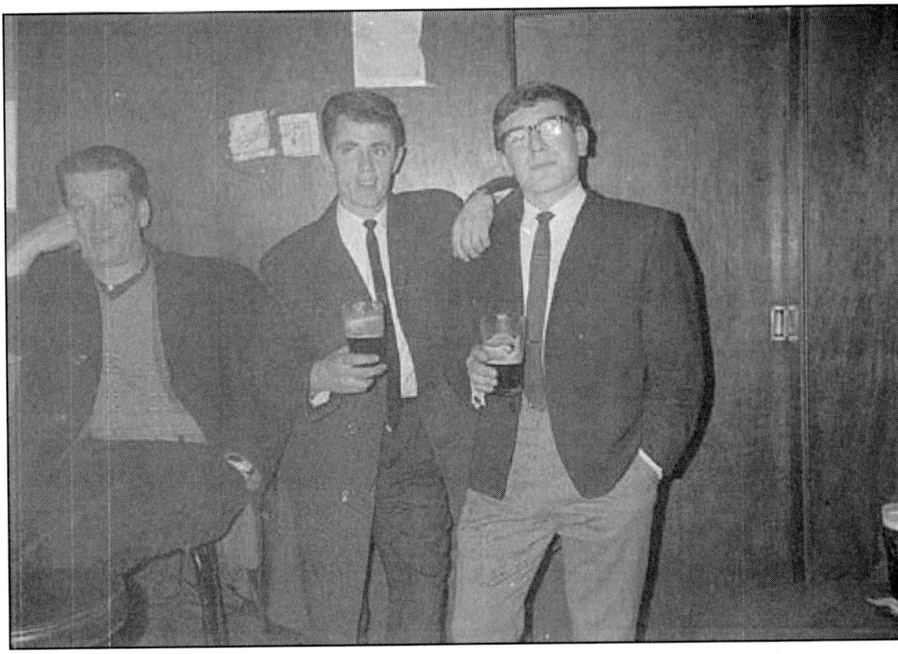

***The lads having a drink.***

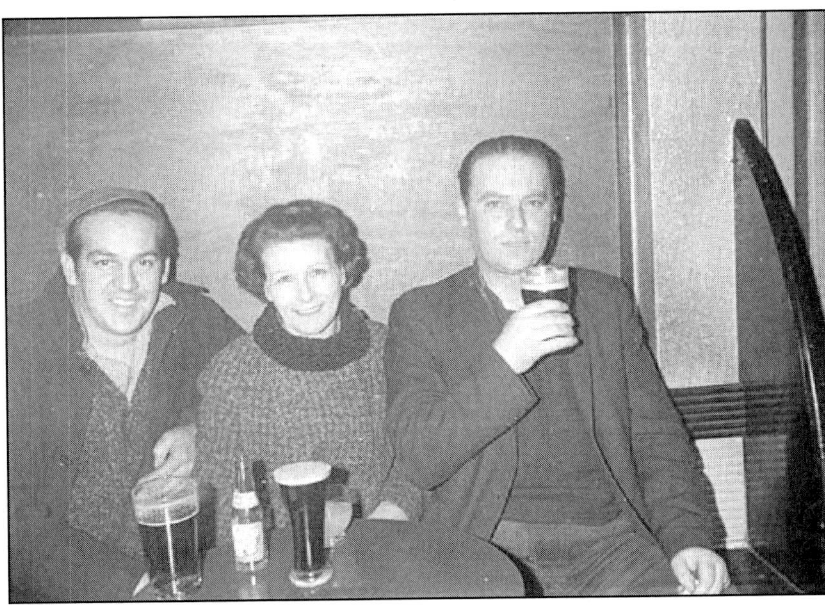

***Wacker and Dinah Rooney with Tom Byrne.***

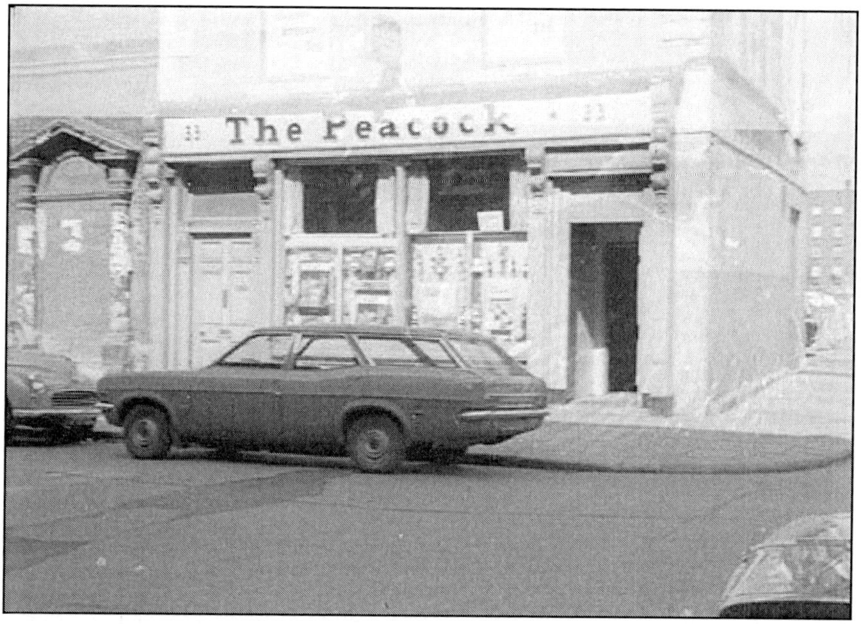


*The Peacock pub on the corner of Marlborough Street and Waterford Street.*

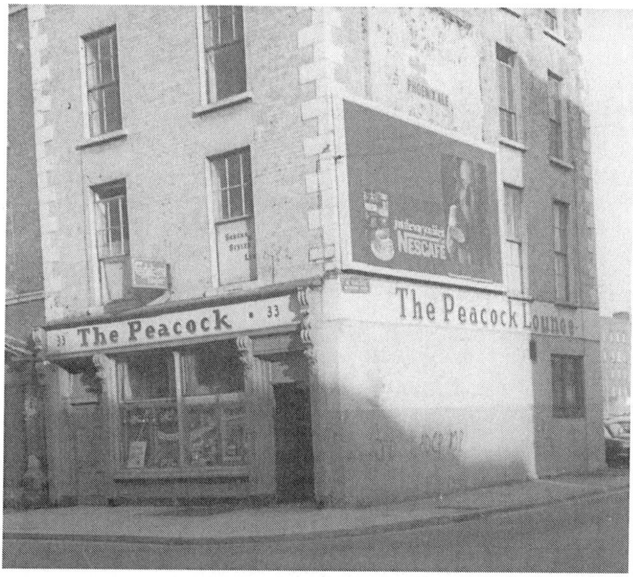


*Mitchell's Rosary Bead factory was situated behind the Dandy garage in Waterford Street.*

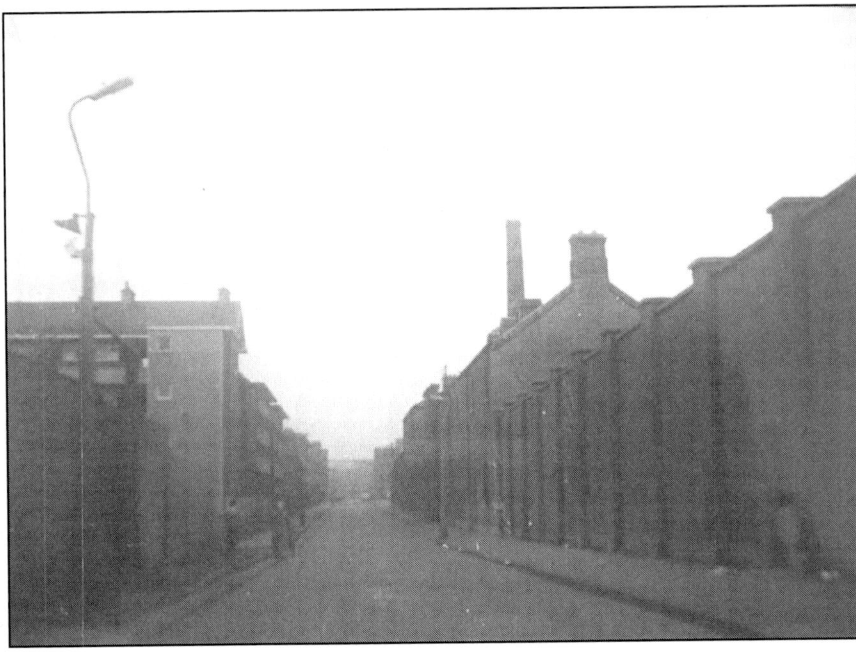

***Railway Street.***

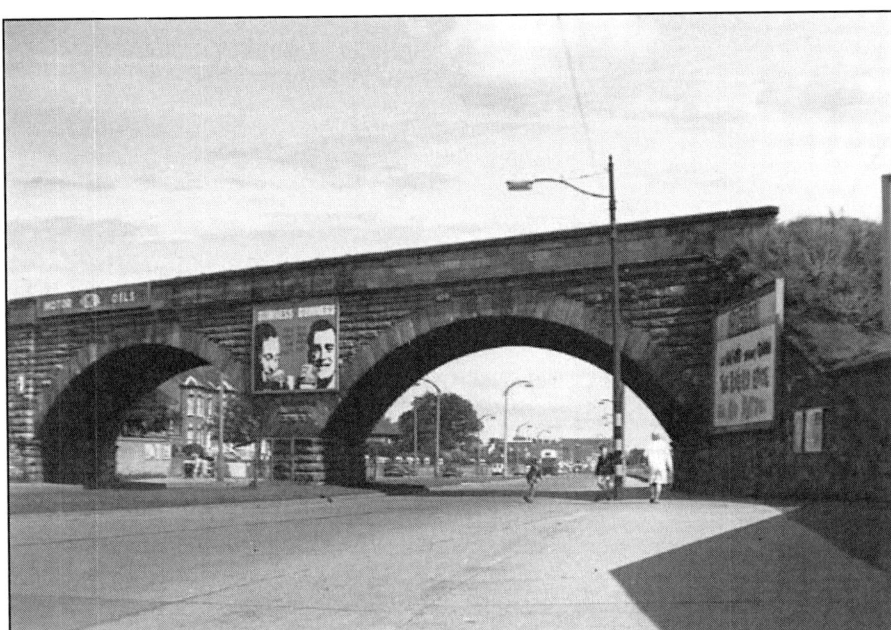


***Clontarf Bridge.***

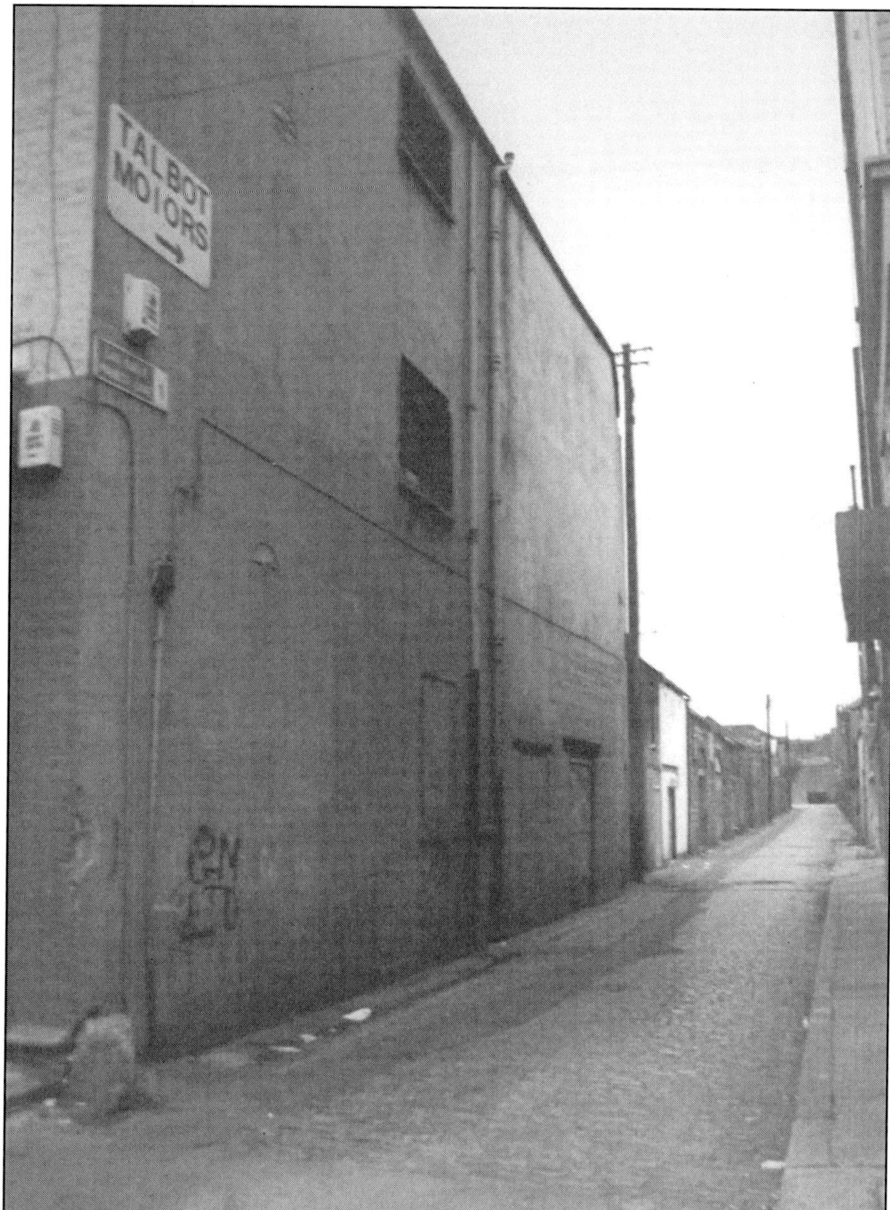


***Mabbott Lane, Dublin.***

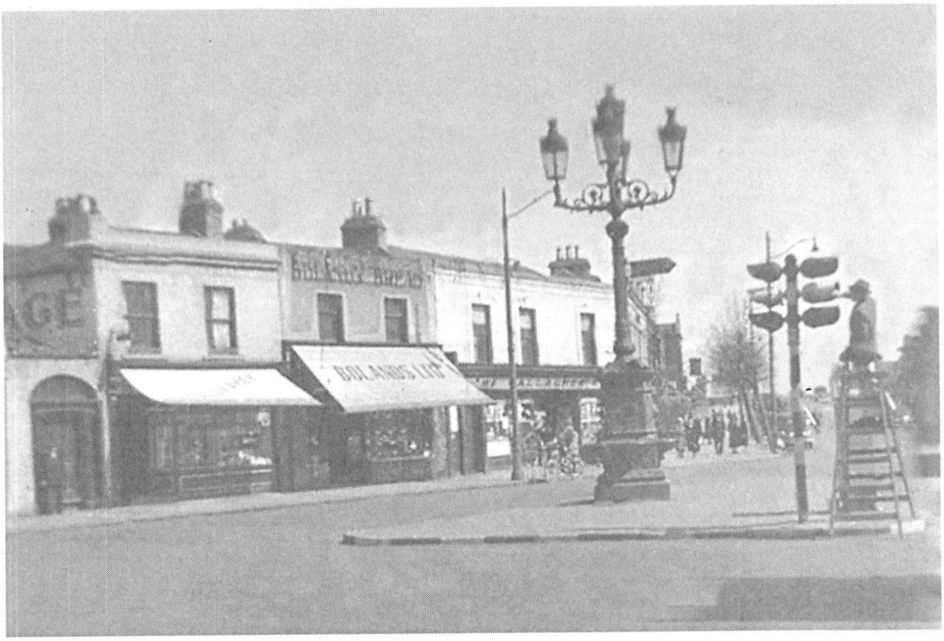

**'The Five Lamps', North Strand, Dublin.**

**Andy Gunnery**

**(Born in 1913)**

*'We lived in Corporation Buildings, it was built like a prison. My father and mother used to sit on a double wooden stool when we were having our dinner and we used to stand at the table because we had no chairs. We had to sleep on the floor on a thing like a bag or a striped mattress. There was a place in Store Street that we used to go to and buy a sheaf of straw to put in the bags so we could sleep on them.*

*Things were very bad back then. We used to go to where Fairview Park is now but back then it was called "The Slob Lands". It was a dump where everything was thrown out. Jacob's Biscuit factory had all their stuff dumped there. We used to go out and pick up old Jam Jars, empty Porter Bottles, bits of old timber and Cinders. We'd be looking for anything to sell and make a few bob'.*

*I probably started school when I was about four years old. I went to Rutland Street School. I remember one teacher name Mister Herbert. He used to pull me by the ear because I was left handed and left footed. He tried to force me to use my right hand when I'd be writing and that. The headmaster was Mister Scully and I remember a teacher named Miss Fish. There was also a Mister Frame who was related to the Frame family that owned the Hammond lane Foundry'.*

**(Extracts from: How' ya Doc? by Gerry Walsh KSG.)**

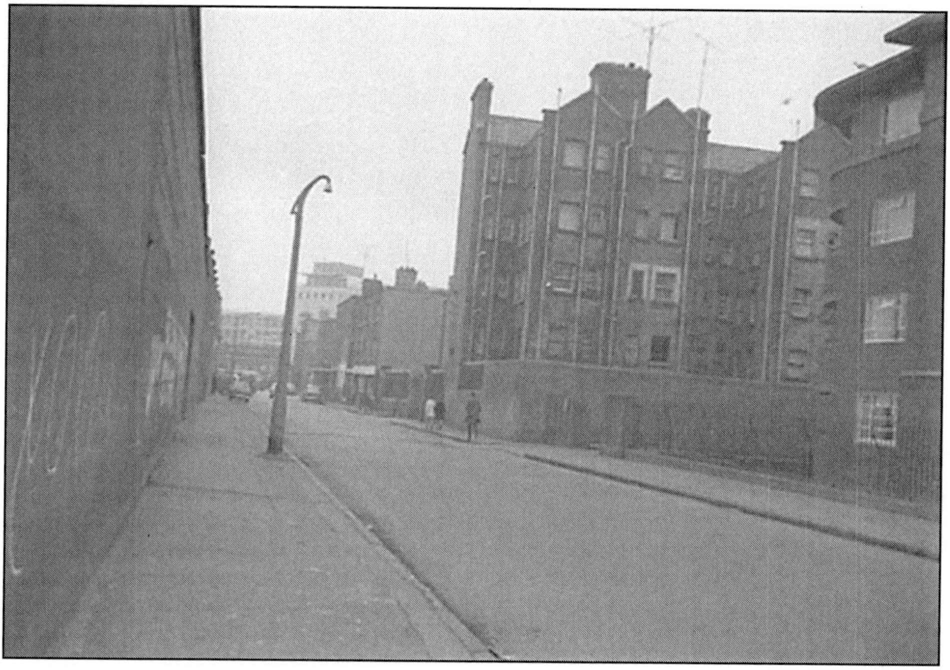

***Railway Street.***

Railway Street was previously known as Mecklenburgh Street and was once a very busy street with dairies, carpenter shops, dressmakers and printers. In the early 19th century Mecklenburgh Street was considered to be a very fashionable street of beautiful Georgian houses owned by the cream of society. In 1801 the Act of Union abolished the Irish Parliament and Ireland came under direct rule from London. This was a tragic blow for Ireland and especially Dublin as it prompted a mass exodus of many of the wealthy and prominent Anglo Irish from the city. In its wake it left behind streets of empty houses that were gradually turned into tenement slums.

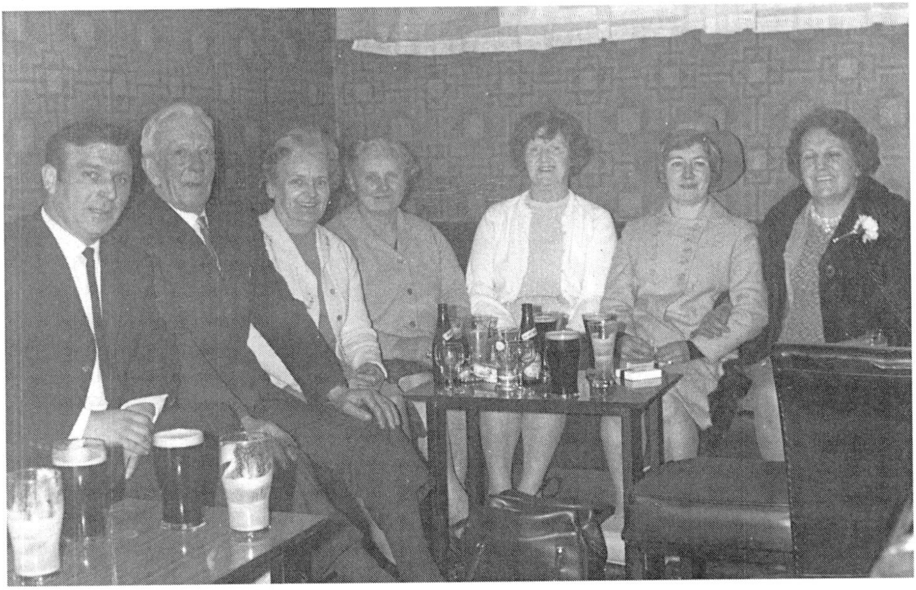

***L-R: Billy Dillon, Tom Fagan, Rooie Kane, Biddy Coffey, Jessy Fagan, Chrissie Dillon and Mrs McDonald.***

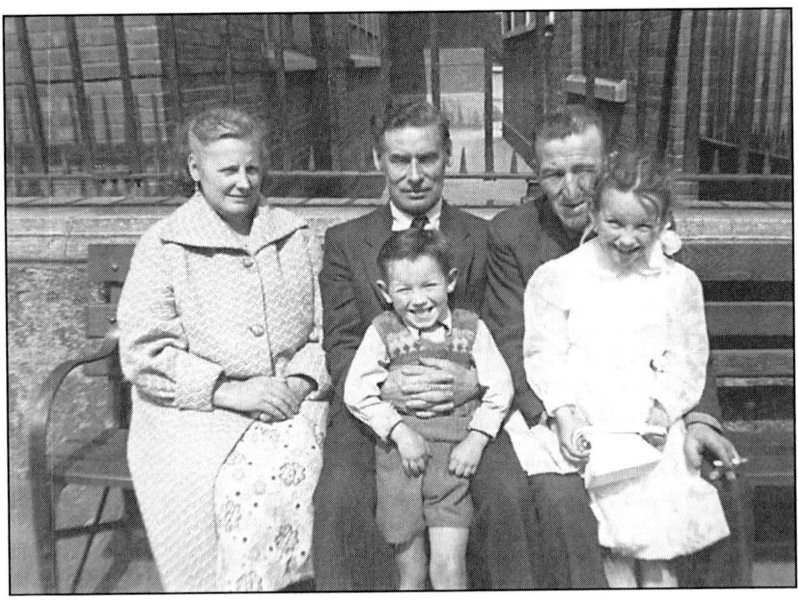

***Biddy and Paddy Coffey with***

***Alfie Kane and his two children Paddy and Angela.***

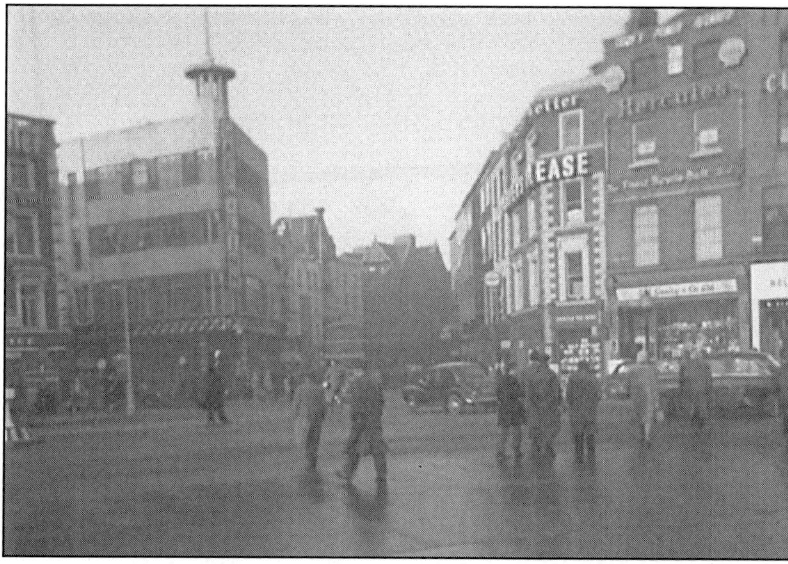

***Saint Stephen's Green, Dublin.***

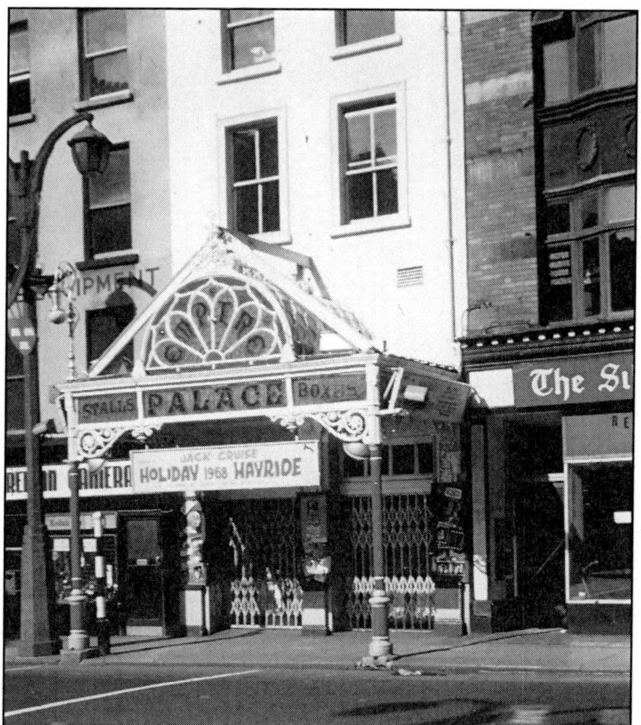


***The Palace in Dame Street, Dublin.***

# Chapter 5

## From Shore to Shore

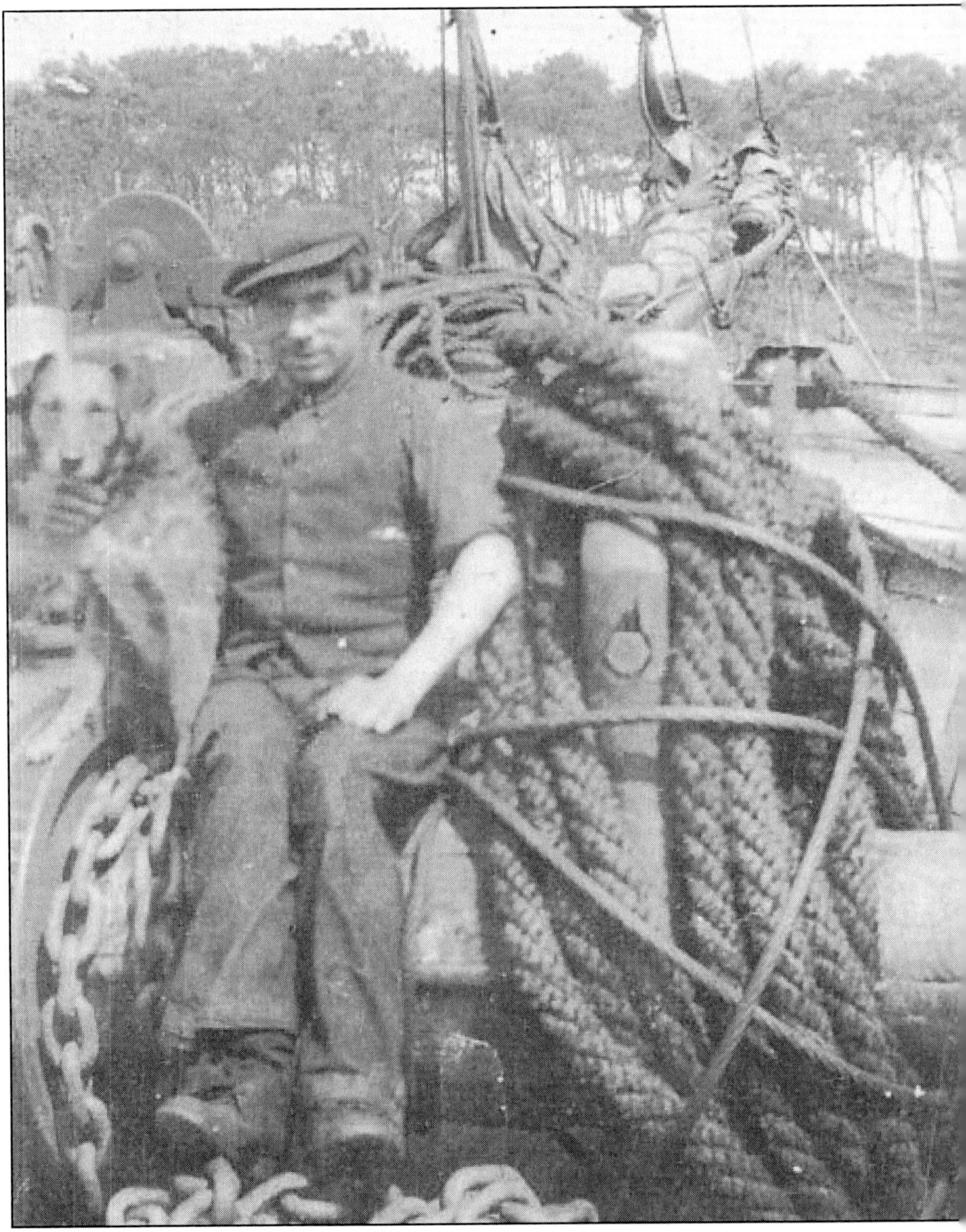

*Paddy Coffey in 1931.*

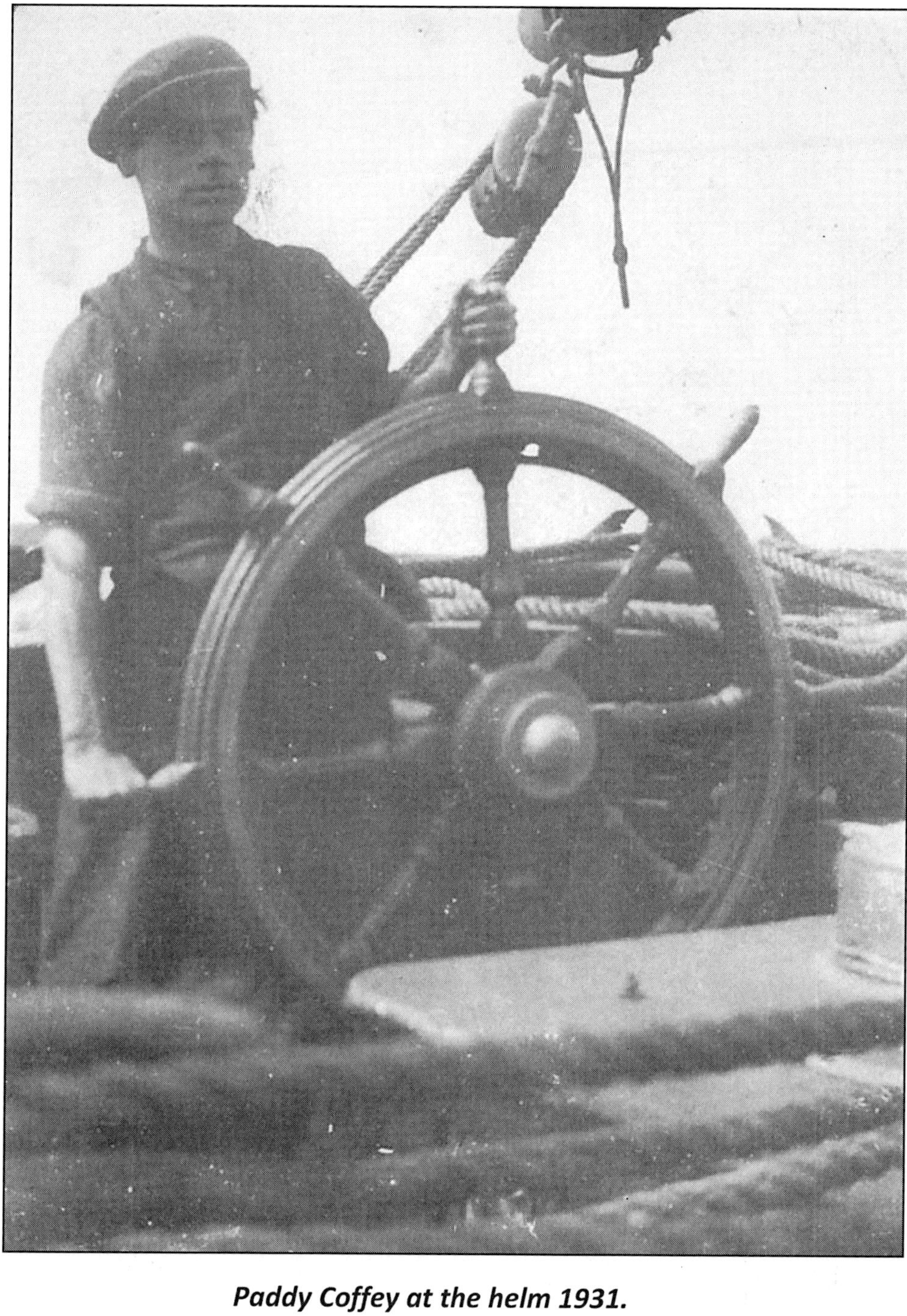

***Paddy Coffey at the helm 1931.***

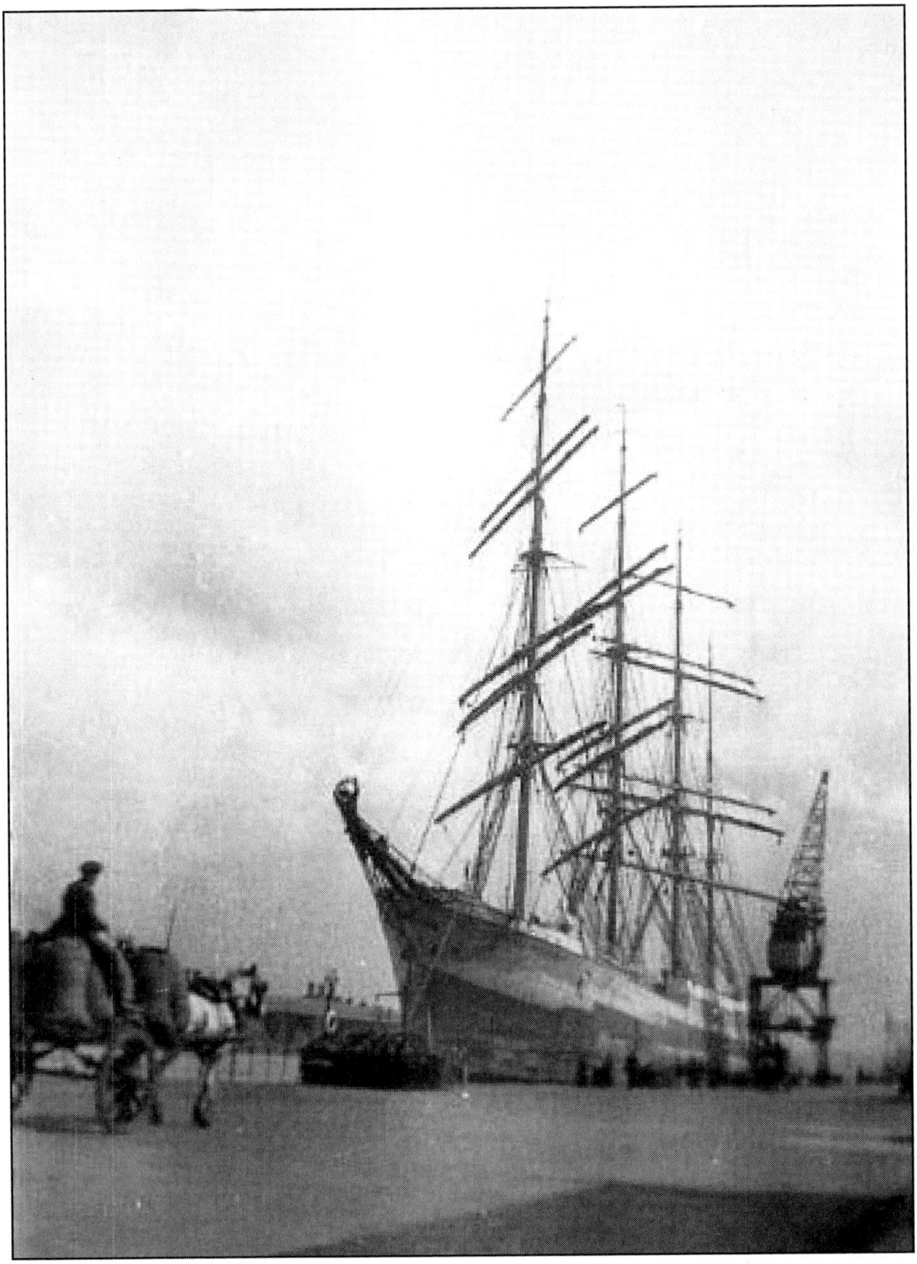

*City Quay, Dublin 1930's.*

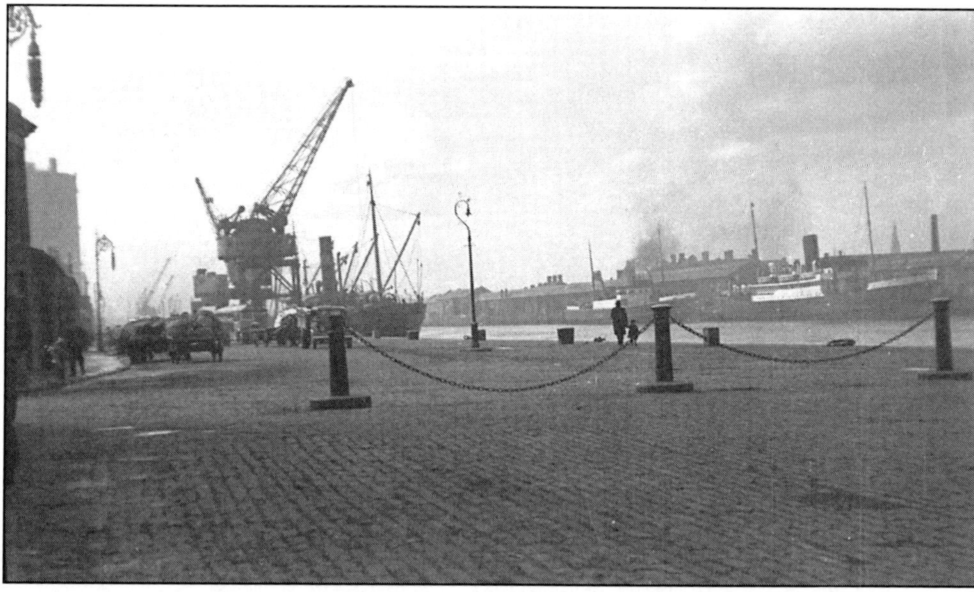

*Looking north across the River Liffey from City Quay 1930's.*

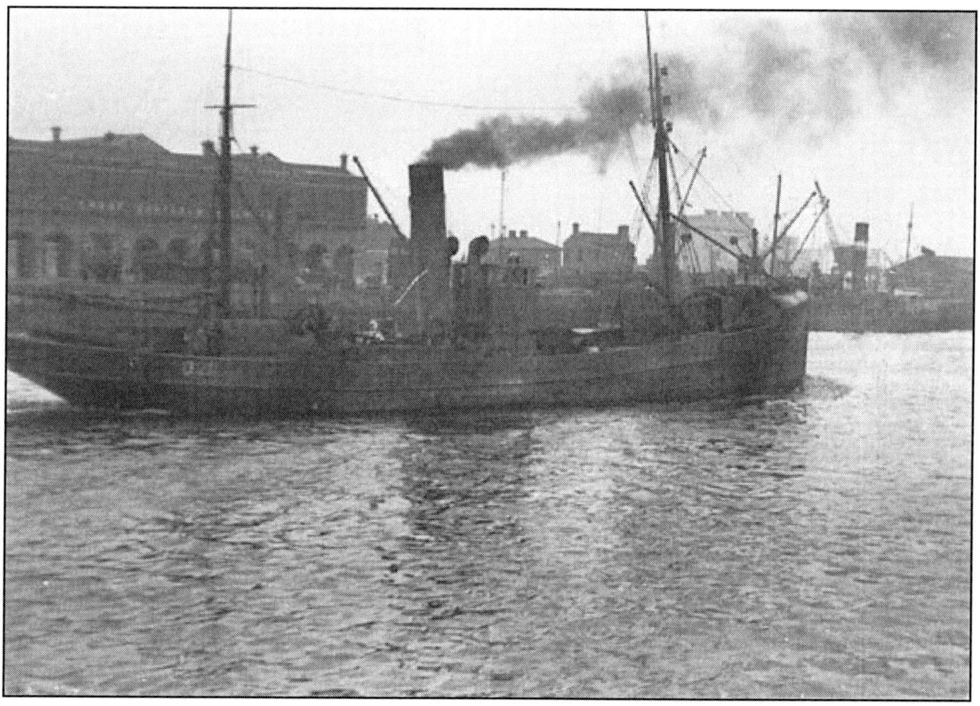

*Sailing past the Point Depot in Dublin.*

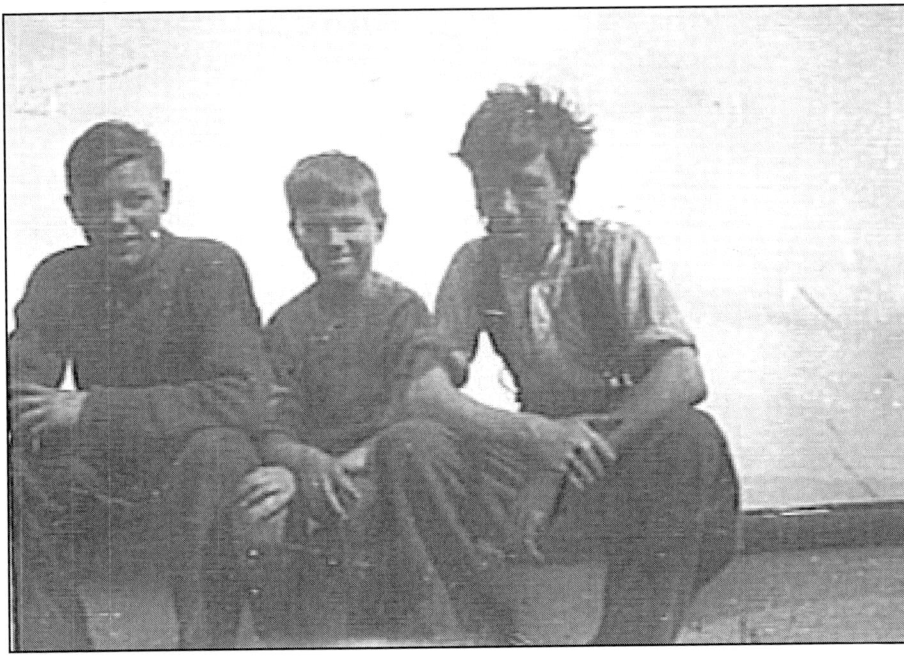

***Three young boys aboard the Squirrel.***

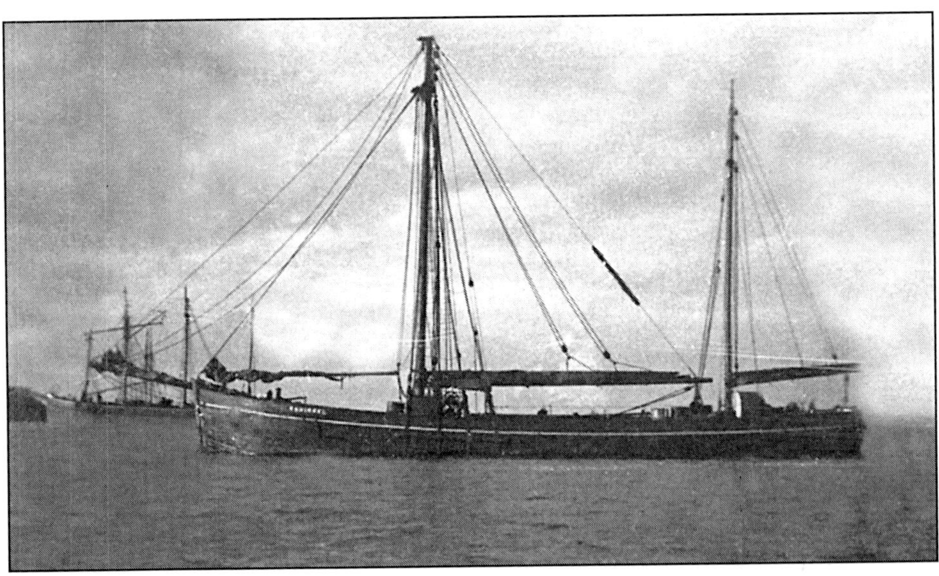

***The Squirrel in Mostyn, North Wales in 1939.***

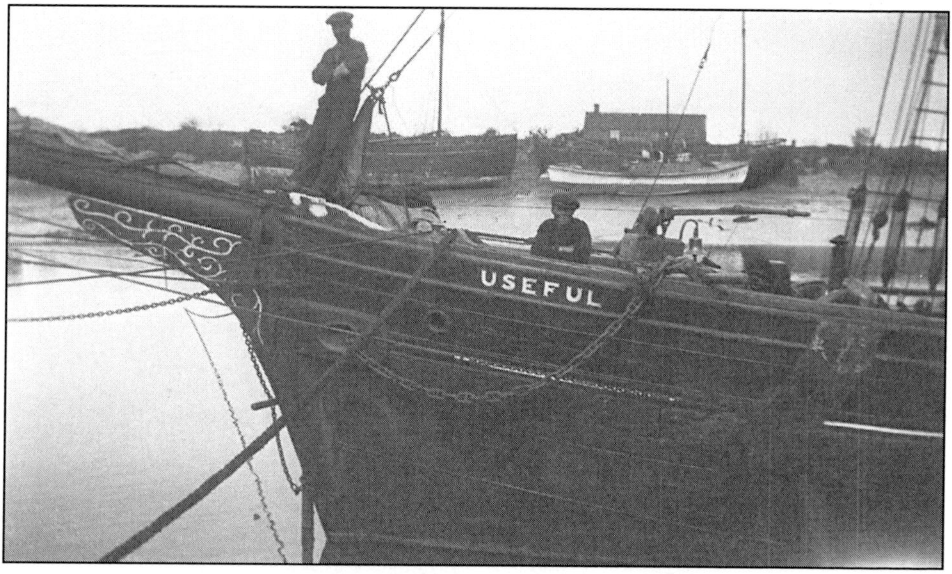


*Paddy Coffey proudly posing on the Useful.*

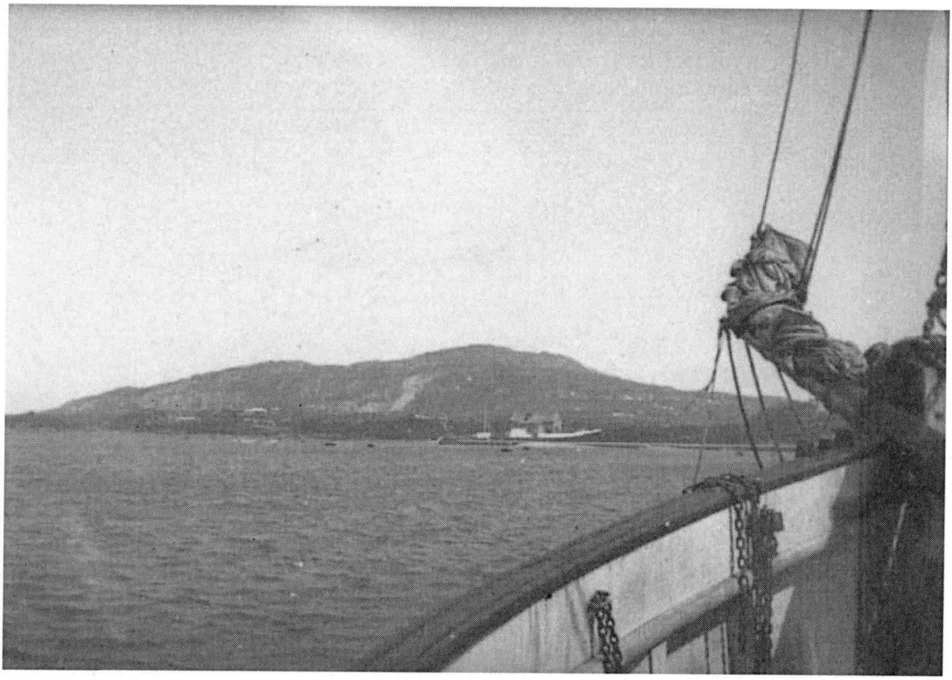

*Sailing out of Dublin.*

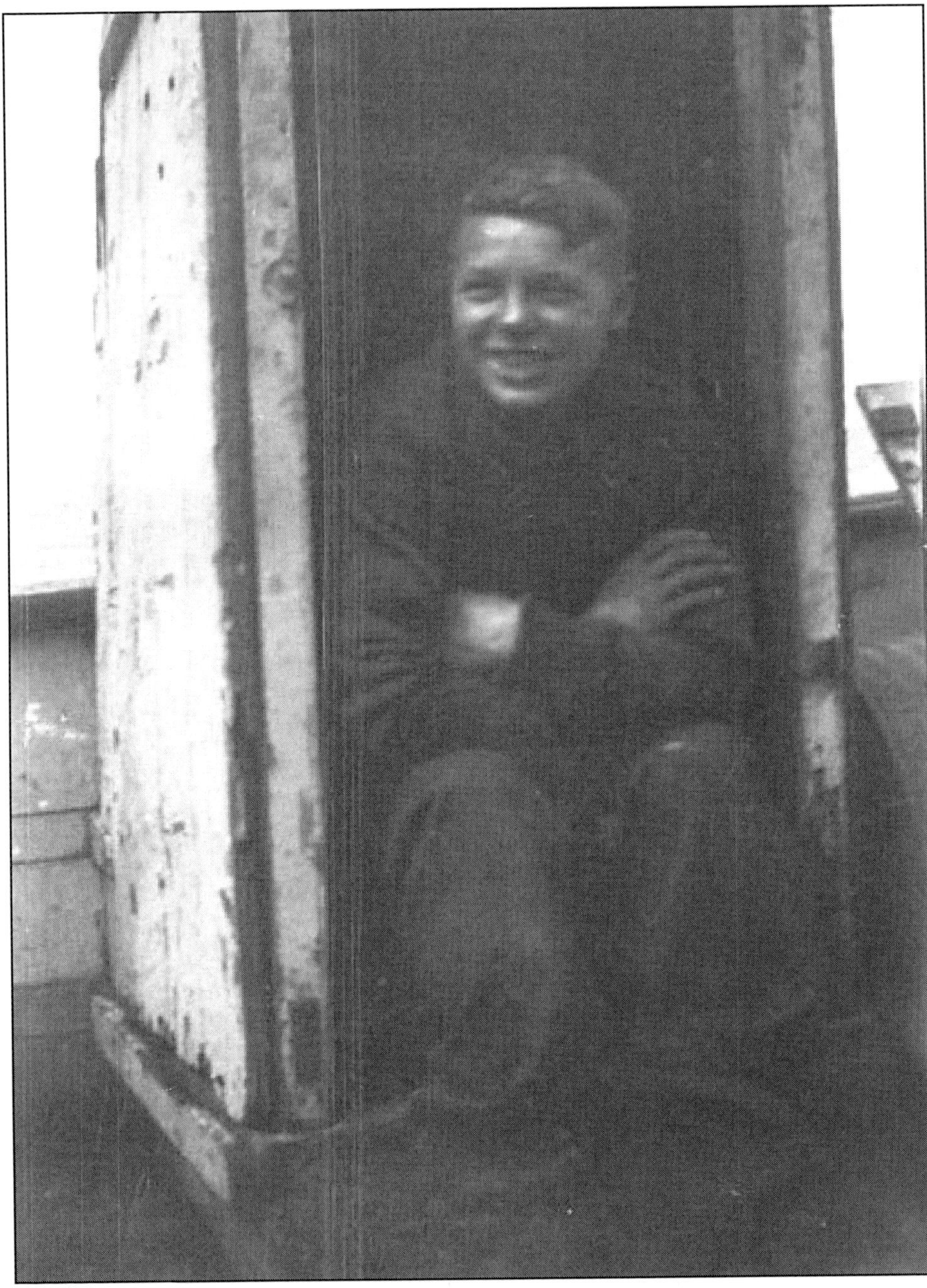

***A young boy sitting on the ships toilet.***

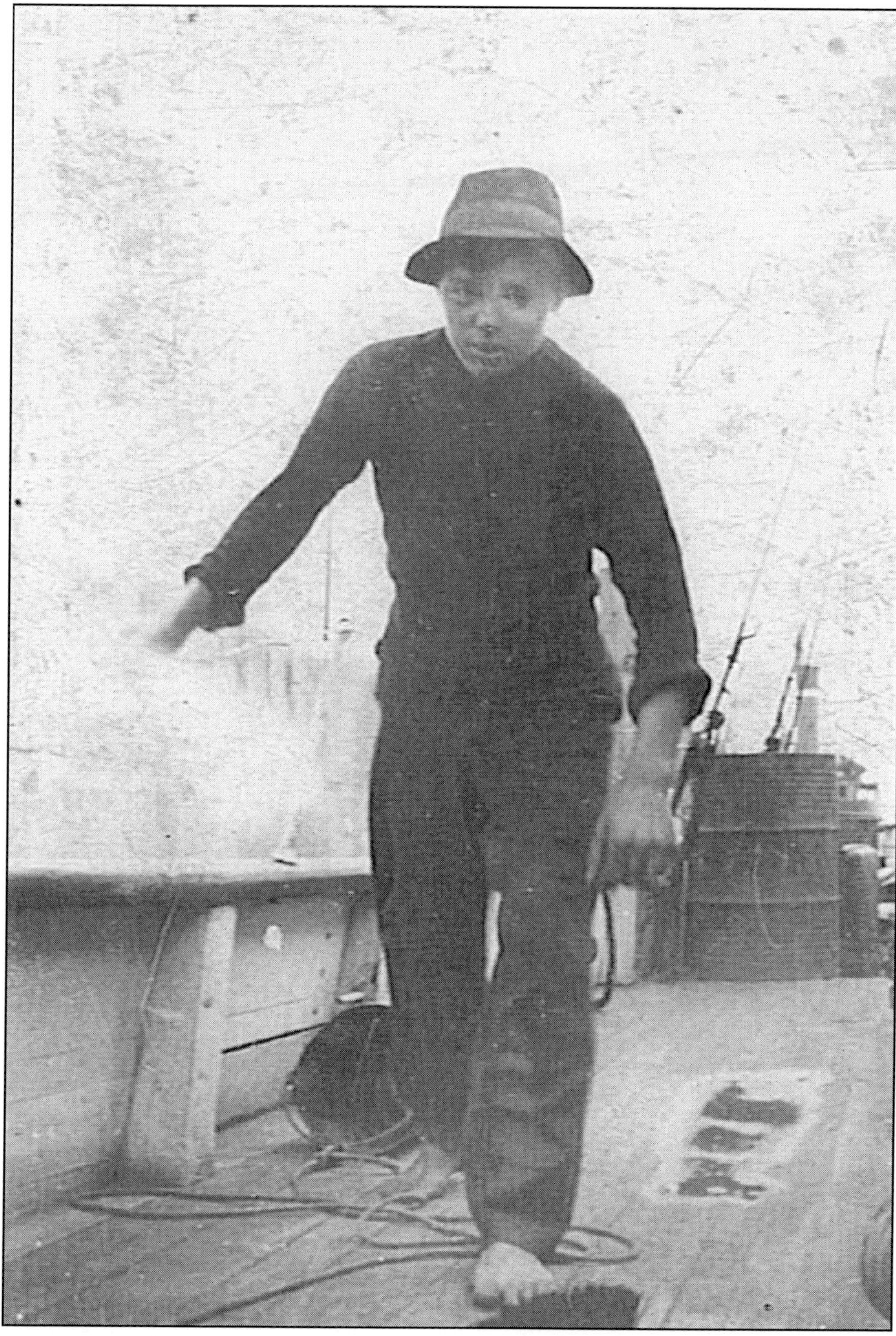

***A very young Deck Hand.***

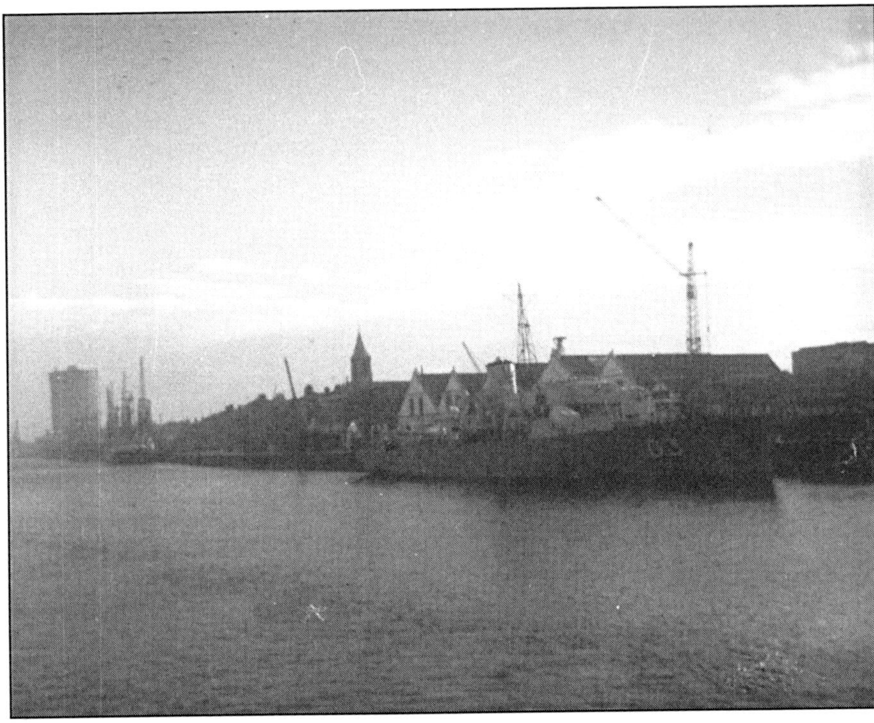

***Looking south across the River Liffey.***

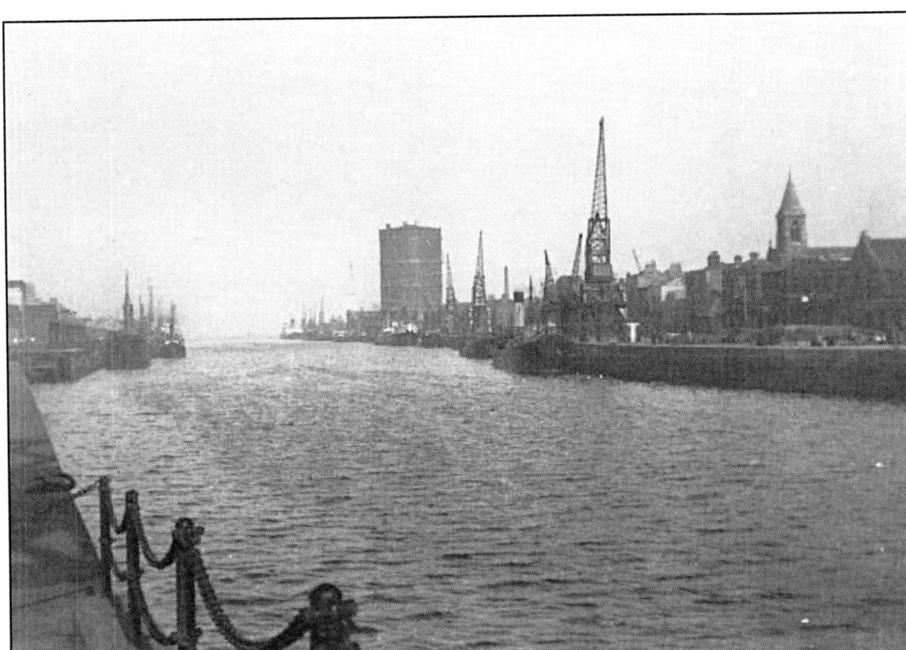

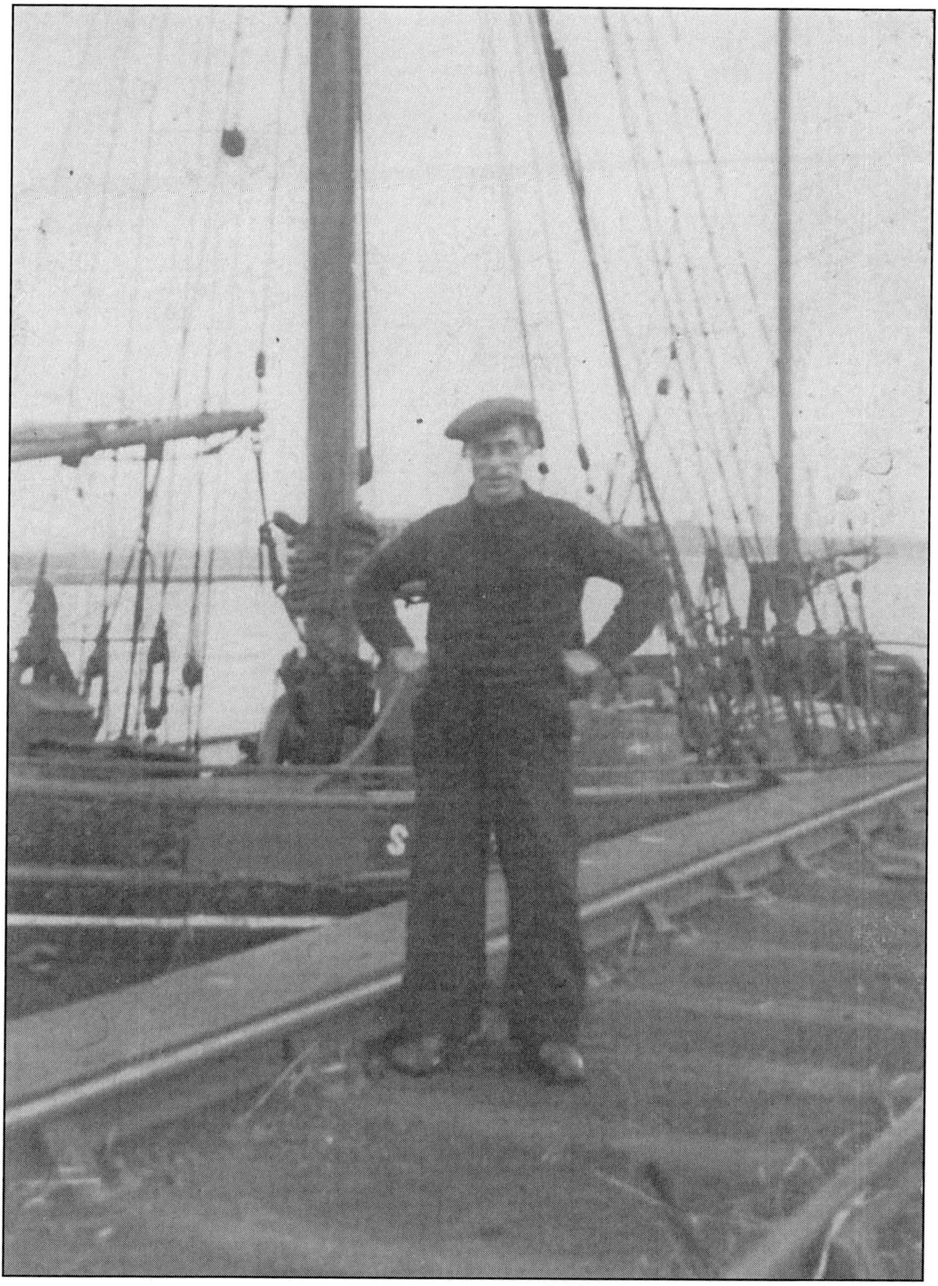

***Paddy Coffey 1931.***

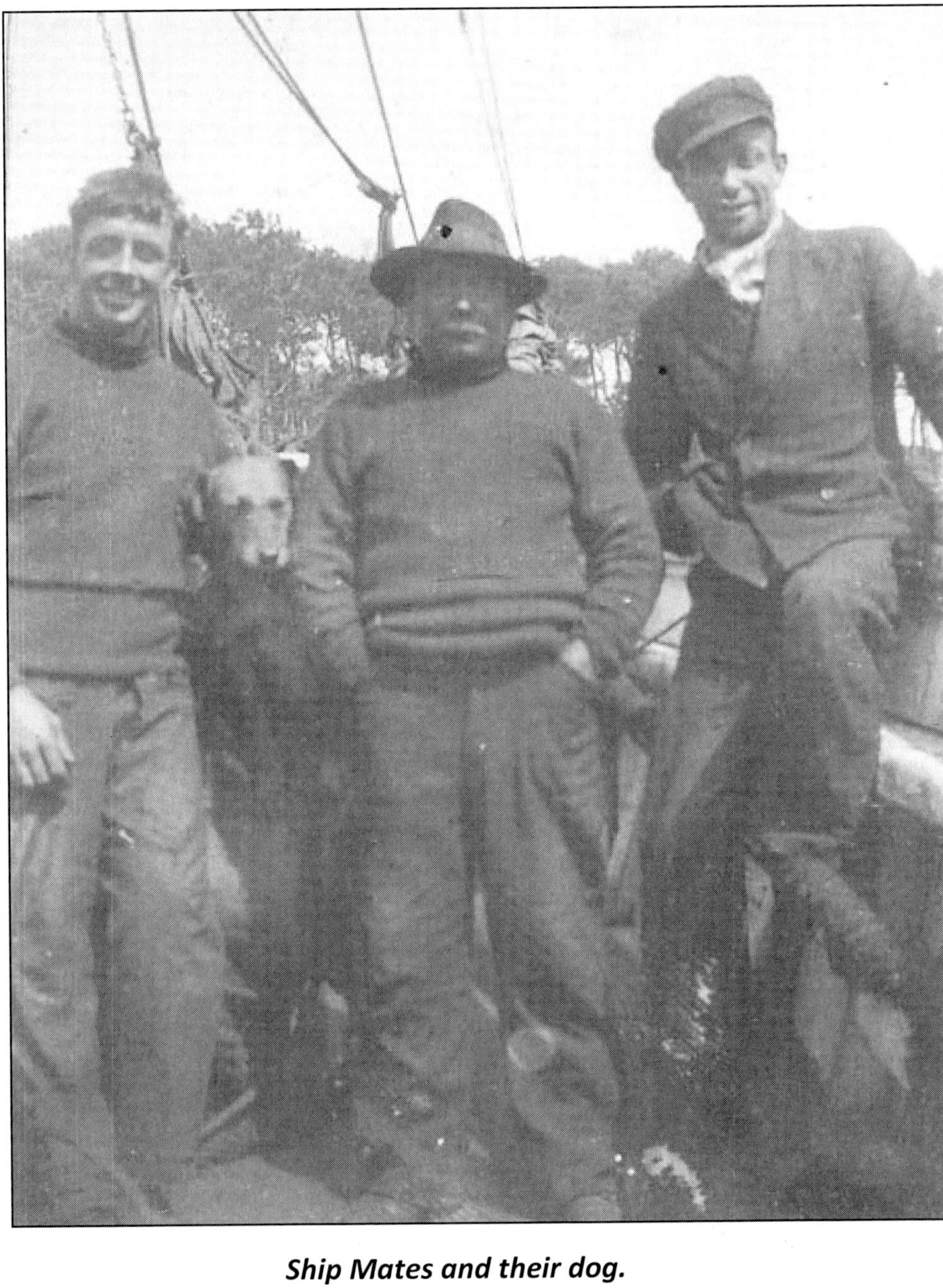

***Ship Mates and their dog.***

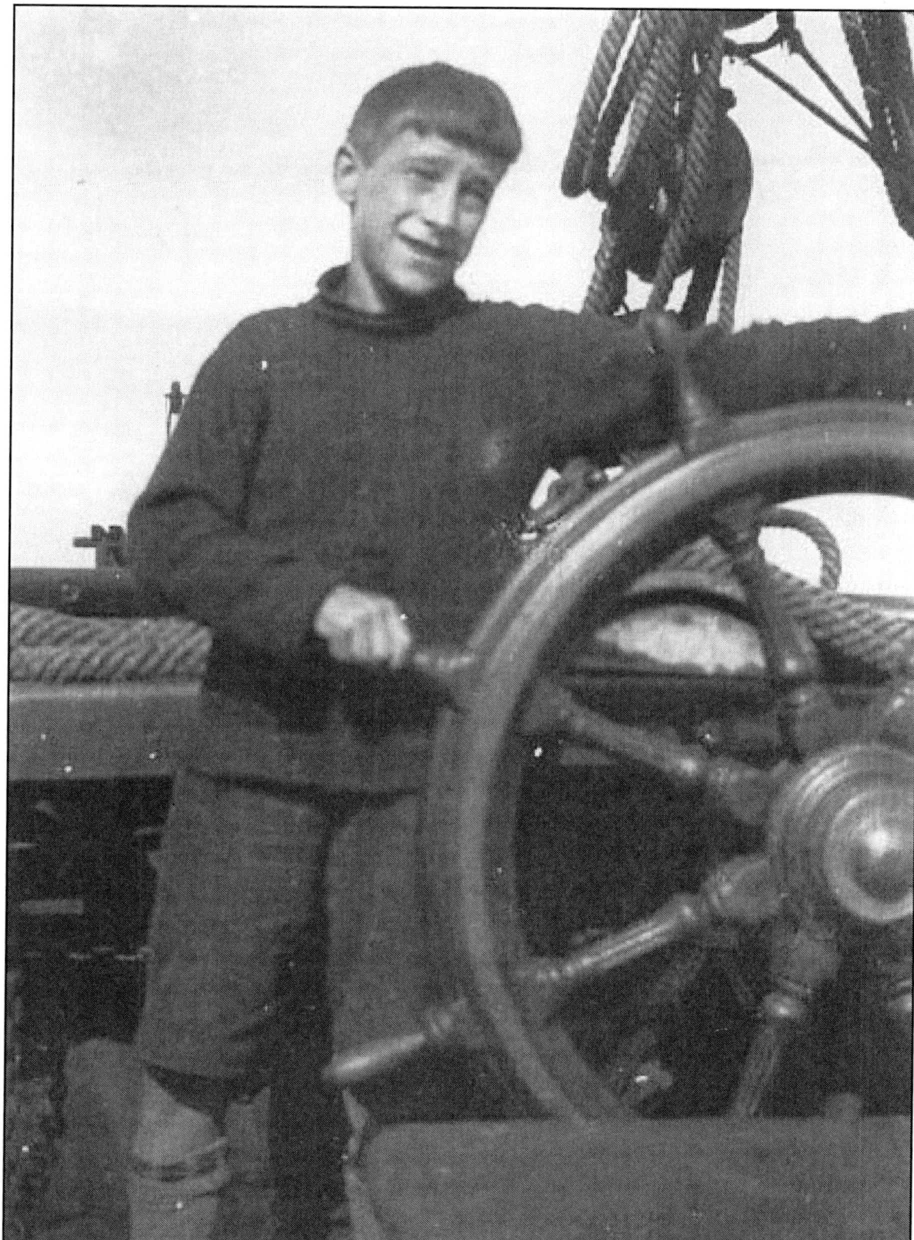

***A young boy at the wheel.***

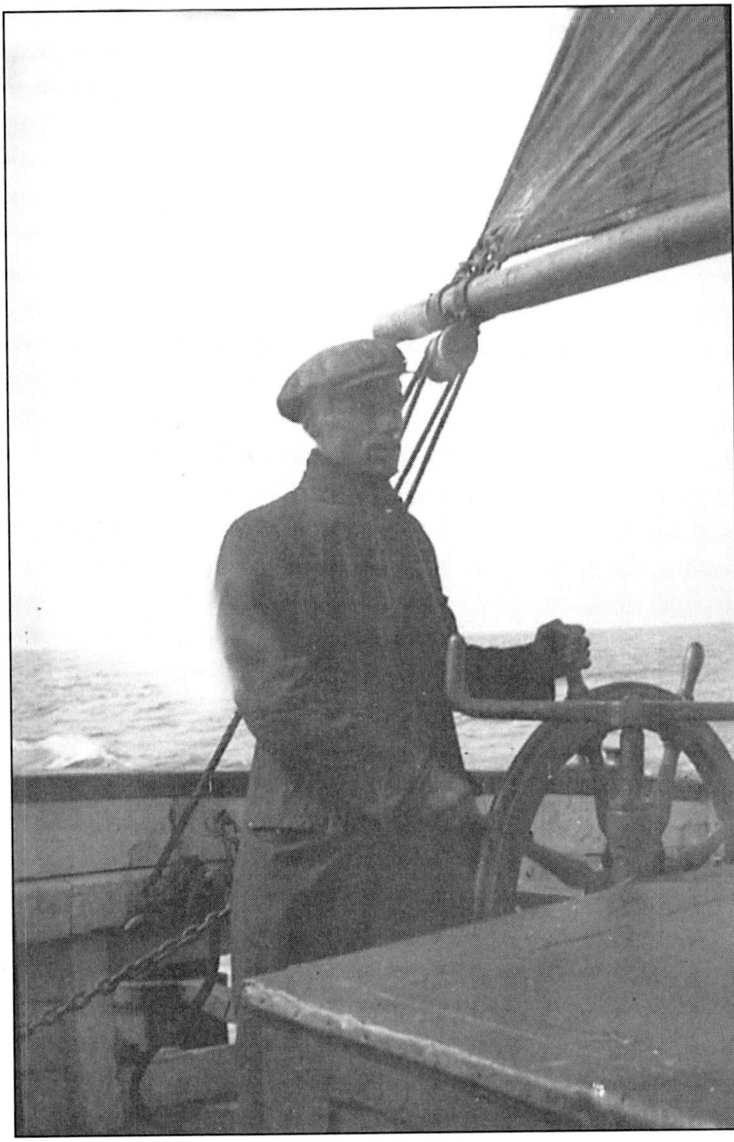

***Paddy Coffey taking the wheel.***

In his early years away at sea Paddy Coffey mainly sailed with fellow Dubliners. Most of the men and boys in his early sailing photographs are all Dubliners. Two of the early vessels he worked on, the Squirrel and the Useful sailed in and out of City Quay. They travelled up and down the east coast going as far north as Drogheda and Belfast and south to Arklow and Wexford collecting scrap iron.

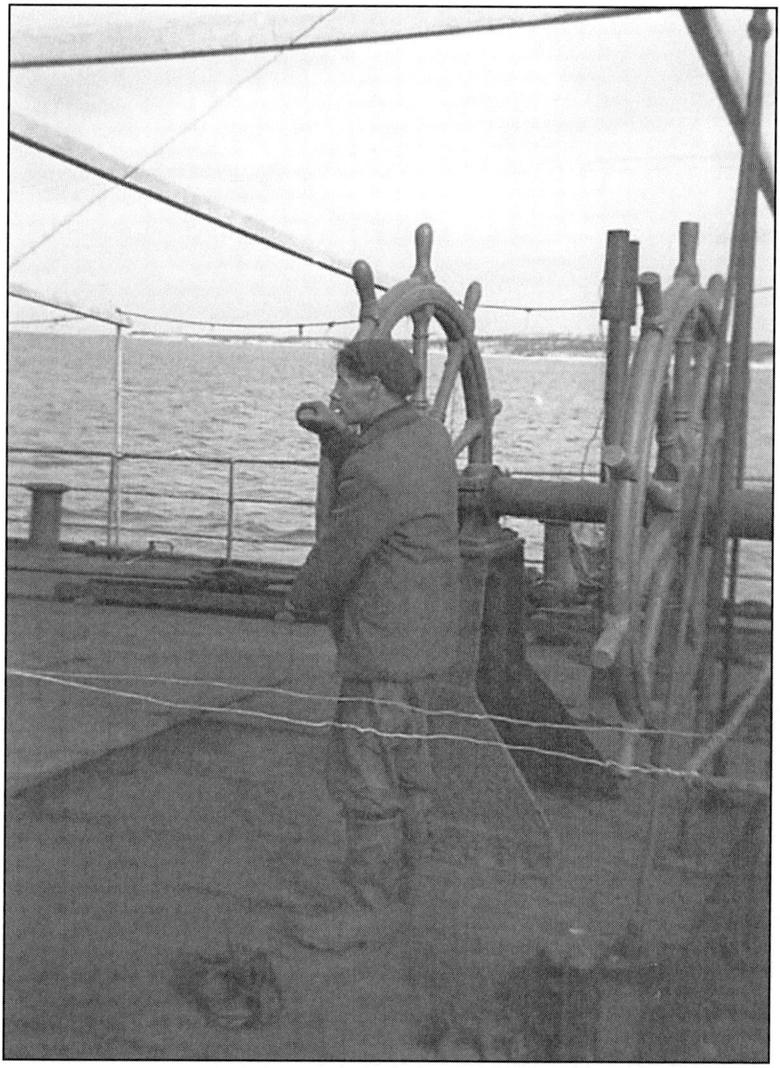

***Paddy Coffey.***

On one return trip to Liverpool in the 1930's the ships engine stalled and cut out. It was late at night with a full moon and a starry sky. The captain sent up distress flares but nobody responded to their call for assistance. Paddy Coffey set up two cloth sails and using the stars as his compass points he successfully guided the ship into a safe port. One Liverpool newspaper heard of the story and put it into print.

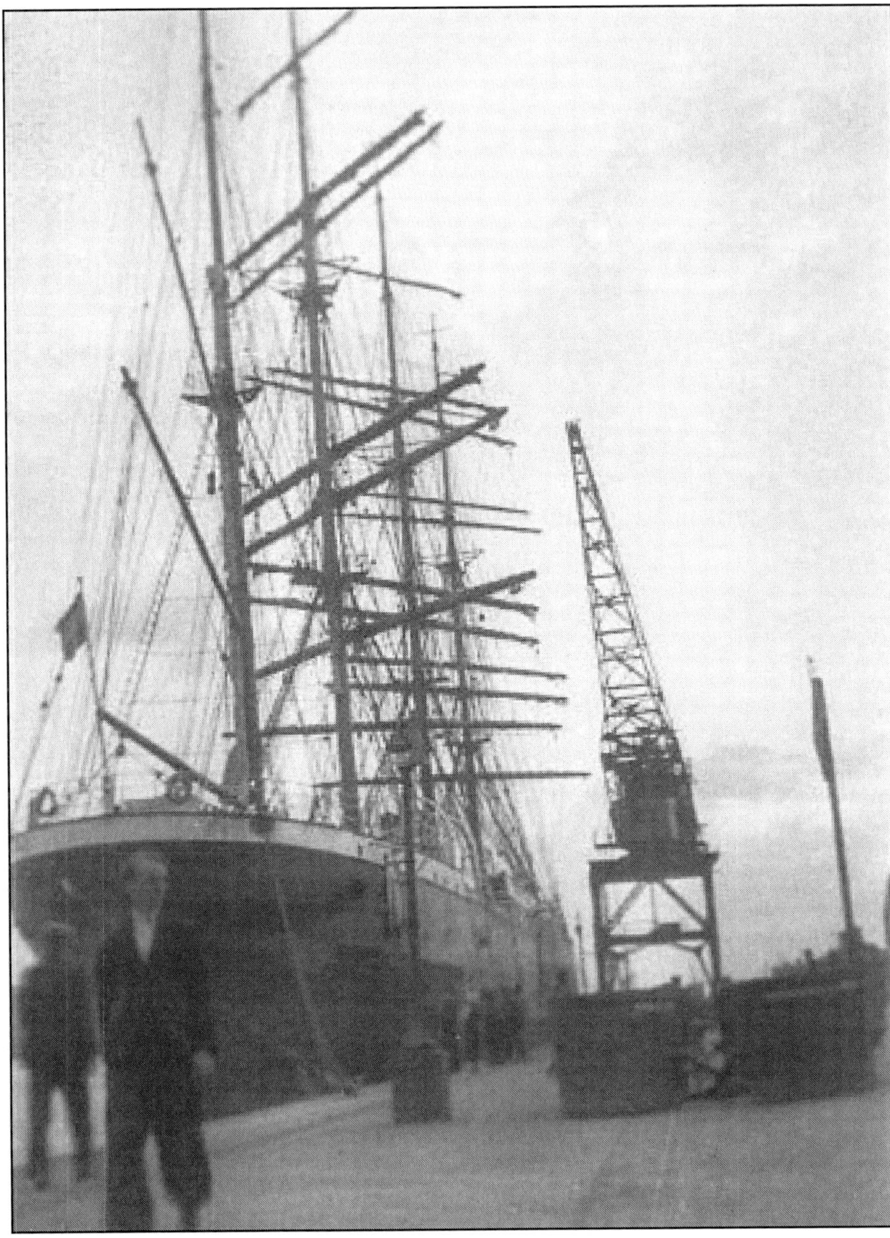

***The Pamir, City Quay, Dublin 1930's.***

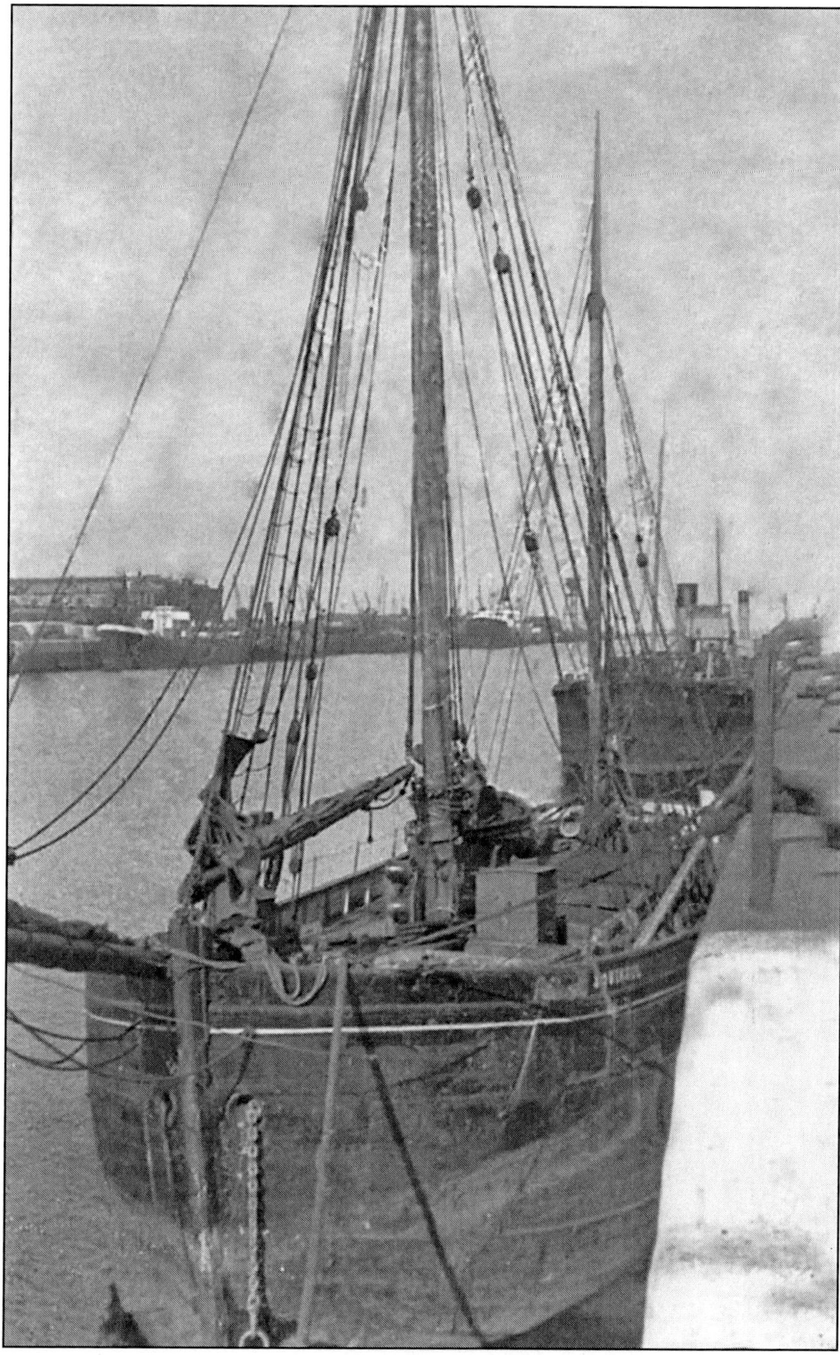

***The Squirrel.***

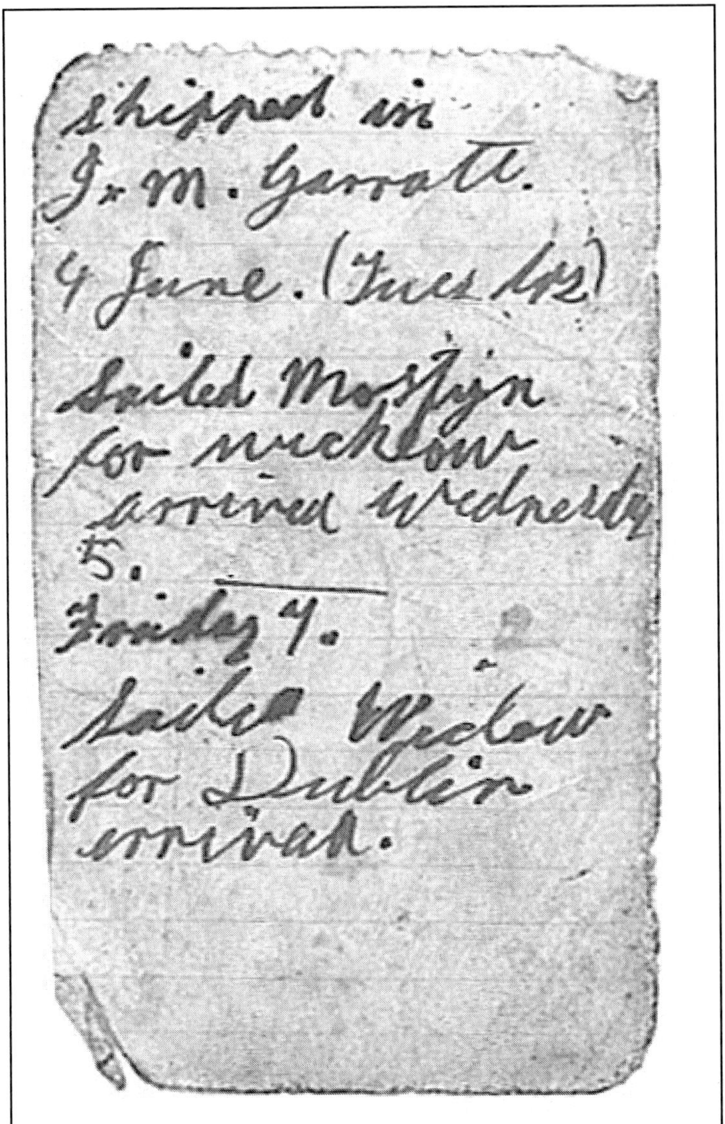
Shipped in
J & M. Garratt.
4 June. (Tues [illegible])
Sailed Mostyn
for Wicklow
arrived Wednesday
5.
Friday 7.
Sailed Wiclow
for Dublin
arrival.

A small notebook was discovered belonging to Paddy Coffey in which he wrote down short notes relating to his various seafaring journeys in 1940. On this page he writes:

1) *'Shipped in J&M Garrett, 4$^{th}$ June (Tues Sailed Mostyn for Wicklow arrived Wednesday 5$^{th}$.*
2) *'Friday 7$^{th...}$ Sailed Wicklow for Dublin...arrived.*

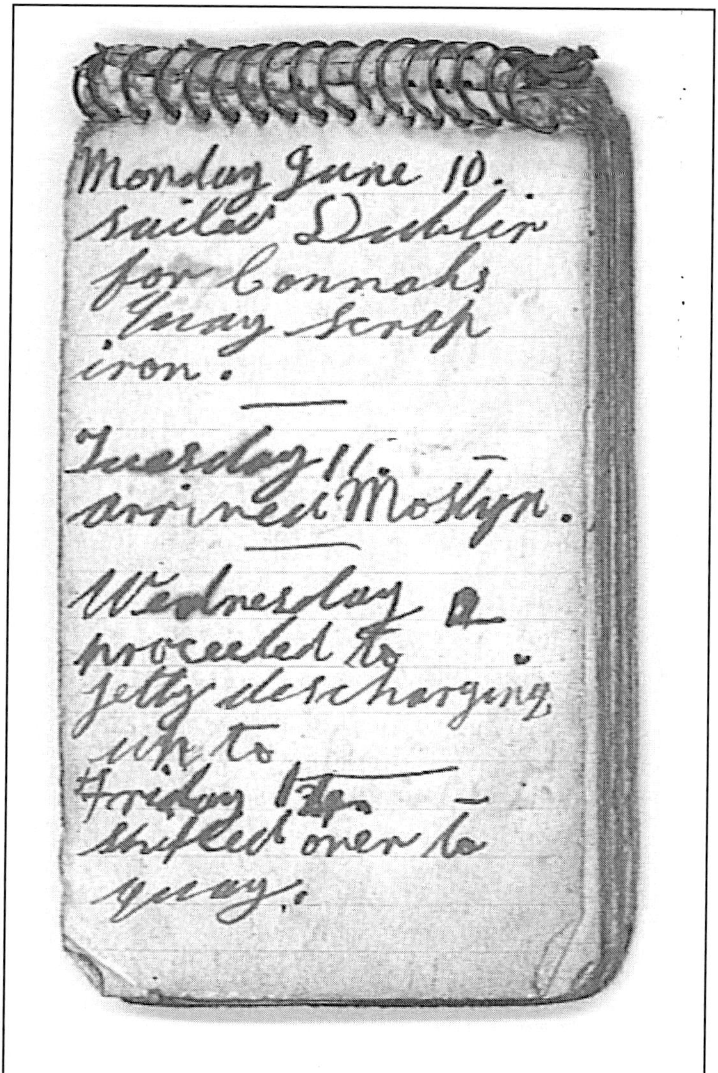


1) ***Monday June 10th…sailed Dublin for Connah's Quay…scrap iron.***
2) ***Tuesday 11th arrived Mostyn.***
3) ***Wednesday 12th proceeded to jetty discharging u0p to …***
4) ***Friday 13th Shipped over to quay.***

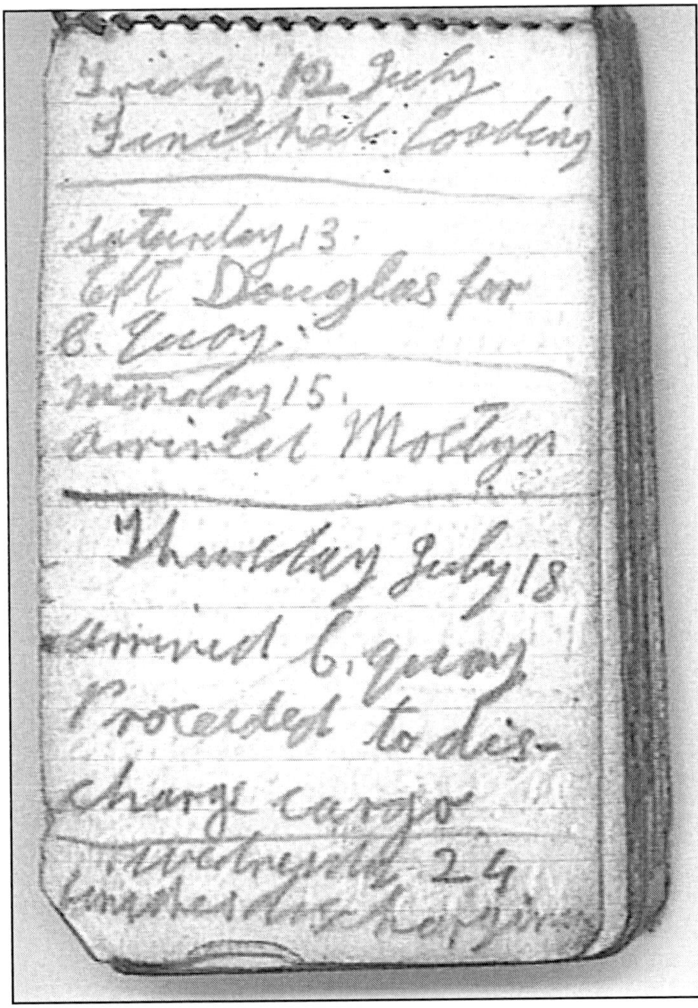
Friday 12 July
Finished loading
Saturday 13.
Left Douglas for
C. Quay.
Monday 15.
Arrived Mostyn
Thursday July 18
Arrived C. Quay
Proceeded to dis-
charge cargo
Wednesday 24
Finished discharging

1) ***Friday 12th July…Finished loading***
2) ***Saturday 13th…Left Douglas for C. Quay.***
3) ***Monday 15th…Arrived Mostyn.***
4) ***Thursday July 18th…Arrived C. Quay. Proceeded to discharge cargo.***
5) ***Wednesday 24th…Finished discharging.***

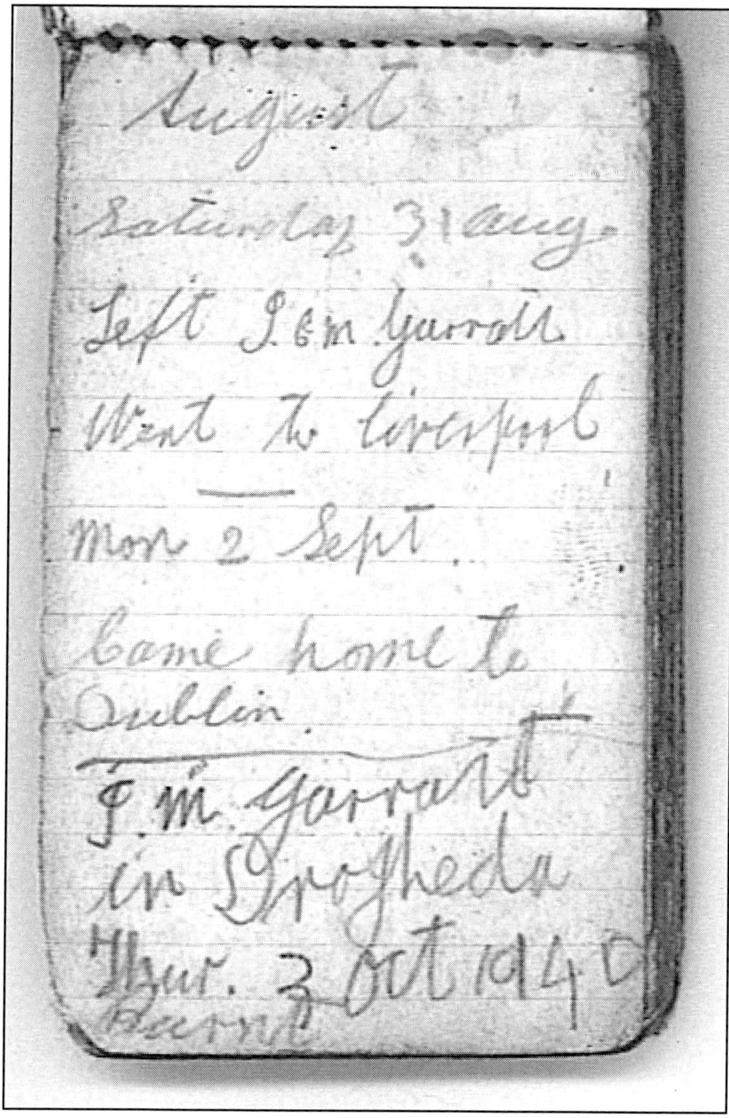


***August***

1) ***Saturday 31st…Left J&M Garrett. Went to Liverpool.***
2) ***Monday 2nd Sept…Came home to Dublin.***
3) ***J&M Garrett in Drogheda, Thursday 3rd October 1940…Burnt.***

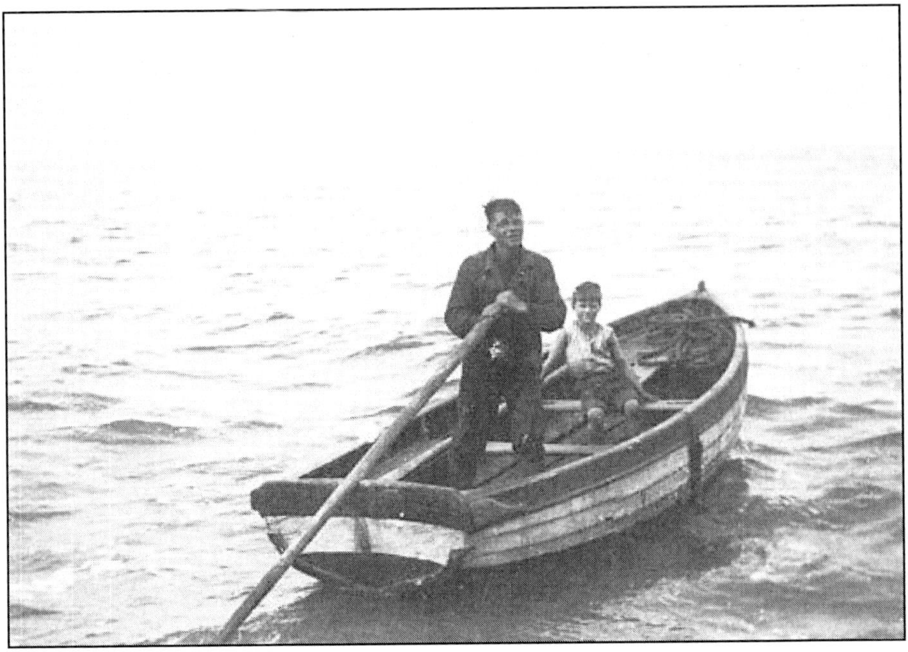

***Two young boys.***

Paddy Coffey gives us no names or any indication as to who these young boys may be. The younger of these two boys looks to be no more than maybe ten or twelve years old. He appears to be quite relaxed and at home on the water, almost an already seasoned young mariner. Perhaps his father is one of the adult crew on board the ship. It was not unusual for young boys to run away from home and head off on some ship or other. Paddy Coffey left home at a relatively young age because of his stepmother. It was a common sight back then to see young boys helping out on the dockside loading and unloading goods onto some horse and cart to earn themselves some money.

*'I remember me father used to work down on the docks. But sometimes he wouldn't have any work down there and he'd still be expected to go down and stand around just in case. I can remember my Auntie Mary used to be working down the Quay and she'd often bring me down and she'd have something for my father, maybe a bowl of Stew or a bowl of Coddle, you know and if you didn't have that you'd have a big can full of tea and a few cuts of Bread and Butter, well Bread and Marge. We'd go down there and maybe she'd be able to give him the price of a pint. I remember my mother saying that the night before he died he had been six weeks idle and eh they*

*went for a ramble down around Talbot Street and he was looking at the things in Guiney's and he was saying "Now there's warm underwear, now when I get the work I can come and throw a few bob off them". I think it was Gorman's or O'Gorman's used to be across the road, another shop where you could go in and throw a few bob off the clothes. He was pointing out what he would get for the winter for us. Six weeks he was idle. My mother said it was the dust from the wheat that killed him, he had a weak chest you see'.*

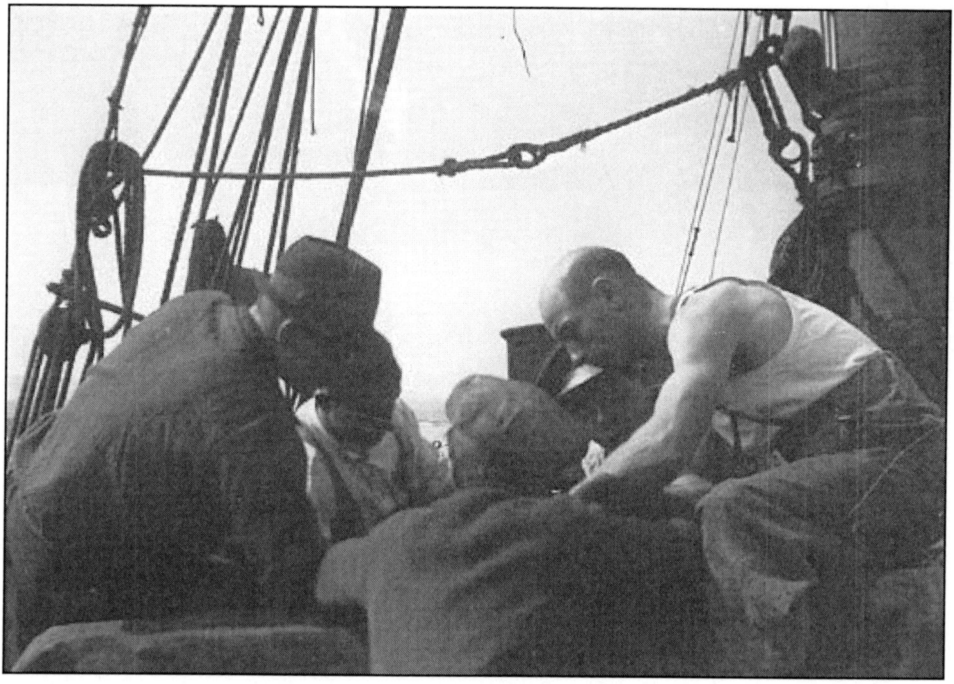

***Some of the crew enjoying a game of cards.***

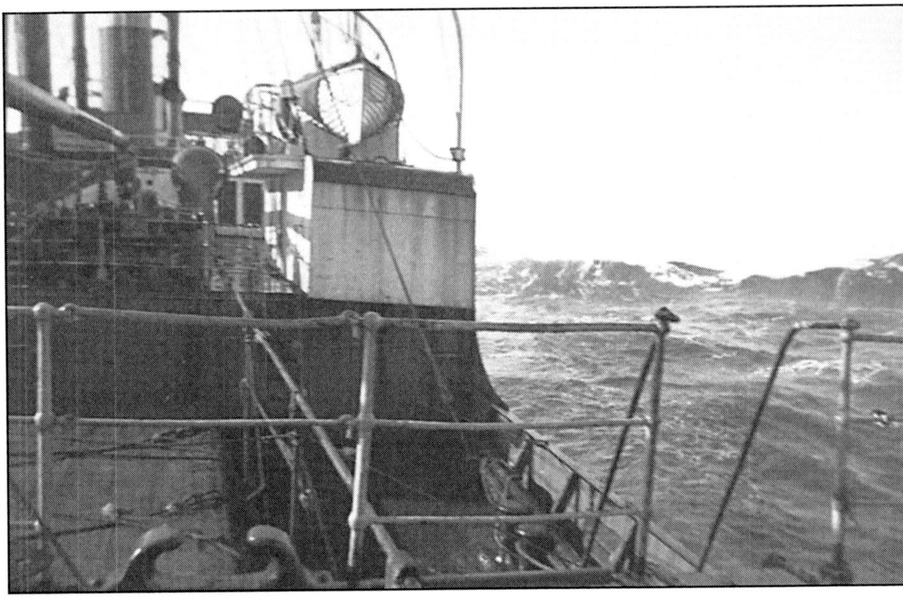

***In the eye of the storm.***

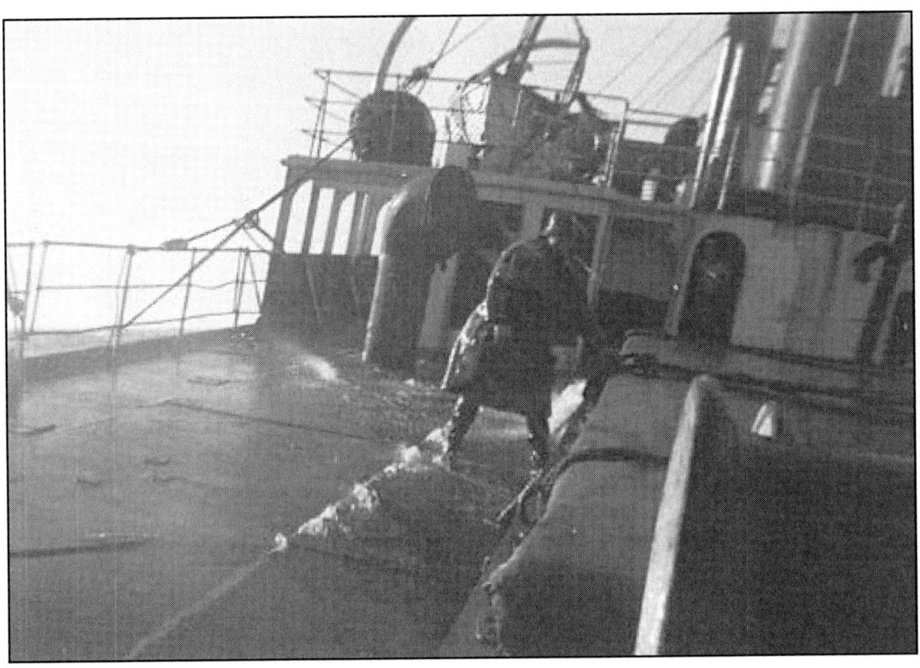

***Out on deck taking a photograph.***

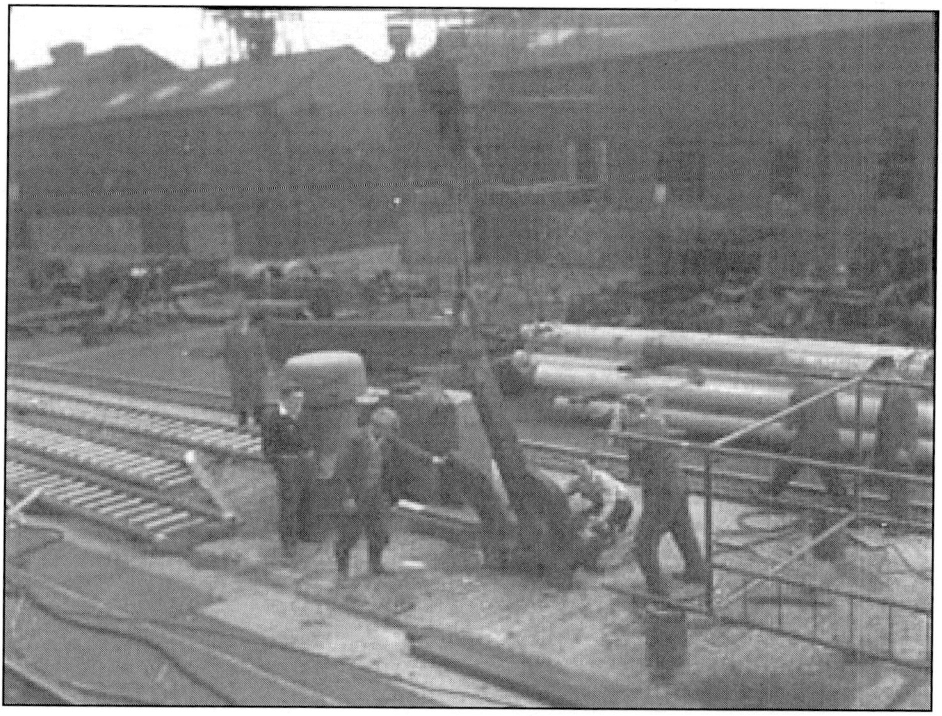

***Striking the Anchor.***

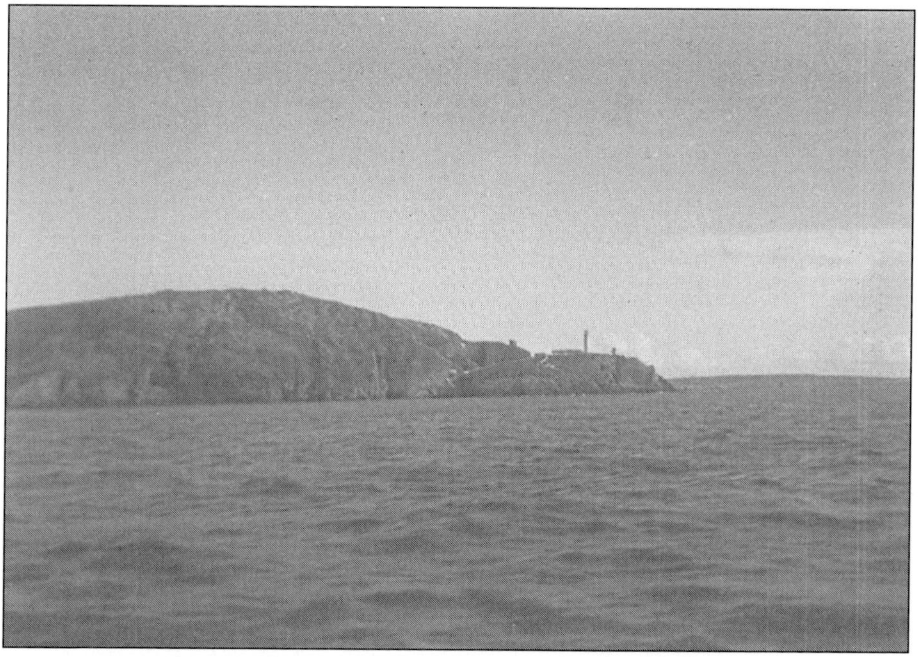

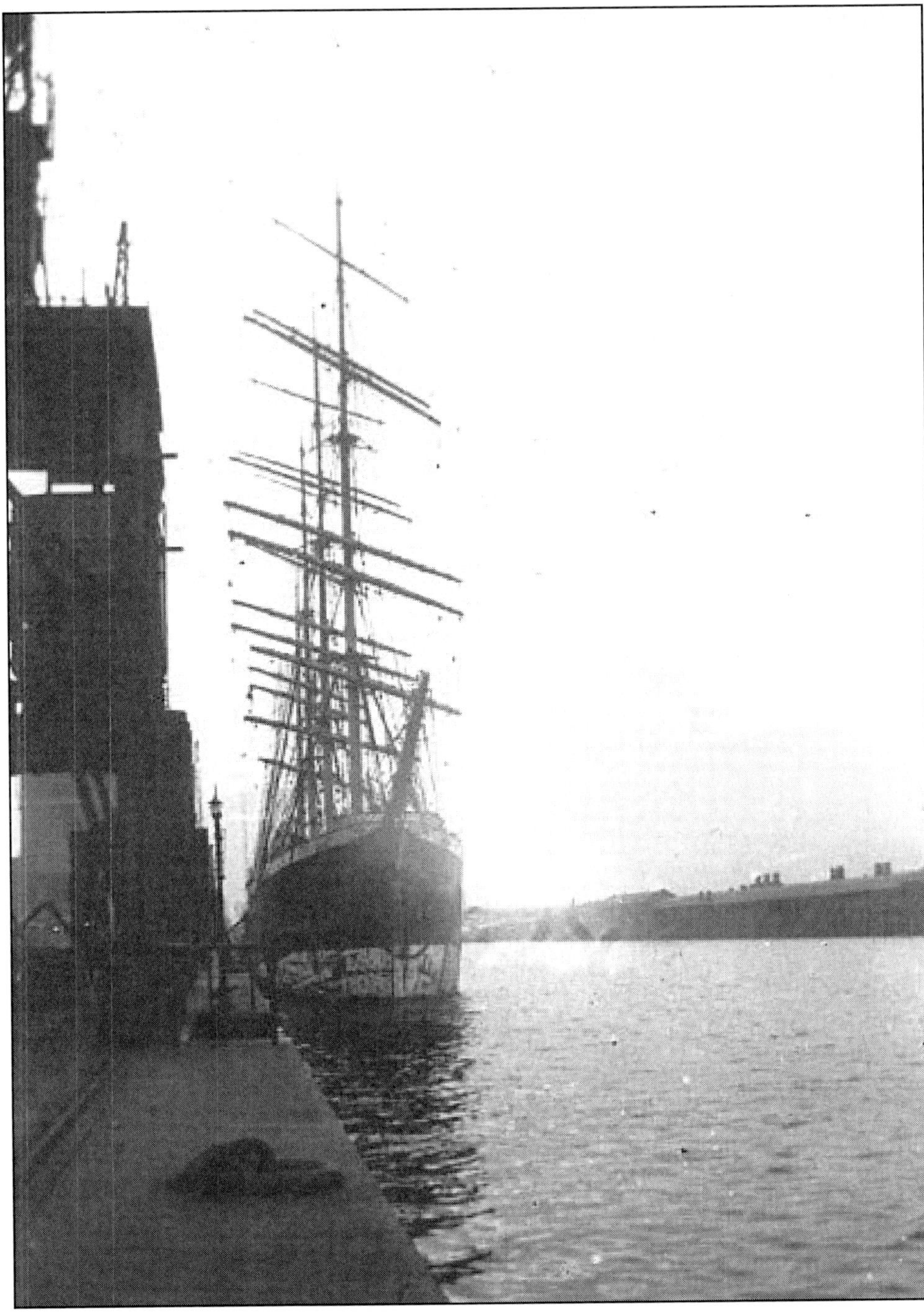

***Sunset on City Quay with the Pamir.***

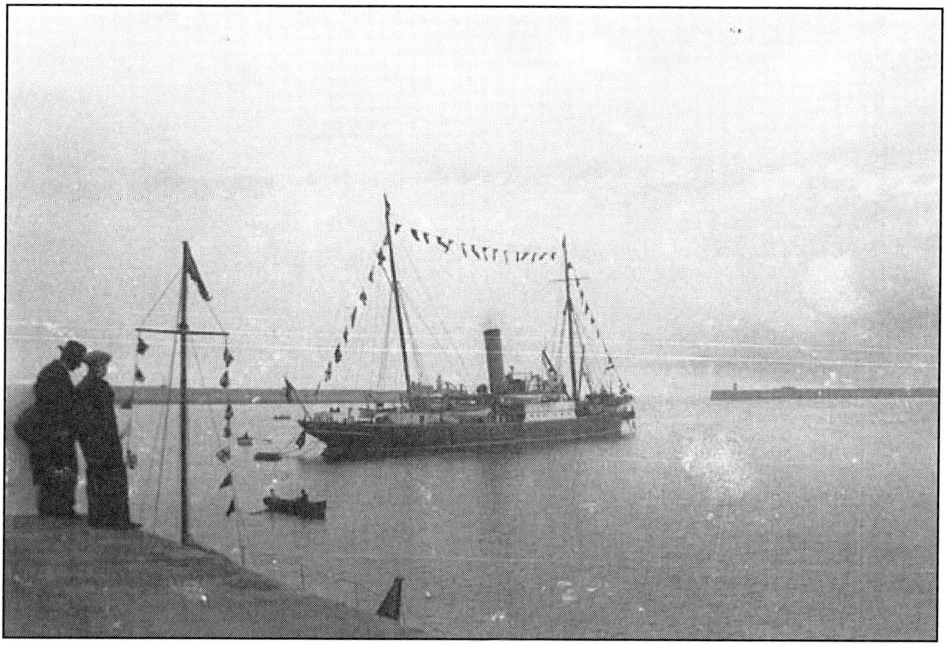

***Dropped Anchor.***

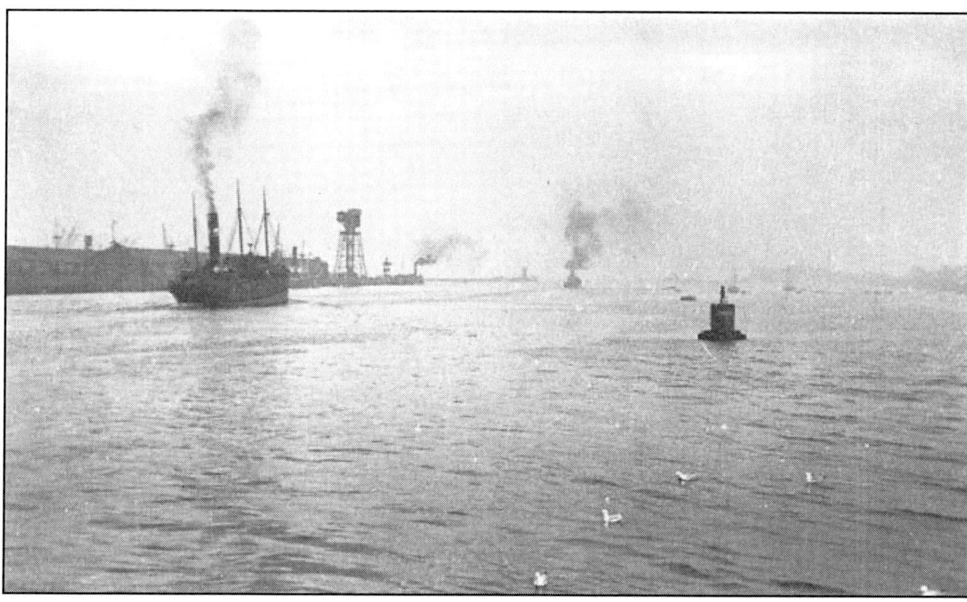

***Steaming into Port.***

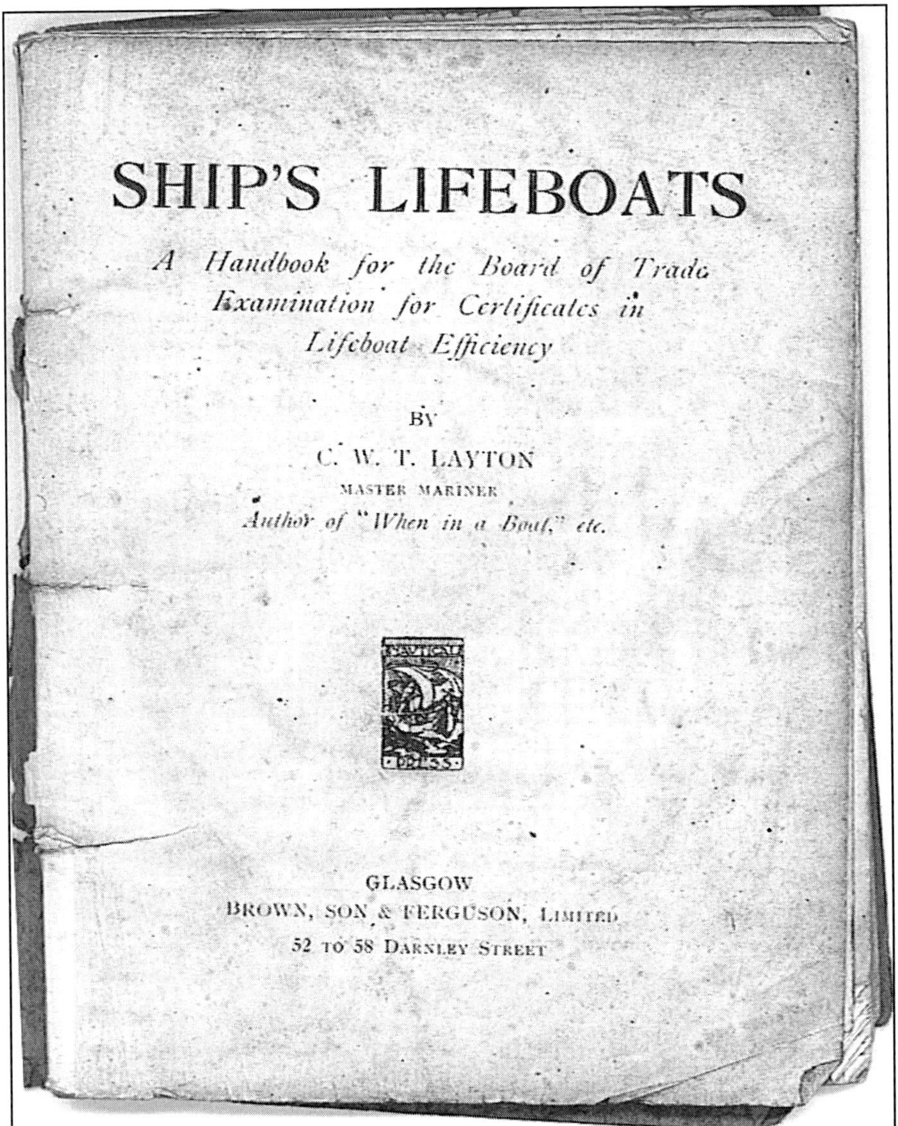


***One of the examinations that Paddy Coffey had to take In order to qualify as an Able Bodied Seaman was the Ship's Lifeboat Certificate Examination. This required a thorough knowledge of the correct procedure to be taken in the event of the crew being ordered to lower a Lifeboat into the water and to know how to handle the boat once that procedure was carried out.***

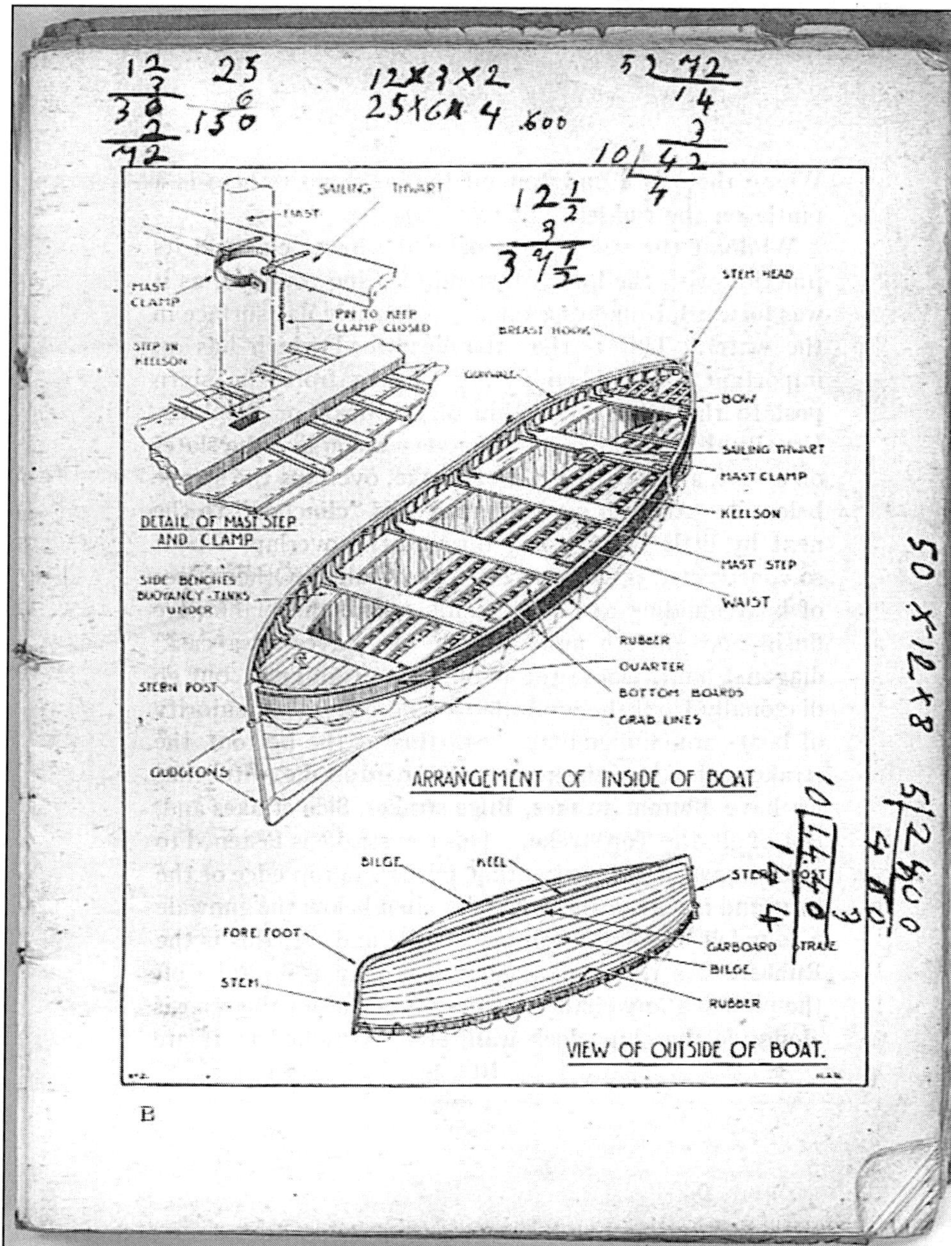


***The correct layout of a Lifeboat.***

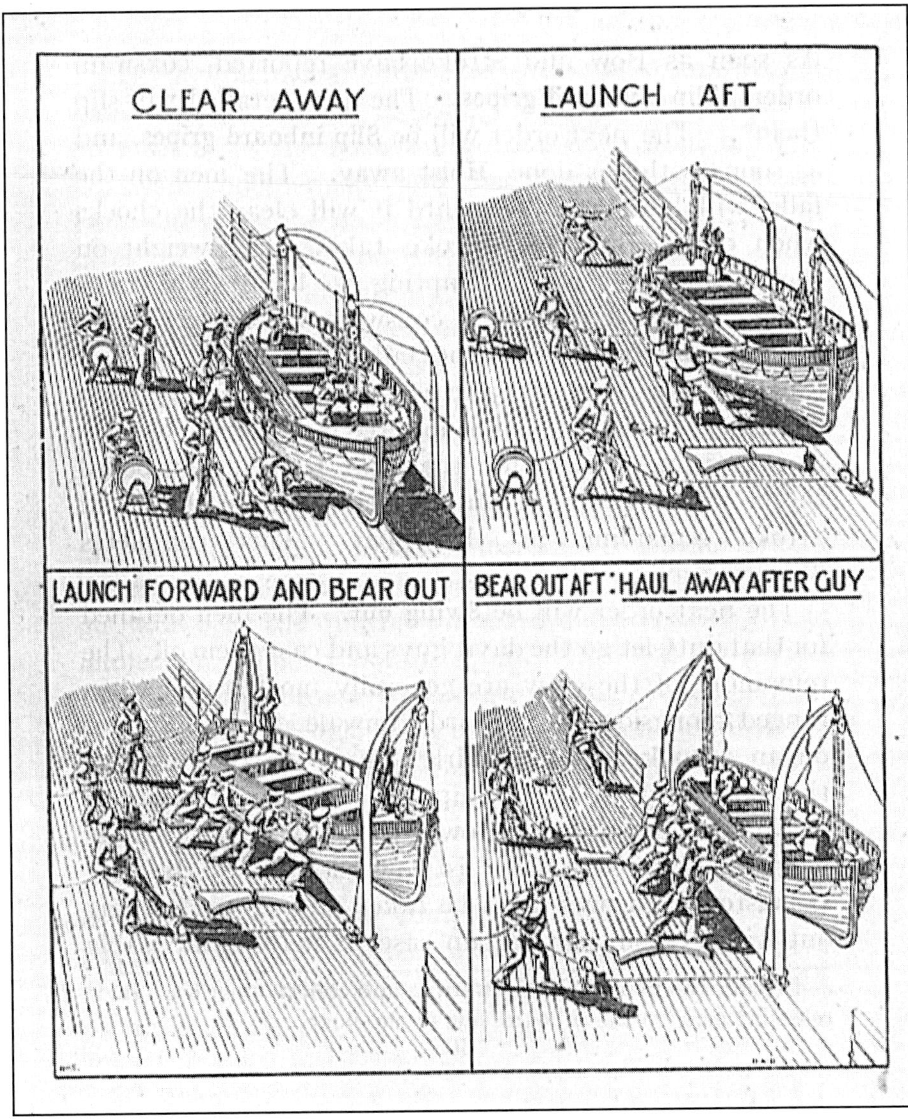


***The correct procedure for launching a Lifeboat.***

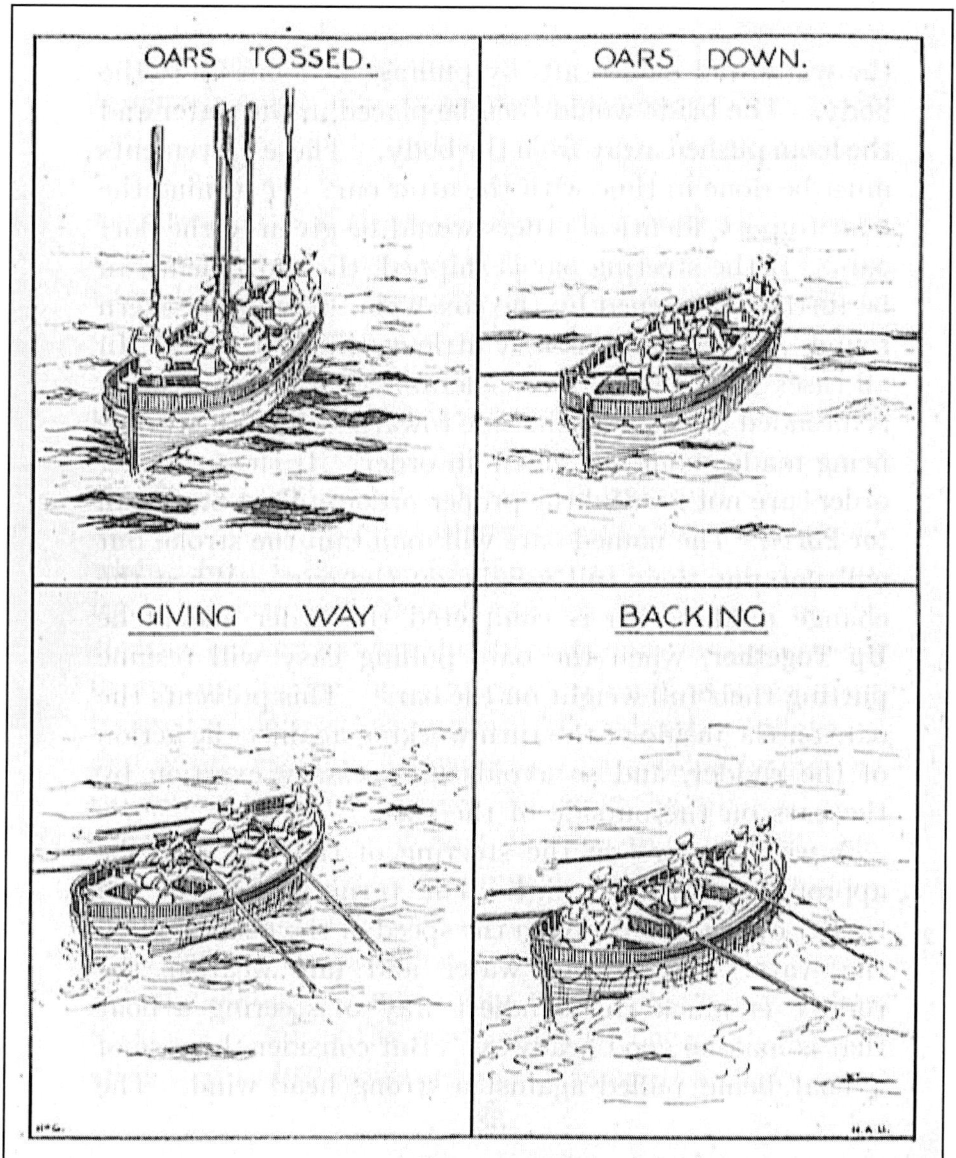


*Correct use of the oars.*

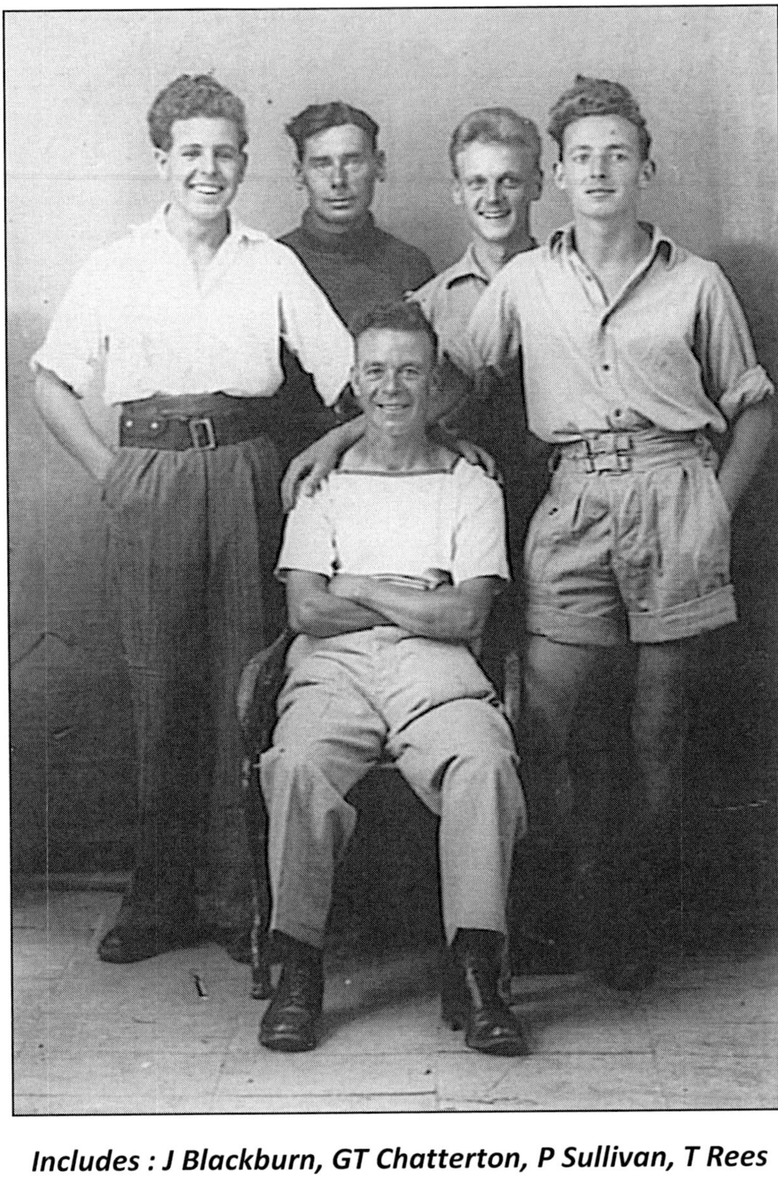

***Includes : J Blackburn, GT Chatterton, P Sullivan, T Rees and Paddy Coffey standing at the back.***

In 1944 Paddy Coffey sailed with these lads on the Saint Vincent. They carried coal from the north of England to the Cape Verde Islands that are situated off the west coast of Africa. The coal was stored on the island as part of an emergency supply for British Warships during WWII.

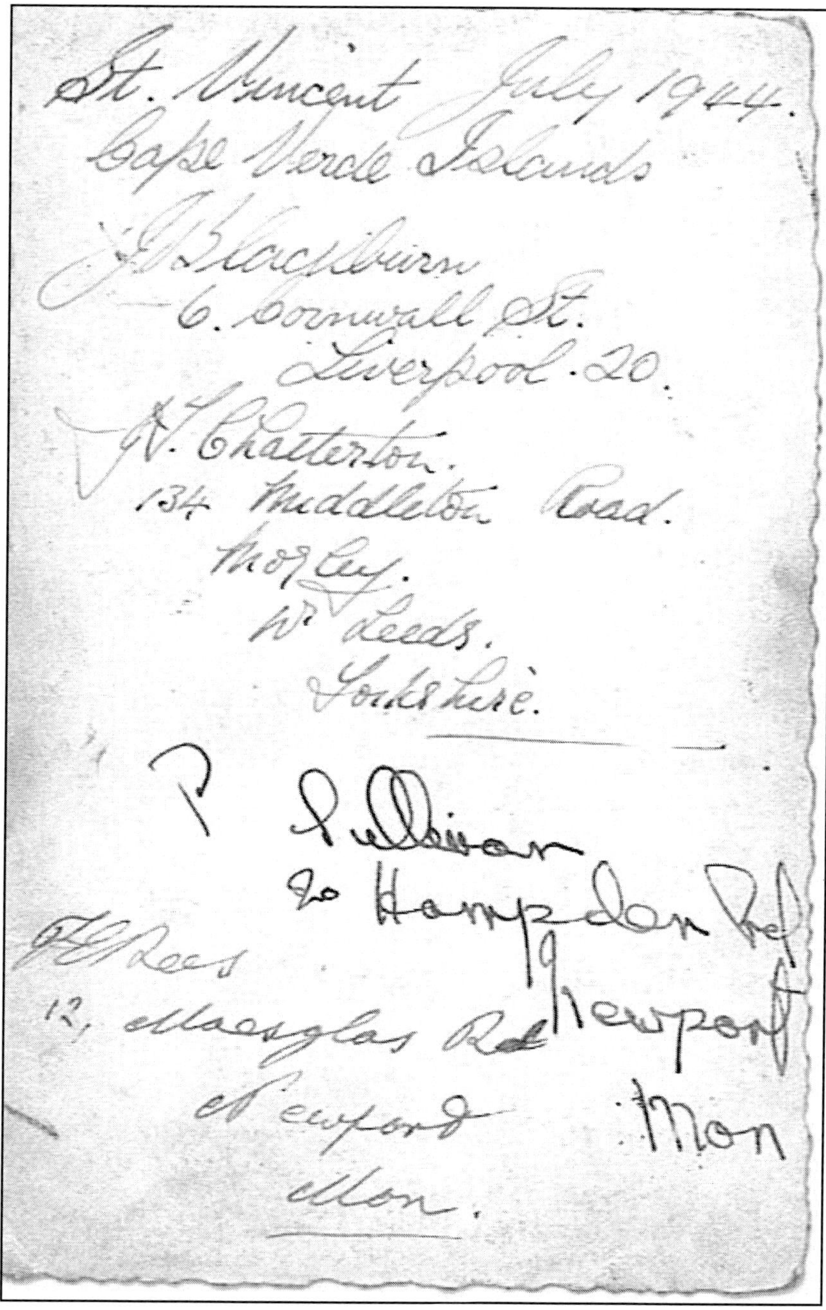

St. Vincent July 1944.
Cape Verde Islands
J. Blackburn
6. Cornwall St.
Liverpool. 20.
A. Chatterton.
134 Middleton Road.
Morley.
Nr Leeds.
Yorkshire.
P. Sullivan
20 Hampden Rd
Newport
Mon
F. G. Rees
12, Maesglas Rd
Newport
Mon.

***Names on the back of the photograph.***

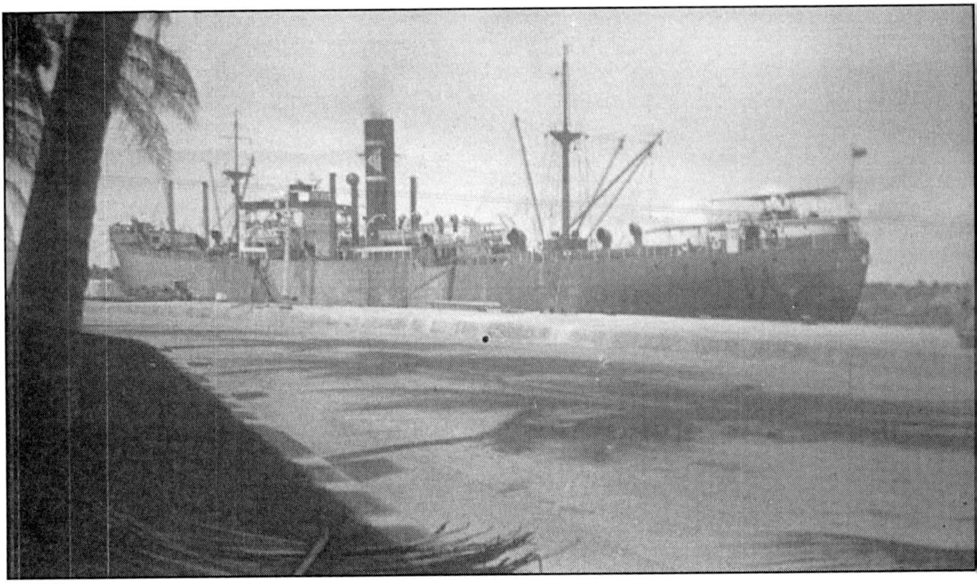

***The Saint Vincent in Cape Verde 1944.***

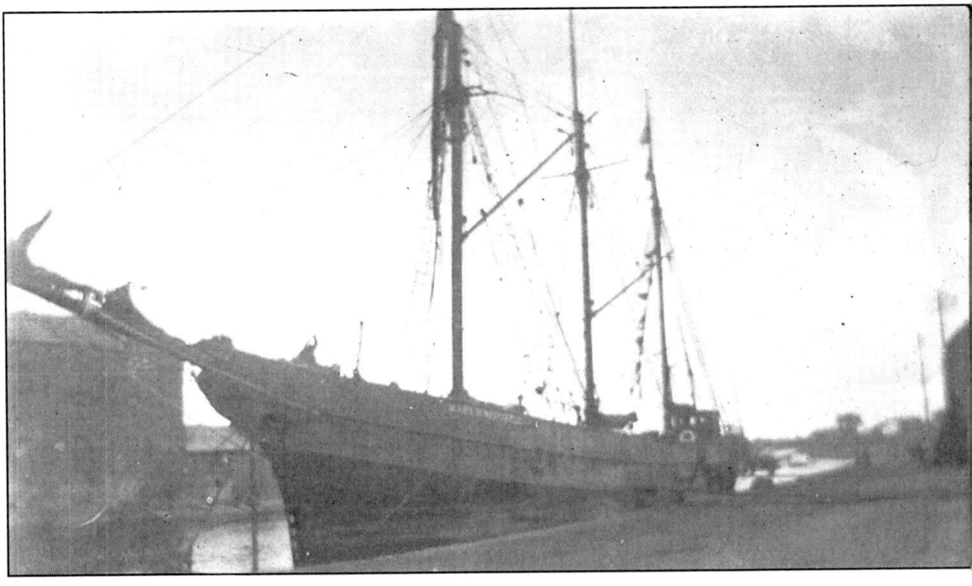

***The Mary B. Mitchell?***

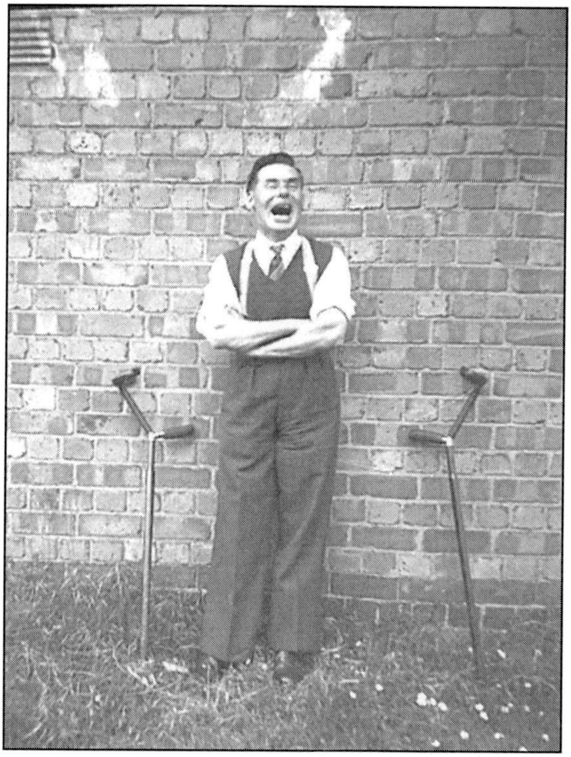

***Paddy Coffey.***

Paddy Coffey was shipwrecked on at least three occasions. During WWII while his ship was sailing into the English Channel it was struck by a torpedo from a German U Boat. At the time of the hit Paddy was working up on deck and was thrown into the air from the impact. As he crash landed onto the deck a wave smashed up onto the ship and sent Paddy reeling along the deck. One of his legs became entangled in some of the ships equipment causing Paddy to break his hip. As he lay there in agony two of his shipmates came to his rescue. As their ship was going down the surviving crew lowered a lifeboat into the water. Paddy pleaded with one of his mates to go below deck and rescue his camera, which he did. Many other members of the crew were either killed in the explosion or washed overboard and their bodies were never recovered. Paddy spent several weeks as a patient in the Royal Hospital, Gloucester, England.

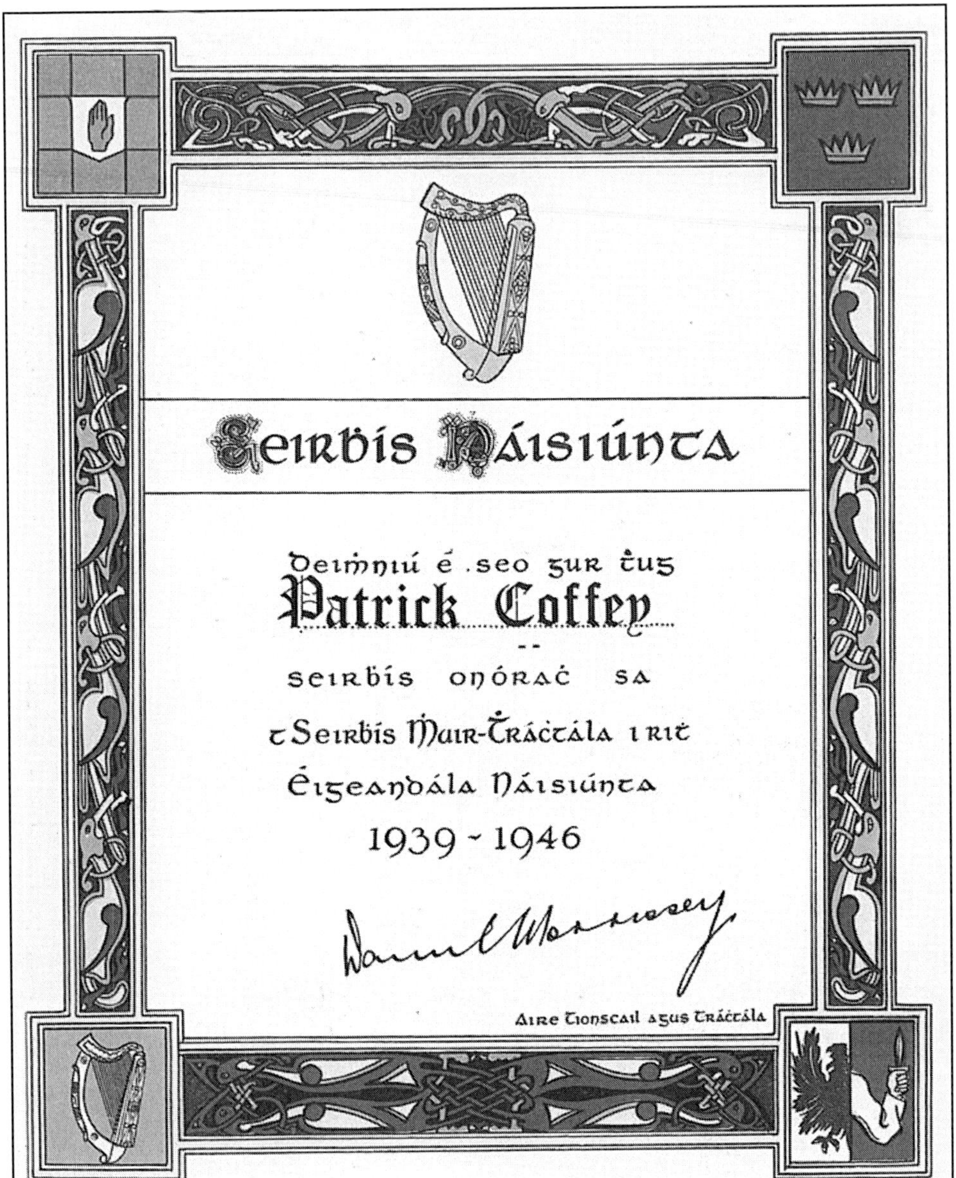

Seirḃís Náisiúnta

Deiṁniú é seo gur ṫug

Patrick Coffey

seirḃís onóraċ sa

tSeirḃís Ṁuir-Ṫráċtála i riṫ

Éigeandála Náisiúnta

1939 - 1946

Aire Tionscail agus Tráċtála

*National Service Certificate.*

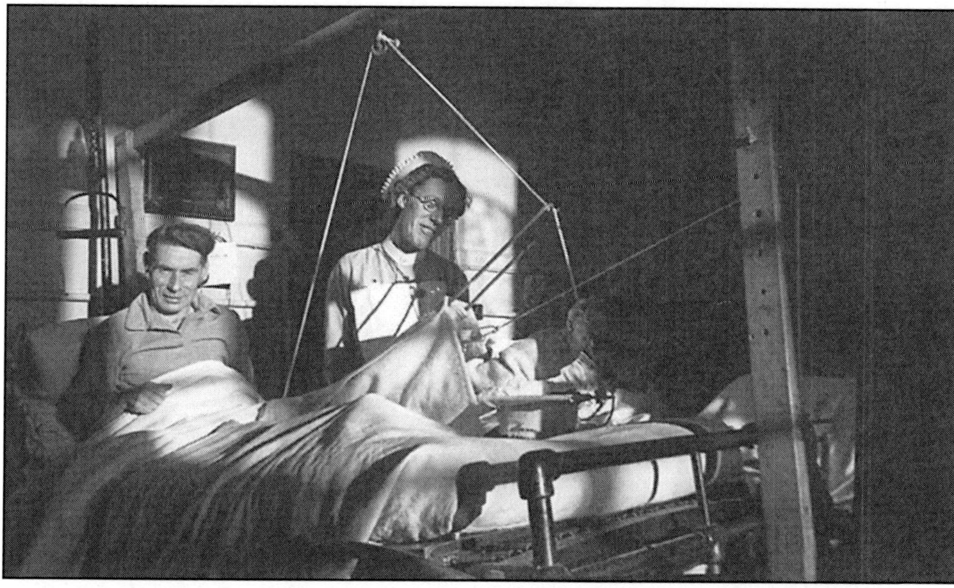

***Laid up in hospital with a pretty young nurse to look after him.***

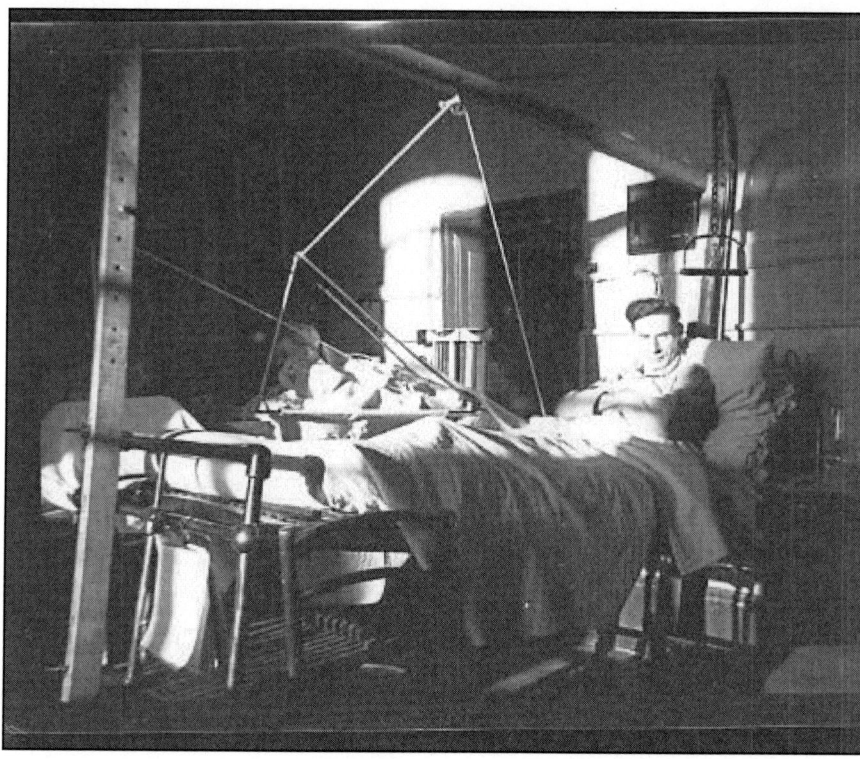

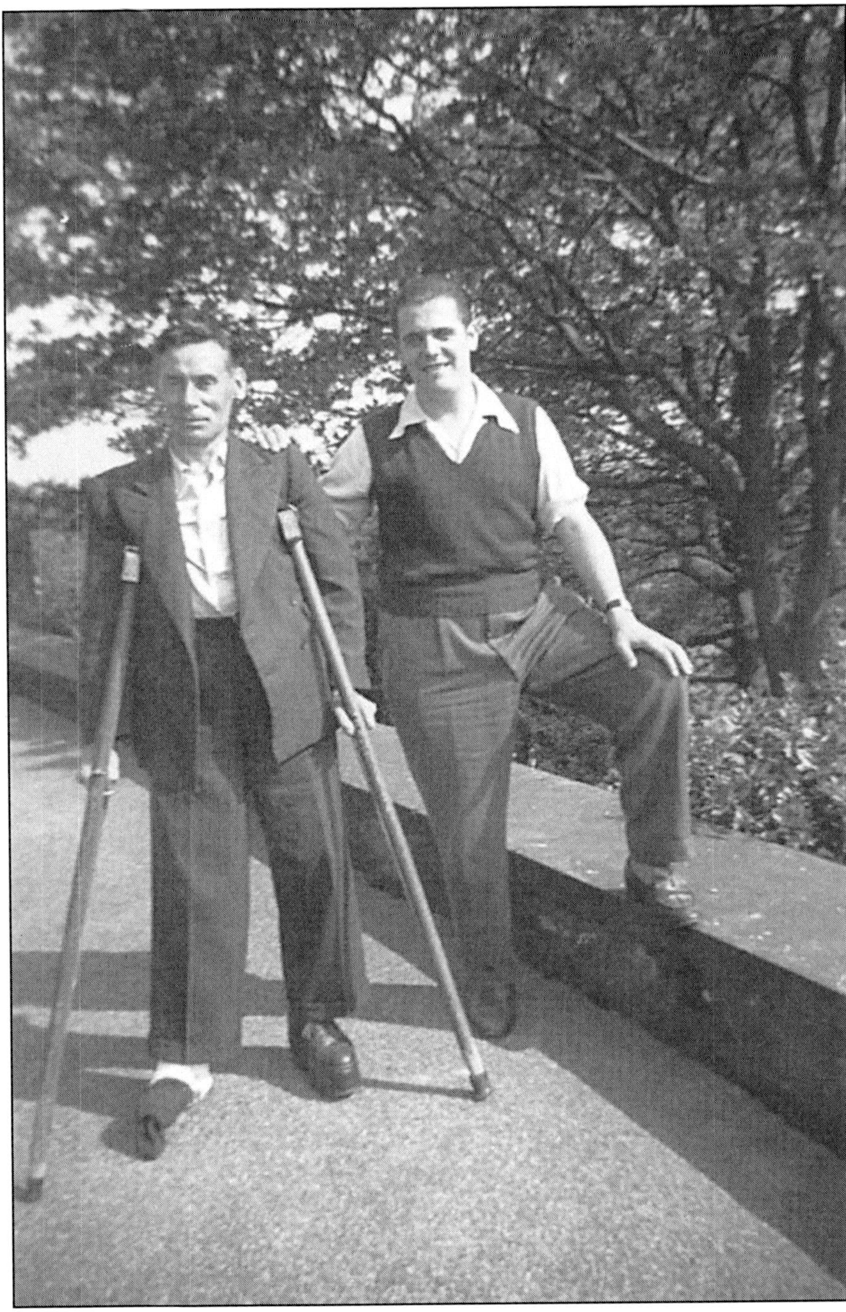

***Paddy Coffey on crutches posing with his friend.***

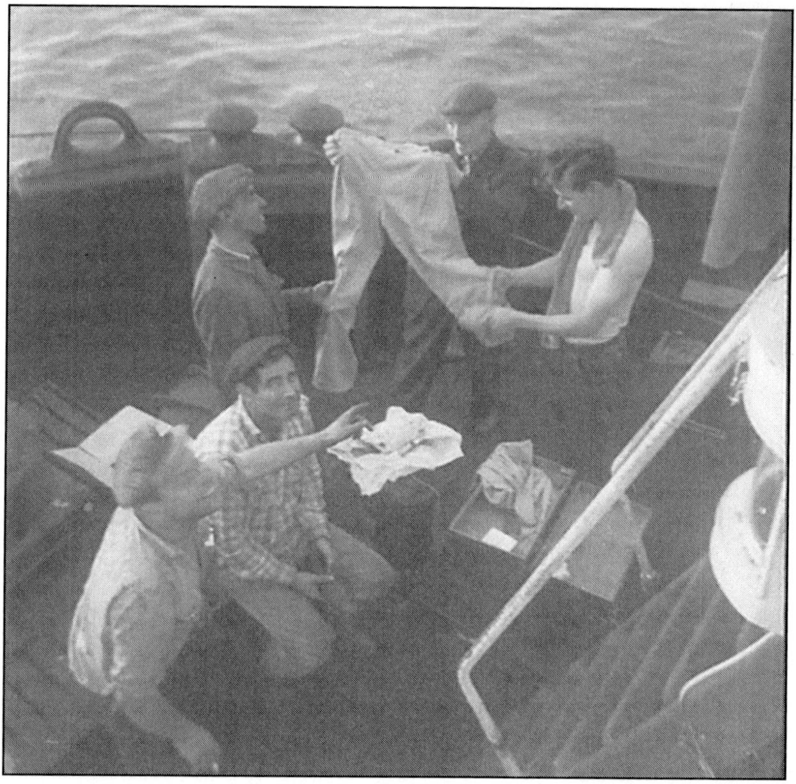

***Pirate's Booty.***

Paddy Coffey would often buy second-hand clothes from the street market in Cumberland Street and bring them away to sea with him. Sometimes he would share them out with his fellow shipmates. On most occasions he would take them on a trip to the African coast and exchange them with the natives for hand-made African craftwork. He brought home small elephants made from black ebony wood whose tusks were made from ivory.

Wherever he travelled to Paddy Coffey would always try and find a piece of local craftwork to bring home to Dublin and display it in the cabinet that he had in his bedroom in Sean McDermot Street. Each one of these pieces would then become the centrepiece of a story to be told to his young nieces and nephews when they came to visit him.

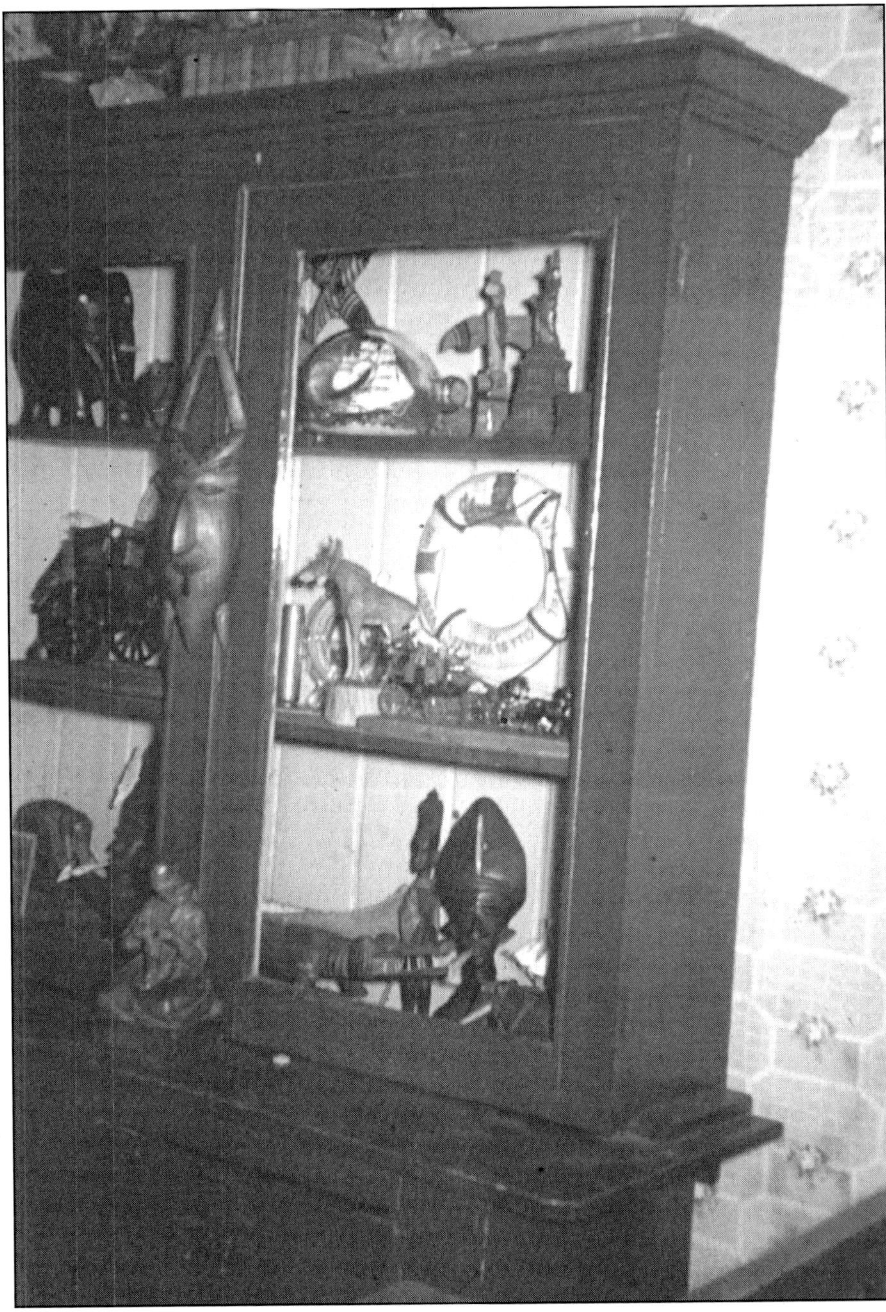

***An assortment of souvenirs brought home from his worldwide travels.***

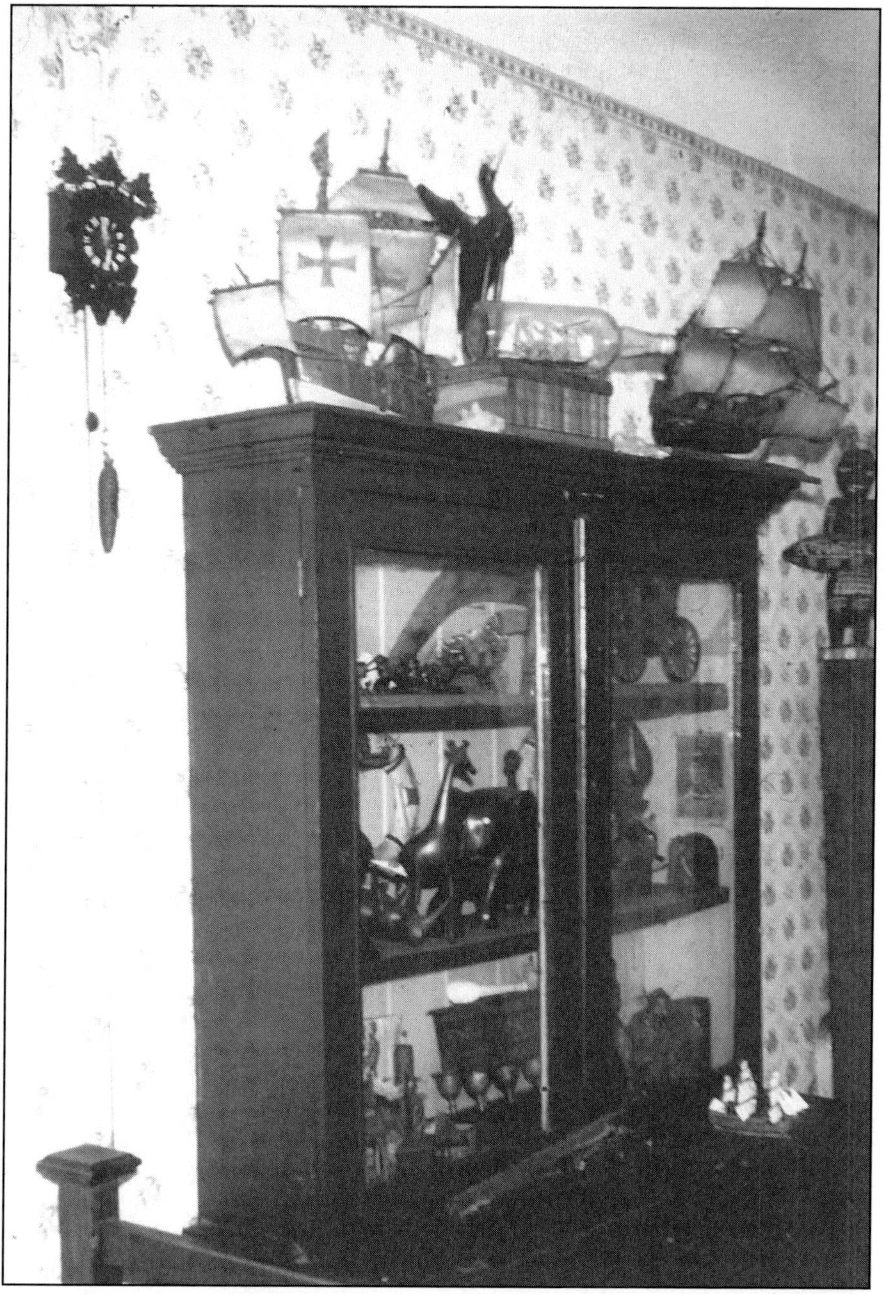

***Another view of the display cabinet in Paddy Coffey's bedroom.***

***(Note the ship in the bottle on top of the cabinet made by Paddy Coffey)***

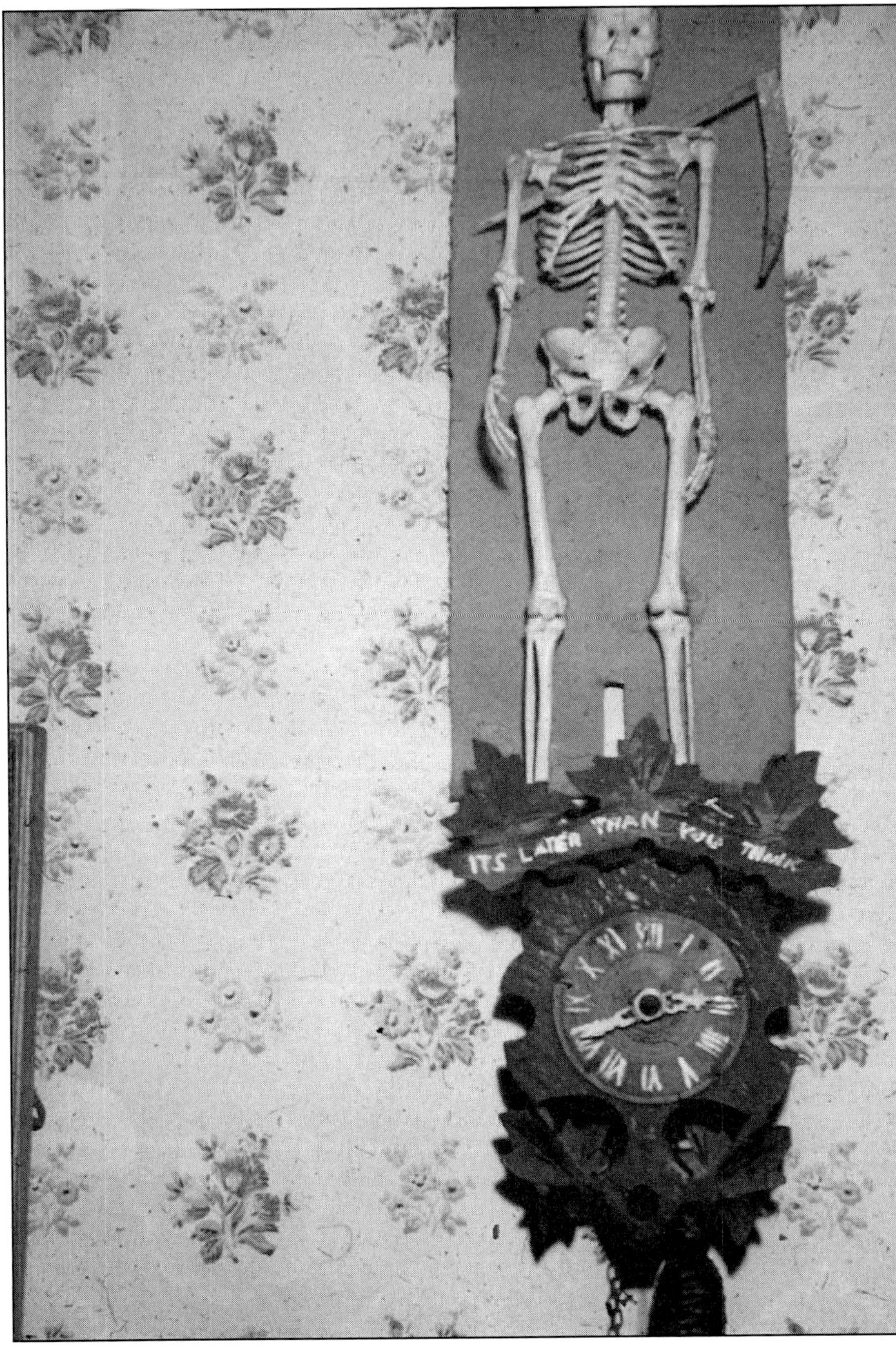


***'It's later than you think…'***

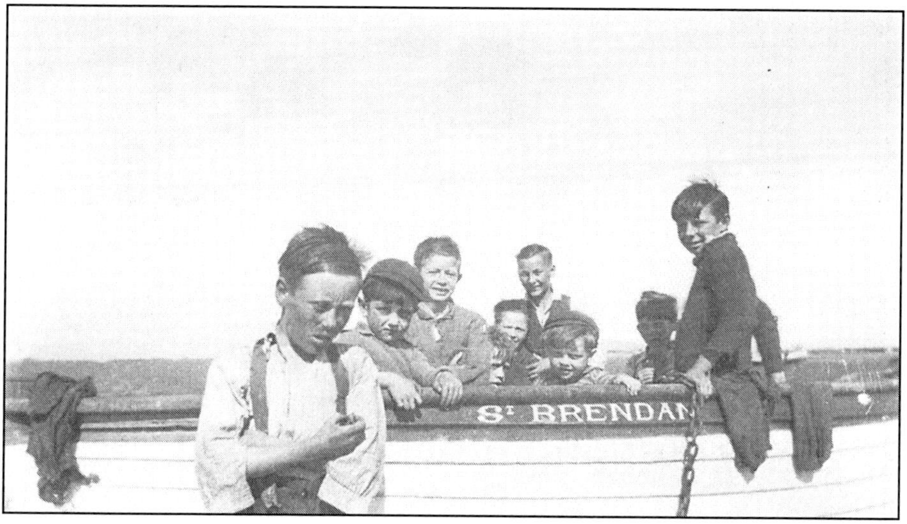


***A group of young boys from Dublin's North Inner City. The boy on the left with the cap is Blacker Doyle and the little boy with the cap in the centre is his brother Barney Doyle from Liberty House in Railway Street.***

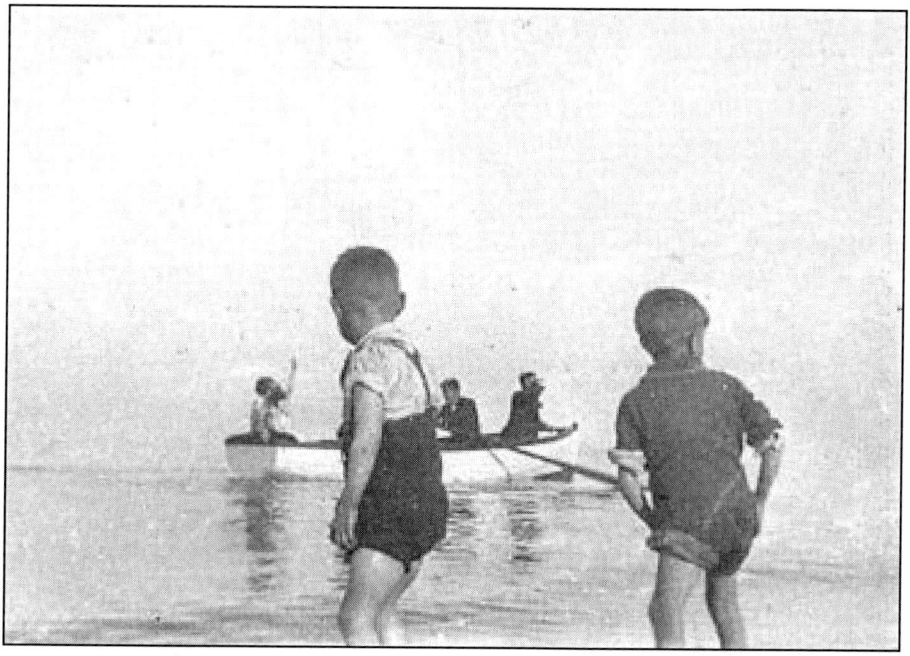

***Blacker Doyle on the right spending time in Bray.***

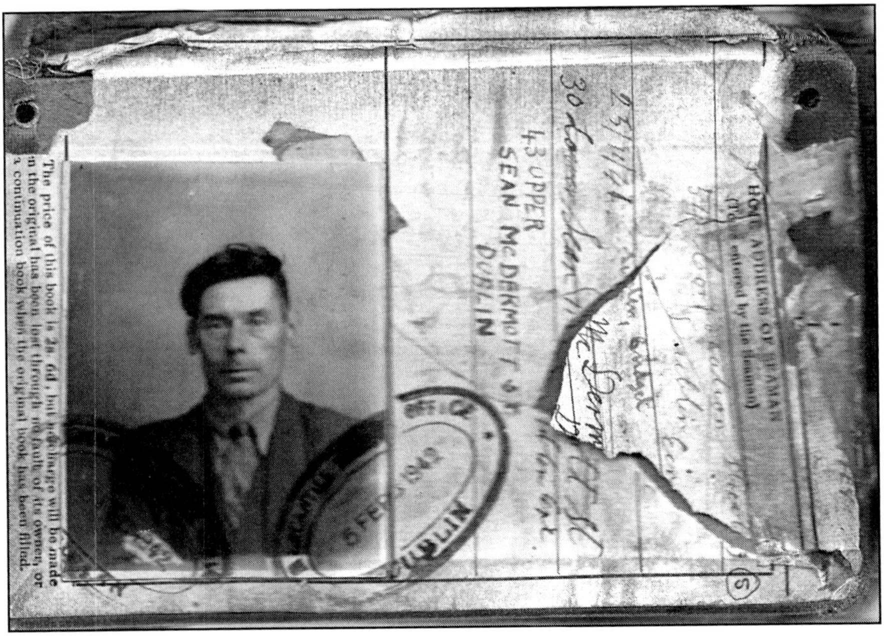


***Seaman's identity book 5th February 1942.***

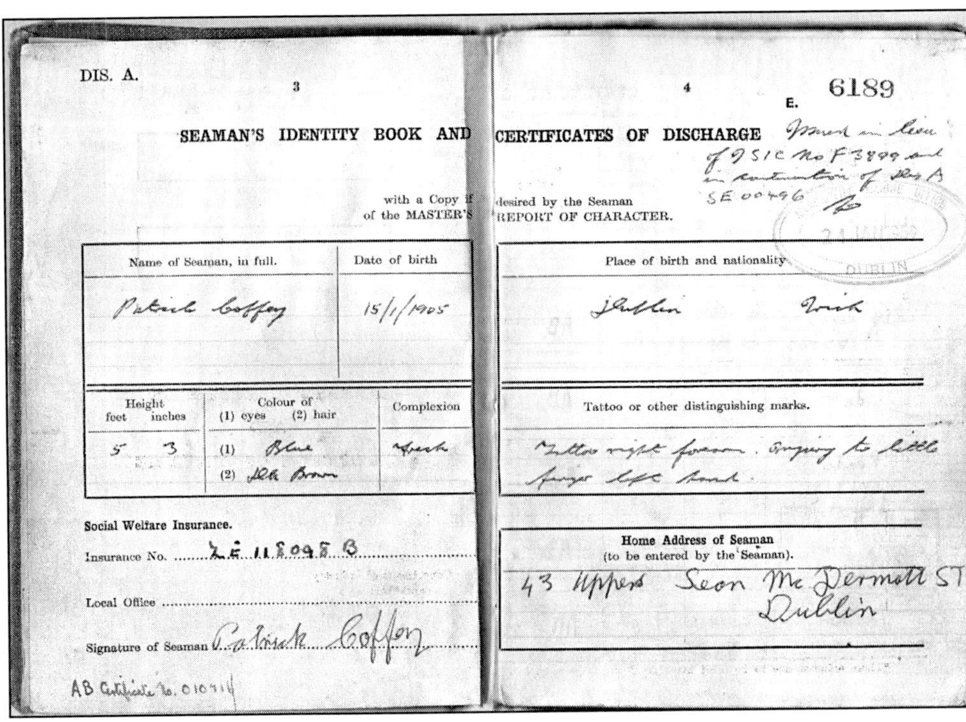

DIS. A. 3 4 E. 6189

SEAMAN'S IDENTITY BOOK AND CERTIFICATES OF DISCHARGE

Issued in lieu of DSIC No F 3899 and in continuation of Dis A SE 00496

with a Copy if desired by the Seaman of the MASTER'S REPORT OF CHARACTER.

| Name of Seaman, in full. | Date of birth | Place of birth and nationality |
|---|---|---|
| Patrick Coffey | 15/1/1905 | Dublin Irish |

| Height feet | Height inches | Colour of (1) eyes (2) hair | Complexion | Tattoo or other distinguishing marks. |
|---|---|---|---|---|
| 5 | 3 | (1) Blue (2) Dk Brown | Fresh | Tattoo right forearm. Injury to little finger left hand |

Social Welfare Insurance.

Insurance No. ZE 118098 B

Local Office

Signature of Seaman Patrick Coffey

AB Certificate No. 010914

Home Address of Seaman
(to be entered by the Seaman).

43 Upper Sean Mc Dermott ST
Dublin

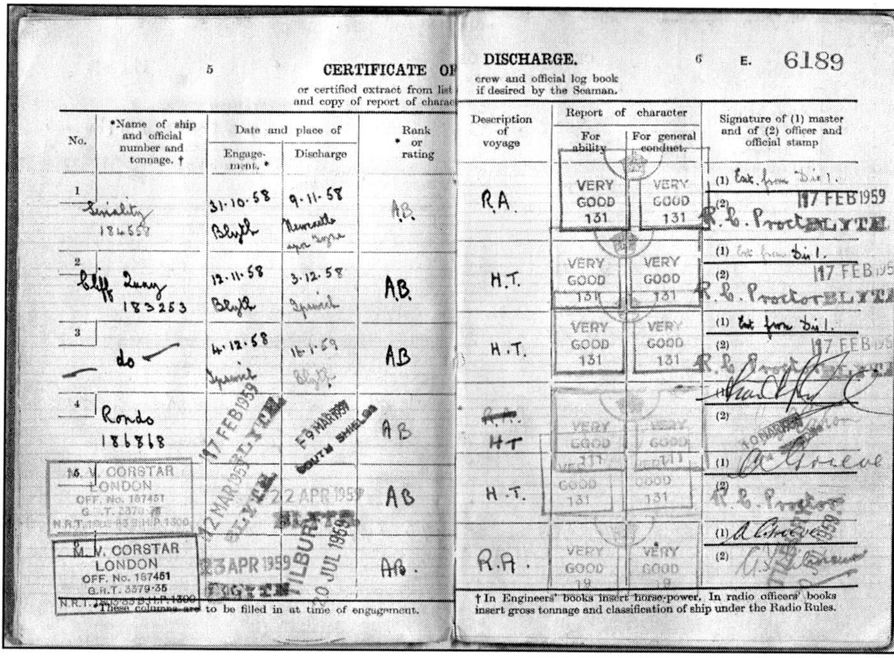

5 CERTIFICATE OF DISCHARGE. 6 E. 6189

or certified extract from list of crew and official log book and copy of report of character if desired by the Seaman.

| No. | *Name of ship and official number and tonnage. † | Date and place of Engagement. * | Date and place of Discharge | Rank * or rating | Description of voyage | Report of character For ability | Report of character For general conduct. | Signature of (1) master and of (2) officer and official stamp |
|---|---|---|---|---|---|---|---|---|
| 1 | Eniality 184557 | 31.10.58 Blyth | 9.11.58 Newcastle upon Tyne | AB | R.A. | VERY GOOD 131 | VERY GOOD 131 | (1) Ext. from Dis 1. (2) 17 FEB 1959 R. E. Proctor BLYTH |
| 2 | Cliff Quay 183253 | 12.11.58 Blyth | 3.12.58 Ipswich | AB | H.T. | VERY GOOD 131 | VERY GOOD 131 | (1) Ext. from Dis 1. (2) 17 FEB 1959 R. E. Proctor BLYTH |
| 3 | do | 4.12.58 Ipswich | 16.1.59 Blyth | AB | H.T. | VERY GOOD 131 | VERY GOOD 131 | (1) Ext. from Dis 1. (2) 17 FEB 1959 |
| 4 | Rondo 186868 | 17 FEB 1959 BLYTH | F9 MAR 1959 SOUTH SHIELDS | AB | H.T | VERY GOOD | VERY GOOD | (2) |
| 5 | M.V. CORSTAR LONDON OFF. No. 187451 | 12 MAR 1959 BLYTH | 22 APR 1959 BLYTH | AB | H.T. | VERY GOOD 131 | VERY GOOD 131 | (1) (2) R. E. Proctor |
| 6 | M.V. CORSTAR LONDON OFF. No. 187451 G.R.T. 3379·35 | 23 APR 1959 BLYTH | TILBURY 30 JUL 1959 | AB. | R.A. | VERY GOOD | VERY GOOD | (1) (2) |

*These columns are to be filled in at time of engagement.

† In Engineers' books insert horse-power. In radio officers' books insert gross tonnage and classification of ship under the Radio Rules.

*Certificates of discharge.*

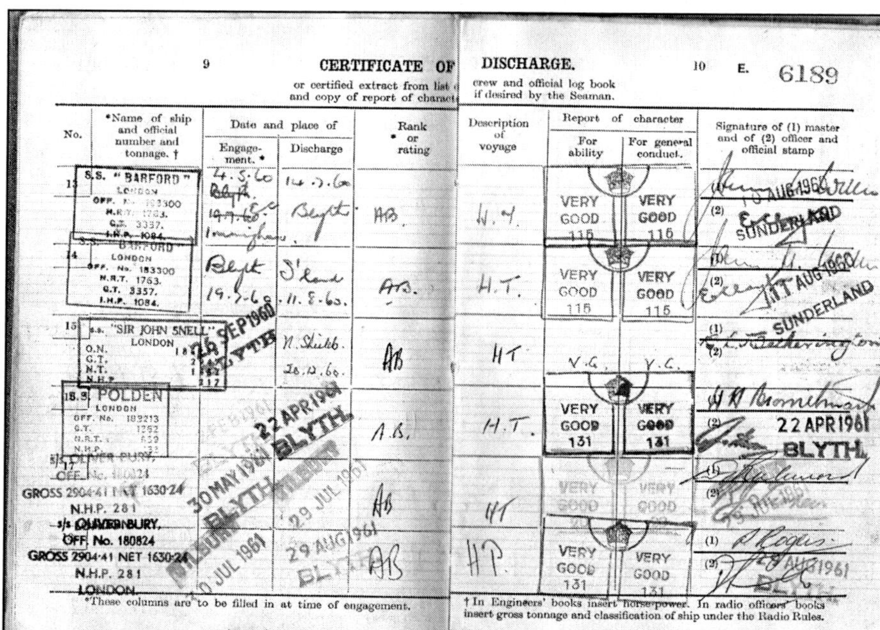

9 CERTIFICATE OF DISCHARGE. 10 E. 6189

or certified extract from list of crew and official log book and copy of report of character if desired by the Seaman.

| No. | *Name of ship and official number and tonnage. † | Date and place of Engagement. * | Date and place of Discharge | Rank * or rating | Description of voyage | Report of character For ability | Report of character For general conduct. | Signature of (1) master and of (2) officer and official stamp |
|---|---|---|---|---|---|---|---|---|
| 13 | S.S. "BARFORD" LONDON OFF. No. 183300 N.R.T. 1763. G.T. 3357. I.H.P. 1084. | 4.5.60 Blyth | 14.7.60 Blyth | AB. | H.T. | VERY GOOD 115 | VERY GOOD 115 | (2) 10 AUG 1960 SUNDERLAND |
| 14 | S.S. "BARFORD" LONDON OFF. No. 183300 N.R.T. 1763. G.T. 3357. I.H.P. 1084. | Blyth 19.7.60 | S'land 11.8.60. | AB. | H.T. | VERY GOOD 115 | VERY GOOD 115 | (1) (2) 11 AUG 1960 SUNDERLAND |
| 15 | S.S. "SIR JOHN SNELL" LONDON | 26 SEP 1960 BLYTH | N. Shields 28.12.60. | AB | HT | V.G. | V.G. | (1) (2) |
| 16 | S.S. POLDEN LONDON OFF. No. 183213 | 22 APR 1961 BLYTH | 30 MAY 1961 BLYTH | A.B. | H.T. | VERY GOOD 131 | VERY GOOD 131 | (1) (2) 22 APR 1961 BLYTH |
| 17 | S/S OLIVER BURY. OFF. No. 180824 GROSS 2904·41 NET 1630·24 N.H.P. 281 | TILBURY 29 JUL 1961 | | AB | HT | VERY GOOD | VERY GOOD | (1) (2) |
| 18 | S/S OLIVERBURY. OFF. No. 180824 GROSS 2904·41 NET 1630·24 N.H.P. 281 LONDON. | 30 JUL 1961 | 29 AUG 1961 BLYTH | AB | HT | VERY GOOD 131 | VERY GOOD 131 | (1) (2) 29 AUG 1961 |

*These columns are to be filled in at time of engagement.

† In Engineers' books insert horse-power. In radio officers' books insert gross tonnage and classification of ship under the Radio Rules.

29

**Photograph of Holder.**

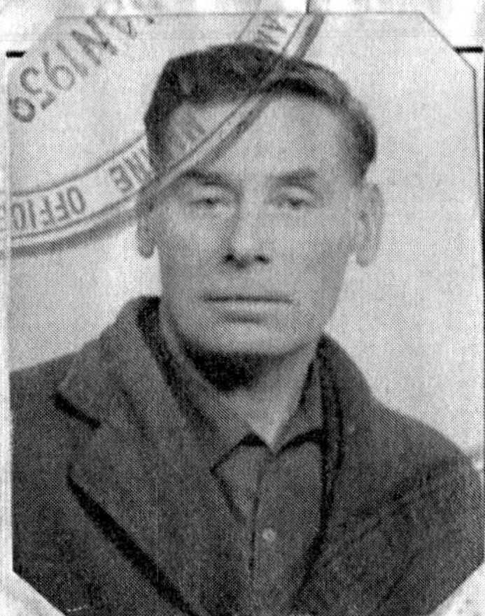

**Declaration.**

**I declare** (i) that the person to whom this Identity Book relates has satisfied me that he is a seaman and (ii) that the photograph affixed bearing my official stamp is a true likeness of that person, that the signature within is his true signature, that the finger-prints within are his, that he possesses the physical characteristics entered within and has stated to me the date and place of his birth as entered within.

Signature of Superintendent at Mercantile Marine Office—

.......................................

*Date*.......................................

24 JAN 1959

**Thumbs—Plain Impressions.**

**Left Thumb.** **Right Thumb.**

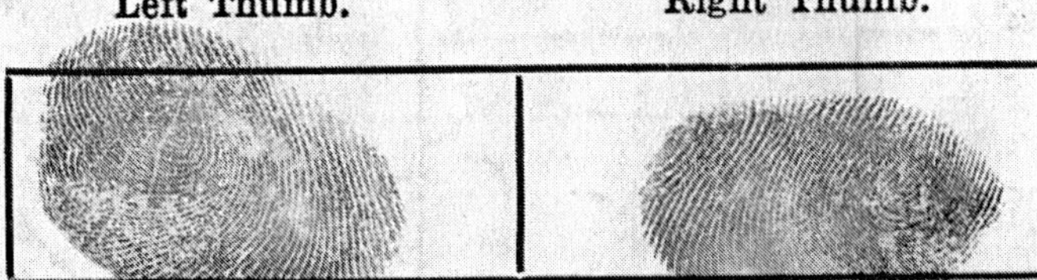

The price of this book is 2s. 6d., but no charge will be made when the original has been lost through shipwreck or fire at sea or for a continuation book when the original book has been filled.

***Paddy Coffey 1959.***

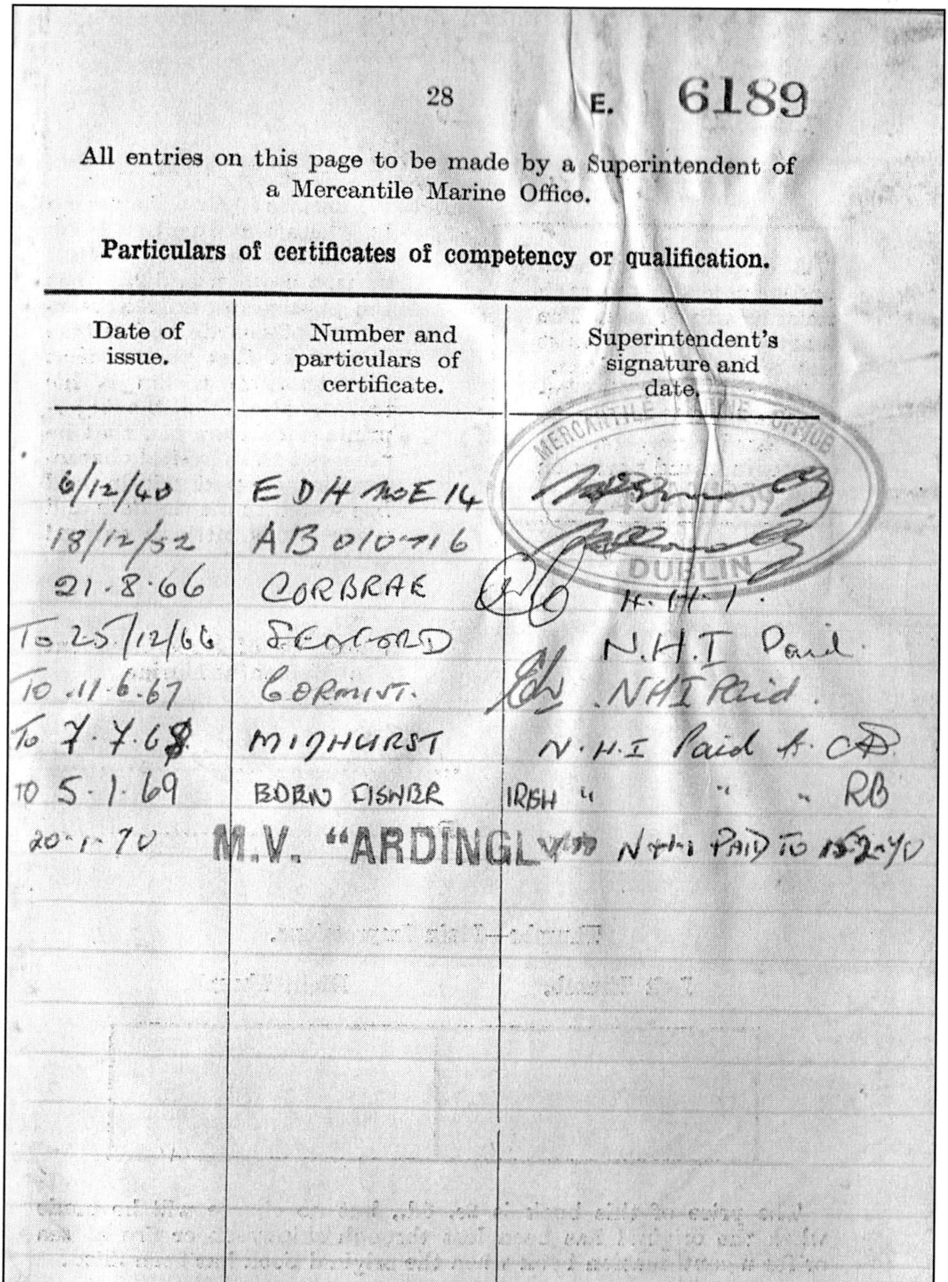

28 E. 6189

All entries on this page to be made by a Superintendent of a Mercantile Marine Office.

**Particulars of certificates of competency or qualification.**

| Date of issue. | Number and particulars of certificate. | Superintendent's signature and date. |
|---|---|---|
| 6/12/40 | EDH No E 14 | [illegible] |
| 18/12/52 | AB 010716 | [illegible] |
| 21.8.66 | CORBRAE | [illegible] N.H.I. |
| To 25/12/66 | SEAFORD | N.H.I Paid |
| To 11.6.67 | CORMIST. | [illegible] NHI Paid. |
| To 7.7.68 | MIDHURST | N.H.I Paid A.C.D. |
| TO 5.1.69 | BORN FISHER | IRISH " " " RB |
| 20.1.70 | M.V. "ARDINGLY" | NHI PAID TO 15.2.70 |

MERCANTILE MARINE OFFICE DUBLIN

*Particulars of Certificates of Competency and Qualification 1940 – 1970.*

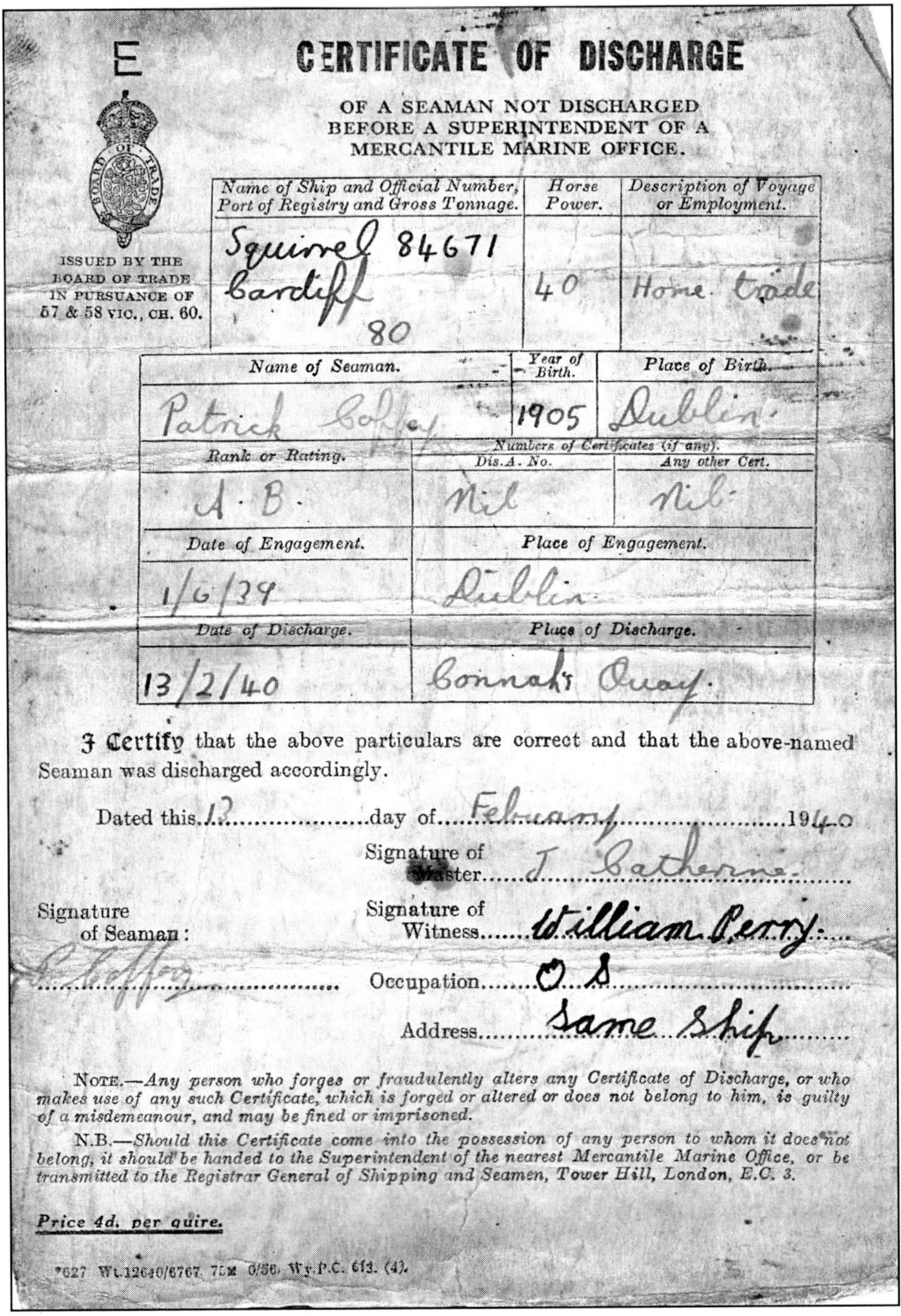

E

# CERTIFICATE OF DISCHARGE

OF A SEAMAN NOT DISCHARGED BEFORE A SUPERINTENDENT OF A MERCANTILE MARINE OFFICE.

BOARD OF TRADE

ISSUED BY THE BOARD OF TRADE IN PURSUANCE OF 57 & 58 VIC., CH. 60.

| *Name of Ship and Official Number, Port of Registry and Gross Tonnage.* | *Horse Power.* | *Description of Voyage or Employment.* |
|---|---|---|
| Squirrel 84671 Cardiff 80 | 40 | Home trade |

| *Name of Seaman.* | *Year of Birth.* | *Place of Birth.* |
|---|---|---|
| Patrick Coffey | 1905 | Dublin |

| *Rank or Rating.* | *Numbers of Certificates (if any).* Dis.A. No. | *Any other Cert.* |
|---|---|---|
| A. B. | Nil | Nil |

| *Date of Engagement.* | *Place of Engagement.* |
|---|---|
| 1/6/39 | Dublin |
| *Date of Discharge.* | *Place of Discharge.* |
| 13/2/40 | Connahs Quay. |

I Certify that the above particulars are correct and that the above-named Seaman was discharged accordingly.

Dated this 13 day of February 1940

Signature of Master J. Catherne

Signature of Seaman: P. Coffey

Signature of Witness William Perry

Occupation O S

Address Same Ship

NOTE.—*Any person who forges or fraudulently alters any Certificate of Discharge, or who makes use of any such Certificate, which is forged or altered or does not belong to him, is guilty of a misdemeanour, and may be fined or imprisoned.*

N.B.—*Should this Certificate come into the possession of any person to whom it does not belong, it should be handed to the Superintendent of the nearest Mercantile Marine Office, or be transmitted to the Registrar General of Shipping and Seamen, Tower Hill, London, E.C. 3.*

*Price 4d. per quire.*

7627 Wt.12640/6767 75M 6/36. Wy.P.C. 613. (4).

***Certificate of Discharge 1940.***

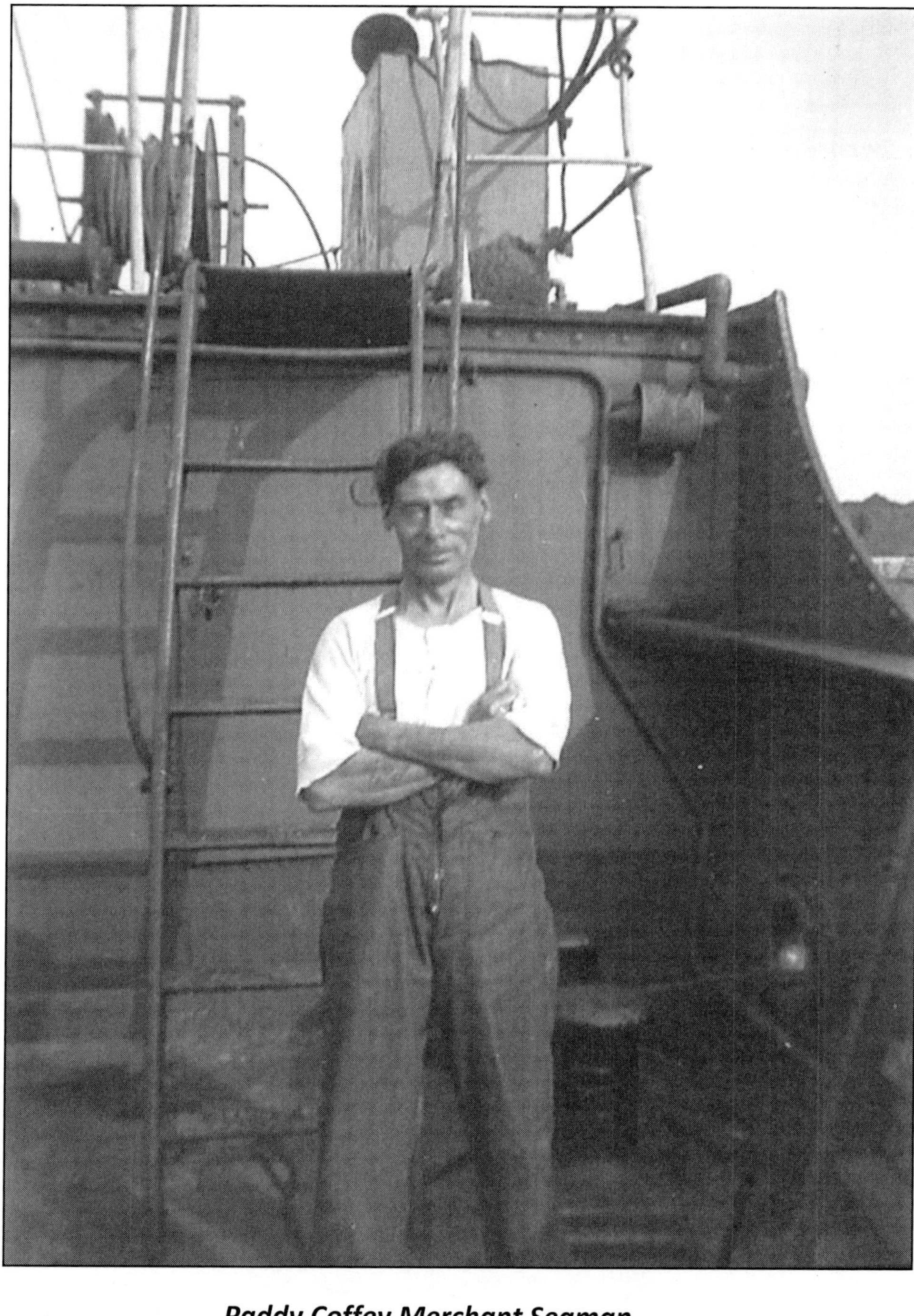

***Paddy Coffey Merchant Seaman.***

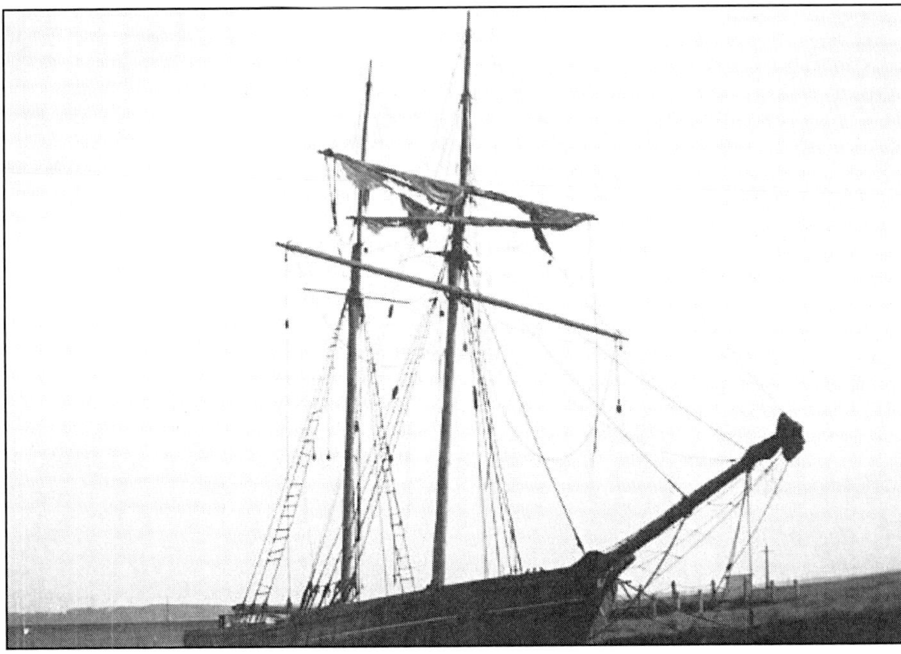

***Waiting to be scrapped in Liverpool.***

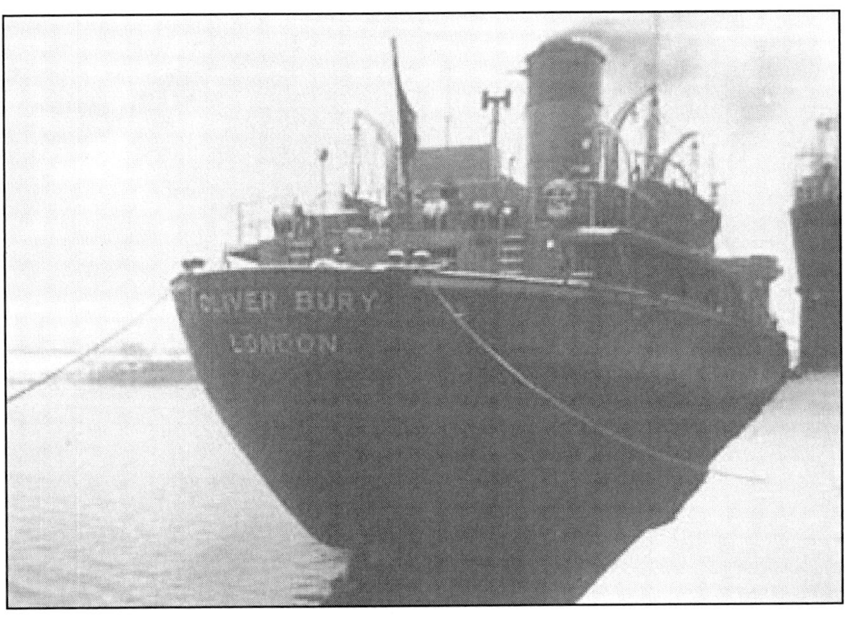


***The Oliver Bury.***

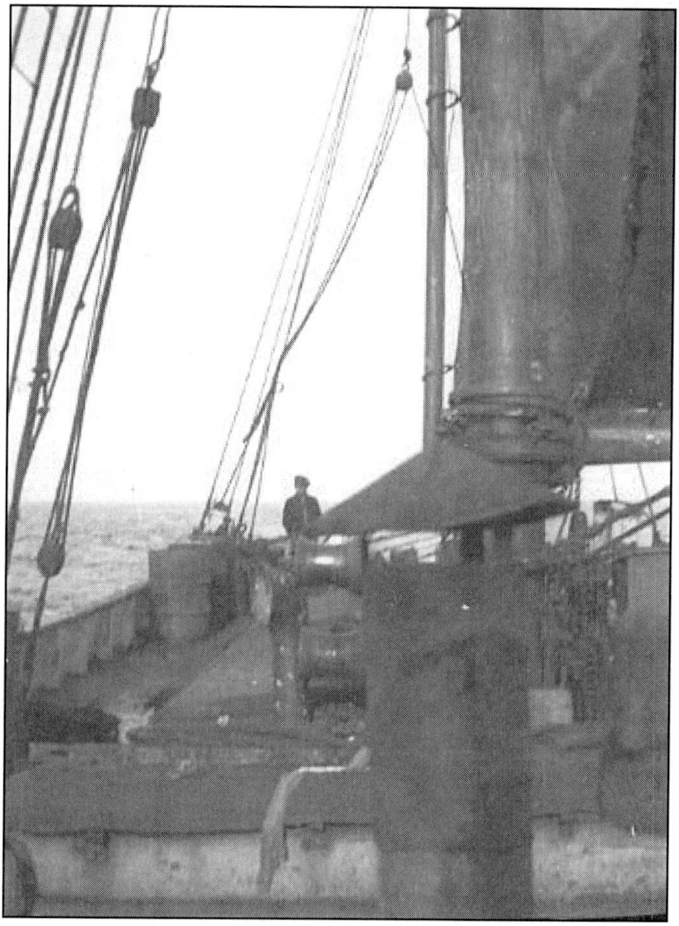

***Posing on board ship.***

While on his first visit to the Canadian coastline Paddy Coffey climbed up the ships rigging on orders of his captain. There was some problem or other that he wanted Paddy to sort out. This however was Paddy's first time to climb up that height sober. He lost his footing and fell down onto the deck below injuring his back. He ended up in a Canadian hospital for three weeks. At the end of the three weeks some of his shipmates arrived at the hospital and carried him back to their ship as they feared he might become 'Too soft' from lying in bed so long.

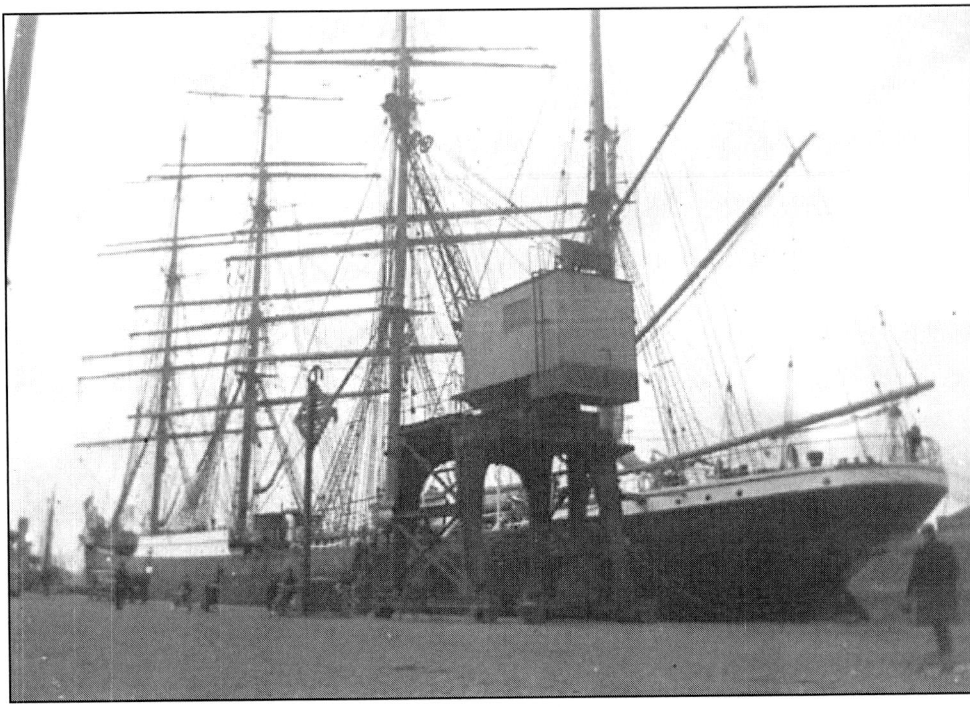

***Ships tied up in Dublin Port 1940's.***

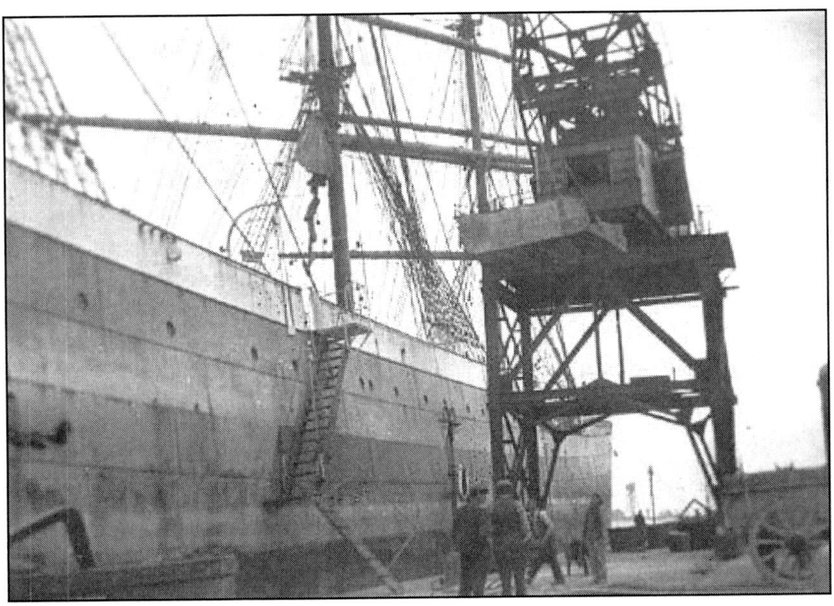

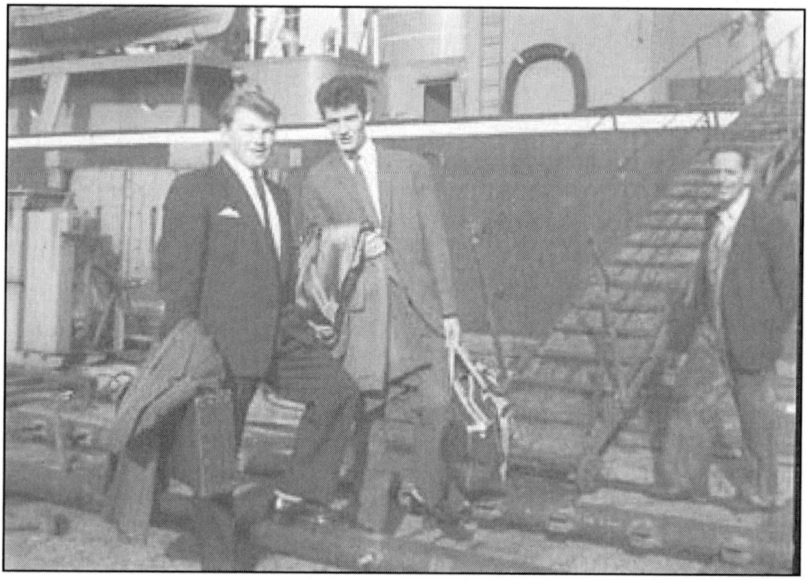

***Heading out to sea.***

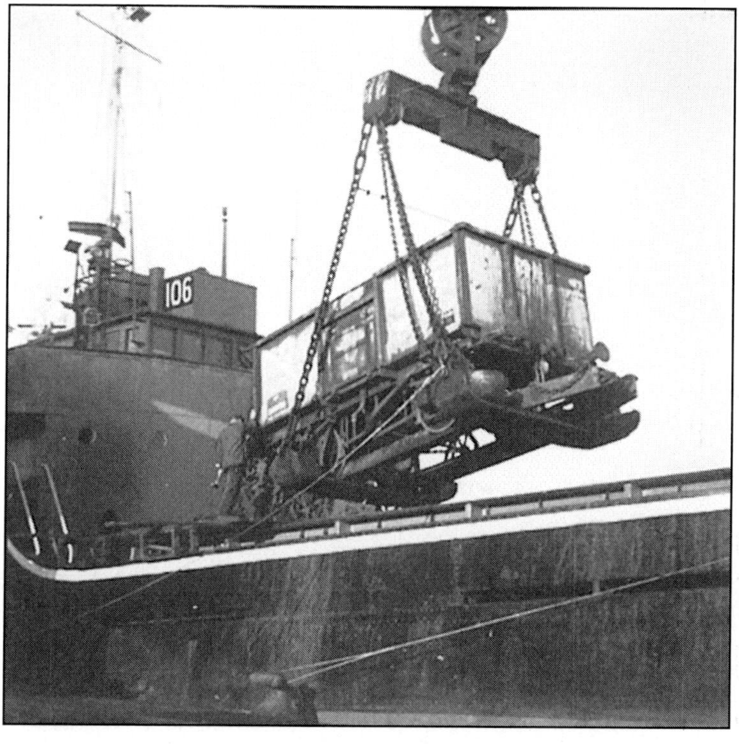


***Container loading.***

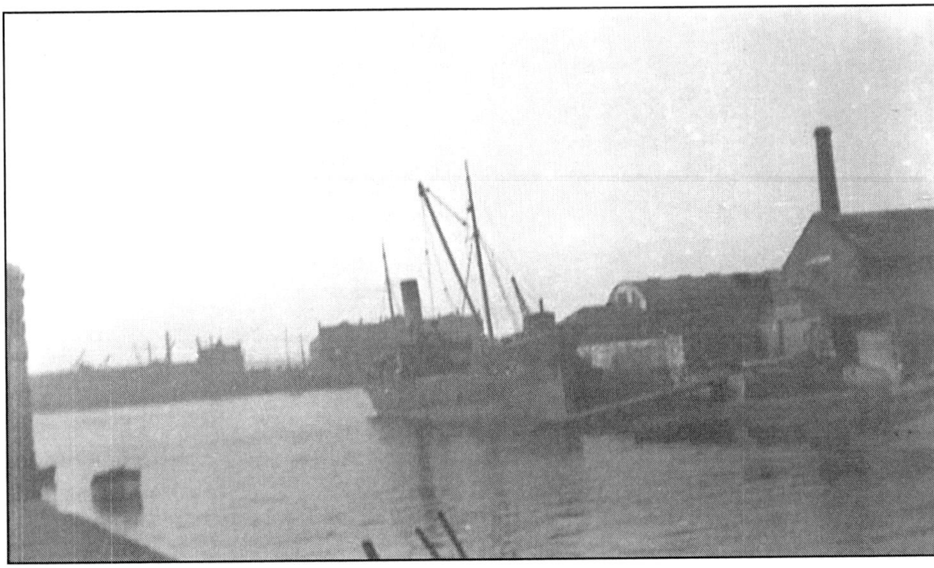

***Location unknown but possibly Ringsend.***

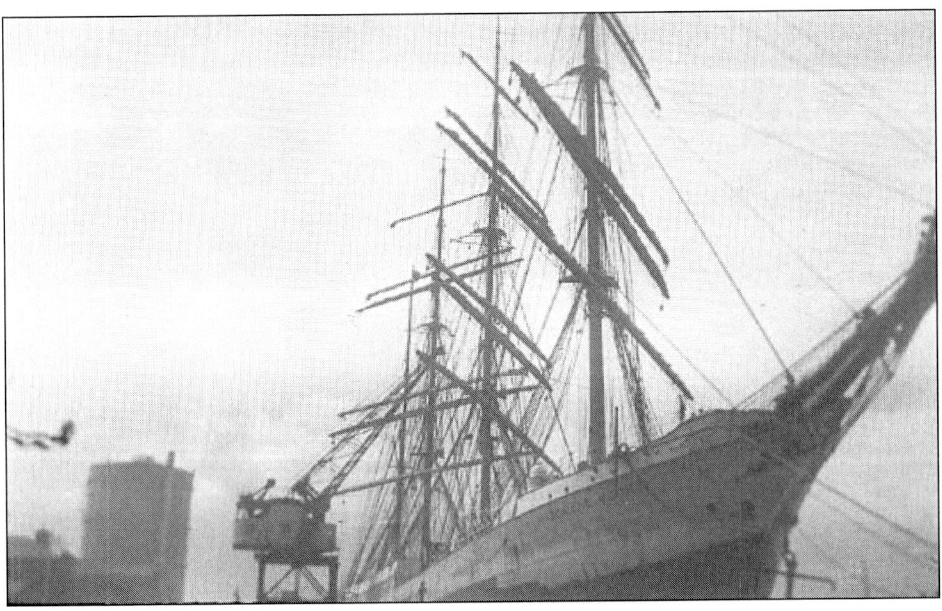

***The Magdelene? in Dublin Port.***

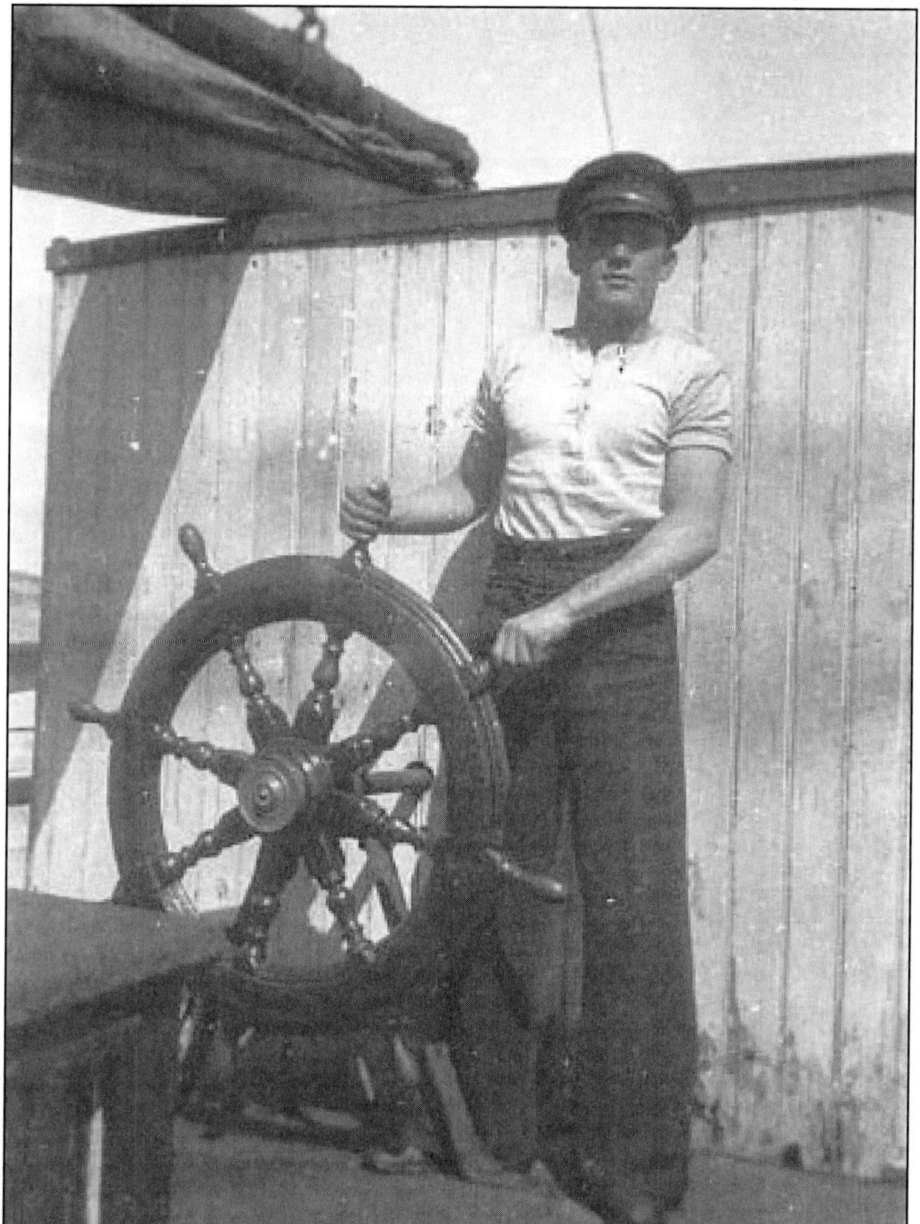

***Sailor at the wheel.***

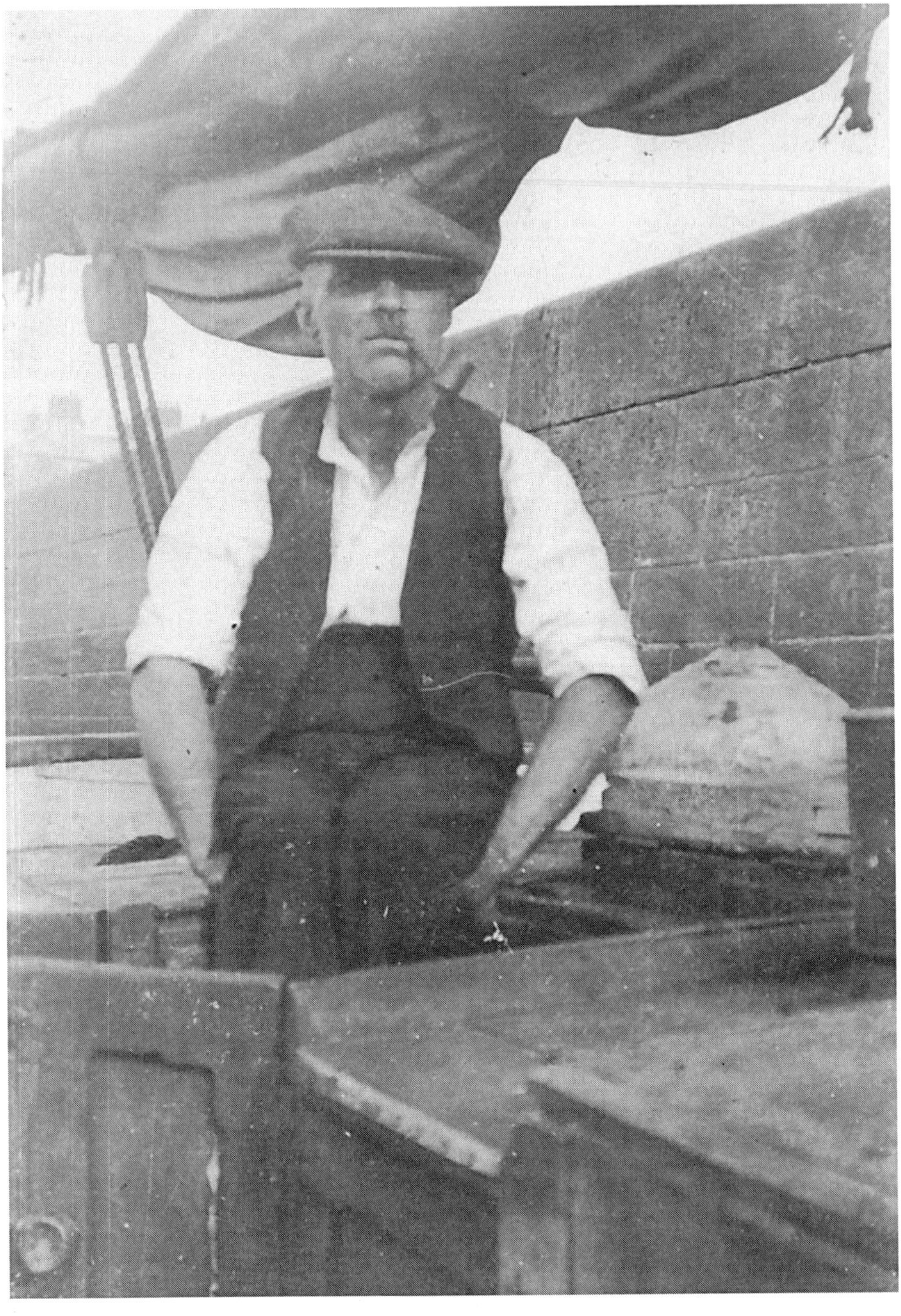

***One journey over and another yet to begin.***

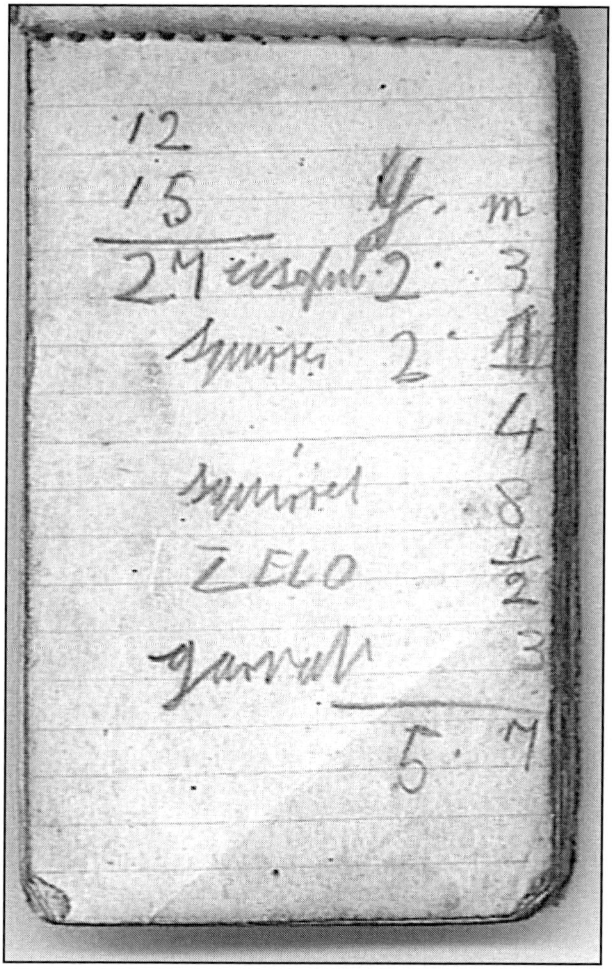

When I first discovered this small diary/travel-log belonging to Paddy Coffey, which he wrote in 1940 I was somewhat puzzled by this particular page. It took me some time to decipher its exact meaning. The names on the left represent the ships he had worked on up to 1940 and the numbers in the right-hand column represent the years and months he sailed with each vessel. This information is of course all pre WWII era and does not include every vessel he sailed on from his first sea voyage. If his calculations are correct then he first sailed with the *Useful* in 1934 when he was 19 years old, he sailed on this for 2 years and 3 months. According to Paddy Coffey's calculations it covers a period of five years and seven months.

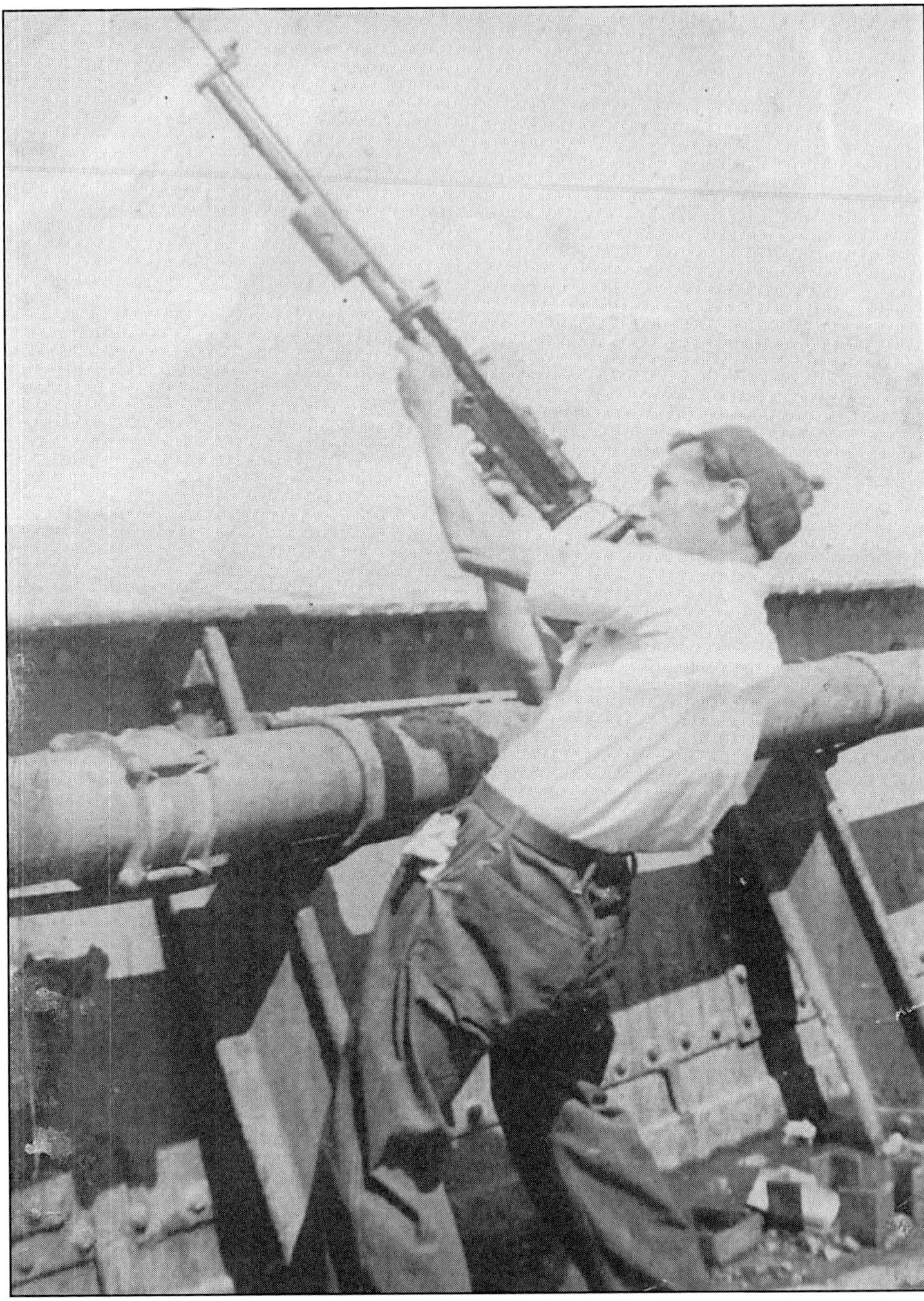

***Paddy Coffey firing an Anti-Aircraft gun.***

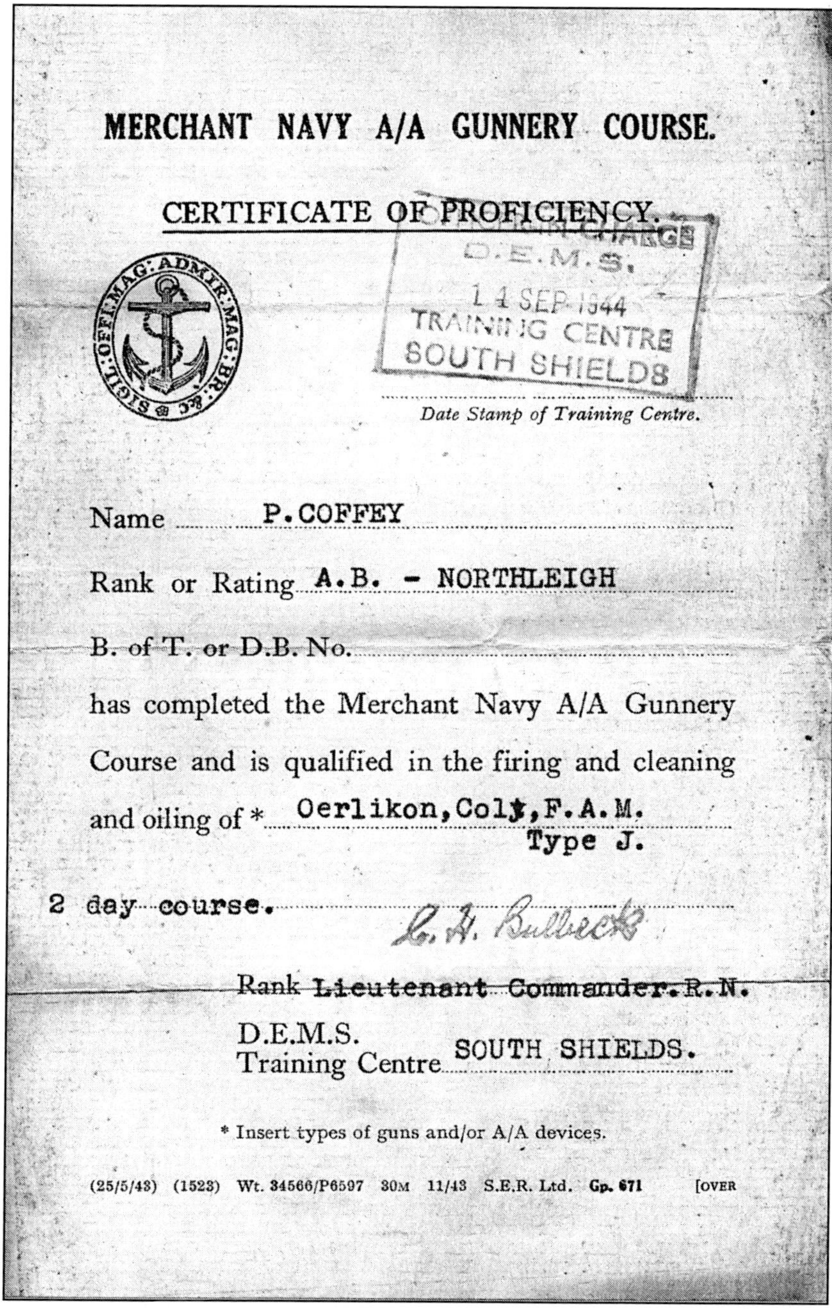
MERCHANT NAVY A/A GUNNERY COURSE.

CERTIFICATE OF PROFICIENCY.

SIGIL. OFF. MAG. ADMIR. MAG. BR. &c

OFFICER IN CHARGE
D.E.M.S.
14 SEP 1944
TRAINING CENTRE
SOUTH SHIELDS

Date Stamp of Training Centre.

Name P. COFFEY

Rank or Rating A.B. - NORTHLEIGH

B. of T. or D.B. No.

has completed the Merchant Navy A/A Gunnery Course and is qualified in the firing and cleaning and oiling of * Oerlikon, Colt, F.A.M. Type J.

2 day course.

C. H. Bulbeck

Rank Lieutenant Commander. R.N.

D.E.M.S.
Training Centre SOUTH SHIELDS.

* Insert types of guns and/or A/A devices.

(25/5/43) (1523) Wt. 34566/P6597 30M 11/43 S.E.R. Ltd. Gp. 671 [OVER

*Merchant Navy Gunnery Course Certificate WWII.*

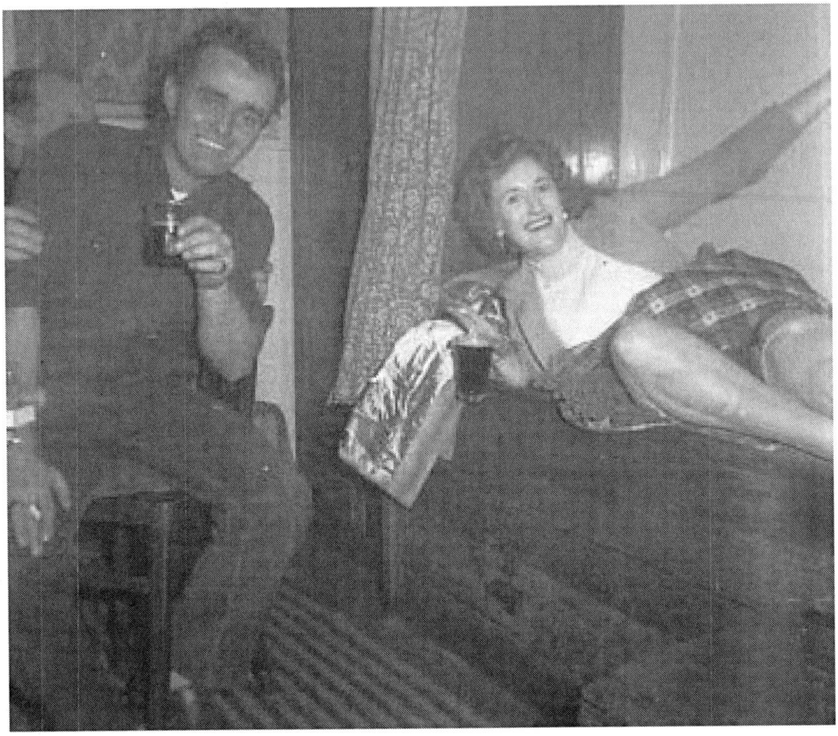

***It was considered 'Bad Luck' to bring a woman on board a ship.***

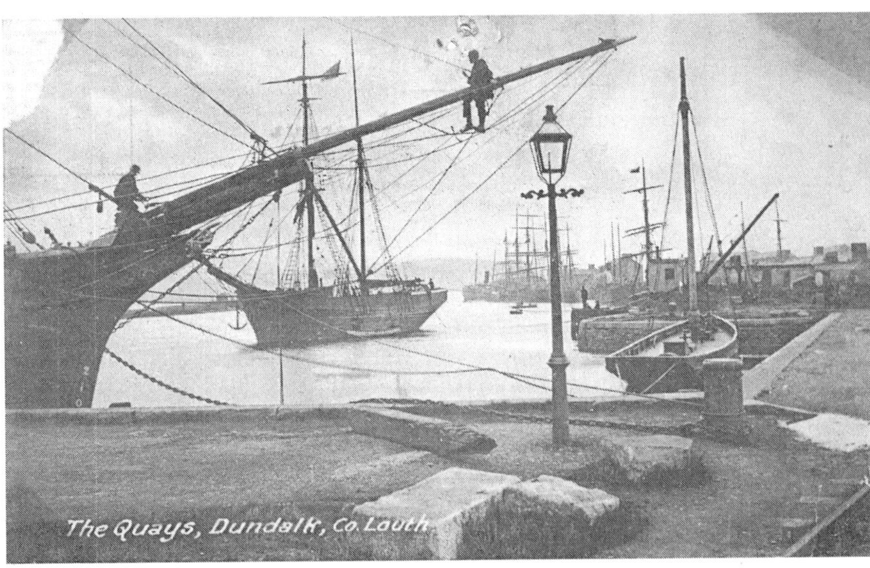


***Paddy Coffey postcard from Dundalk, date unknown.***

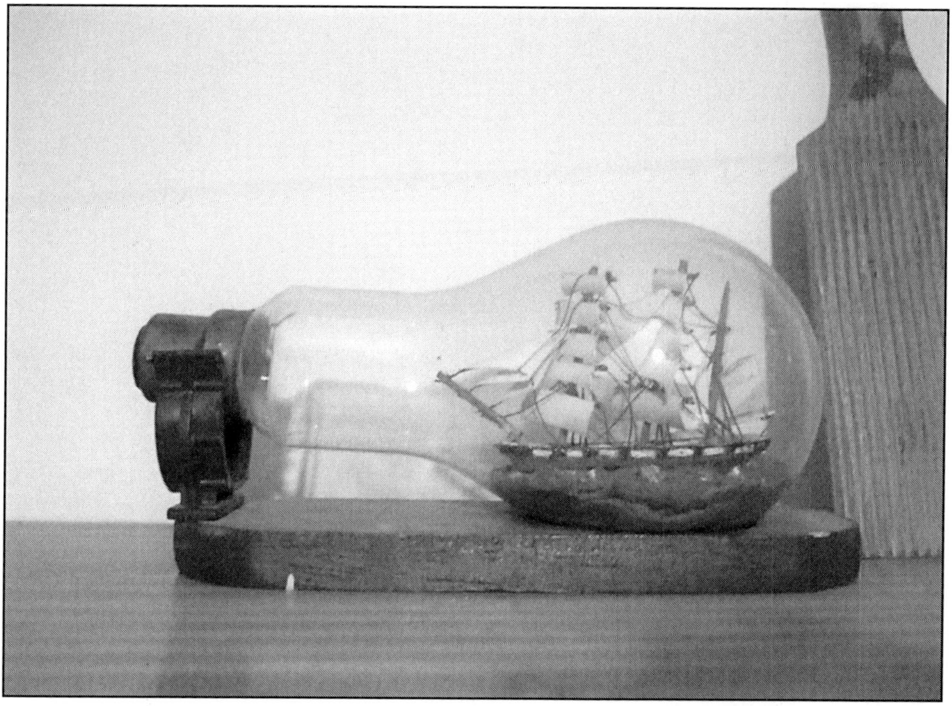

*'Ship in a Bulb' made by Paddy Coffey 1974.*

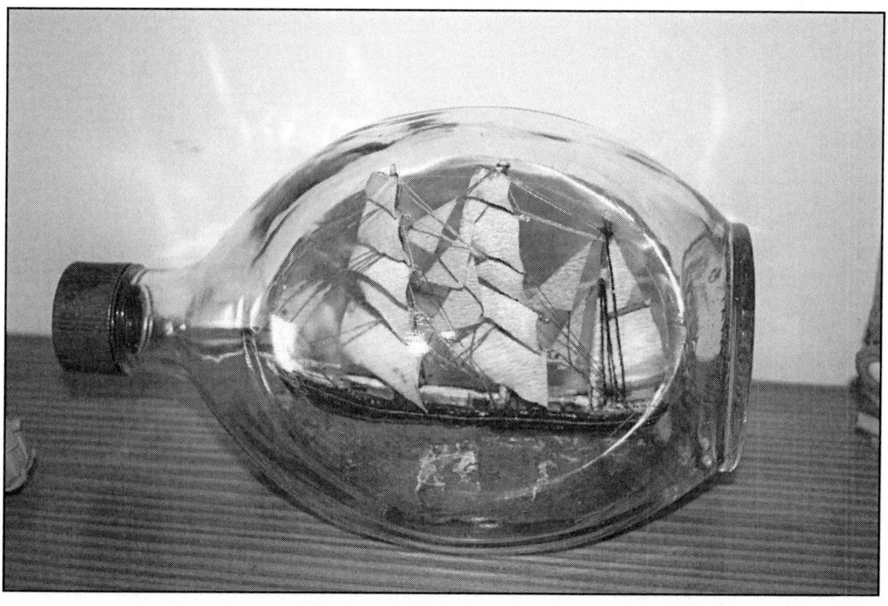

*'Ship in a Bottle' made by Paddy Coffey 1974.*

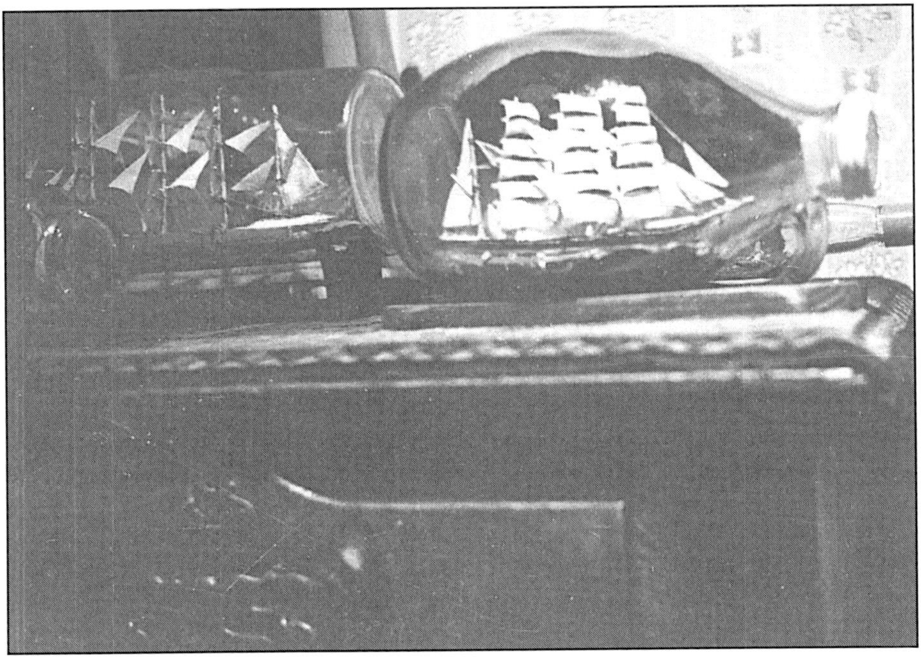

***Ships in Bottles made by Paddy Coffey 1940's.***

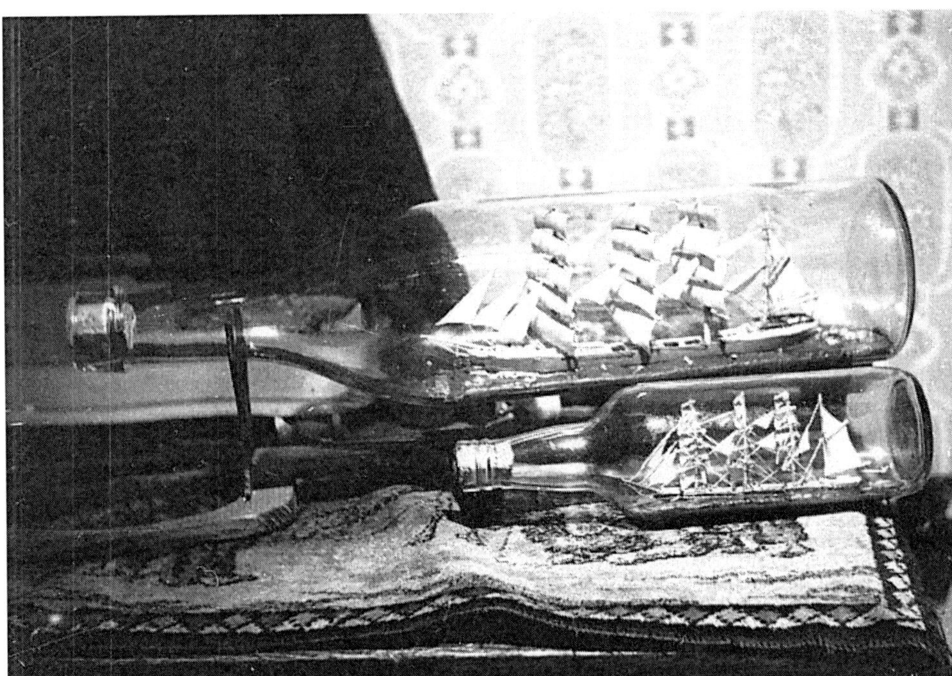

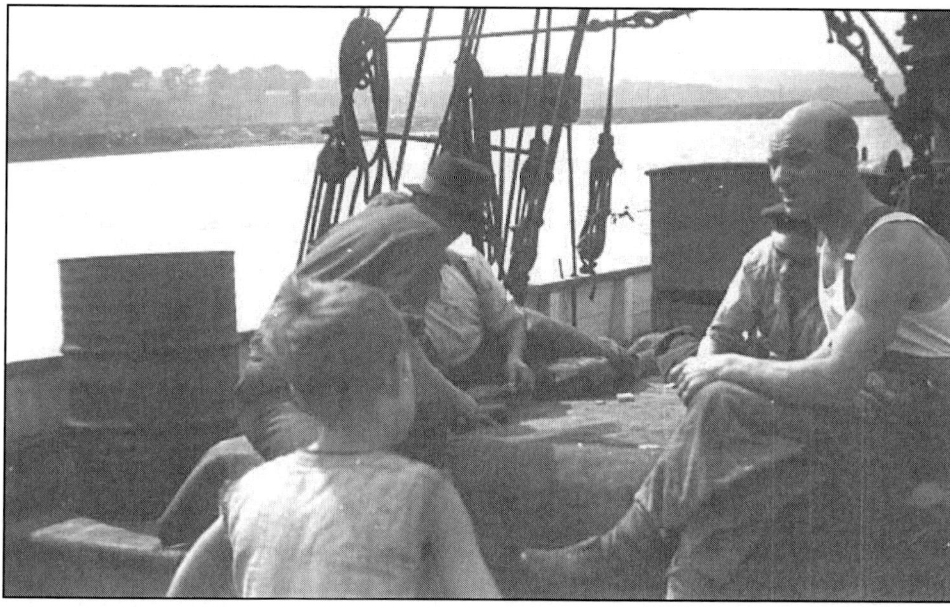

***A young boy chatting with the men.***

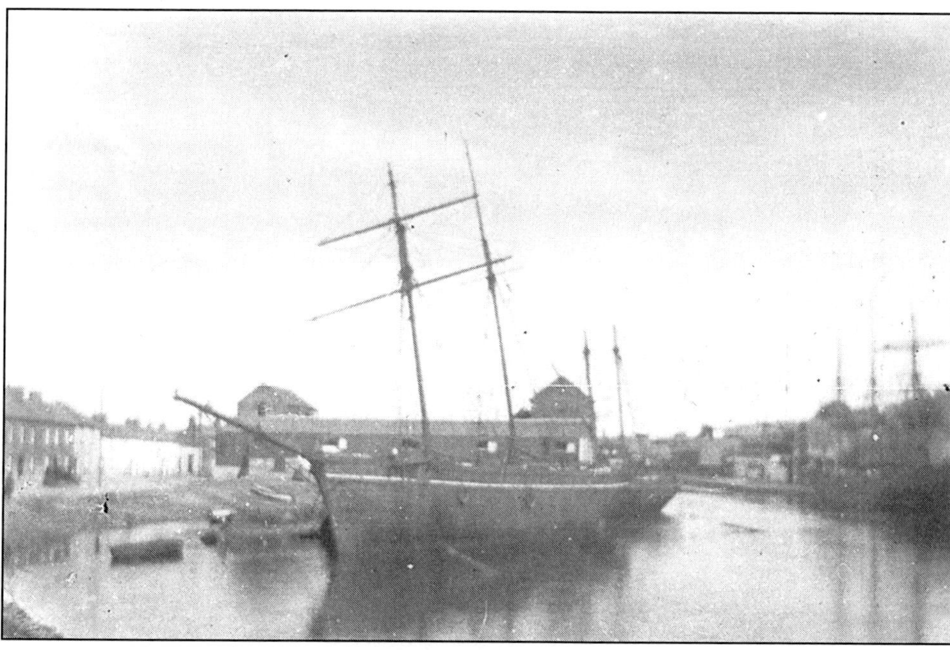

***Ships tied up.***

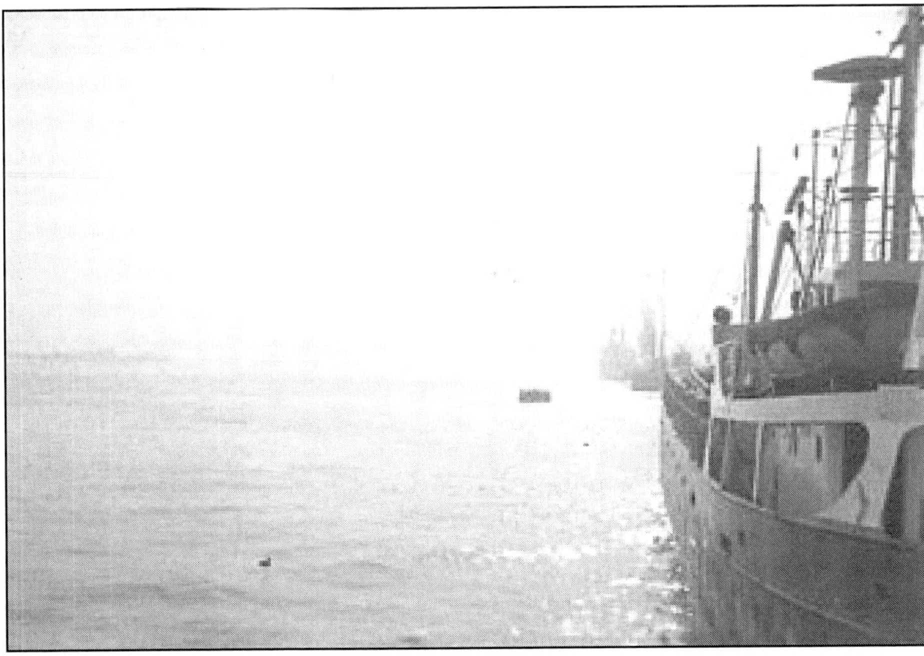

***Ships travelling in convoy during WWII.***

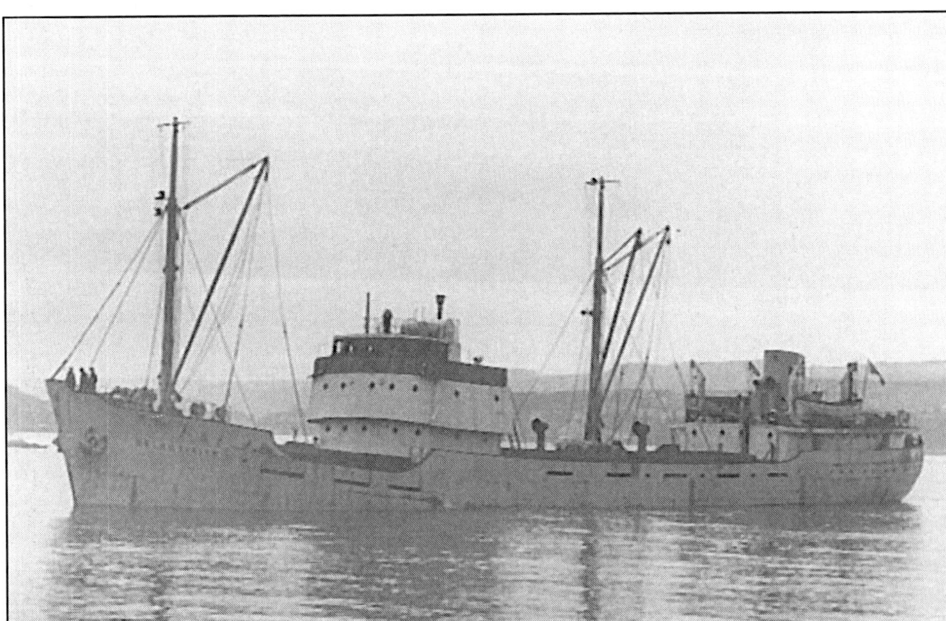

***The Selectivity runs aground.***

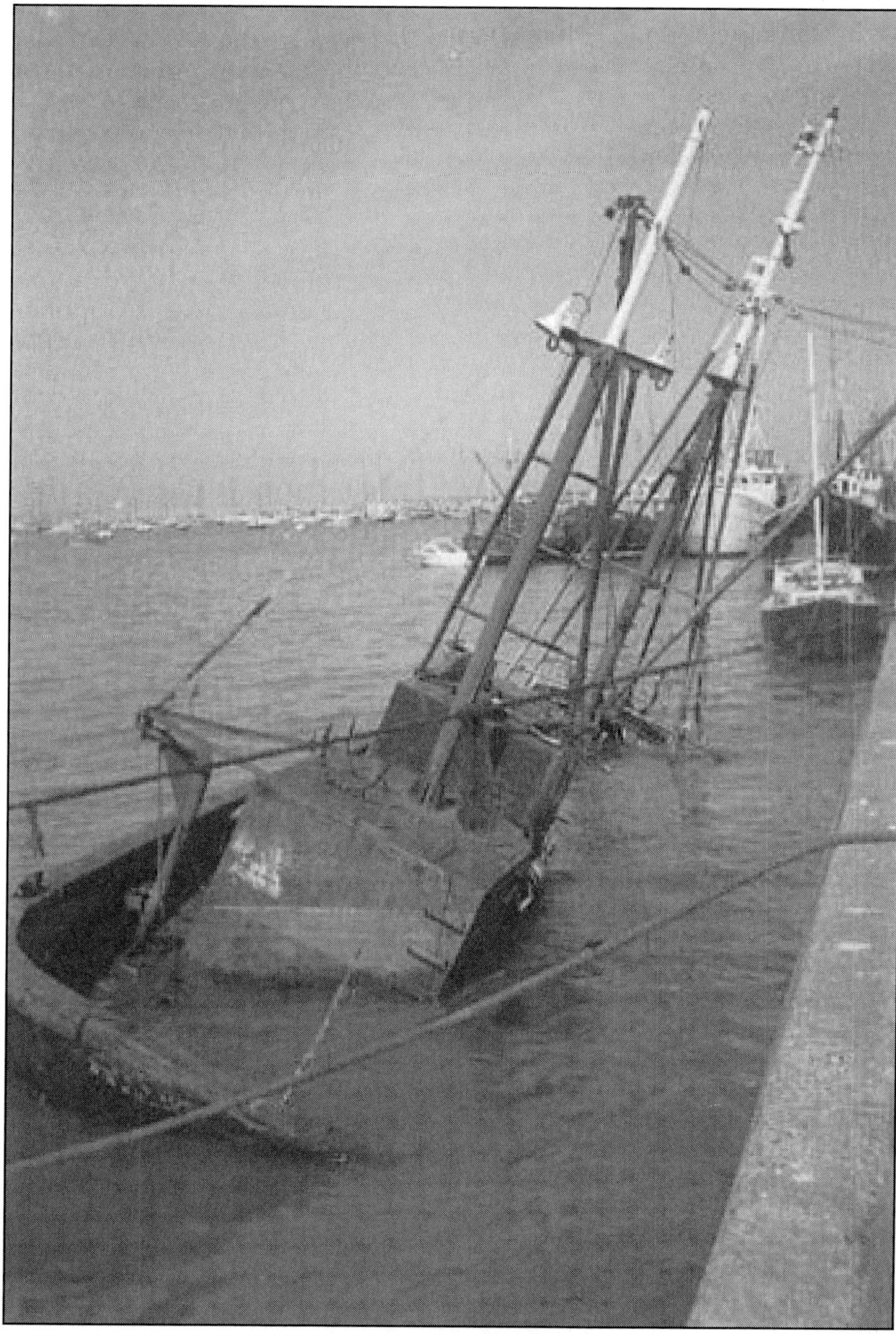

***Trawler in trouble.***

# Chapter 6

## Other Photographs

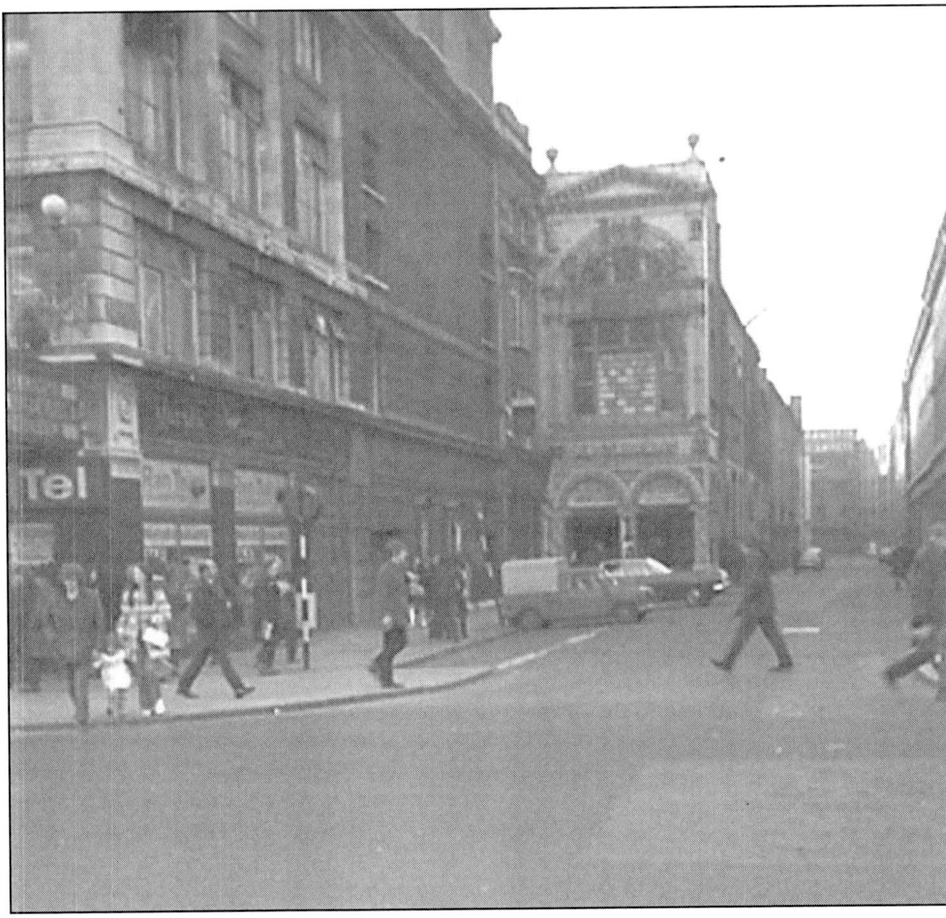


***The Capitol Cinema, Dublin.***

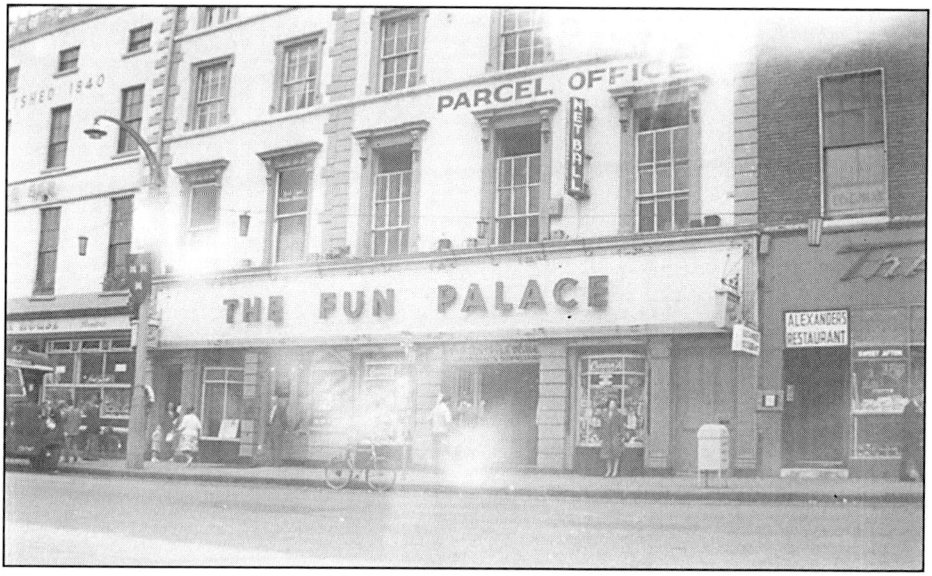


***The Fun Palace.***

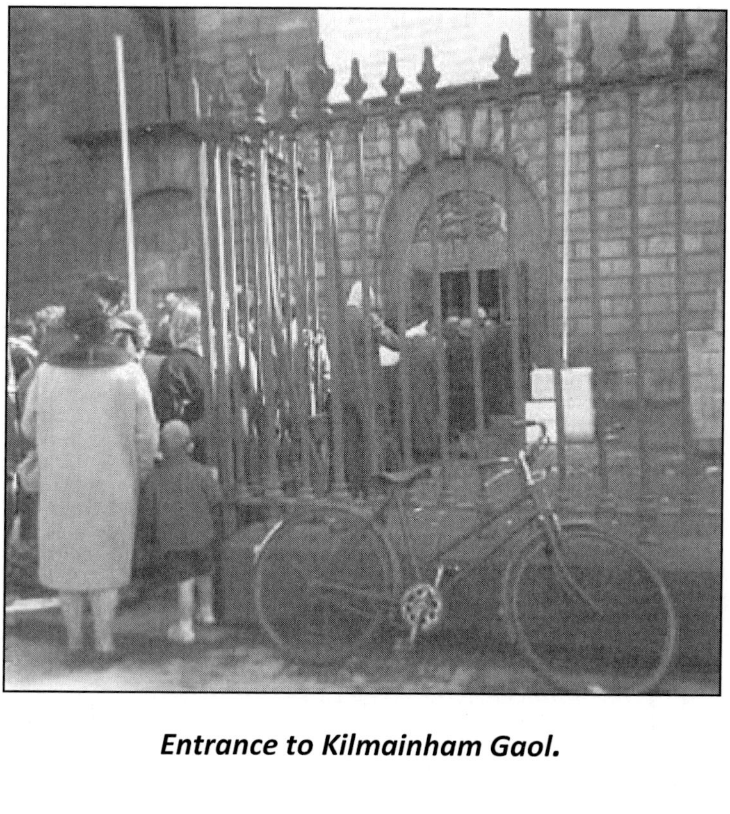

***Entrance to Kilmainham Gaol.***

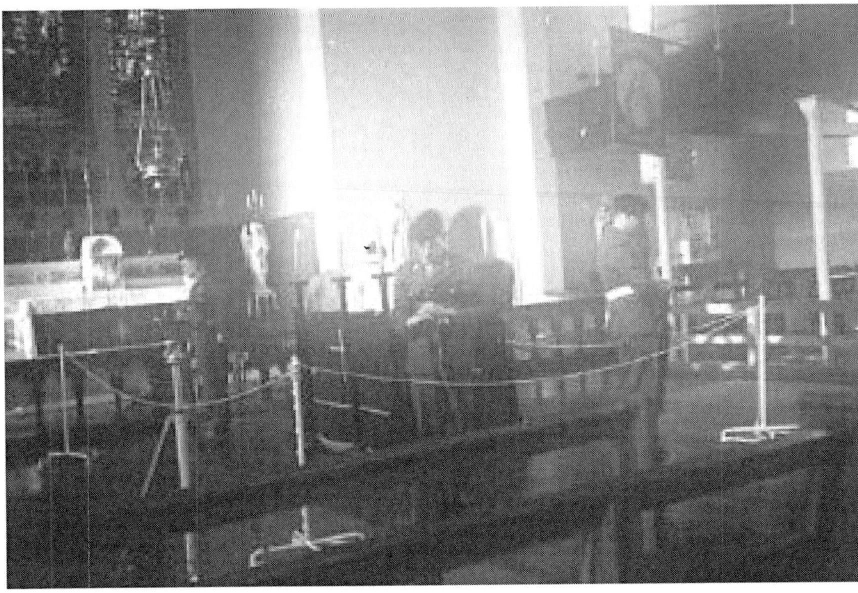

***President Eamon de Valera lying in state.***

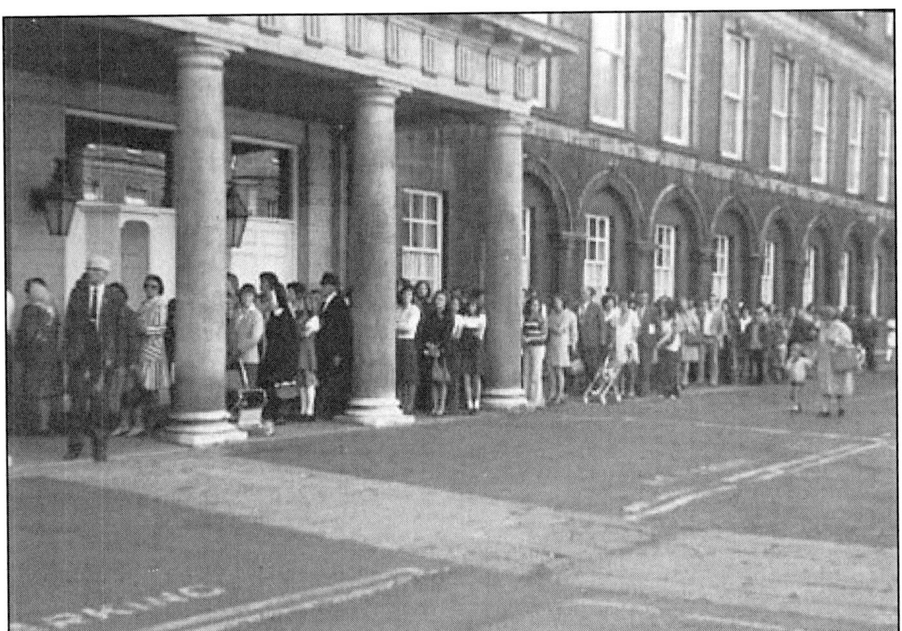

***Queuing up at Dublin Castle to see President Eamon de Valera lying in state.***

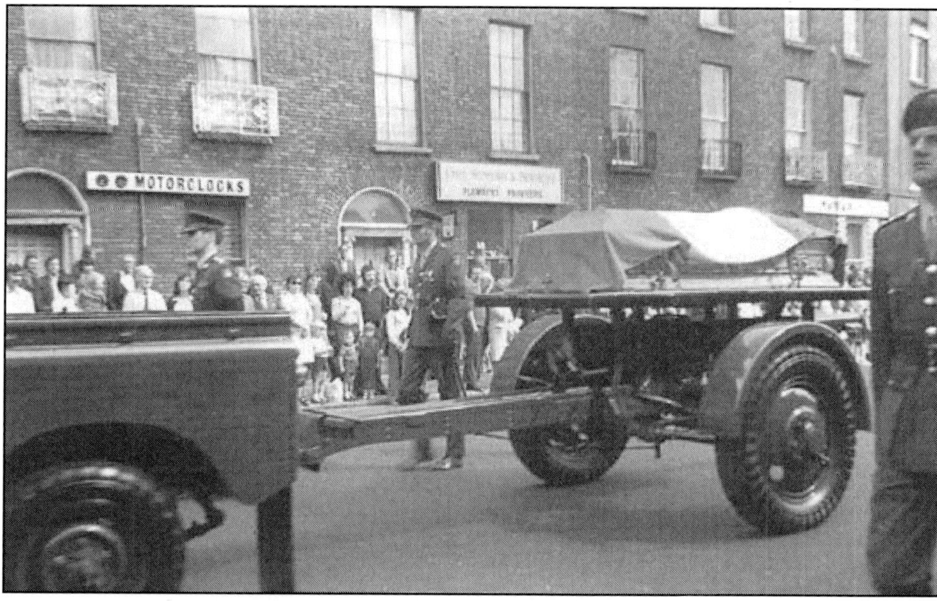


State Funeral for Roger Casement.

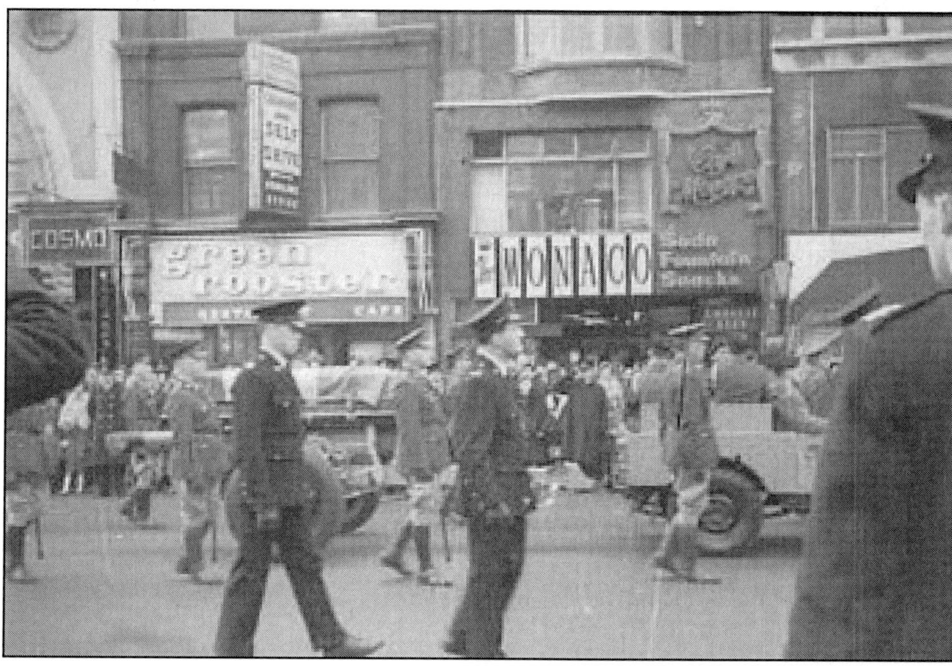

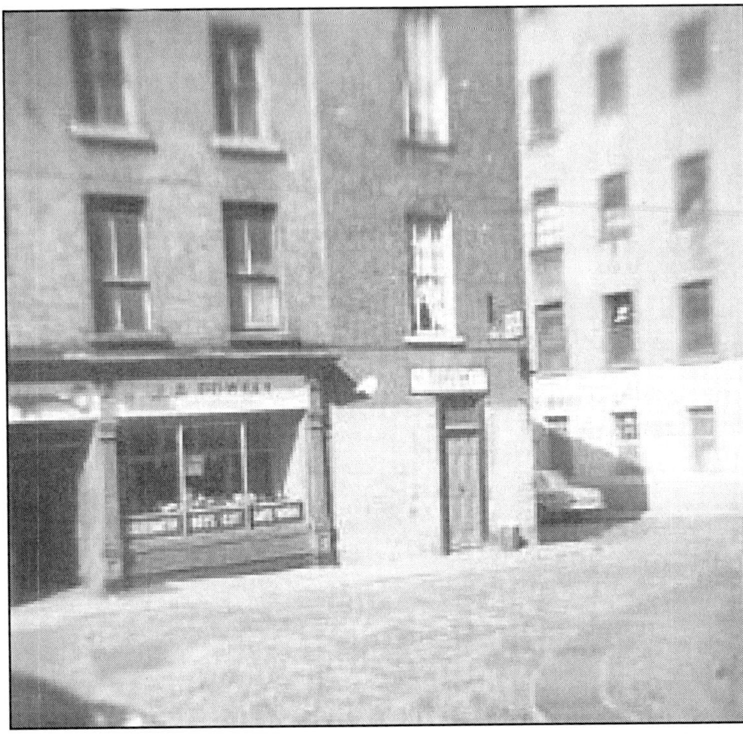

***Powell's Shop.***

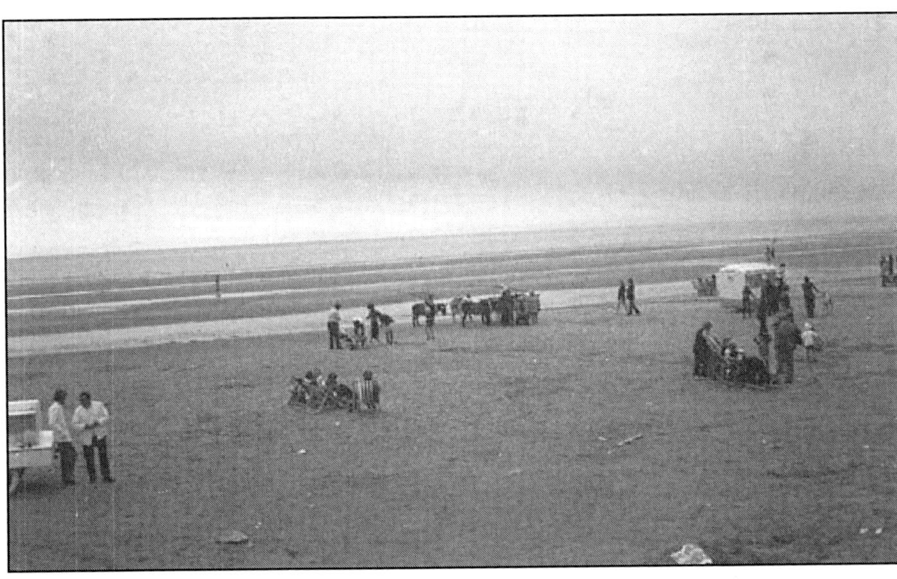

***Dollymount Strand.***

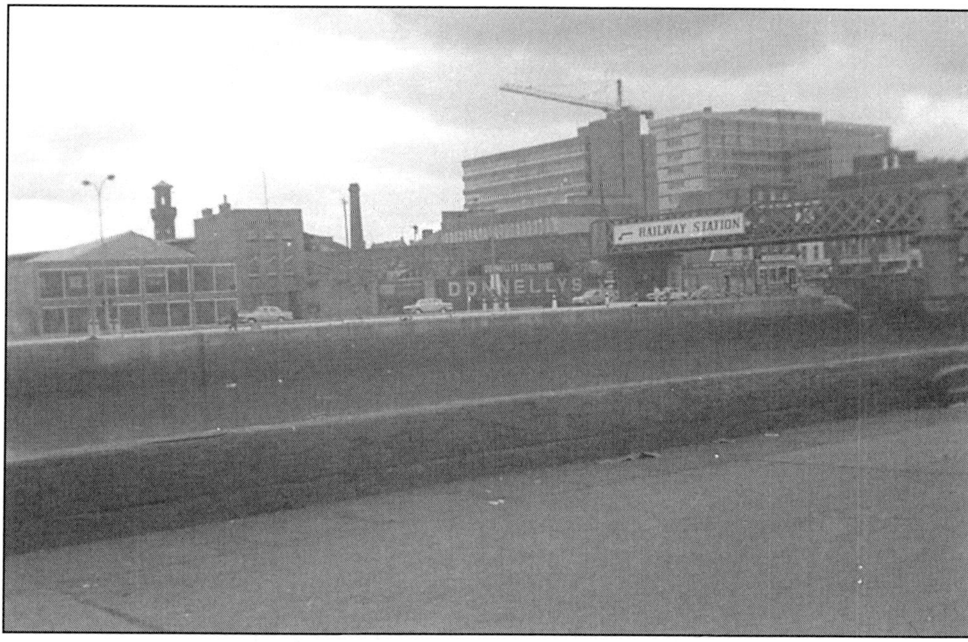


***Donnelly's coal yard on Sir John Rogerson's Quay.***

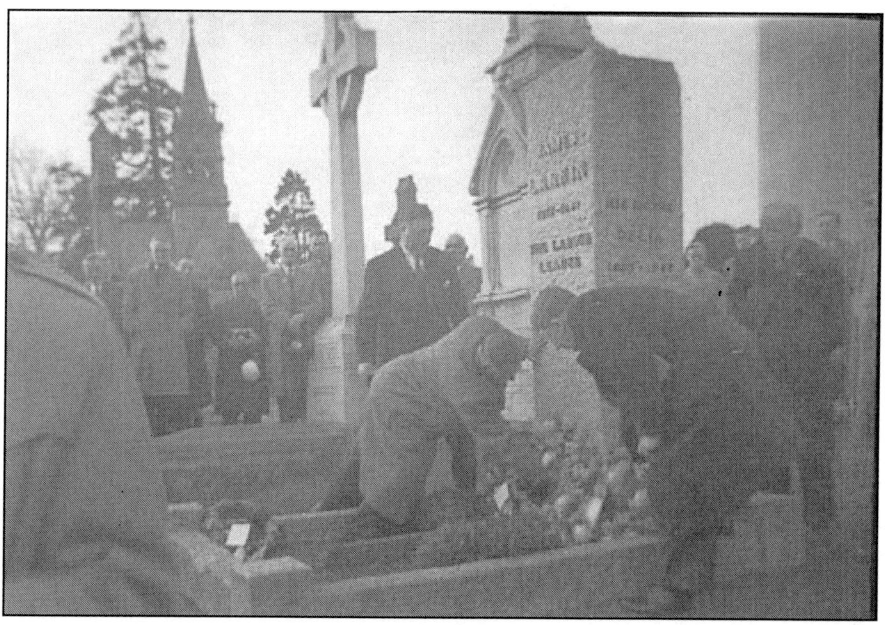

***Laying wreaths at James Larkin's graveside in Glasnevin, Dublin.***

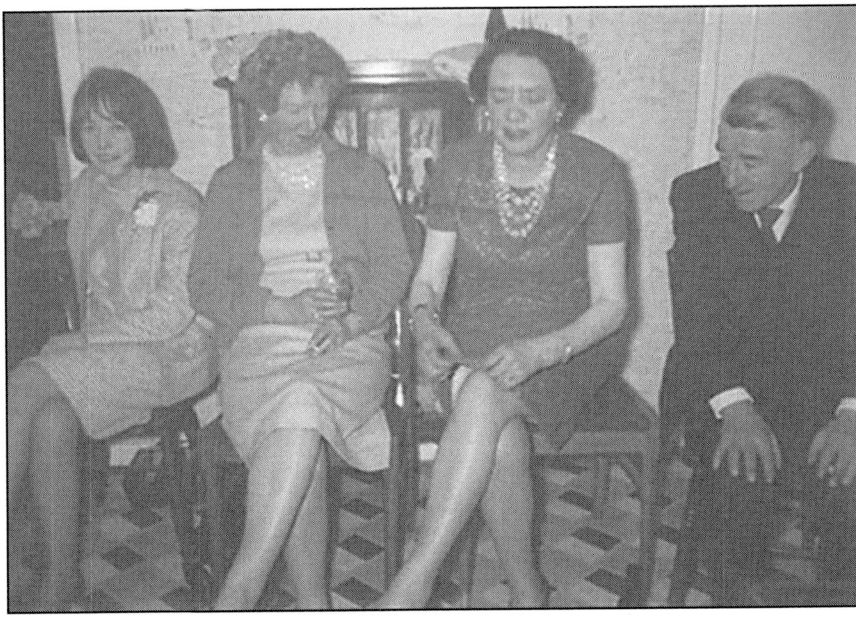

***Mary Boyle sitting next to Alfie Kane.***

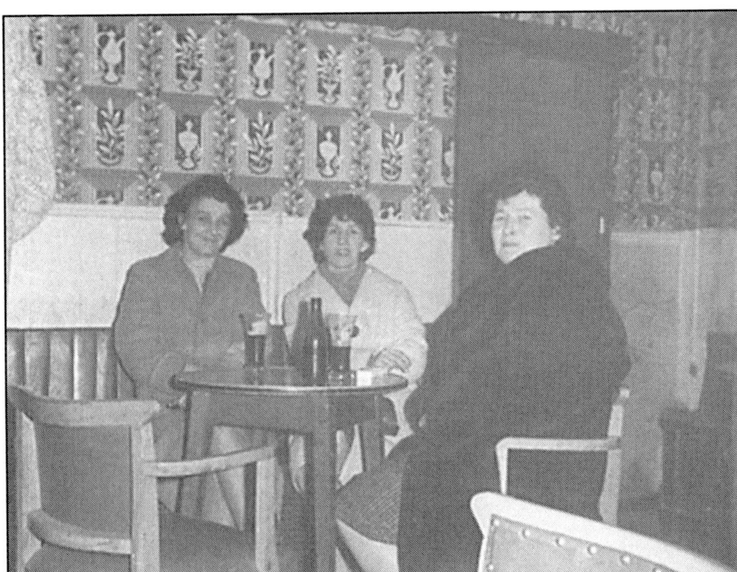

***Maureen Murdiff, Mrs Campion and Mrs Cunningham in Mulvihill's Pub.***

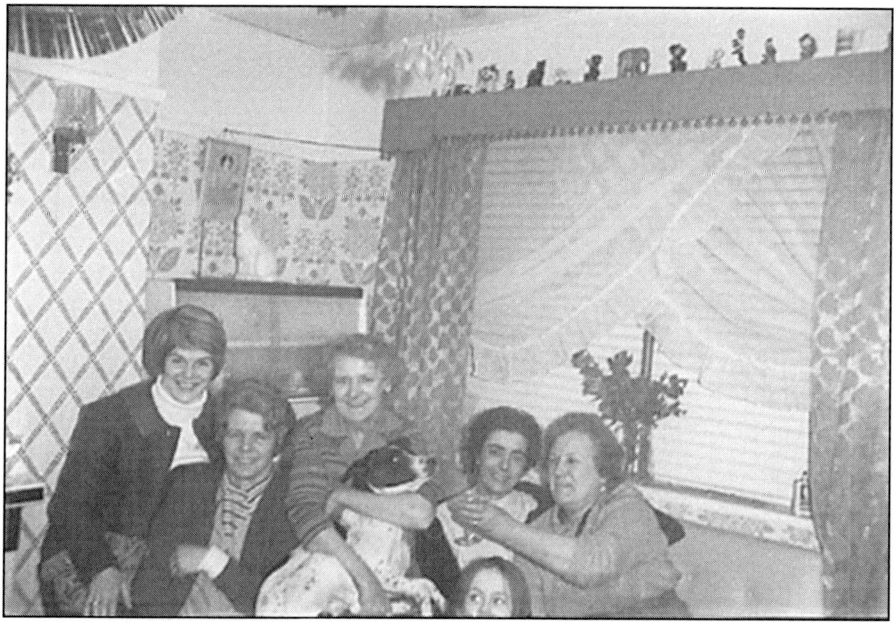

***Jenny Kane, Mrs Dunne, Rooie Kane, Mrs Flood, Mrs McDonald, Angie Dillon and 'Trooper' the Dog.***

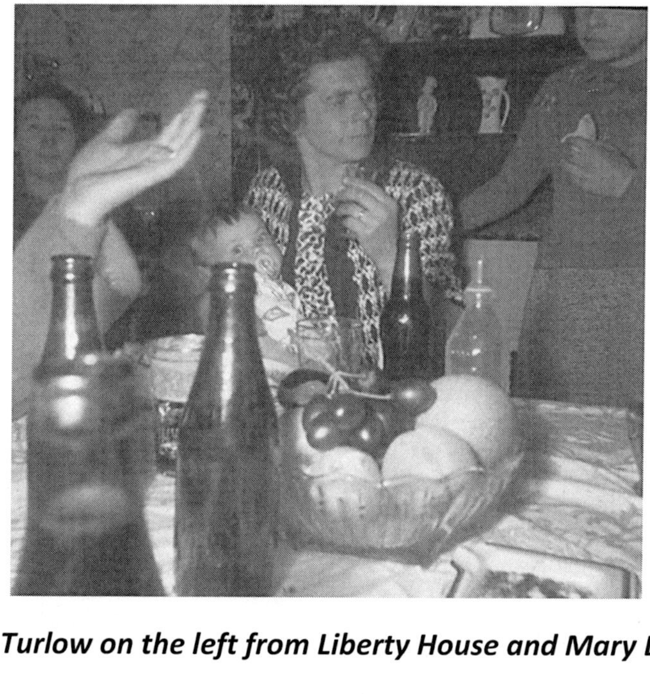

***Peggy Turlow on the left from Liberty House and Mary Dunne.***

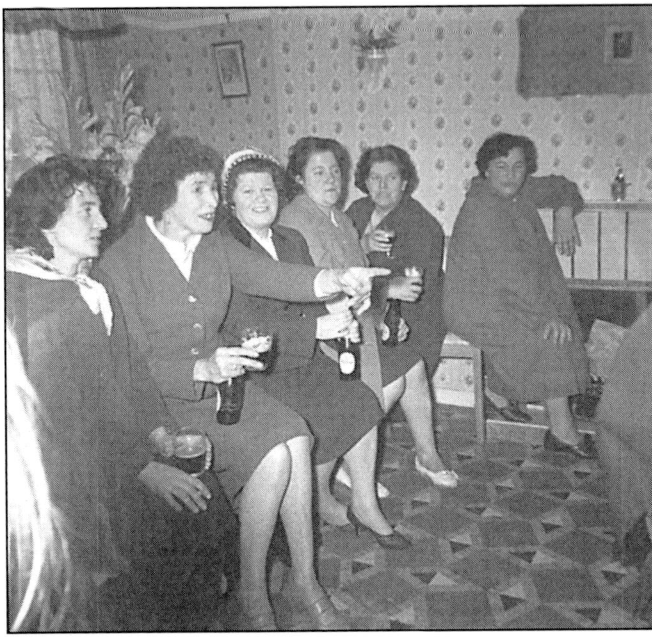

***Including: Bridie Doyle, May Jones, Nan Devine, Biddy Lawless, Martha Mallon and Maggie Connor in 1961.***

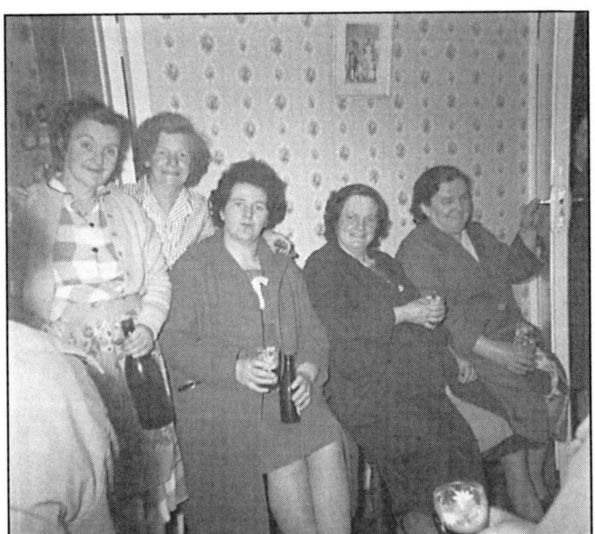

***Including: Molly Harris, Mary Boylan, Dinah Rooney, Bella Kavanagh and Maggie Connor 1961.***

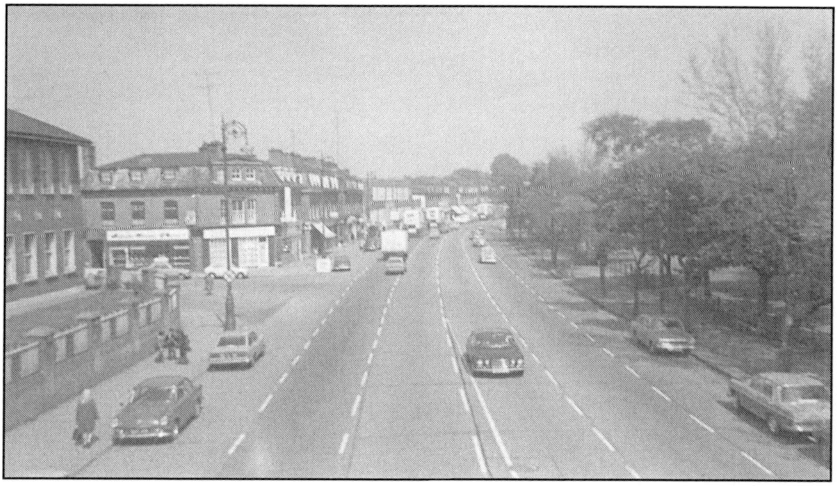

***Fairview Strand.***

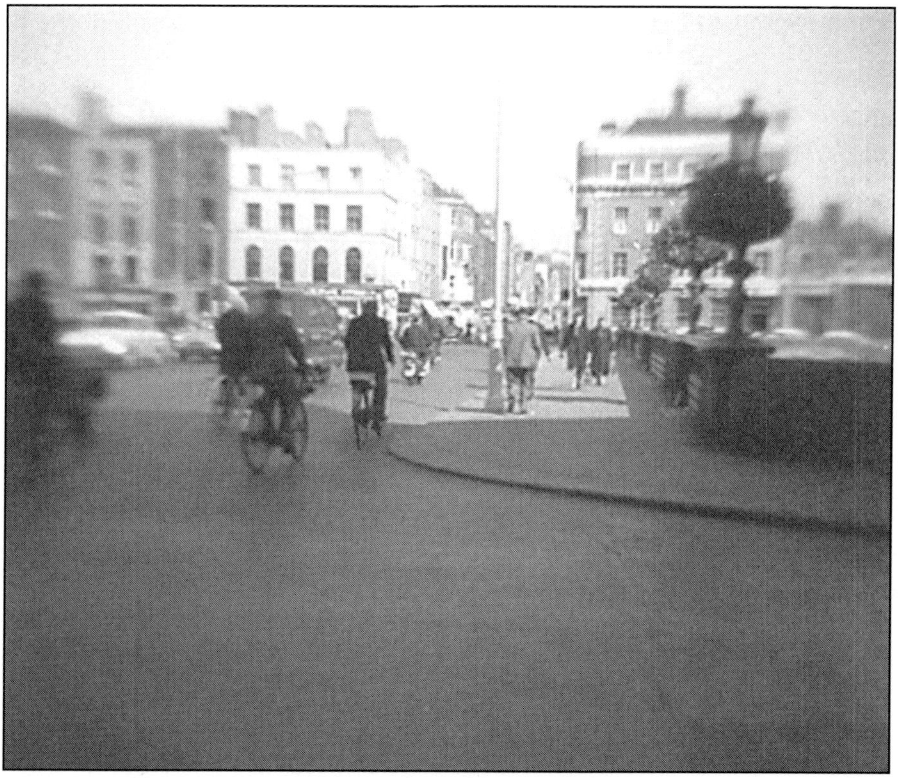

***Looking across Grattan Bridge.***

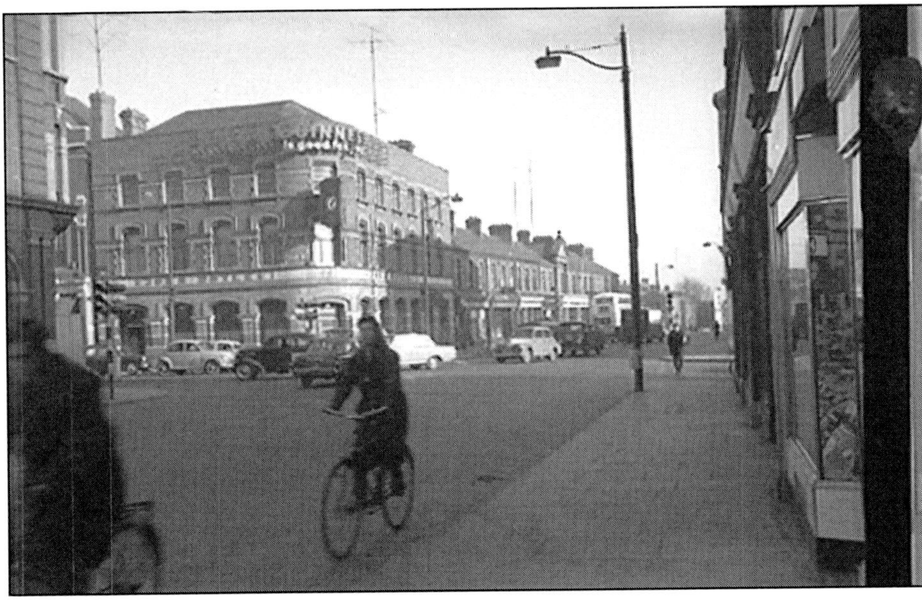

***Doyle's Corner, Phibsborough.***

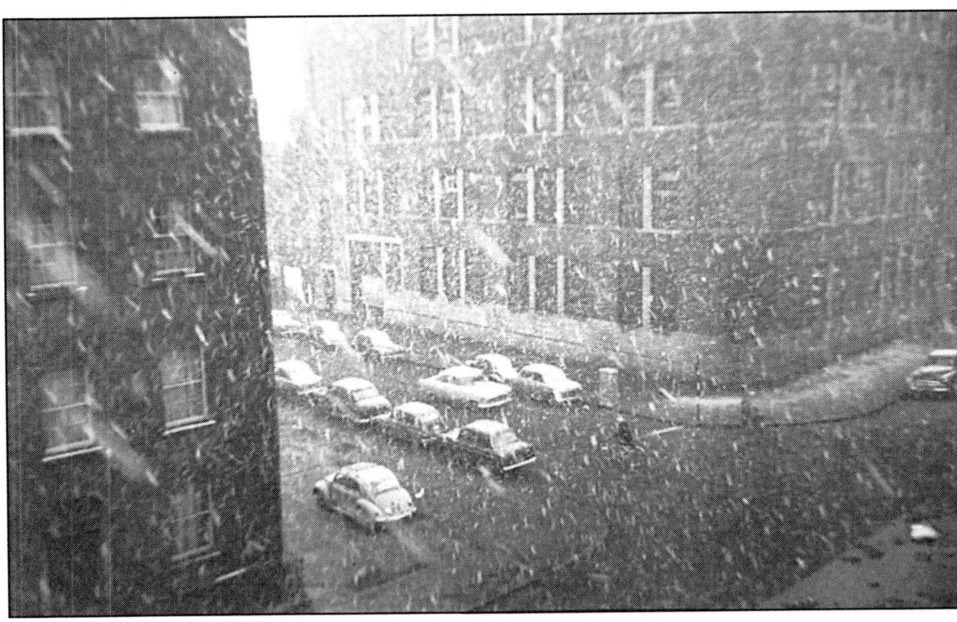

***Tenement houses in the snow.***

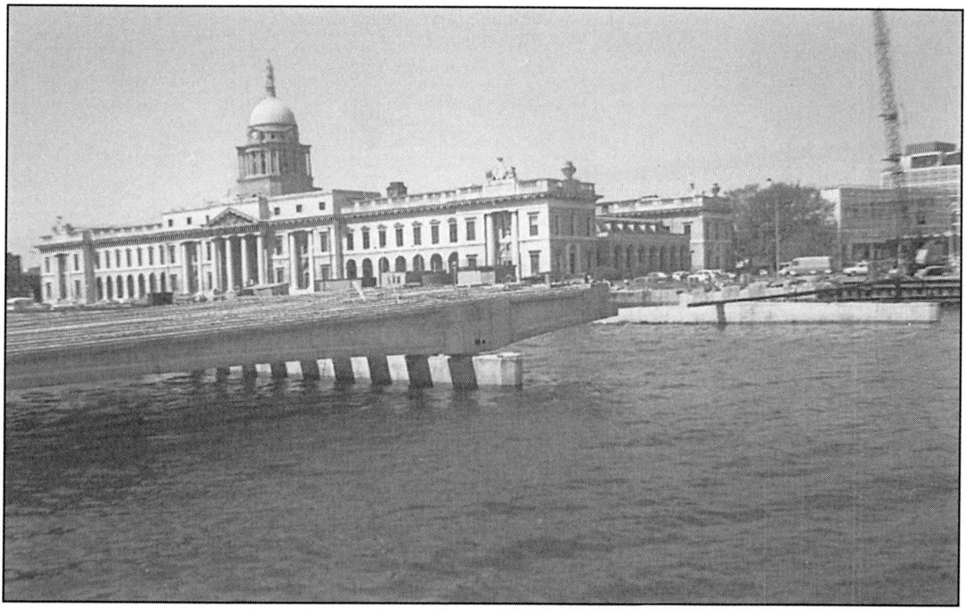

***Matt Talbot Bridge under construction, completed in 1978.***

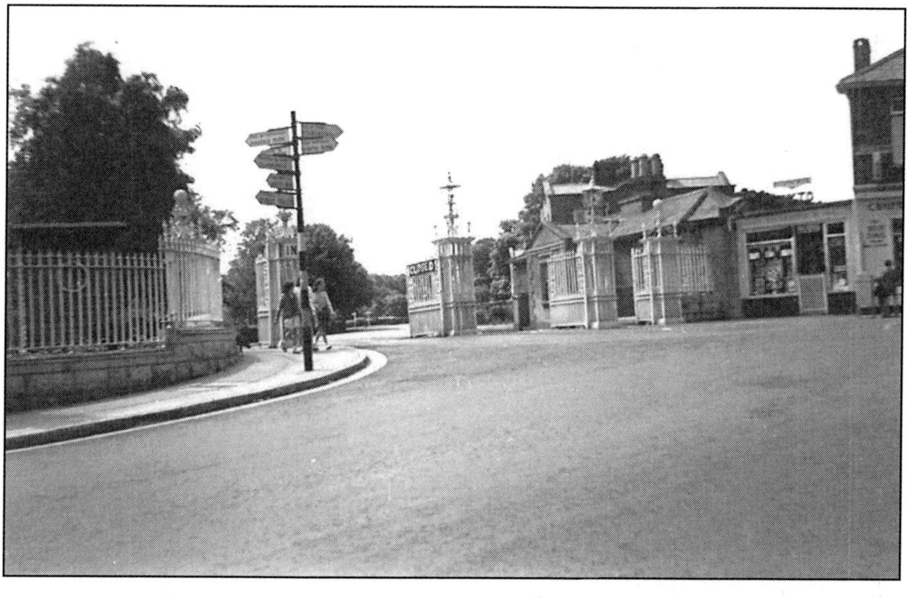

***The Phoenix Park gate on the North Circular Road, Dublin.***

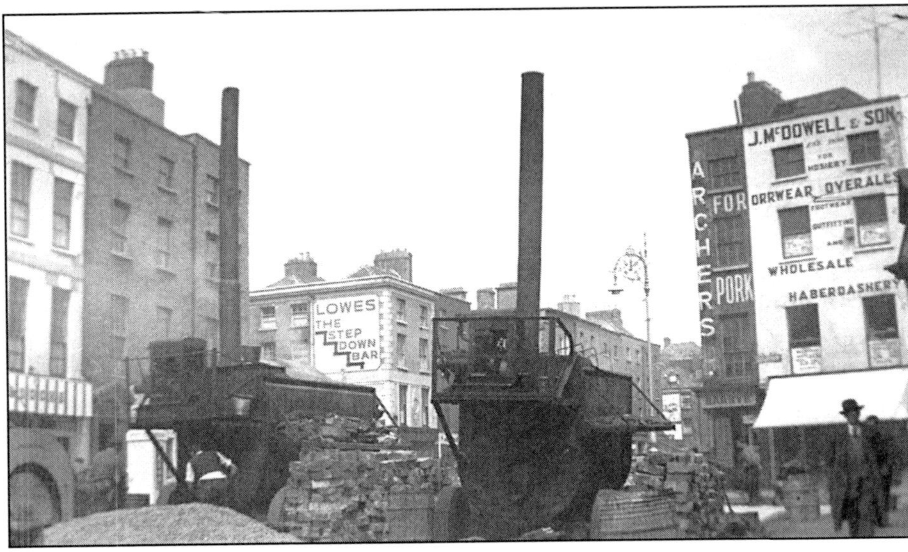


***Road works on Parnell Street, Dublin.***

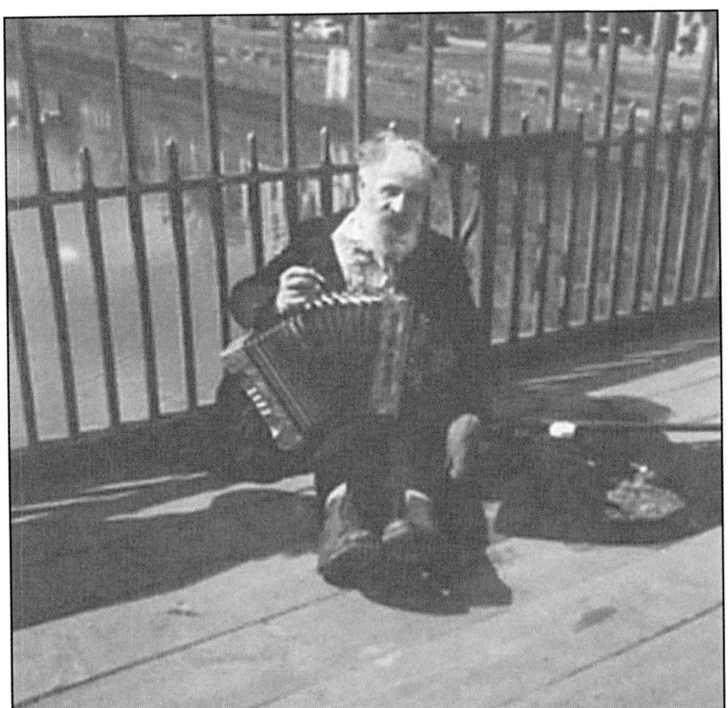

***Dublin accordion player on the Ha'penny Bridge.***

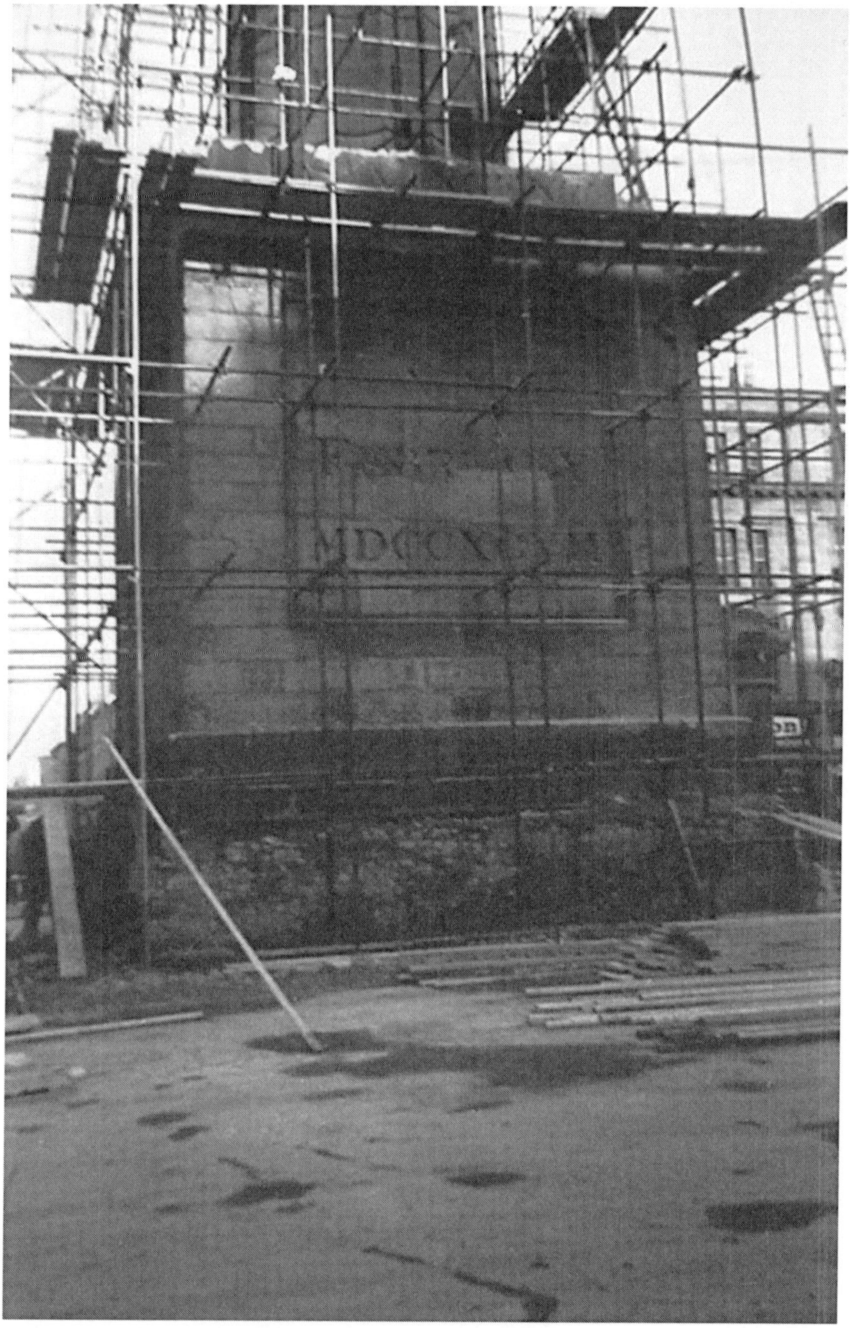

***The base of Nelson's Pillar 1966.***

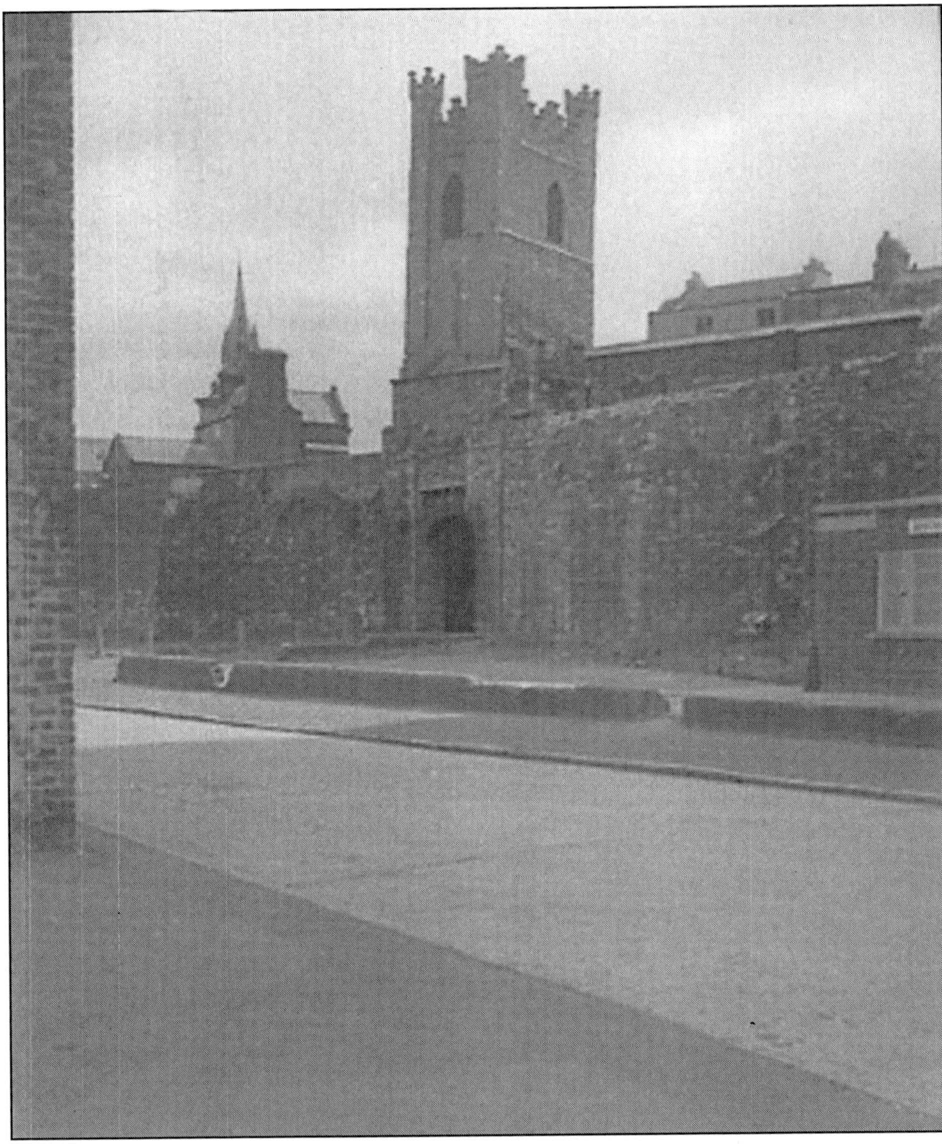

***Saint Audeon's Church in High Street and the only surviving gate that once led into medieval Dublin.***

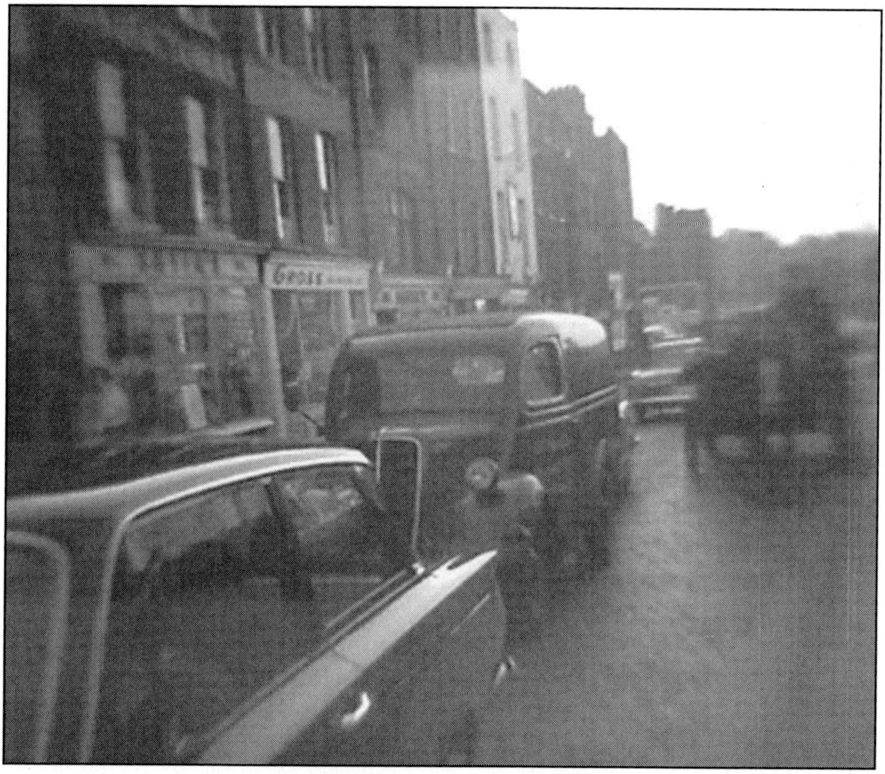

***Traffic jam on the Quays.***

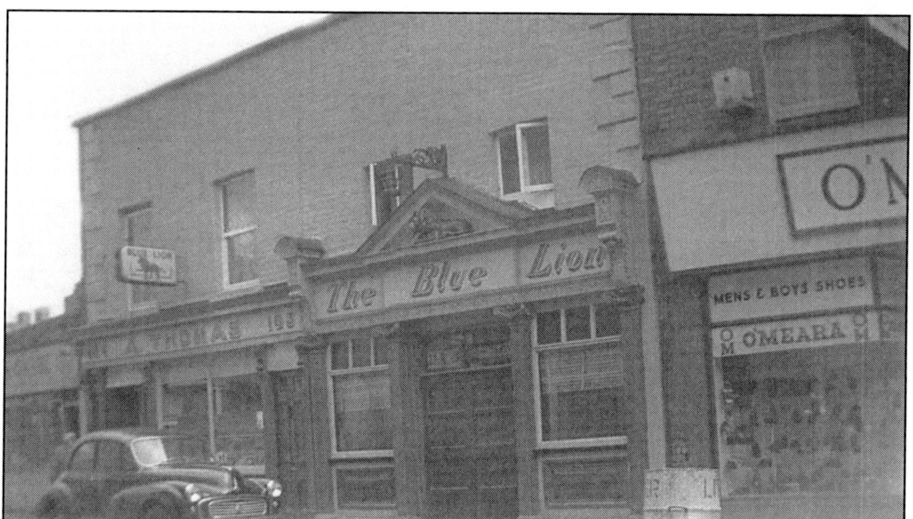


***The Blue Lion.***

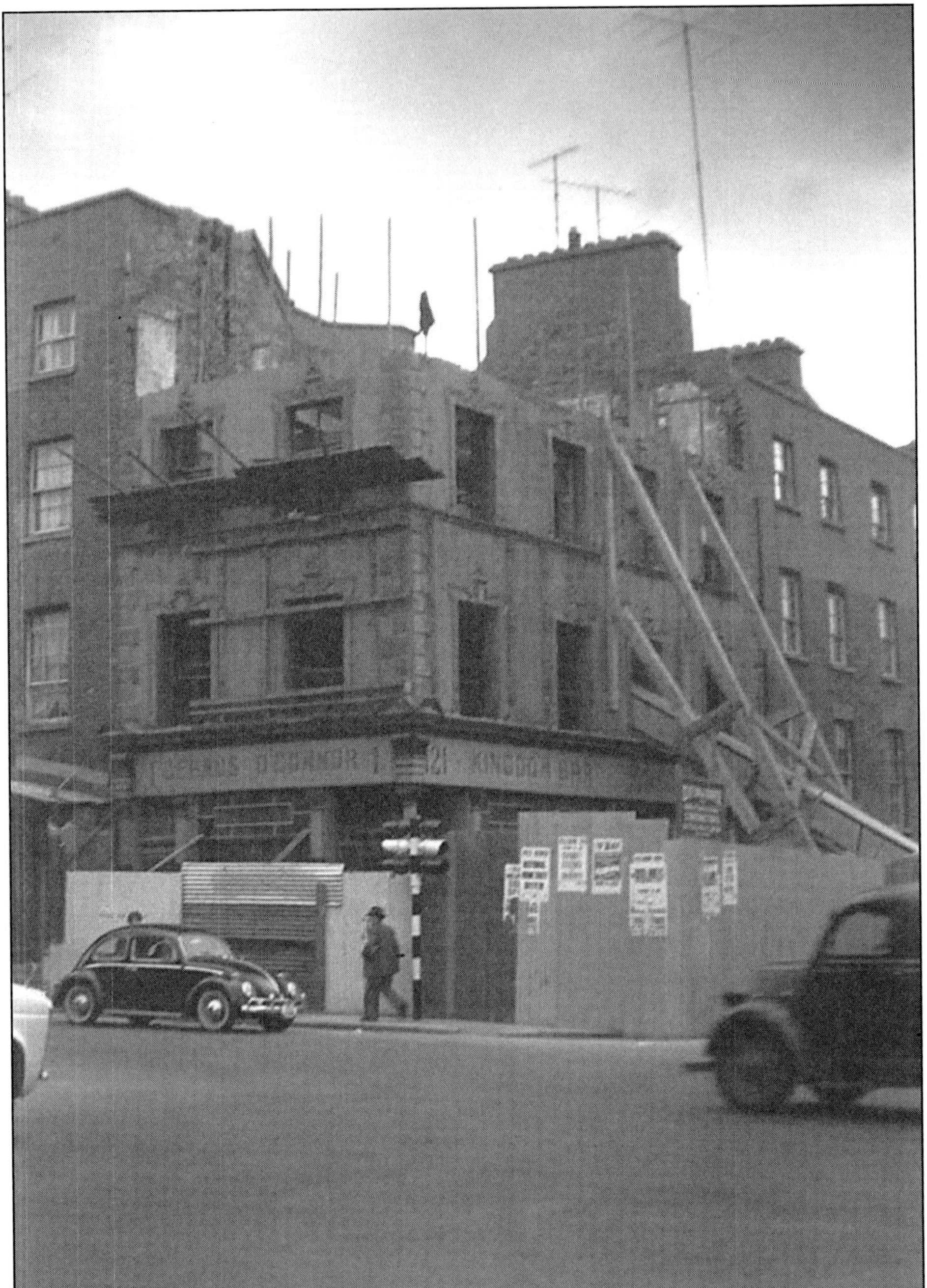

***The demise of the Kingdom Bar.***

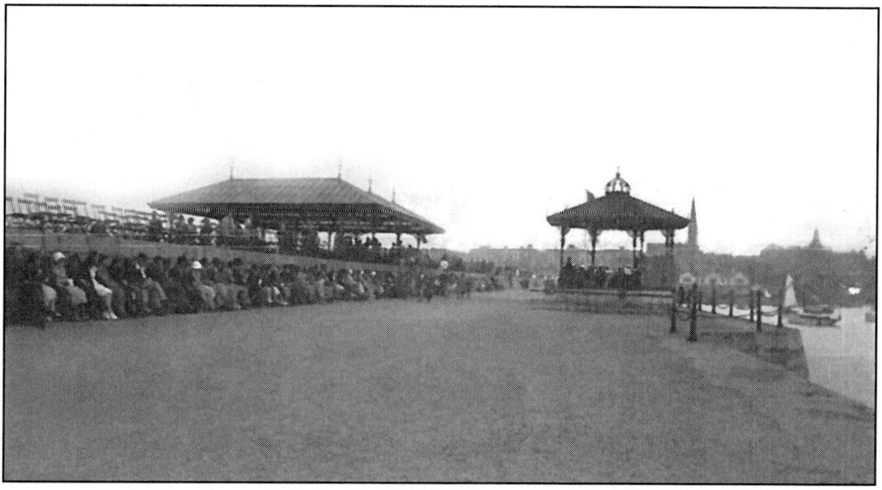

***Crowds being entertained on Dunlaoghaire pier.***

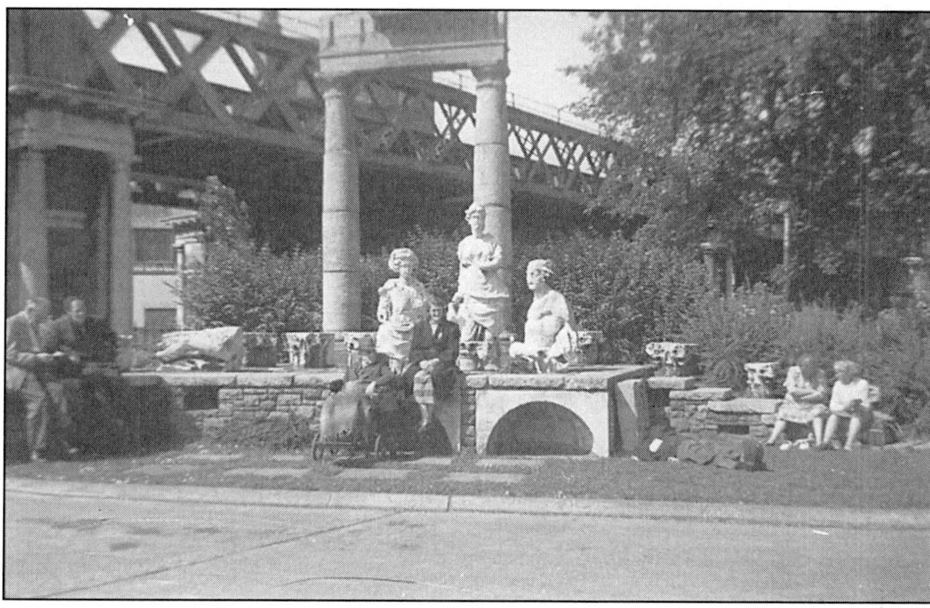

***Broken Statues.***

This photograph was taken in the Customs House Park. The two ladies on the right are Biddy Coffey and her sister Rooie Kane. Next to Biddy is a man asleep on the grass with a coat over his face. It was from the above bridge in 1916 that William Barter was shot.

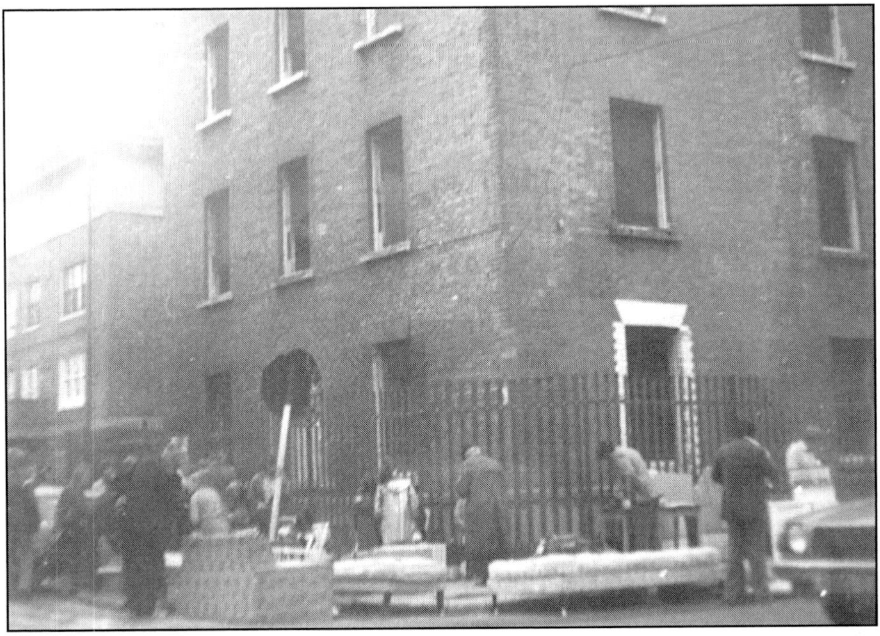

***Beds and sofas for sale on the corner of Cumberland Street and Cathal Brugha Street.***

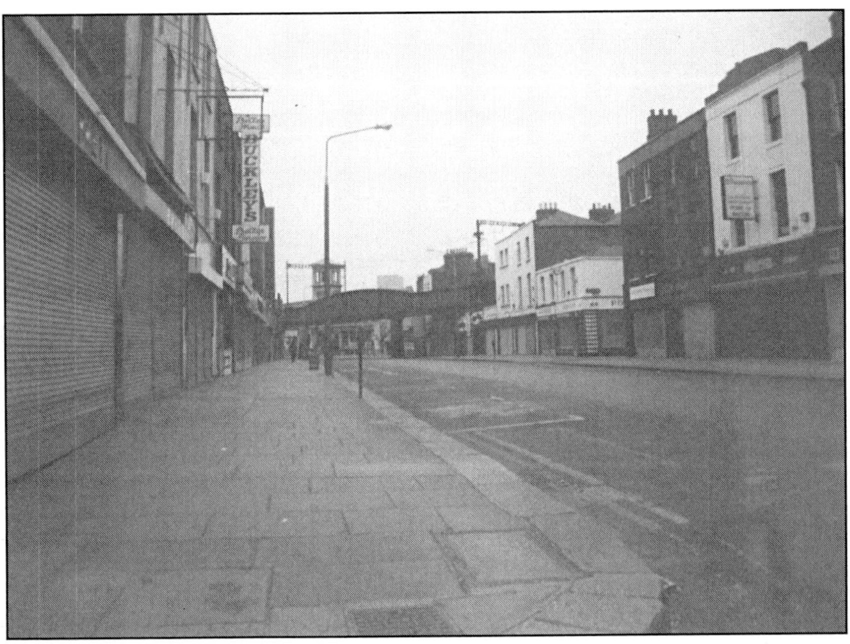

***Talbot Street.***

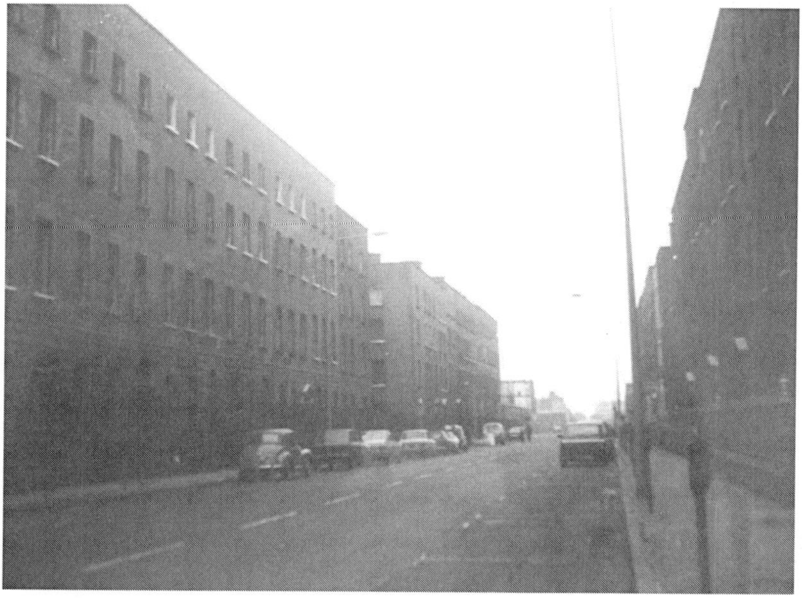

***Tenement houses in Sean McDermot Street 1970's.***

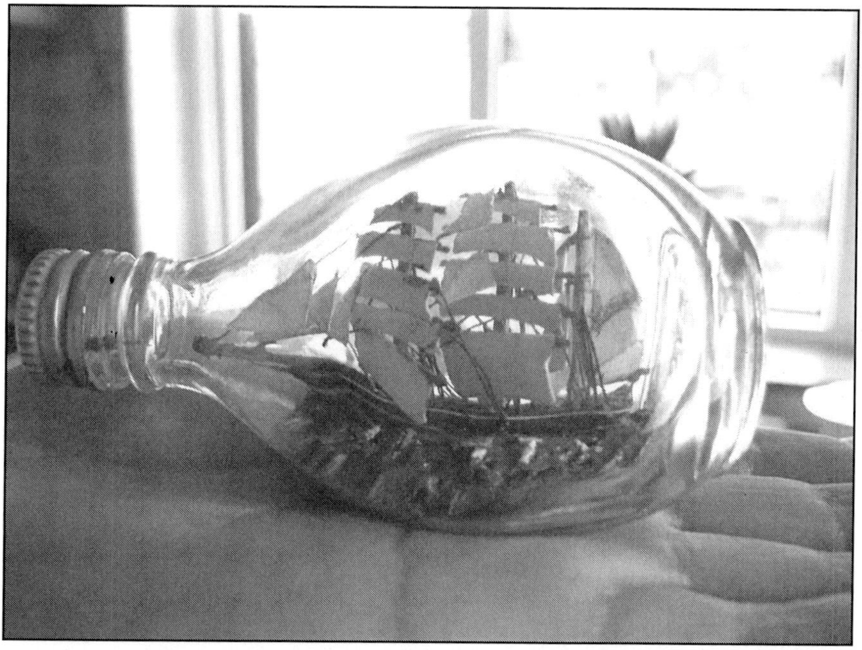

***Ship in a bottle made by Paddy Coffey.***
***(Photo by Martin Coffey)***

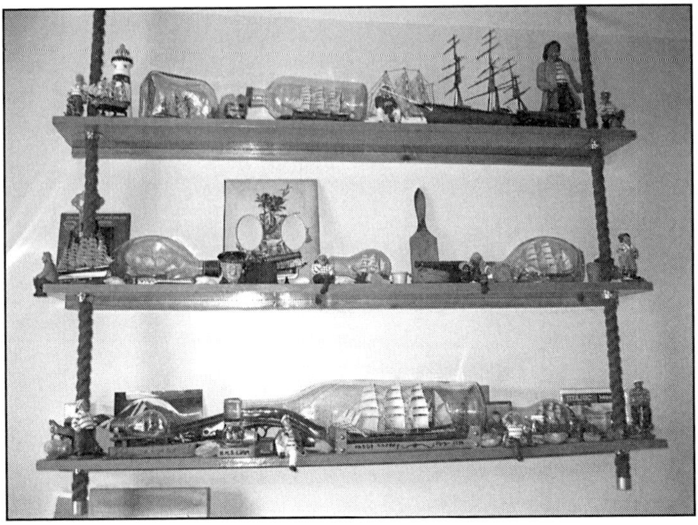

***A collection of ships in bottles and bulbs.***

One ship in particular that Paddy Coffey had great admiration for was the '***Cutty Sark'*** and so much so that he repeatedly built tiny models of it again and again. These tiny models were ever so gently placed inside bottles and bulbs. He learned this craft in his early days away at sea during quiet periods when some of the more seasoned sailors would sit out on the deck and show him how it was done. This collection is in the author's possession and probably represents a small number of the total amount of ships that Paddy Coffey would have made like these.

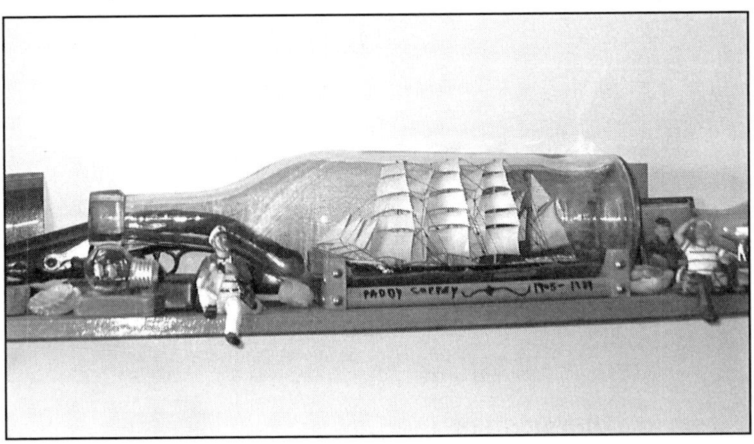

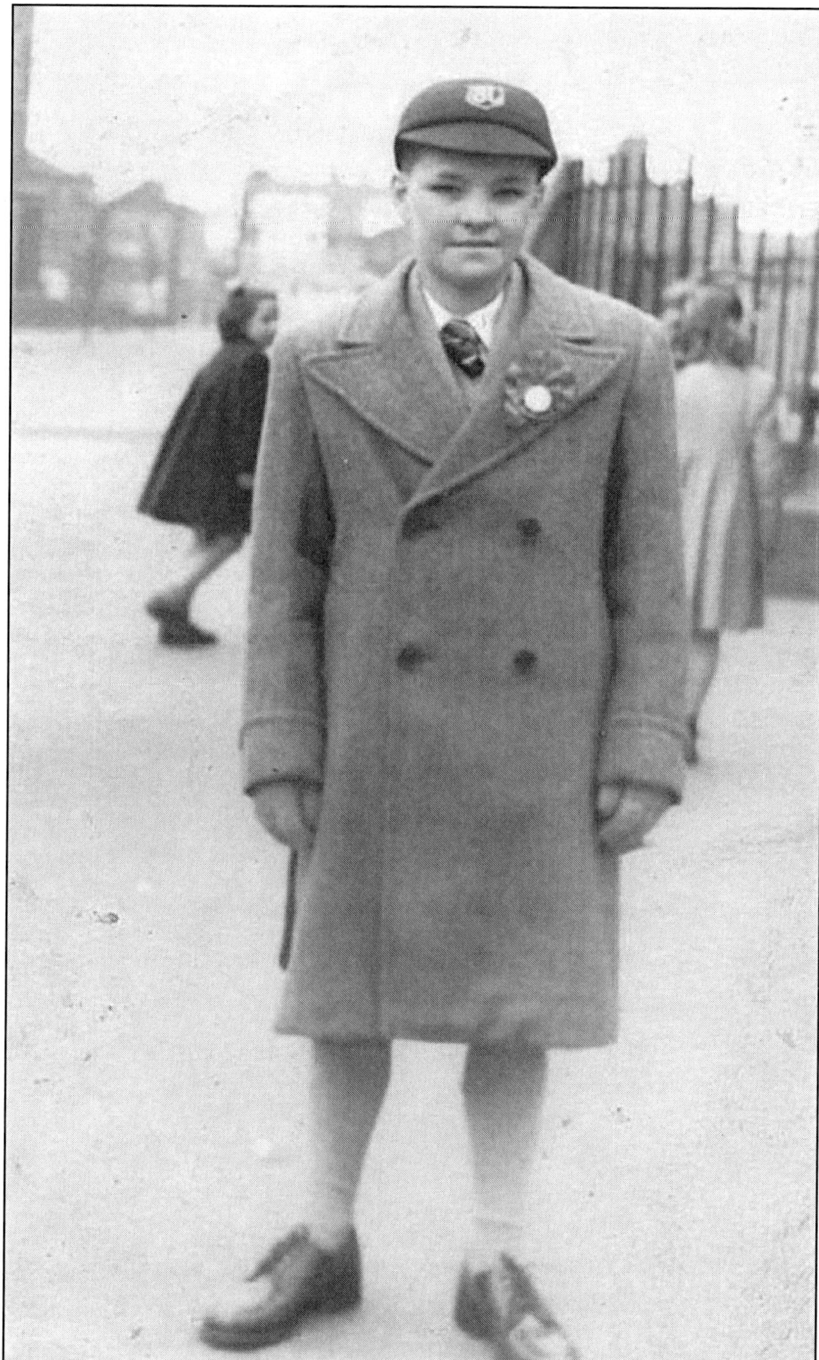

***Gussy Farrelly.***

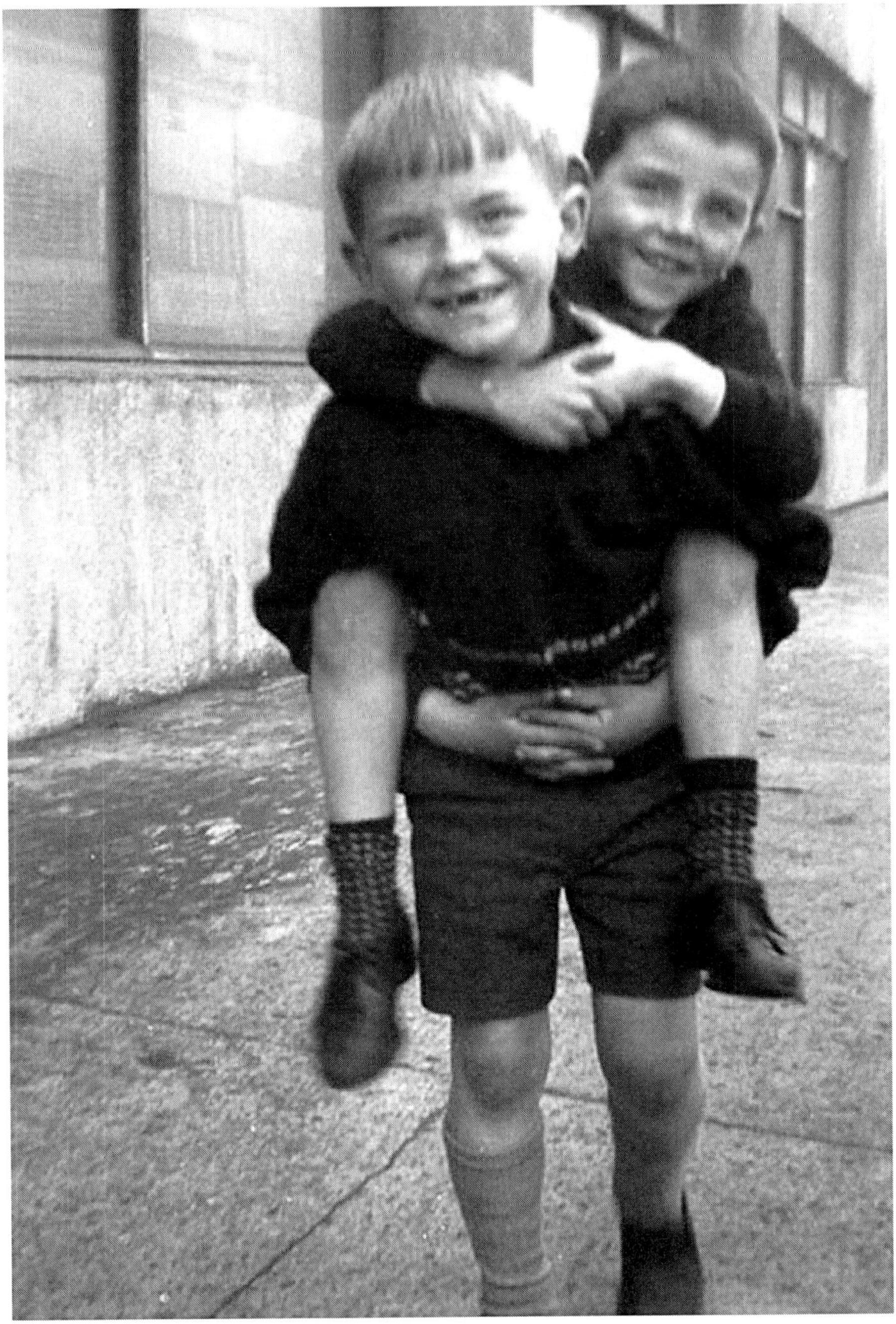

***Paul and Stephen Kelly.***

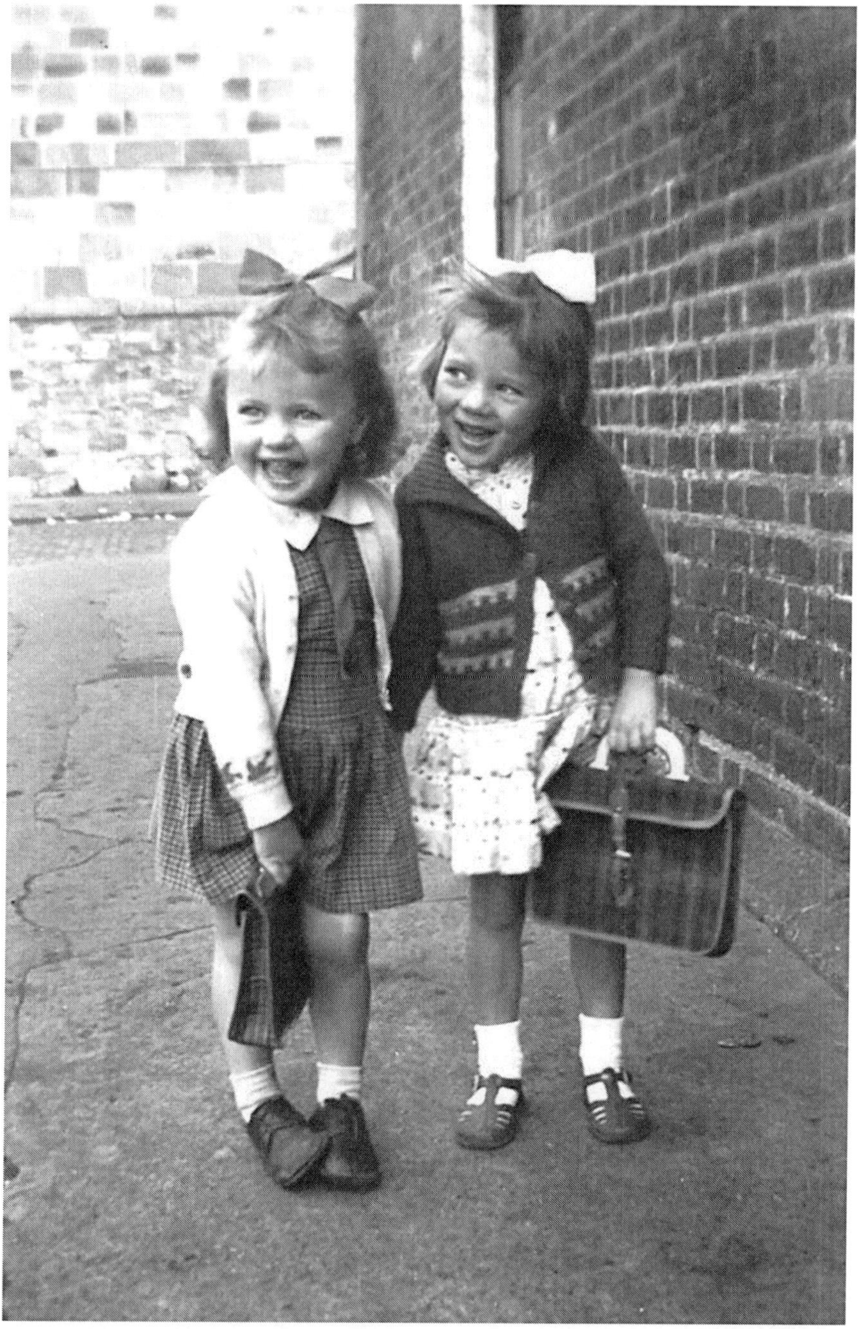

***Kathleen Dillon and Jonie Tormey on their first day in school.***

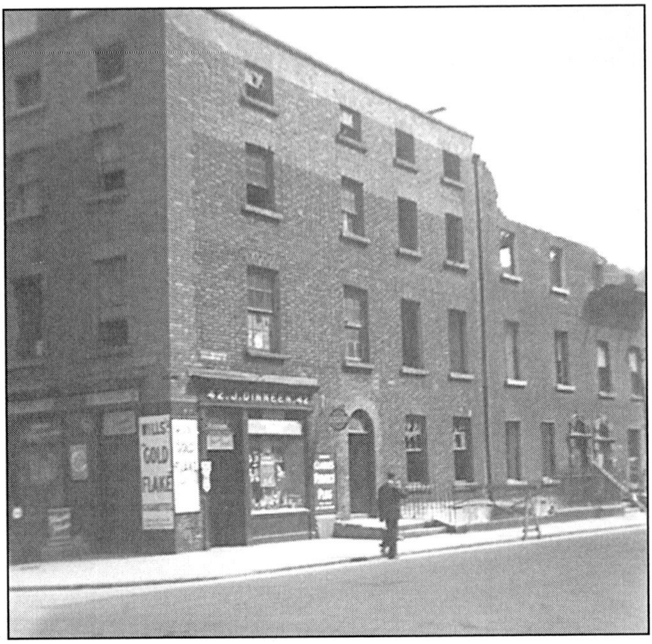


*Dineen's Corner Shop.*

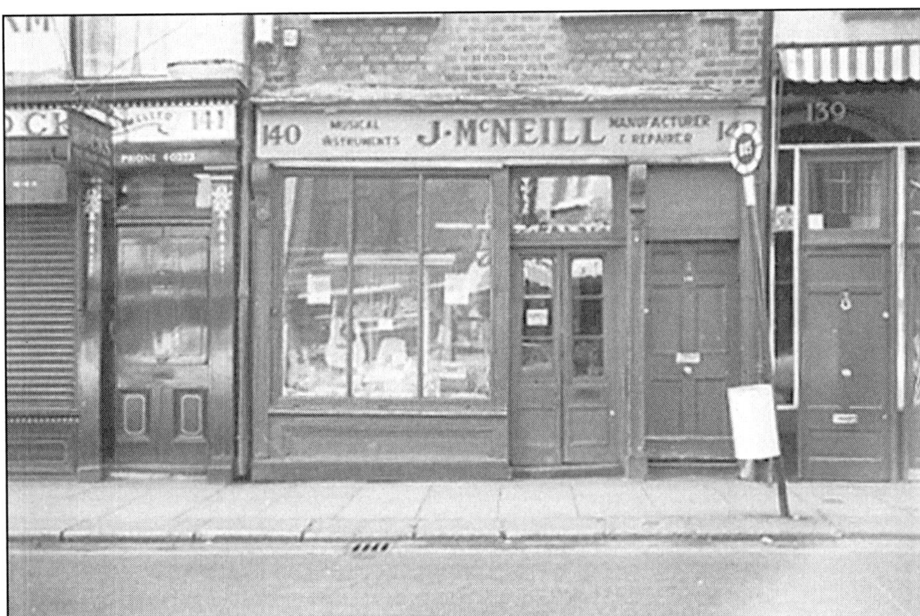


*Mc Neill's music store in Capel Street, 1960's.*

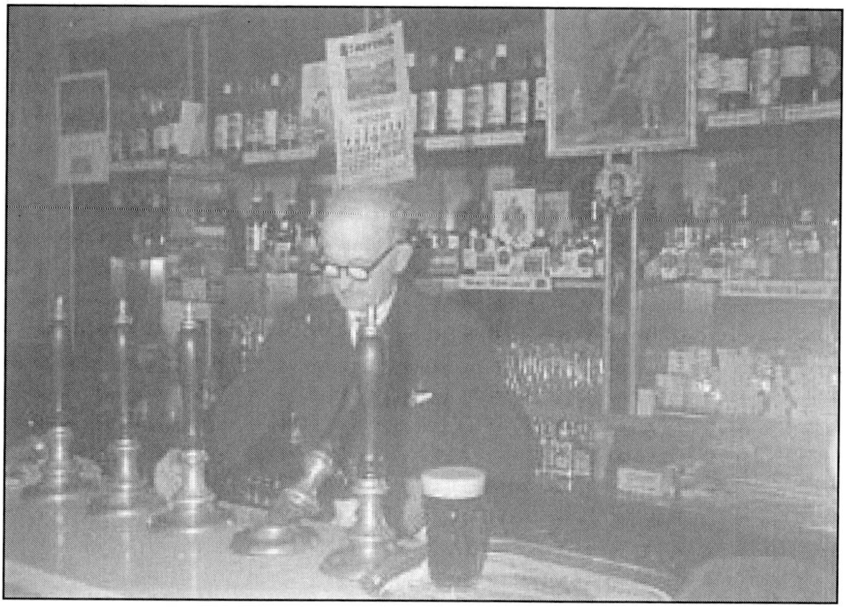

***Pulling a pint in the Sunset Pub, Dublin.***

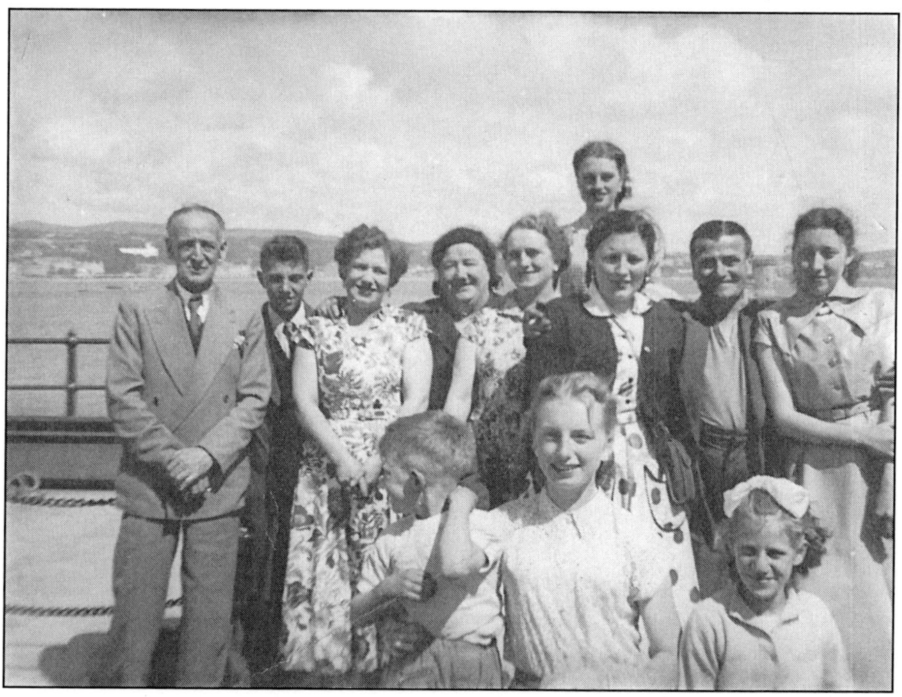

***Day trip to the Isle of Man.***

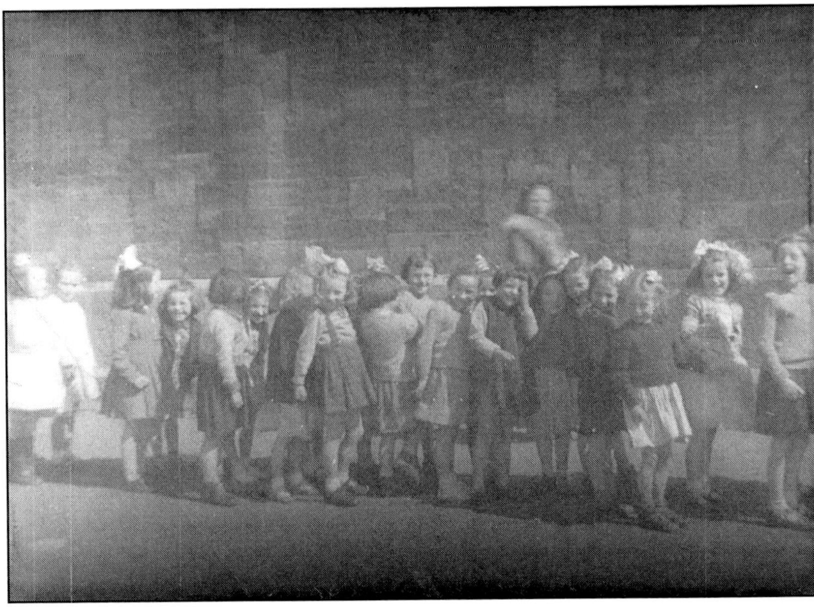

***School Girls from Seville Place.***

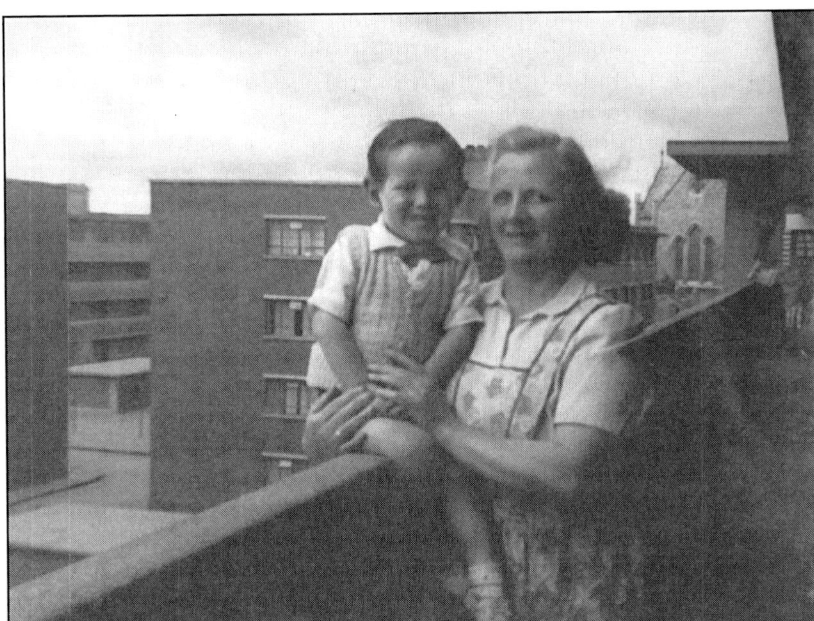

***Paddy Kane with his aunt Biddy Coffey.***

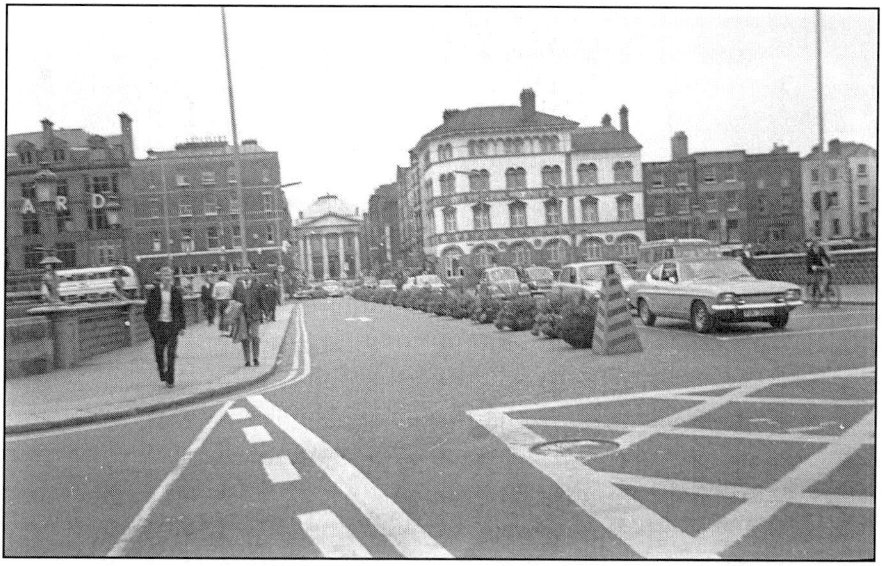

***Capel Street Bridge, Dublin.***

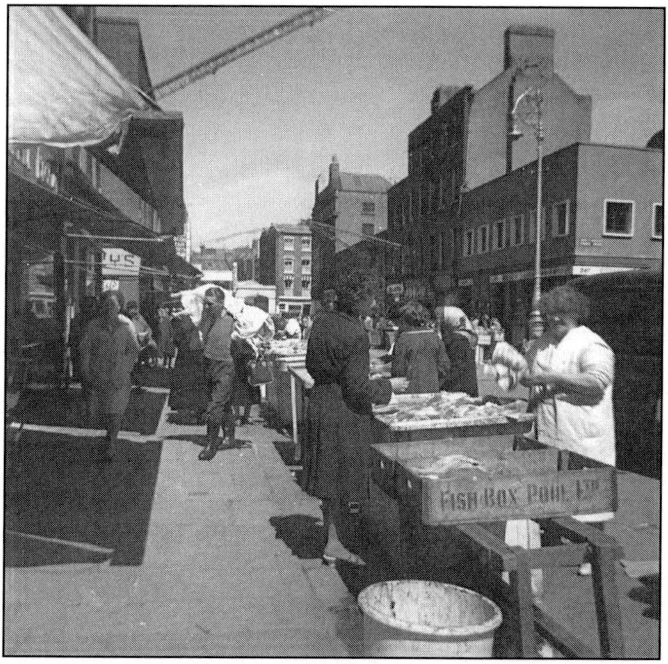

***A Fish Stall in Moore Street, Dublin.***

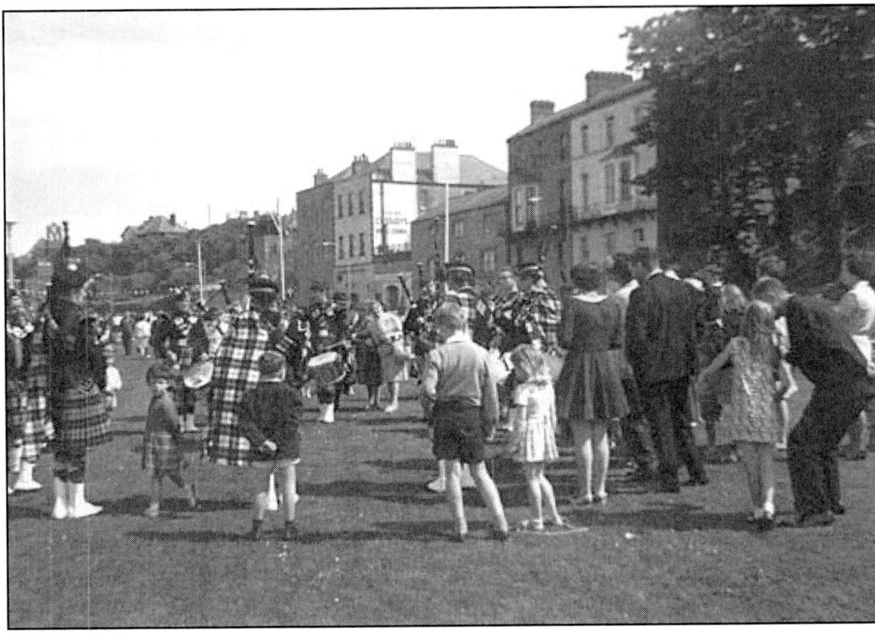

***Howth Pipe Band.***

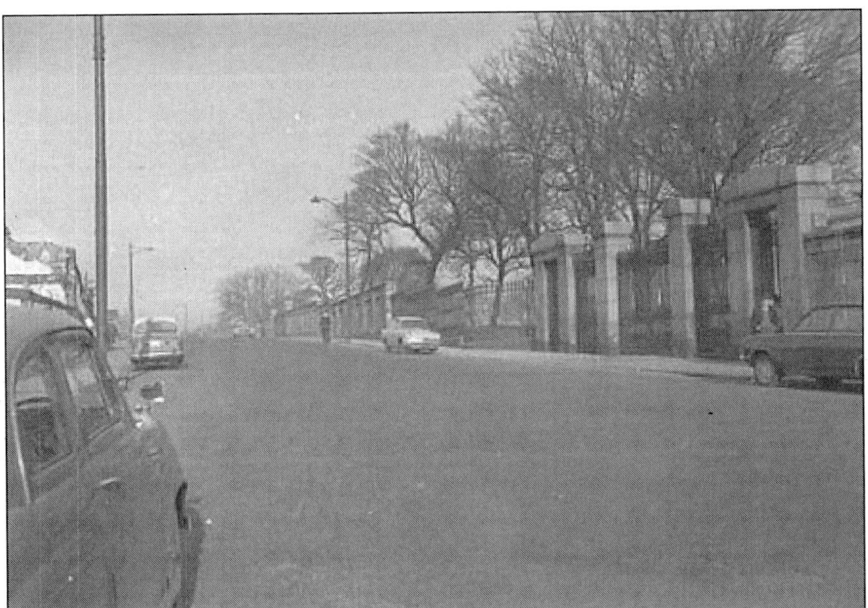

***Constitution Hill.***

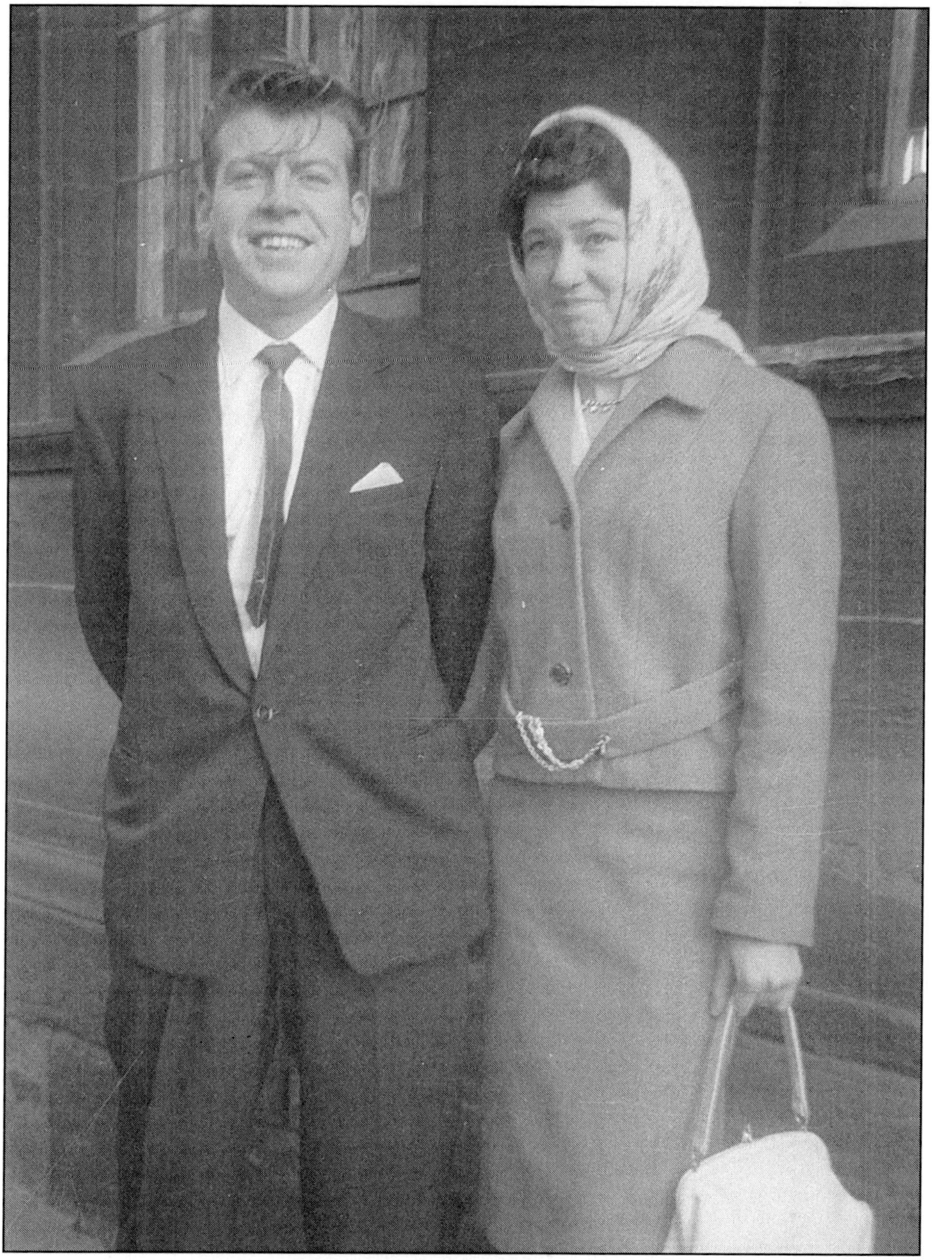

***A happy young couple from Dublin.***

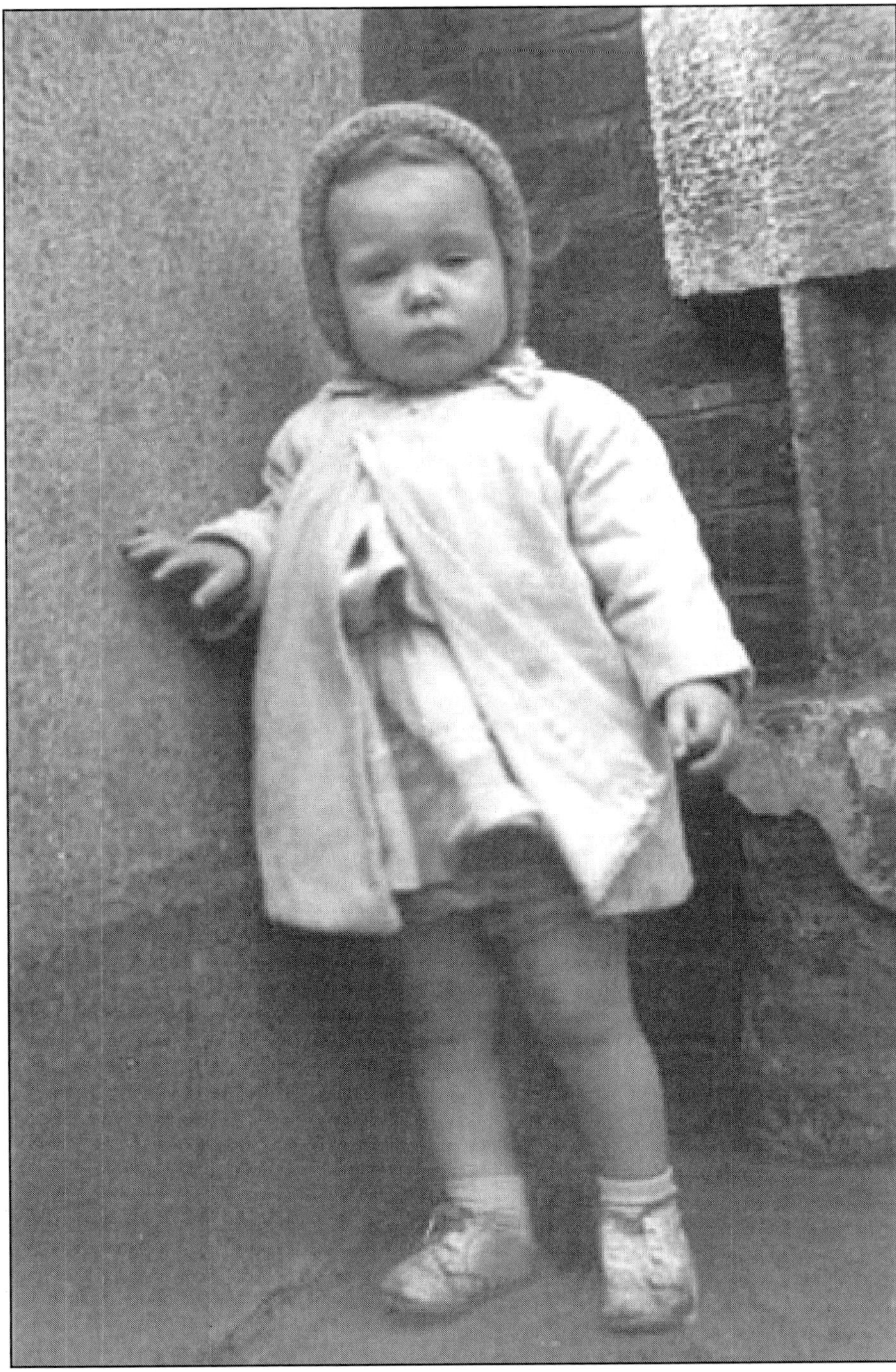

***A little girl in Sean McDermott Street.***

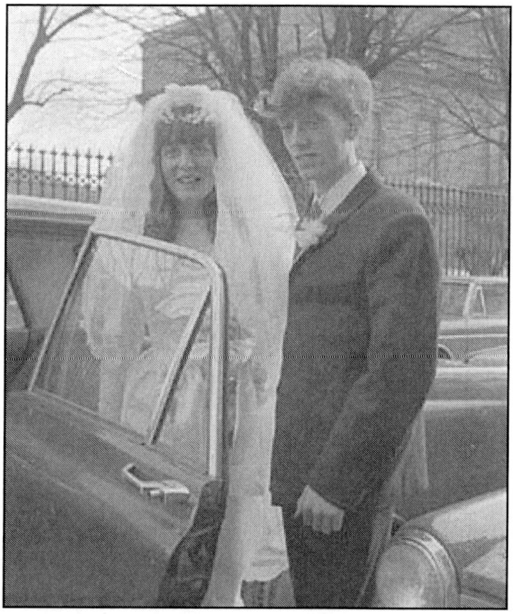

***Newly Weds***

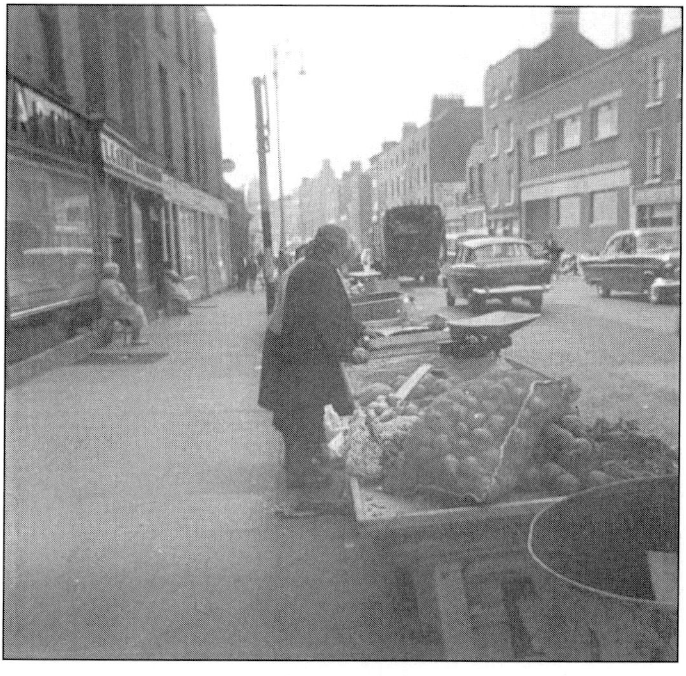

***Street Dealer.***

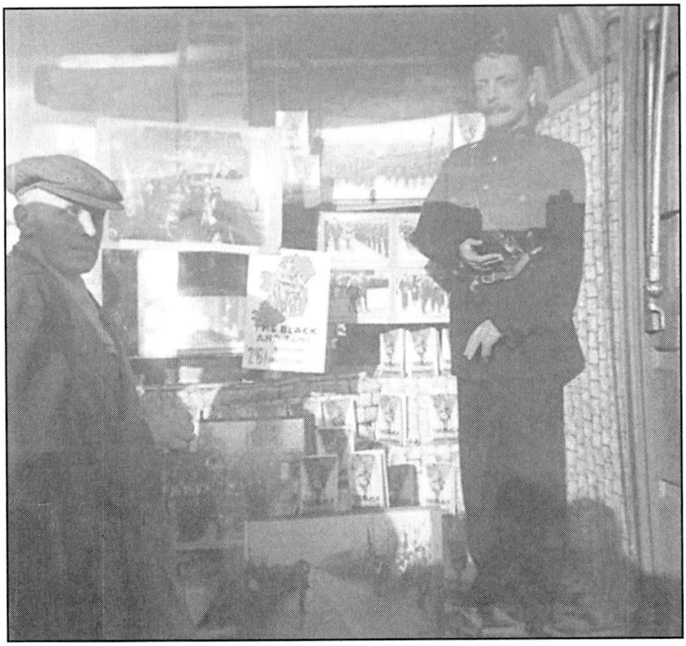

***The Black and Tans on display in Dublin 1966.***

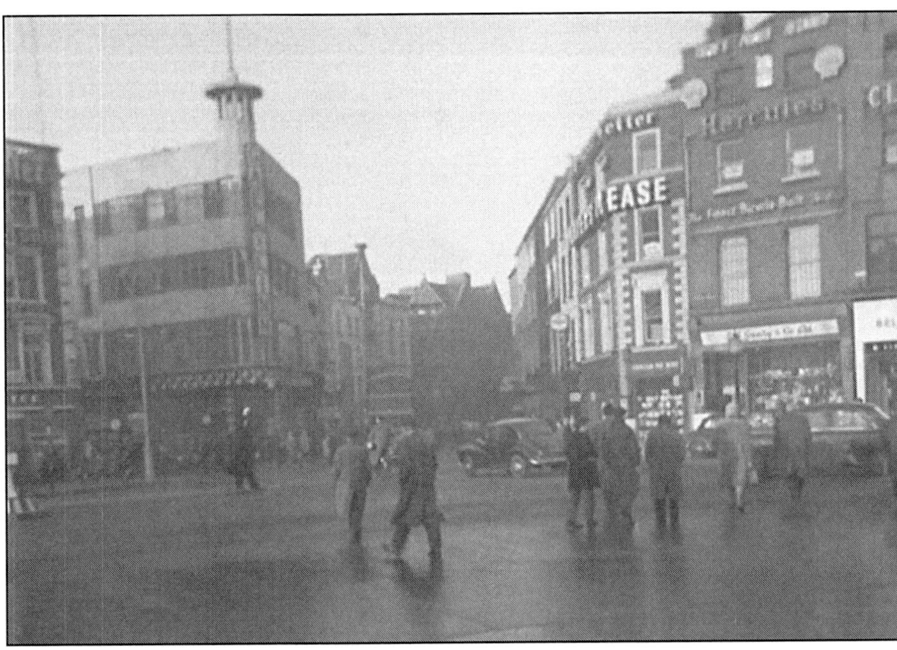

***St Stephen's Green, Dublin.***

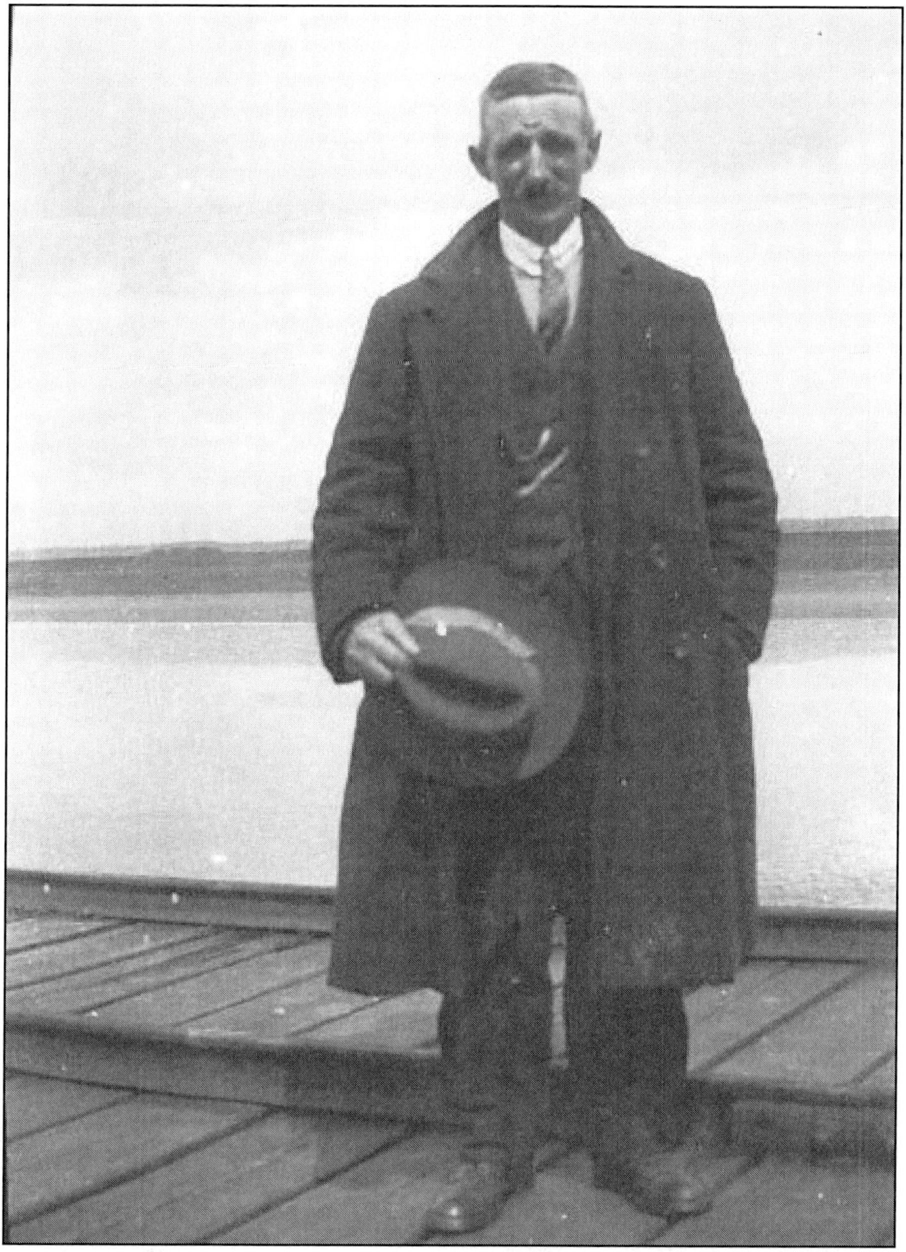

***Posing for the camera.***

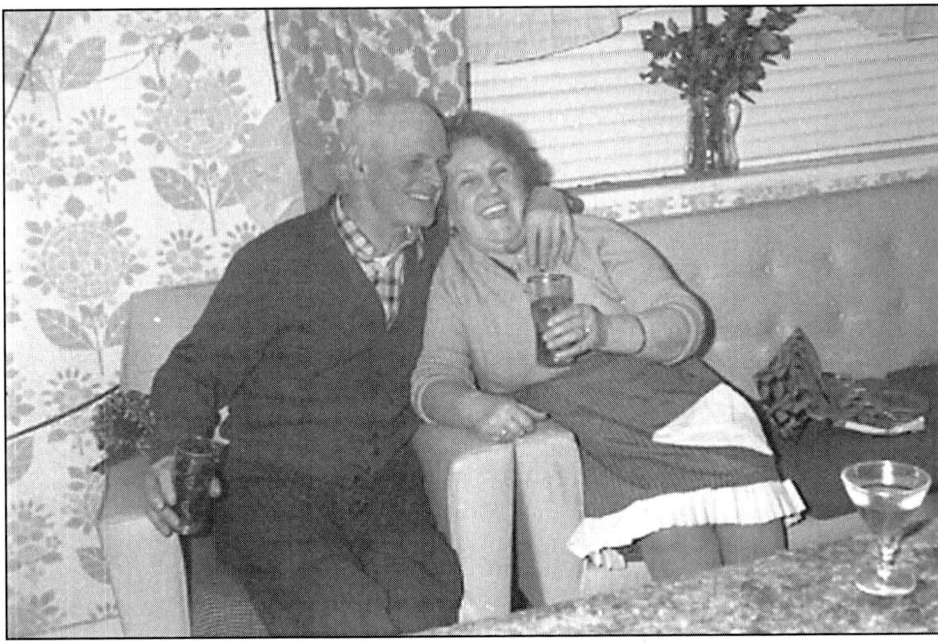

***Old friends are best.***

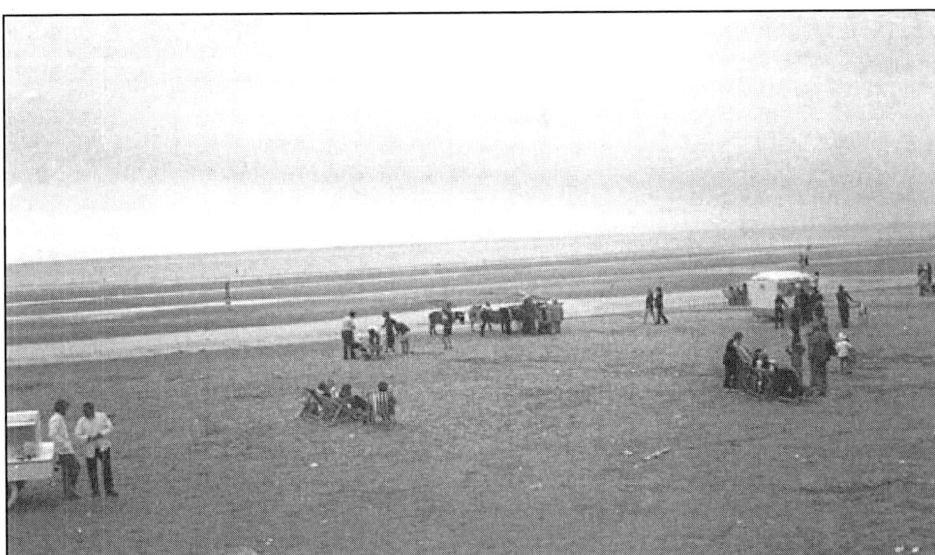

***Dollymount Strand.***

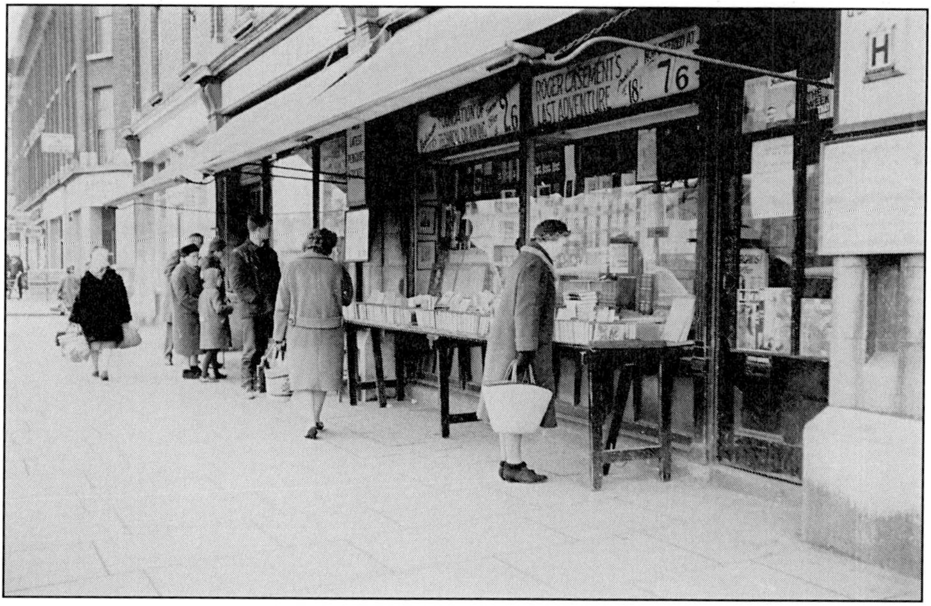


***Nothing like a good read.***

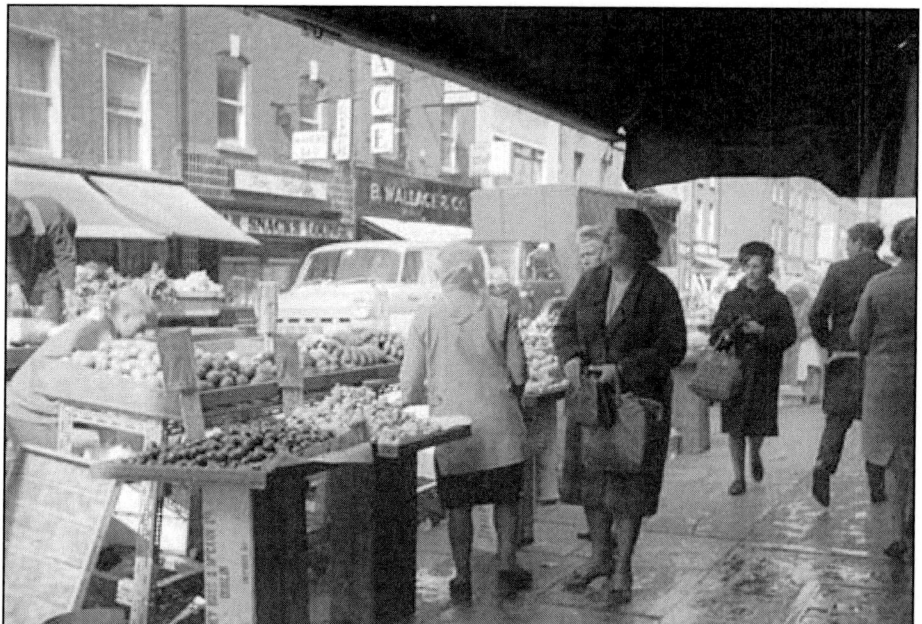


***Alive Alivo.***

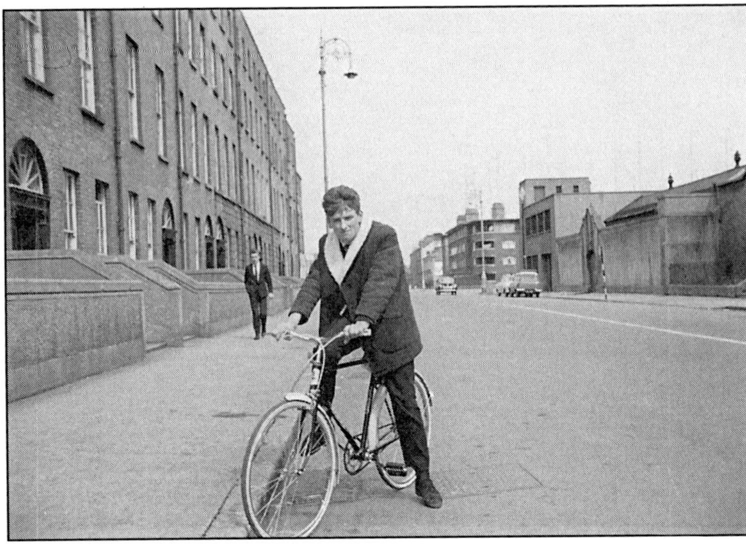

***The Old and New.***
***In this photograph can be seen the old style tenement houses on the left and further down the street in centre picture can be seen the more modern flats.***

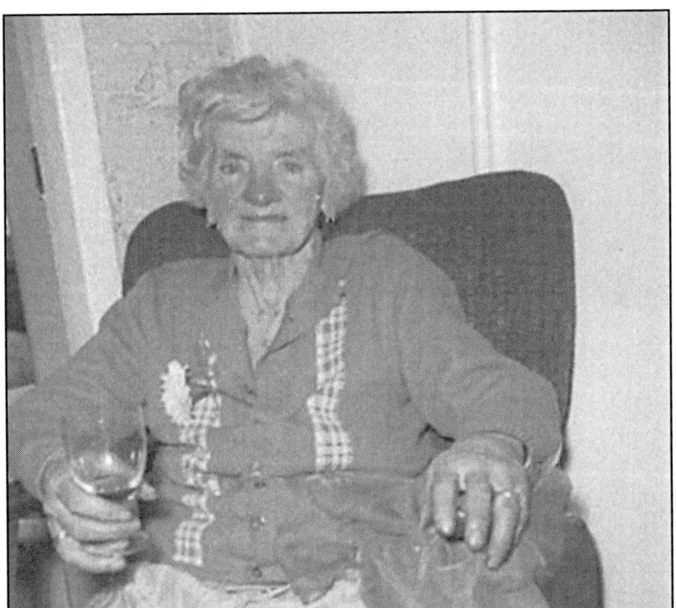

***Cheers.***

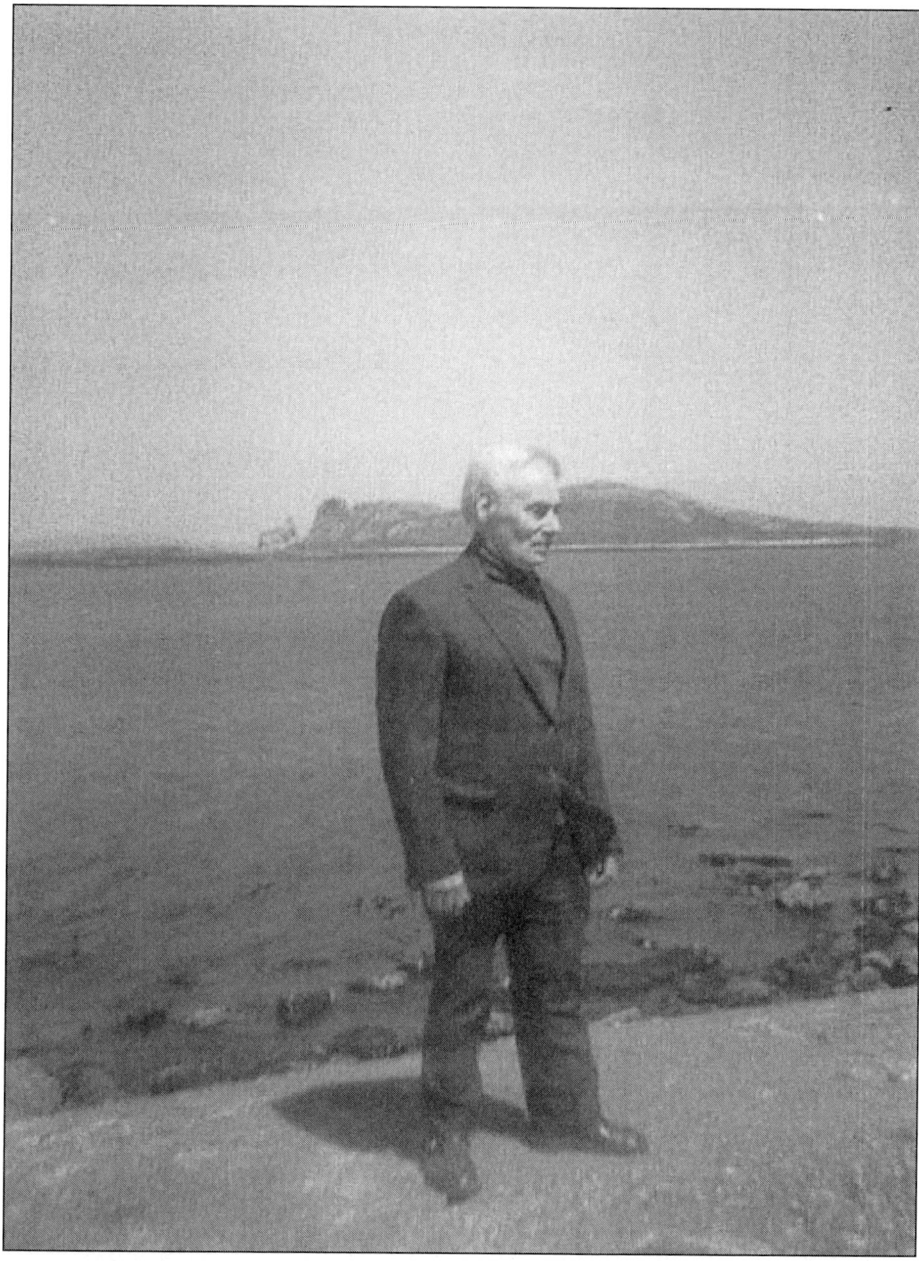

***Paddy Coffey soon after his final retirement as a Merchant Seaman.***

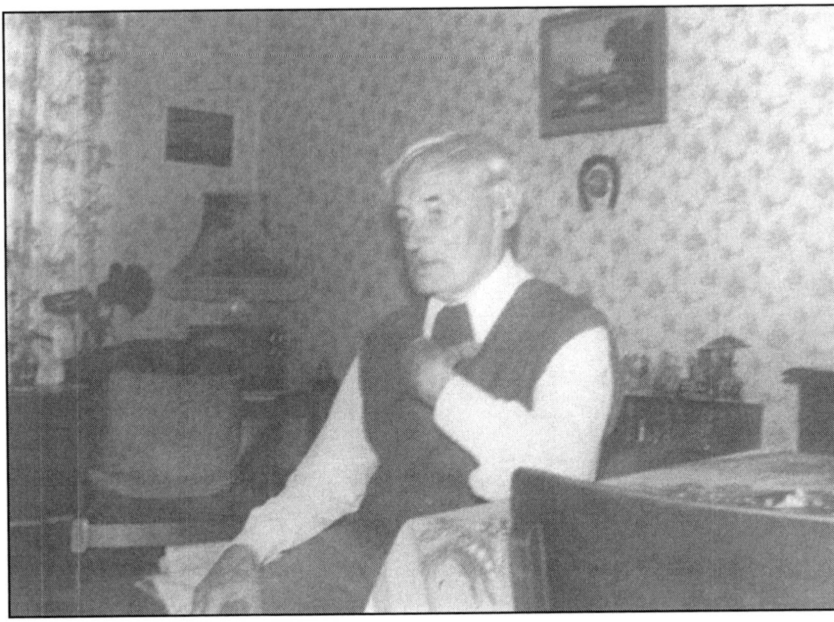

***Paddy Coffey 1988.***

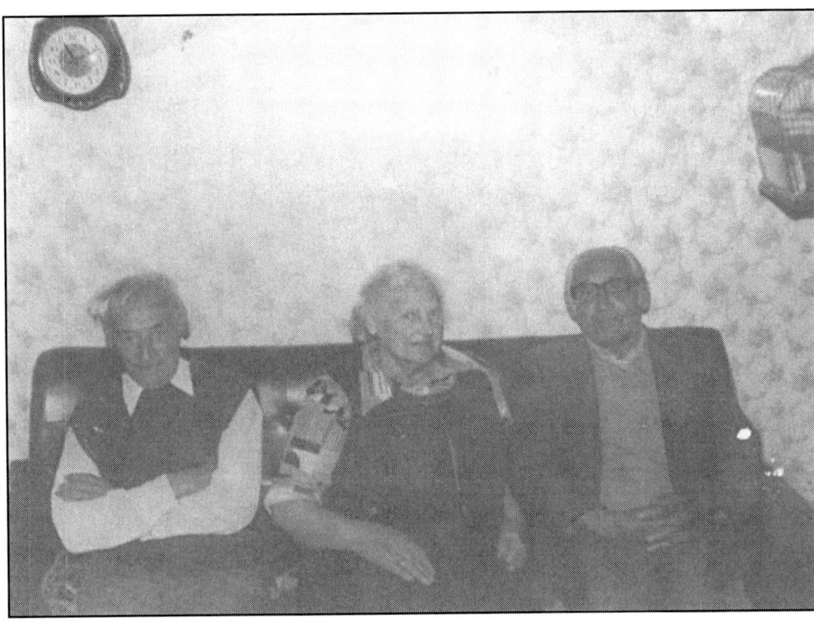

***L-R: Paddy Coffey 1905-1989, Biddy Coffey 1906-1989, Bernard 'Archie' Coffey 1912-1989.***

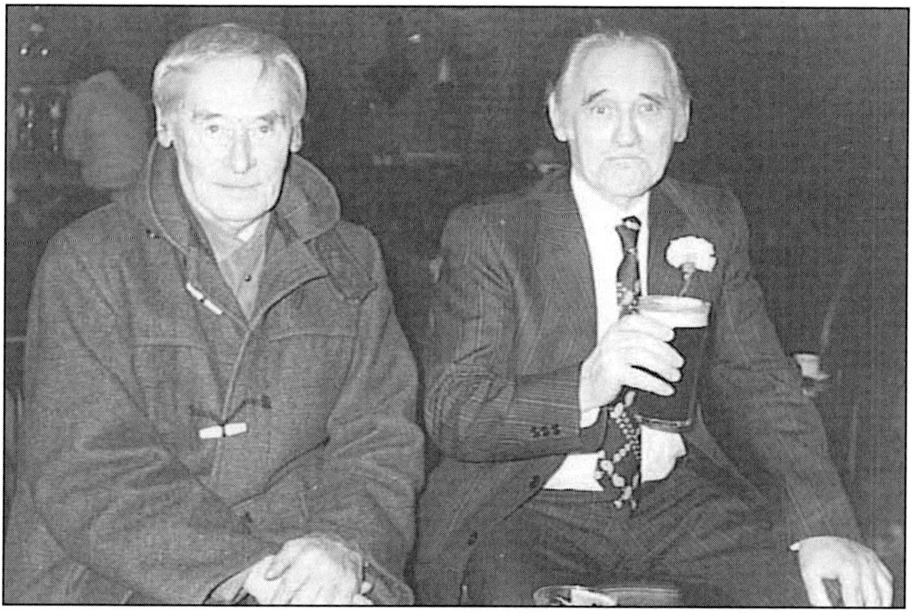

***Paddy Coffey having a pint with his youngest brother Bernard 1981.***

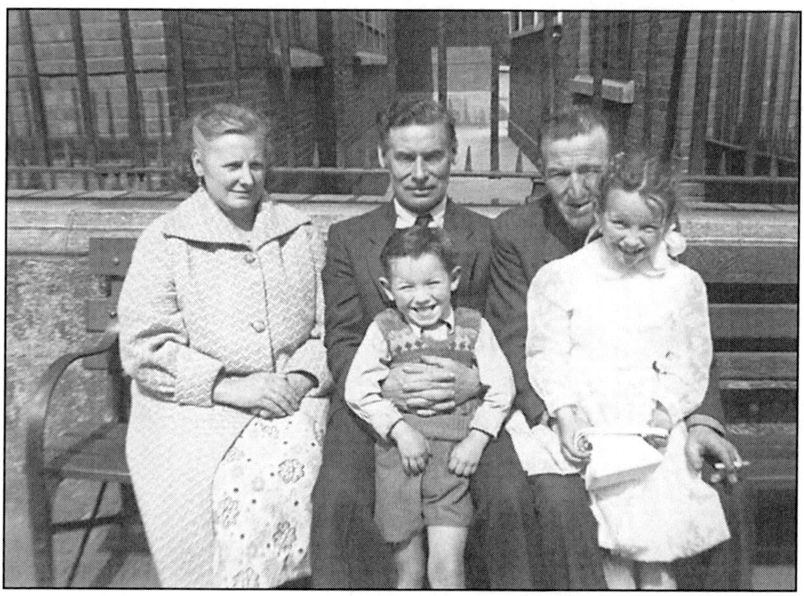

***Biddy Coffey, Paddy Coffey, Alfie Kane,***
***Paddy Kane and Angela Kane.***

***Other books by this author.***

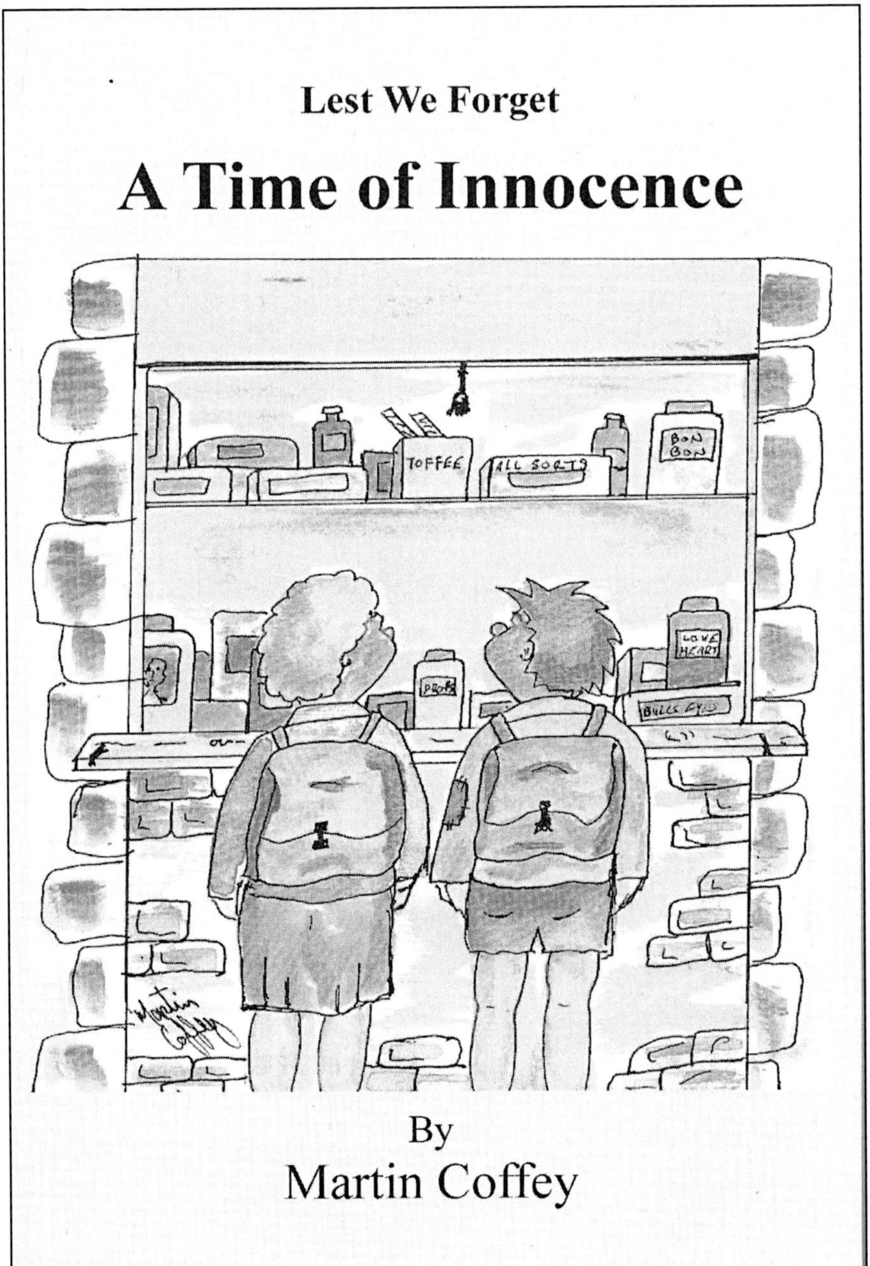


***A Time of Innocence 2007.***

# A Time To Remember

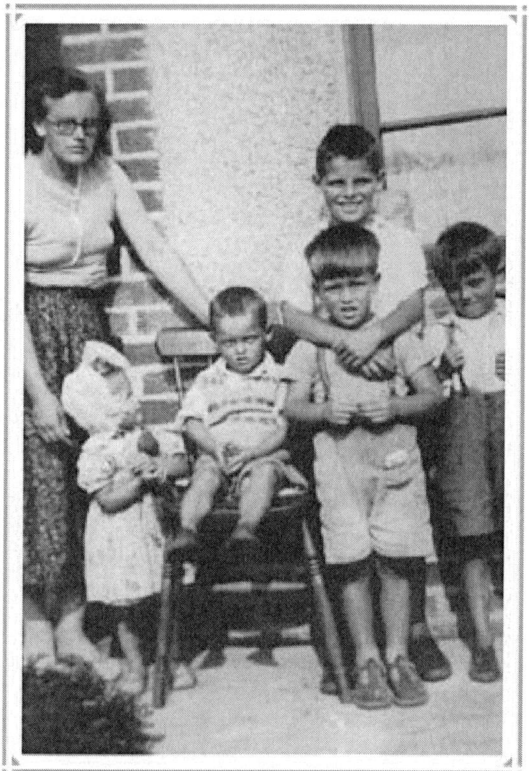

## Cabra and its People

By

Martin Coffey B.A.

***A Time to Remember 2009.***

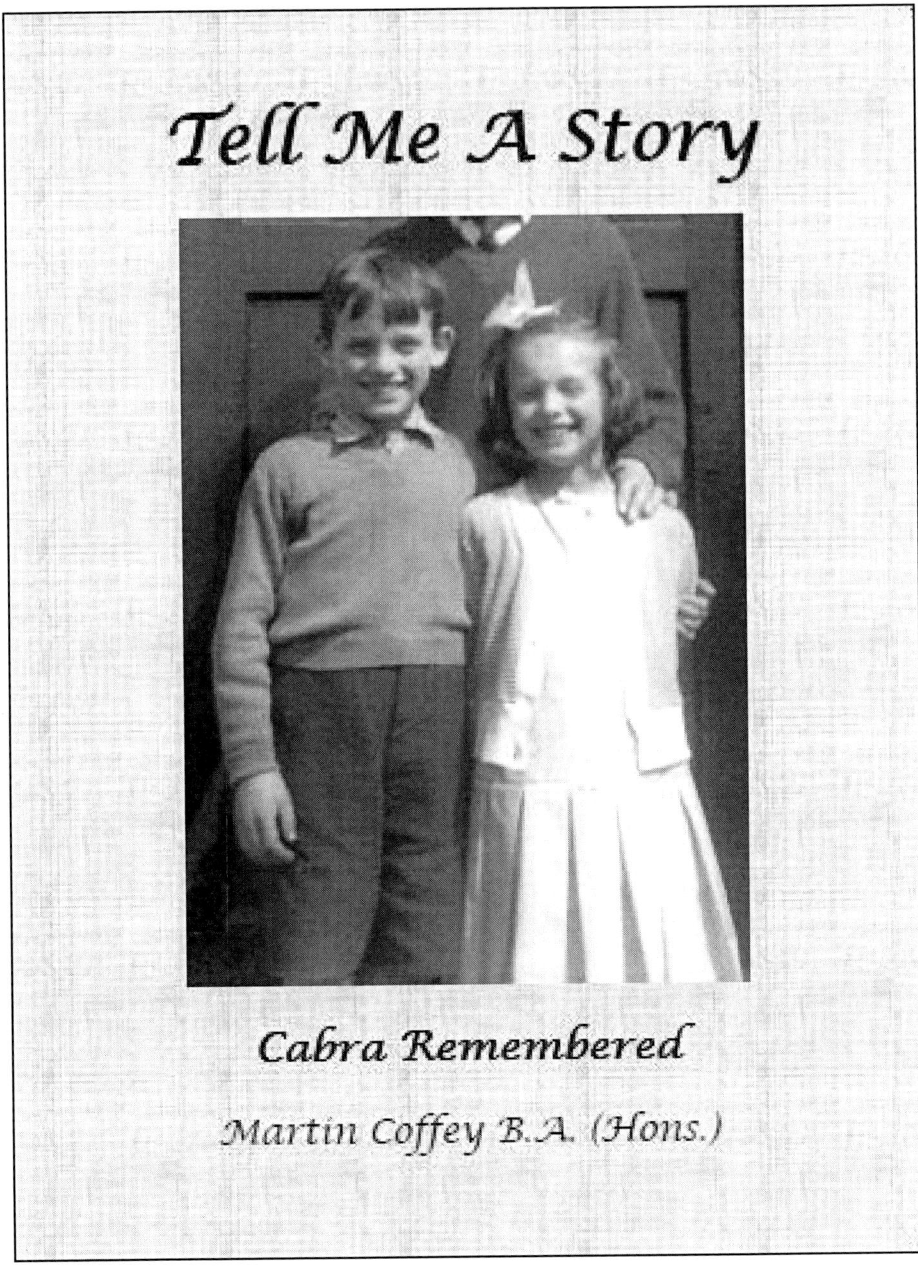


***Tell Me A Story 2012.***

# Ambrose O Shea

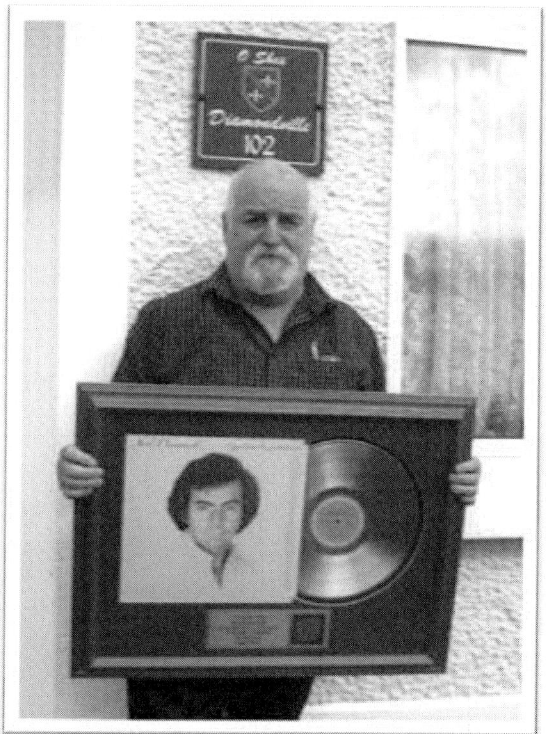

***'My Neil Diamond Experience'***

Written and compiled by

**Martin Coffey B.A (Hons.)**

***Ambrose O Shea 2014.***

## *Notes*

## *Notes*